# Emigrant Tales of the
# PLATTE RIVER
# RAIDS

## An 1864 Trail Diary Companion

## Janelle Molony

Foreword by Kylie Louise McCormick

 M Press Publishing

Cover Design and Interior: J. Molony
Cover Image: Boyd, Mcgowan, D, George H Hildt, and Leopold Gast & Brother. *Map of the United States west of the Mississippi...*, St. Louis, Leopold Gast & Bro, 1859. Map. LOC: 71000833 [Public Domain Image]

ISBN: 978-1-7344638-7-3 (paperback, M Press)
Library of Congress: 2023918917

Non-Fiction: Trade
Genres: United States History, Literary Collection
Keywords: Wyoming, Iowa, Oregon, Civil War, Sioux War, Wagon Train, Westward Expansion, Oregon Trail, Overland-California Trail, Mormon Trail, Family History, Genealogy, Research

# *Praise for* Emigrant Tales

"It's like having a front row seat for the action."

**Julia Brunia Thompsen,** Descendant of the Roorda Family (2023)

"This is an important story to tell! Anyone who studies American History will enjoy this book."

**Kathy Lay,** Descendant of the Shoemaker Family (2023)

"Janelle allows the reader to feel the excitement, and often times the anxiety, the emigrants experienced."

**Alan Ver Ploeg,** Descendant from the Jongewaard Train (2023)

"Anyone who enjoys 19th Century Westerns will enjoy [this book]. ... It is a GOOD story."

**Dana Cahoon,** Descendant from the Ridgley Party (2023)

"The amount of research ... is astounding."

**Steve Borders**, Descendant of the Morris & Hastings Families (2022)

"Perfect ... I couldn't put it down."

**Barbara Yates-Romine,** Descendant of the Kelly Family (2022)

"This incident, and the balance of the journey, will be welcomed by trail fans."

**Robert Clark,** Overland-California Trails Association, Editor of *Overland Journal* (2020)

## Other Books by the Author

**From Where I Sat** (Forthcoming)
*The fictionalized retelling of the Pella Company's 1864 Trip Across the Plains. While everyone might be heading in the same direction, they are all on their own, separate journey. Will their friendships last? Are grit and mettle enough to make it through when every last resource is extinguished?*

**Cross Family Wives' Tales** (Forthcoming)
*Oral histories highlighting the lives and history of the Cross Tobacco Plantation in North Keys, Maryland. Features first-person accounts of the farming experience from 1902 to 2023.*

**The 1864 Diary of Mrs. Sarah Rousseau, Unabridged** (2023)
*The complete, transcribed and edited diary of Sarah Jane Daglish Rousseau, wife of prominent Iowa physician and members of the Pella Company covered wagon train to California. Ft. surnames: Earp, Curtis, Rousseau, Hamilton, Parker, Ellis, Hatton, Young, Wells, and more.*

**Poems from the Asylum** (2021)
*The true story of a first-generation German-American woman who claimed she no longer needed to eat, drink, or sleep. Speaking out resulted in an insane asylum committal and becoming an international news sensation. Her poetic testimonies from inside the asylum would later shock the world.*

**Un-Adoptable? Faith Beyond Foster Care** (2020)
*Creative nonfiction/memoir. One woman faces an incredible challenge and finds that faith to see what is beyond the present moment can be the lifeline and path to redemption that everyone needs... especially for children in foster care.*

# Dedication

To my uncle, Richard "Dick" Molony (1926-2015):

Thank you for introducing me to this incredible story.
I wish you could have seen where it has taken us all!

# Maps of the "Black Hills" of Idaho Territory

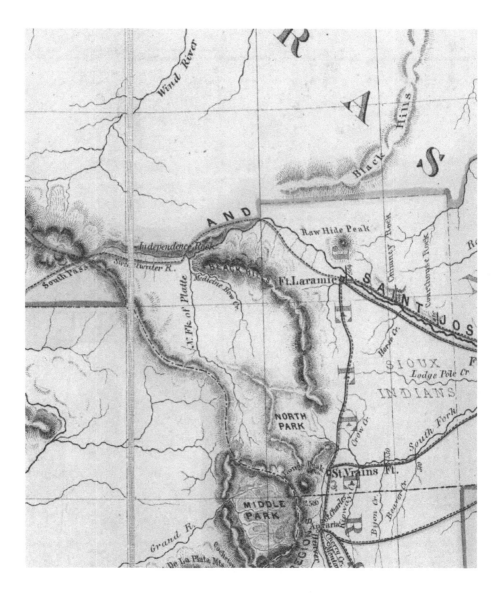

**Nebraska Territory-Wyoming, 1859.** Boyd, Mcgowan, D., George H. Hildt, and Leopold Gast & Brother. *Map of the United States west of the Mississippi...*, St. Louis, Leopold Gast & Bro, 1859. Map. LOC: 71000833 [Public Domain Image]

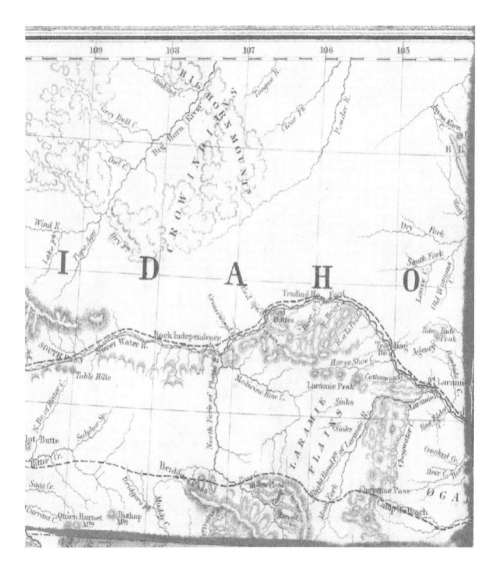

**Idaho Territory-Wyoming, 1863.** Lionel Pincus and Princess Firyal Map Division, The New York Public Library. "Map of Kansas, Nebraska, and Colorado. Showing also the eastern portion of Idaho." [Public Domain Image]

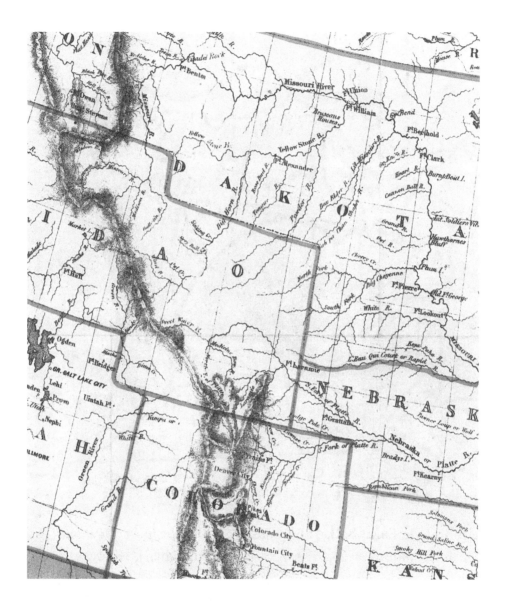

**Idaho Territory-Wyoming, 1864.** Bacon & Co. *Map of the United States, showing the territory in possession of the Federal Union, January.* [London Lithographed by Bacon & Co, 1864] Map. LOC 99447141.

**Map by John Lyle Campbell, 1864.** *Idaho: Six Months in the New Gold Diggings. The Emigrant's Guide Overland.* (New York: Self Published), 1864.

# Emigrant Tales of the

# PLATTE RIVER
# RAIDS

## An 1864 Trail Diary Companion

## Janelle Molony

Foreword by Kylie Louise McCormick

# Contents

# Preface

This book is the result of seven years of research into my Rousseau family ancestry. In the process of gathering notes for that project, I accumulated source materials that expounded on their covered wagon journey from Iowa to California in 1864.  The overlapping accounts added important context and confirmed that their shared experiences during the Platte River Raids were far more significant than previously believed.

By combining the testimonies, I could see a clearly defined picture of the events, leading factors, and subsequent reactions to the Raids, however, this task was made exceedingly difficult because prior to writing this book, nothing had been said about these events, in full context, by any other trail historian to date (excluding my own prior articles on the topic).

The only researchers that have come close to understanding the depth and range of this topic are Dr. Grace Raymond Hebard and Earl Brininstool, co-authors of *The Bozeman Trail* (1922), and Susan Badger Doyle, editor of *Journeys to the Land of Gold* (2000). Still, their research stopped before the Raids started, leaving me no choice but to take up that mantle and continue the story.

I wish to acknowledge that there is a side to this story that is not well represented. An authoritative, descendant-informed, and mapped-out account from the perspective of the Northern Plains Indians is desperately needed before too many conclusions can be made. If there is any perception that I am speaking on behalf of their people, it is unintentional. Until that enrichment occurs, the narrative of the emigrants, as presented here, must humbly be considered lacking and biased.

**Respectfully, Janelle Molony, M.S.L.**
3rd great-granddaughter of James & Sarah Rousseau
(in the Pella Company)

# Acknowledgements

The work held in your hands, could not have been completed with such depth of perspective and quality of interpretation without the generous assistance and prepared works of descendants and historians listed here:

**Descendants**
Curtis: Pamela Greenwood
Kelly: Barbara Yates-Romine
Howard: Christopher Courtney
Mahan: Cheryl Endres
Merill: Irving Merrill
Morris & Hastings: Steve Borders
Oliver: Robin Poindexter & Lisa Groves
Ridgley: Dana Cohoon & Alan Ridgley Griswold
Roorda: Alan Ver Ploeg & Julia Brunia-Thompson
Roe: Yvonne Reeman Rose & Betty Wilkins
Rousseau: Richard Molony, Kathleen Rousseau, Tiffany Hall & Stephen Daglish
Shoemaker: Kathy Lay, Ryan Shoemaker, Deb Trout & Art Shoemaker

**Historians:**
Earp: Nicholas Cataldo
Edwards: Janalyn Watson
Parker: Linda Kay Lehman
Pella Dutch: Brian Beltman
Roorda: Kor Postma
Wyoming & Overland-California Trail historian, Kylie Louise McCormick
Trail Grave Historians & Preservationists, Randy Brown, Richard Rieck & Larry Cundall

To all those above and those who have chosen to remain anonymous, thank you!
– Janelle Molony

# Foreword

## By Kylie Louise McCormick

In July of 1864, the Union Army, stretched to their limit, repelled Confederate advances on Washington D. C. and strained to stymie guerilla attacks in border states. As they marched into their battles in the east, hundreds of civilian men, women, and children stepped into another major conflict over 1,700 miles away, on the Western Frontier. The experiences of the families represented in the wagon trains, miner-packers, freighters, and companies that are featured in this volume present a significant fragment of the overarching stories of the United States' many conflicts and conquests.

Since the late 1840s, the Great Platte River Road from the Missouri River to the Red Buttes functioned largely like a toll road through the Plains and eastern Rocky Mountains. Along the road, emigrants grazed their stock, killed game, cut wood, and used waterways. Local bands of Plains Indians who lived along the route and depended on those resources, generally expected compensation such as with gifts or trading with the emigrants. Emigrants on the other hand had been warned about "hostile savages" and many came armed and afraid. Misunderstandings were bound to happen, especially after emigration increased rapidly in 1849 with the California Gold Rush. The increased traffic brought enterprising businessman building trading posts, bridges, and operating ferries. While most of the emigrants treated these "tolls" as necessary and legitimate, many of the same emigrants tried to "dodge" trading with or giving presents to the Indians they met along the route.

This defensive attitude is displayed in the account of former Sergeant Nicholas Earp who led his family and the Pella Company across the Plains in 1864. While traveling, Earp refused to engage in trades and discouraged those traveling with him from believing that a peaceful journey was possible. Before this, members of the Union Army had long been stirring up resentment amongst numerous Plains Indian Nations by disregarding the enduring relationship of Indigenous People with their land and simultaneously sending a message of superiority to Westward emigrants who desired to claim whatever land they stepped on as their own. Combined with a religious belief in Manifest Destiny, emigrants often didn't recognize Indigenous territorial claims because they were prone to believe that their move west was ordained by God.

Many of the prejudicial behaviors surged shortly after the signing of the 1851 Horse Creek Treaty which intended to honor important land-use boundaries so that overland travel could be done peacefully. While most attended the 1851 Horse Creek Treaty in hopes of peace, the treaty's allowance for the U.S. to establish forts along the trail soon escalated minor misunderstandings to war.

Pierre-Jean De Smet, "Map of the upper Great Plains and Rocky Mountains region," 1851. Library of Congress [G4050 1851.S6]. Public Domain.

In August of 1854, a Minniconjou Sioux warrior named High Forehead allegedly stole a sickly cow that was trailing behind a Mormon wagon train, some distance east of Fort Laramie (in what was then, Nebraska Territory). Soon after this crime was reported at Fort Laramie, a well-liked Brulé chief, Conquering Bear (Matȟó Wayúhi) traveled to the fort to name High Forehead as the thief and offer a mule or a horse as restitution. Brevet 2nd Lieutenant Hugh Fleming refused the compensation and insisted on waiting for the arrival of the Indian Agent to settle the matter.

After a heated argument with 2nd Lt. John Grattan, who wanted a show of force, Fleming changed his mind and sent Lt. Grattan and twenty-nine soldiers into the Brulé-Sioux village to arrest High Forehead. When they arrived in the village Conquering Bear again offered restitution, but Grattan refused; demanding that he hand over High Forehead instead. Verbal threats were exchanged and one of Grattan's men fired into the crowd of Brulé by-standers. Conquering Bear was shot three times in the fray, but Grattan and his men were surrounded and soon Brulé warriors killed every one of them.[1] As with many conflicts in the Indian Wars, this event was soon mislabeled a "massacre" with both Fleming's and Grattan's violent escalation glossed over. After the U. S. Army's inflammatory response to an alleged theft that included an apology and offer of restitution, local bands of Plains Indians became increasingly reluctant to put up with emigration activities through and on their treaty-protected lands.

The Grattan Fight marked the beginning of the 1854-1891 Sioux Wars, right on the heels of the congressional signing of the Kansas-Nebraska Act earlier in the year. The Act, a political compromise made in May of 1854, allowed for new territories to decide on the issue of slavery by popular vote. This spurred violent clashes between pro-slavery and anti-slavery factions known as Bleeding Kansas, igniting the unrest that led to the Civil War. After the Grattan Fight, depredations[2] along the trails continued to increase. Many historians, Molony included, correctly argue military intervention escalated Westward Expansion issues into an ongoing war with the Sioux. From then on, relations between Plains Indians and the U. S. Government deteriorated rapidly.

Though separated by distance and motivation, the Civil War and the Sioux Wars are inextricably linked by Westward Expansion. The idea of controlling the land from "sea to shining sea" was a politically charged and often religiously motivated idea. The introduction of new territories and states upset the balance of power in Congress between slave-labor and free-labor states. Without a doubt,

---

[1] Douglas R. Cubbison, "The Grattan Fight: Prelude to a Generation of War," *WyoHistory.org*, December 5, 2016, https://www.wyohistory.org/encyclopedia/grattan-fight-prelude-generation-war.
[2] Attacks or thefts of a violent nature.

the Civil War was fought over slavery—however, Westward Expansion increased the pressure on the Union Army. Meanwhile, Westward Expansion is also an antecedent of the Sioux Wars. From the 1600s to the 1850s, the Sioux were pressured to migrate from the Great Lakes into the Powder River Basin in response to European and U. S. emigration.

Prior to the gold rushes turning trails along the Platte River into highways for tens of thousands of emigrants, a Little Ice Age forced sacred Buffalo to migrate into the once lush Powder River Basin, the historic hunting grounds of the Apsáalooke Crow. The Lakota (Brulé, Hunkpapa, Oglala bands of Sioux) who hunted along the North Platte River followed the animals northward and waged war against the Apsáalooke. Allied with the Cheyenne and Arapaho, the Lakota asserted their dominance over the prized territory. Migration patterns of the Buffalo continued to be affected by trail travel through the 1850s. Buffalo grazing opportunities shrunk as emigrants marched their livestock further and further from the trails in search of grass for grazing. This led to further hostilities.

In 1862, six weeks of violent clashes between Anglo-Americans and Dakota-Sioux in Minnesota resulted in the arrest and exile of nearly 2,000 Dakota-Sioux men, women, and children. Biased military tribunals sentenced 303 Dakota-Sioux men to death, but President Abraham Lincoln reviewed each of the sentences, commuting all but thirty-nine. On December 26, 1862, thirty-eight of these men who proclaimed their innocence were mass executed – the thirty-ninth having been given a last-minute reprieve.[3] Six days later, on January 1, 1863, President Lincoln signed the Emancipation Proclamation declaring freedom for anyone enslaved within the rebelling states of the Confederacy.

Tensions between the Sioux and the U. S. Government rose higher that year when the mountain men John Jacobs and John Bozeman trespassed off the main trails and ventured through the Powder River Basin to create a shortcut to the goldfields of present-day Montana. This wagon road known as the Bozeman Trail cut through the Lakota's proudly won hunting ground. The basin area was

---

[3] Pekka Hamalainen, *Lakota America: A New History of Indigenous Power*. (New Haven: Yale University Press, 2019), 254.

considered, at least for the three nations using it, to be one of the last refuges untouched by Westward Expansion.[4]

In 1864, the situation out West became exasperated as greater numbers of civilians desperately fled war-torn states. While some folks on the trails were still bound for the coastal destinations of California or Oregon, others were now attracted to the future states of Idaho, Colorado, and Wyoming. Nations like the Sioux or Cheyenne who tolerated travelers passing through, now faced emigrants claiming and settling in their occupied lands. New findings of gold and silver in Idaho and Montana Territories also elicited more aggressive travel behaviors, as seen by Bozeman. The gold strike in Montana Territory drew emigrants from the South like Josiah and Fanny Kelly and the well-esteemed pioneers in the Forbis and Irvine families out onto the trails where death or destiny awaited.

The emigrants traveling on the Great Platte River Road in 1864, were unwittingly exchanging one warzone for another. As Grace Raymond Hebard, PhD., and E. A. Brininstool described in their book on the Bozeman Trail, "...anyone who dared to appear on the trails to the south ... became a marked man upon whom the hand of hate and vengeance descended, resulting in torture, mutilation and death."[5] This volume traces fifteen notable emigrating parties over a period of two weeks in July of 1864 along two branches of the famous trail that follows the North Platte River. During the Platte River Raids, more than 370 innocent civilians coming around the Laramie Mountains experienced the "hand of vengeance" in a way that shocked the Union Army rendering it incapable of stopping it.

The attacks were "soon felt all along the great trail when the rifle, tomahawk, arrow, and scalping knife did their relentless slaughter."[6] Emigrant victims looked to each other to escape, fight, or survive any way they knew how. In isolation, their stories promise to leave a lasting impression on readers that vilifies specific individuals. When read in context, however, readers' biases and pre-conceived notions will be challenged.

--------

[4] Charles Collins Jr., "Fort Phil Kearny Besieged," in *Atlas of the Sioux Wars*, 2 ed. (Fort Leavenworth:Combat Studies Institute Press, 2006).
[5] Grace Raymond Hebard and E. A. Brininstool, *The Bozeman Trail*, (Cleveland: Arthur Clark, 1922), 125.
[6] Ibid.

As a descendant of the Rousseau family, Janelle Molony has worked for years to gather the testimonies found in this volume and corroborate her family's experience as described in Sarah Rousseau's diary. Molony presents a never-before-seen accounting of the Platte River Raids by weaving diary entries, letters, and later recorded testimonies together into an exquisite play-by-play. An extensive appendix and Molony's hefty use of primary sources makes this a go-to reference for everyone studying the trails across the United States, the travelers who risked everything to use them, or the rich history of the Indigenous People who were displaced by them. Though the emigrant tales are one-sided, Molony's expanded review of them is essential reading for deepening our understanding of the complex Sioux Wars and how they affected the psyche of the nation.

**Kylie Louise McCormick** is a public speaker and historian at KLM Wyoming Historian and the Assistant Editor for *WyoHistory.org*, a project of the Wyoming Historical Society. More on her work and speaking engagements can be found at www.KylieTheHistorian.com.

# Meet the People
## on the
# South Bank Trails

(in alphabetical order)

# George Forman

Surname Included: Forman

**Zero wagons, one soul**
**From St. Louis, Missouri to Boise, Idaho**

**George Forman** is a lone traveler destined for Idaho's Boise Basin in search of gold. His wife **Ellen** stays back in Ontario (Canada West) while he travels south to St. Louis, Missouri, a common starting point for emigrants to get equipped for their journey ahead.

On paper, **George** can be classified as a disorganized opportunist who makes plans by the seat of his pants, only to see them fall apart at the seams. Rather than buying a wagon outfit, **George** opts to both save and make money by taking on jobs driving for other trains along the way. Leaving St. Louis, he accepts a "bull whacker" gig, driving one of ten ox-drawn freighters for **Mathias Ferris'** shipping company.[7] After one day, he realizes how slow the operation moves and abandons **Mathias** to help drive for the faster moving Peck family. When jumping ship, **George** races the Peck family wagon down the road to escape the ire of his first employer. The delay prevents **Mathias** from reaching Fort Laramie until July 20.[8]

After a while, **George** tires of his traveling company and their constant rest breaks for the animals. Thinking he can walk faster and farther on his own, **George** leaves the family. By the end of one day walking, he realizes he isn't cut out for the physical demand. His next plan includes trading his Ballard rifle and $50.00 cash (around $2,000, present-day) for an Indian pony that he later discovers is unrideable. The pony throws tantrums, stomps on **George's** bag, and cannot – will not – wear a saddle. The only

---

[7] Matthias Ferris eventually reaches the Black Hills with the Ringo Company.
[8] His story is then told by members of the Ringo Company.

upside, he finds, is that it can eat almost any greenery around. Without his hunting rifle, however, Forman goes entire days without meals.

At a settlement near the South Platte, **George** is tempted to trade his fussy animal for an Indian wife. He reasons that a wife would carry his pack and be less trouble overall. When making the trade arrangement, the woman learns just how far **George** expects her to travel and vehemently backs out of the deal. He is ultimately stuck with a disobedient horse, unable to hunt, and at the mercy of other wagon trains who either show compassion or hire him on for a distance. Sometimes his hitchhiking turns into a calamity. In one scenario, he is hired to drive a wagon for a widow and her children. Then, when he falls ill, his wages are deducted for each day they feed and haul him along.

From July 6 to 10, **George** travels in company with **Mr. Shoemaker**, who leaves him at Fort Laramie to take the North Bank Trails. In the Black Hills, **George** makes new friends with the **Merrill Team,** then after the Platte River Raids, he remains close to the **Granger Company** for a while.

The testimony of **George Forman** comes from his personal biographical sketch based off a diary that was never officially published. At mail stations along the way, **George** tears out the completed pages of his journal and mails them to his wife for safe keeping. Later in life, he reviews the documents and expands on his memories with information that would have been unknown at the time of original composition. The complete manuscript is available for researchers at the American Heritage Center and the University of Idaho and excerpts are found in easily accessible online publications.

**Primary Sources:**

Forman, George, "Biographical Sketch of the Life and Ancestry of Geo. Forman of Stratford, Ontario, Canada," 1883. Unpublished manuscript.

**Secondary Sources:**

Forman, George. "Across the Plains in 1864." Edited by Neal Miller, in *Annals of Wyoming, (*April 1968): 5-21.

Forman, George. "Across the Plains in 1864." Transcribed by Dean Galliver (1883). American Heritage Center [box 17, folder 4, #400029].

Forman, George. "Across the Plains in 1864, in Use of the Lander Trail as Reflected in Emigrant Accounts." Edited by Peter Harstad. Star Valley: Idaho State University, 1966, 52-55.

Forman, George. "George Forman: The Great Pedestrian." Edited by William E. Davis, in *Idaho Yesterdays*, 10, no. 1 (Spring 1966): 2–11.

"Historic Context Statements: Craters of the Moon National Monument." Seattle: National Park Service, 1995, 85-86.

Molony, Janelle. "1864 Mule Train 'Captain' Rescues Stranded Emigrants." *GenTales Magazine*, August 25, 2023.

Molony, Janelle. "Jesse Shoemaker: Pioneer of Merrick County's Hospitality & Tourism Industry," in *History Nebraska!* 105, no. 2, Lincoln: Nebraska State Historical Society (Summer, 2024).

# George Forman Roster

## Party 1: Ontario, CAN to Boise Basin, ID

| Full Name | Birth Year, Approx. Age |
|---|---|
| George S. Forman | 1830, 34 |
| *Lone Traveler* | |

# Granger Company

Surnames: Granger – Marsh - Jewell - Hawley - Rockwood - Logan

**At least eight wagons, twenty-nine souls**
**From Centralia, Illinois to Northern California**

The **Granger Company** comprises five families departing from Centralia in Marion Co., Illinois, to various destinations in Northern California. From Fort Laramie to Deer Creek garrison, the Company travels on the Oregon Trail system through the forested area of Wyoming's Black Hills (around Laramie Mountain). **Samuel Granger** is elected the captain of the train because he is, as **Aaron Rockwood** puts in a letter, "The man who owned the most of the train."

According to one descendant, **Samuel's** father Minard was a crime leader in a counterfeiting operation in New York.[9] While Minard is imprisoned, **Samuel's** mother remarries and, for the most part, the family distances themselves from the disreputable New York side of the family. In DeKalb, Illinois, **Samuel** cleaves to his wife's family and tries convincing her parents and several of her siblings to make the move to California with them. In 1861, his brother-in-law, **Omar Jewell** had made a trip there via the Panama Canal and established a place for his family in Bolinas. When **Omar** comes back for his family, **Samuel** has readied the wagons. The **Grangers** settle in Petaluma, while the **Jewells** establish a dairy ranch in the Olema Valley and establish the town of Jewell, California.

**Aaron Rockwood**, one of the memoirists in the Company, is originally from Vermont. In 1862, he musters out as an injured captain of the 4th Illinois Cavalry. During his service, he makes a promise to bring all his men home, dead or alive, and keeps that promise for better or worse. **Aaron's** story about the Platte River Raids is published in both the

---

[9] Leonard Granger. Personal commentary on "Minard Granger abt. 1804-1885," as shared on *WikiTree.com* (October 6, 2013). Accessed September 9, 2022. https://www.wikitree.com/wiki/Granger-897#Descendants

*Chicago Tribune* and *Cincinnati Enquirer* newspapers. His testimony contains details of their early morning robbery on July 14th. He reports a loss of sixty heads of horses, all but two of his own.

**James Logan**, another memoirist, is an undertaker and furniture maker by trade. **James** reportedly contracted either pyemia or septicemia (blood poisoning) from his interactions with corpses and may be self-treating with injections of the toxin Bromine. Before the journey, **James** invests in sixteen mules and four wagonloads of "drugs, liquors, etc." so he can set up a new undertaking business in San Jose, California.[10] His biography in the 1891 book, *Memorial and Biographical History of Northern California* helps pinpoint this train's March departure date. **James**' testimonial was published in the *Salem Weekly Advocate.* In his version, he reports fifty-two animals stolen, but none from his personal stock. He writes on August 1st: "they happened to miss me which was the only train that escaped for many miles."

In 1861, **John Hawley** is a hotelier of the famed Planter's House in St. Louis, Missouri, but at the outbreak of war, he abandons the position and moves to a Union state. By 1862, the **Hawleys** are living in Illinois where they prepare for a trek to Los Angeles, California. **John** is believed to have dogs with him on this journey. After news of the Platte River Raids reaches Fort Laramie and a detachment of soldiers is sent out, the **Granger Company** is detained for about two days. On July 17, when their military order to stay in place is lifted, **John** takes the wrong road at a fork, which separates him from the **Company** and takes him two miles out from Little Box Elder Creek. When he realizes his mistake, he cuts across a hill to get back on track and in the process, his dogs find the mutilated body of a little girl: **Mary Hurley Kelly**, of the **Kelly-Larimer Train**.

---

[10] *Memorial and Biographical History of Northern California…* (The Lewis Publishing Company: Chicago, IL), 1891. 341-342.

## Primary Sources:

Logan, James. "From the Rocky Mountains," letter to the editor, in *Salem Weekly Advocate,* November 10, 1864. (See the Appendix)

Rockwood, Aaron L. "From the Plains," letter to the editor in *Chicago Tribune*, September 10, 1864. (See the Appendix)

## Secondary Sources:

"John Hawley," *Memorial and Biographical History of Northern California.* Chicago: The Lewis Publishing Company, 1891. 341-342.

Livingston, Dewey S. "Jewell Ranch," in *A Good Life: Dairy Farming in the Olema Valley*, National Park Service (1995): 390-397.

Stedman Rothwell, Bertha. "Biographical Sketch of Omar Jewell." Manuscript in *Pioneering in Marin County* (1959): 228-238. (Copies available through the Marin County History Museum.)

"Woman Who as Girl Traversed Prairie Passes," Jennie Hawley Wildermuth obituary in *Los Angeles Times*, May 29, 1924.

# Granger Company Roster

### Party 1: Centralia, IL to Petaluma, CA

| Full Name | Birth Year, Approx. Age |
|---|---|
| Samuel Granger<br>*Captain, Head of Household* | 1833, 29 |
| Mary Matilda Marsh<br>*Wife, sister of Vienna Marsh* | 1840, 24 |
| Frank Minard Granger<br>*Son* | 1858, 6 |
| Elmer Eugene Granger<br>*Son* | 1862, 2 |

## Party 2: Wheatland, IL to Bolinas, CA

Omar Jewell                          1821, 43
*Head of Household, brother-in-law to Samuel Granger*

Vienna Marsh Jewell                  1824, 40
*Wife, sister of Mary Marsh*

Alva Jewell                          1848, 16
*Son*

Viana Jewell                         1849, 15
*Daughter*

Emma "Emily" Jewell                  1851, 13
*Daughter*

Olive Jewell                         1853, 11
*Daughter*

William H. Jewell                    1853, 10
*Son*

Anna "Annie" Jewell                  1857, 7
*Daughter*


## Party 3: Centralia, IL to Los Angeles, CA

John Milton Hawley                   1817, 47
*Head of Household*

Anna Maria Bruce Hawley              1819, 45
*Wife*

Jennie Bruce Hawley                  1853, 11
*Daughter*

Robert Bruce Hawley                  1859, 5
*Son*

*[Continued]*

## Party 4: Centralia, IL to Monterey, CA

Aaron Leeland Rockwood          1824, 40
*Head of Household, Memoirist*

Anna S. Mapes Rockwood          1825, 39
*Wife*

Henry & Unnamed Man             N/A
*2 Teamster-drivers*


## Party 5: Centralia, IL to St. Helena, CA

James Ignatius Logan      1829, 35
*Head of Household, Memoirist*

Unity Jane Livesay Logan         1833, 31
*Wife*

James Melvin Logan               1851, 13
*Son*

Milburn Hill Logan               1855, 9
*Son*

Minnie Adell Logan               1860, 4
*Daughter*

Charles Mead Logan               1863, 1
*Son*

Unnamed Men                      N/A
*3 Teamster-drivers*

# Kelly-Larimer Train

Surnames: Kelly - Larimer - Wakefield - Sharp – Taylor - Lawrence

**Five wagons, eleven souls
From Kansas to Montana**

The **Kelly-Larimer Train** includes two families from Allen County, Kansas, one clergyman, one neighbor and three extra teamsters, leaving in May of 1864. All are from nearby cities of Iola, Owl Creek and Geneva and recognize each other early on the journey. They join into one group for companionship and protection.

**Josiah** and **Frances ("Fanny") Kelly** are newlyweds on the trail from Geneva, Kansas. In 1863, **Josiah** musters out of the Union Army with an illness requiring a therapeutic change of climate.[11] **Fanny** is a Canadian immigrant who is about half his age when they marry. Shortly after the wedding, **Fanny's** younger sister is widowed and the **Kellys** adopt one of her children, **Mary Hurley**.[12] According to a Kelly family descendant, **Fanny's father** is a known abolitionist in the area and the family gets caught up in border warfare prompted, in part, by John Brown's demonstrations (murders) at Pottawatomie Creek in 1856.[13] This ongoing

---

[11] In the Victorian Era/Civil War Era, climatotherapy, or a prescriptive "change of air" as a medical treatment was a common recommendation for respiratory diseases and disorders, though it did not apply exclusively to these concerns. Those with inflammatory disorders such as asthma, arthritis and even tuberculosis would be prescribed a dry air, salted air, or warm air climate such as those found in California, Arizona, and Nevada. By the 1880s, many patients sought the remedy of a vacation or resort stay to improve their mental health when they suffered from "melancholy." Some wealthy patients required travel to recover from the stress of marital attachments. The less wealthy could end up getting a change of scenery in an insane asylum.
[12] Mary Ann Wiggins Hurley (1836-1902). Her first husband, William Hurley, dies in 1864.
[13] Ronald T. Shawan, "The Descendants of Frederick Shawhan (1760-1840)," in vol. 2 of *The History and Genealogy of the Shawhan and Related Families* (publisher unlisted; place of publication unlisted, 2000), 320-257.

violence may have been extra motivation for her father to see her off and away.

On the journey, **Fanny** keeps a diary that has since been lost.[14] In the 1871 memoir she bases on the diary, she explains, "My husband was looked upon as a leader, as he was principal owner of the train."[15] He can also be considered the most experienced for such a role because of an 1856 trek to California in search of gold. **Josiah,** retired Army, has plans to start a retail operation in one of the major mining "boom towns" in Montana Territory, so they've packed up two large wagons with an enormous store of supplies, including twenty-five sacks of flour weighing in at one hundred pounds each, canned goods, three kegs of liquor, and "ready-made" clothes.[16] The wagons are both pulled by four yoke of oxen. In addition, they are herding fifty milk cows and twenty-five calves for a potential dairying operation.

The **Kellys** bring along with them two Black freedmen as hired helpers. They drive the herd of fifty dairy cows and twenty-five calves and help cook meals. **Fanny** only identifies them as a father and teen son, **Franklin** and **Andy**, who were once "slaves among the Cherokee."[17] Further research suggests these men are **Franklin and Andy Lawrence**, from Mississippi and Arkansas (respectively), who may have been owned by a wealthy Cherokee plantation owner that brought slaves from the South into "Indian Territory" (Oklahoma) during the Trail of Tears.

In 1863, the Five Civilized Nations in Oklahoma[18] were coerced to emancipate their slaves in exchange for protection from the Union Army. Union troops escorted the freed men and women into Kansas. There, the former slaves had no resources nor citizenship rights, leading to a crisis

---

[14] Barbara Yates-Romine, a 3rd great-grandniece to Josiah and Fanny Kelly, claims the original item was supposed to be donated to an archive, but disappeared before that could be done.
[15] Fanny Kelly, *Narrative of My Captivity Among The Sioux Indians*, (Cincinnati: Wilstach, Baldwin & Co., 1871), 21.
[16] When Fanny Kelly petitions the government for compensation in 1866, these are identified on a list of personal items lost in the Raids.
[17] Ibid., 24.
[18] The Five Civilized Tribes were: Cherokee, Creek, Choctaw, Chicasaw, and Seminole.

of identity and economic security. It is believed the **Lawrences** jump on the travel opportunity seeking a fresh start.

**William** and **Sarah Larimer** are originally from Pennsylvania. In 1859, the couple moves to Iola, Kansas and **Sarah** opens up a photography studio. This move is prompted by **William's** health. Similar to **Josiah's** story, he is a veteran Union soldier, discharged from the Army years before the Civil War due to asthma and arthritis that allegedly made his hands curl, deeming him unable to perform manual labor.[19] "Physicians assured him that a change of climate was necessary," Sarah records in her 1870 memoir.[20] Unfortunately, the Kansas climate does not produce a full recovery for **William**, so they look for a better option, farther west. With them is their only child, **Frank**.

The **Larimers** initially leave Iola with a large emigrant train, possibly captained by a man named Ely, but part ways a few weeks into the journey. They join the **Kellys** who, by then, have picked up a "most agreeable companion" **Gardner Wakefield** (from Geneva),[21] and the "aged and almost blind" **Reverend Andrew Sharp** (from Owl Creek).[22] Around this same time, the **Larimers** hire on **Noah Taylor** (from Coffey Co.), to drive their wagon with glass, foils, chemicals, and other daguerreotype photography equipment from **Sarah's** business.[23]

The five-wagon **Kelly-Larimer Train** is the first group of emigrants in this collection to encounter hundreds of Indians descending upon the trails on July 12, 1864.[24] The emigrants are alarmed by the sight of such an army, but after receiving friendly greetings in the English language,

---

[19] Loretta L. Evans, "Sarah Luse Larimer 1836-1913: Indian Captive, Photographer, and Business woman," in *Pegasus* (Dallas: Dallas Genealogical Society, vol. 1, no. 1, 2013), 21-37.
[20] Sarah L. Larimer, *The Capture and Escape; or Life Among The Sioux,* (Philadelphia: Claxton, Remsen, & Haffelfinger, 1870), 16.
[21] Fanny Kelly, *Narrative of My Captivity*, 1871, 15. In Julius Merrill's journal entry from July 18, he also describes the Reverend as, "blind in one eye and so cross-eyed."
[22] Sarah Larimer, *The Capture and Escape*, 1870, 44.
[23] Noah Taylor is suspected to have been originally hired on as a driver for a Mr. Ely from Burlington, Kansas. Their working relationship dissolves and he accepts an offer from the Larimers to continue on.
[24] Other headcounts have been reported from two hundred-thirty to three hundred-fifty. One news article even claims there were six hundred.

they are put somewhat at ease. After meeting, the large band of warriors from different tribes breaks up and leaves in small groups.[25] These detachments proceed farther down the Overland and Oregon Trails, and set signal fires on hilltops and mountain peaks then position themselves near frequented emigrant camps.[26]

The war chief (given an assumed or invented name in one book) directs **Josiah** to detour from the main trail that crosses Little Box Elder Creek, a tributary of the North Platte River.[27] **Josiah** corrals the teams near the creek, then the chief insists on joining the families for dinner. Both memoirists, **Fanny** and **Sarah**, highlight how unnerving this is for them and mention their begrudged feelings at the expectation to provide an extraordinarily large meal from their rations. The men in the **Kelly-Larimer Train** comply and disperse to collect firewood, tend to the stock animals, and to prepare the expensive meal.

Meanwhile, the Indians in camp curiously inspect the contents of the overstocked wagons and attempt to make trades for things they like. Every primary source record indicates that the women remain with or inside their wagons and that no emigrant is armed at the time.[28] When one of the Indians reaches for a gun that is near to **Sarah**, she responds fearfully, though no story clarifies what words she uses or actions she takes. "I objected in vain," she remembers, though by conjecture or

---

[25] There is a high variability for which tribes are involved based on which emigrant tells the tale. Evidence from arrowheads and descriptions provided narrow the possibility to Cheyenne, Lakota-Sioux, Blackfoot-Sioux, Oglala, and Arapaho, all working in coordinated fashion (though there could be others). Some believe that a faction of Cheyenne Dog Soldiers are involved based on the method of attack. An oral history from Yanktonai Sihasapa chief John Grass (Mato Watakpe) claims the kidnappers were Hunkpapa.

[26] George Forman, "Biographical Sketch," 1864, July 15th: "Indians are now all around us making signals from the Hills with large fires to each other."

[27] A tributary is a branch of a river that flows towards and joins the main course of the river. Little Box Elder Creek is a minor tributary flowing west by northwest into the major Box Elder Creek that flows north by northeast and forms Box Elder Canyon.

[28] This contradicts Sarah Larimer's earlier claim that "all the men carried firearms to defend themselves in case of attack," from the point of Old California Crossing and beyond (Larimer, 1870, 25).

common sense, readers might interpret her objection as a startling scream with the possibility of erratic gestures. [29]

Chaos erupts. The Indian releases a "war-whoop" that elicits a simultaneous firing of guns and arrows. The hired man **Sarah** calls "**Black Franklin**" is crippled with arrows and when he falls, the Indians crush his skull. The hired driver **Noah** receives a bullet in his forehead and drops dead in front of **Fanny**. The **Reverend** is shot while in the process of reaching up into his wagon. He falls some distance to the ground. **Gardner** is struck by three arrows that all miss his vital organs. He makes a dash for the hills where he hides overnight.

Oddly, **William**, who is either tending the fire with **Franklin** (per **Fanny's** book) or tending to the mules (per **Sarah's** book), is left unharmed. Nevertheless, he flees with **Gardner** and while he runs, he is struck with an arrow through his thigh, causing him to fall. Like **Gardner**, he crawls to a hiding place for the night. **Josiah** and **Andy**, take advantage of their distance from camp while collecting firewood. They both spring to their feet and run for their lives.

Back in camp, three men lie dead and both **Fanny** and **Sarah** and their two young children are left completely unprotected. The women and children are commanded to get on horseback to be taken away. The war chief orders a pursuit of the runaways and for the camp to be ransacked and burned to the ground. Some Indians steal away with all the loose horses and mules. Others make chase along the Creek and spot the passing **Morris-Hastings Train**, who have seen too much.

In the departure from camp, the kidnappers scatter in different directions to confuse anyone who might come for them. A short distance out, **Fanny** drops her niece off their shared horse with instructions to run and hide, but the guards catch on and some turn around to make sure little **Mary Hurley Kelly** cannot live to tell her tale. After swimming across the North Platte River, the Indians take their kidnappees due north towards the Pine Gulch Ravine (where **Sarah** and her son **Frank** will make their escape).

---

[29] Sarah Larimer, *The Capture and Escape*, 1870, 45.

The **Kelly** and **Larimer** families from Kansas are the better known travelers through the Laramie Mountains because of the sensationalized memoirs **Fanny** and **Sarah** publish to capitalize on their experiences. One review of **Sarah's** 1870 book writes that "It commences with a touch of hifalutin," but it otherwise is, "quite entertaining" (*Richmond Dispatch*, April 8, 1870). **Fanny Kelly's** book receives a review in 1871 that emphasizes its dramatic flair and lauds its portrayal of the "red man" as "bloodthirsty"; reinforcing the dangerous idea that the only good Indians are dead ones (*Lawrence Daily Journal*, March 3, 1871).

Contradictions in the women's books create the condition that if one version is true, then the other's must be fictitious. Readers are encouraged to review corroborating first-person accounts (such as those in this collection) to see past the biases. **Josiah** also writes about his experience in a letter home to his brother, which might be the most authoritative version of the tale amongst the three. His letter has been transcribed and published, but the original item has been lost.

**A final note on the Kelly-Larimer Train:**

In prior literature, the tragic murder of three men in the **Kelly-Larimer Train**, plus the kidnapping of two women and two children on July 12, has been titled a "massacre." In this book, the author will use alternative terms such as "murder" or "incident" and refrain from equating the loss to events from this same time period:

The Fort Pillow Massacre on April 12, 1864. Over three hundred African-American Union soldiers are slaughtered after their garrison surrendered to the Confederacy in Tennessee. Comparatively, their white compatriots are held as prisoners of war.

The Sand Creek Massacre on November 29, 1864. Union Colonel John Chivington orders the cruel decimation of two-hundred-thirty Cheyenne and Arapaho women, children, and elders in Colorado.

**Primary Sources:**

Grass, John. "Fanny Kelly Story." Oral History to Col. Alfred Burton Welch in 1915. Transcribed by Everett Cox in *Welch Dakota Papers*, 2011. https://www.welchdakotapapers.com/2011 /11/chief-john-grass-2/. (See Appendix)

Kelly, Fannie. "Letter to Rezin Wells Kelly, March 10th, 1865." Transcribed by Mrs. Henry Pelton and Dwight Yates in *Genealogy of the John A. Kelly Family*. Ohio: Private Publication, 1950.

Kelly, Fanny. *Narrative of My Captivity Among The Sioux Indians.* Cincinnati: Wilstach, Baldwin & Co., 1871. [30]

Kelly, Josiah Shawan. "Letter to Rezin Wells Kelly, August 15, 1864," Transcribed by Mrs. Henry Pelton and Dwight Yates in *Genealogy of the John A. Kelly Family*. Ohio: Private Publication, 1950. (See Appendix)

Larimer, Sarah L. *The Capture and Escape; or Life Among the Sioux.* Philadelphia: Claxton, Remsen, & Haffelfinger, 1870.

Larimer, Sarah L. "Letter to Sarah Jane Taylor (ca. August 1864)," in "Attack on the Kelly-Larimer Wagon Train." Typescript by Randy Brown, *Overland Journal,* 5, no.1 (1987): 26. (See Appendix)

**Secondary Sources:**

Brown, Randy. "Attack on the Kelly-Larimer Wagon Train." *Overland Journal* 5, no. 1 (Winter 1987): 16-40.

Brown, Randy. "The Kelly Story," 1986. Kansas Historical Society digital collection #303250, DaRT ID: 303250.

Evans, Loretta L. "Sarah Luse Larimer 1836-1913: Indian Captive, Photographer, and Business Woman," *Pegasus* 1, no. 1, (2013): 21-37.

---

[30] There appears to be an unedited book manuscript from Fanny Kelly on file with the National Archives in Record Group 233: Records of the U.S. House of Representatives, 40th Congress.

Molony, Janelle. "The Kelly-Larimer Train: One of Many Murders on the Oregon Trail." *GenTales Magazine,* November 11, 2022.

Pelton, Mrs. Henry and Yates, Dwight. *Genealogy of the John A. Kelly Family.* Ohio: Private Publication, 1950. (KS Historical Society.)

## Kelly-Larimer Train Roster

### Party 1: Geneva, KS to MT

| Full Name | Birth Year, Approx. Age |
|---|---|
| Josiah Shawahan Kelly<br>*Wagon master, Head of Household* | 1824, 40 |
| Fanny A. Wiggins Kelly<br>*Wife, Diarist/Memoirist* | 1842, 22 |
| Mary Ann Hurley Kelly<br>*Adopted daughter, Fanny's niece* | abt. 1857, 7 |
| Franklin Lawrence<br>*Hired help, father of Andy* | abt. 1820, 44 |
| Andy Lawrence<br>*Hired help* | abt. 1847, 15-17 |

### Party 2: Iola, KS to WY

| | |
|---|---|
| William Jasckson Larimer<br>*Head of Household* | 1826, 42 |
| Sarah Elwood Luse Larimer<br>*Wife, Memoirist* | 1836, 28 |
| Frank Eugene Larimer<br>*Son* | 1857, 7 |
| Noah Daniel Taylor<br>*Teamster-driver from Sharpe, Coffe Co., KS* | 1834, 30 |

**Party 3: Woodson Co., KS to WY**

Gardner Wakefield                1836, 28
*Travel companion*

**Party 4:  Neodesha, KS to WY**

Rev. Andrew Sharp                1810, 54
*Travel companion*

# Mahan–Moore Team

Surnames: Mahan - Moore - Mayger

**Two wagons, four souls**
**From Cole County, MO to Virginia City, MT**

On April 18, 1864, brothers, **Garland** and **Augustus "Gus" Mahan** are mining hopefuls who leave their family in Jefferson, Missouri under pressure to avoid the draft. They initially begin their trip with two other "partners:" **John Moore** and **William "Bailey" Taylor** (from Shelby Co. and Cole Co., respectively), **William Mayger "Major"** and **Edward Allen** from elsewhere in Missouri.

**Garland Mahan** keeps a leather-bound "day-to-day diary," written in pencil and later transcribed by his daughter, Carrie Barker. He is a twenty-five-year-old school teacher, while his brother **Gus** is twenty-three and may have been a farm laborer with his father. They start from Missouri with one wagon and four oxen, while **John** brings the second wagon.

**Garland's** writing takes notice of the flora and fauna along the way and he comments on the sweet smell of roses, the shape of "touch me nots," the vining of wild grapes and other perfumes in the air. He also enjoys teasing his non-American companion, **"Major" (William).** He says the Englishman is green as a gourd, or not ready for the journey. On May 3, **Garland** writes that **William** "clawed off" something from the back of his neck and upon looking at the creature in his palm, he asked, "What kind of bug do you call that bites so?"[31] It was his first experience with a tick. Later, the team spies a skunk—the first **William** has ever seen. He throws rocks at it (no doubt, encouraged by the team) and unleashes its defensive spray. He hollers, "What a smell he has!" **Garland** records everyone roaring with laughter.

---

[31] Garland Mahan, *Garland Jefferson Mahan's Diary,* 1864.

The **Mahan-Moore Team** doesn't get too far out from Jefferson City before one of the men is recognized as a deserter. On May 4, **Edward** is caught and arrested in De Kalb, MO. Three weeks later, with no explanation whatsoever, **William "Bailey"** "dissolves" his partnership with **John** and turns back.[32] The team consolidates and continues, reaching Fort Laramie on July 7. In the Black Hills, they struggle to keep a strong pace. After one day's twenty-four mile haul over rough roads, one wagon loses two wheels and the other's axle breaks. The next day, an ox sickens and dies, forcing the train into a layover to recuperate.[33] In retrospect, this delay may be a lucky break concerning the Raids beginning on July 12. It seems Providence accomplished what the Northern Plains Indians were attempting and an attack on the **Mahan-Moore Team** is made unnecessary.

Three days later and more ox dying, the team drags on to La Prele Creek where they are met with "a no. of wagons" that includes **George Forman**, the **Granger Company** and the **Merrill Team**.[34] Collectively, there are over one hundred covered wagons, plus a company of the **11th Ohio** marching north from Fort Laramie. After a military detainment, the **Mahan-Moore Team** continues on past the scene of devastation at Little Box Elder Creek. Here, **Garland** reports that "our train" buries an anonymous man (now identified as **Jacob Hastings' employee**) and a little girl (now identified as **Mary Hurley Kelly**), who are both found near the road.

**Garland** notes that the Indians who made this attack have since broken into "little squads" seen along the roads for the past thirty-five miles. When the **Granger Company** reaches Deer Creek Garrison, **Garland** avidly listens to **Sarah Larimer's** discourse on her capture and escape. He commends her as "an intelligent person."[35]

---

[32] Ibid., May 21.
[33] Ibid., July 11. Prior to this, Garland replaced one of his four oxen suffering from a "foot evil" with a cow. He continues with only two oxen and one cow.
[34] Ibid., July 15.
[35] Ibid., July 15.

Copies of **Garland's** diary are available through the generosity of his second great-granddaughter, Cheryl Endres, and can be found in the Merrill J. Mattes Collection in the Research Library at the National Frontier Trails Museum in Independence, Missouri (digital access via the Oregon-California Trails Association). A brief mention about the trip can also be found in a biographical pioneer sketch about **Gus** that reads: "**Mr. [Augustus] Mahan** has always resided in Cole County, with the exception of about three years, which were spent in Montana Territory, whither he went in 1863 with an ox team, the journey taking about four months."[36]

### Primary Sources:

Mahan, Garland *Garland Jefferson Mahan's Diary: Trip to Montana by Oxen from*
*Cole County Missouri, 1864*. Transcribed by Carrie M. Barker. Fayetteville: Private Publication, 1965.

### Secondary Sources:

"A. A. Mahan." In *History of Cole, Moniteau, Morgan, Benton, Miller, Maries, and Osage Counties, Missouri*. Chicago: Goodspeed, 1889, 871.

## Mahan–Moore Team Roster

### Party 1: Jefferson, MO to Virginia City, MT

| Full Name | Birth Year, Approx. Age |
| --- | --- |
| Garland Jefferson Mahan | 1838, 25 |
| *Diarist, mining team* | |
| Augustus "Gus" Alexander Mahan | 1840, 23 |
| *Brother, mining team* | |

---

[36] "A. A. Mahan," *History of Cole, Moniteau, Morgan, Benton, Miller, Maries, and Osage Counties, Missouri,* (Chicago: Goodspeed, 1889), 871.

## Party 2: MO to Virginia City, MT

John Thompson Moore                    1841, 23
*Mining team, from Shelby Co., MO*

William Newton Mayger ("Major")        1842, 21
*Mining team, from Saint Louis, MO*

## Associates: (Unable to complete the journey)

Edward Allen                           N/A
*Mining team, arrested for desertion*

William Bailey Taylor                  1837, 26
*Mining team (Moore's partner), turns back*

# Merrill Team

Surnames: Merrill - Carey - Durbin

**One wagon, four souls**
**From Milwaukee, WI to Boise City, ID**

**Julius Merrill** is an Idaho gold seeker from Maine. Because of the Civil War and the Conscription Act of 1863, his parents urged their adult son to make haste leaving the United States. **Julius** first heads west to Milwaukee, Wisconsin. There, he joins up with **Charles Carey**, a local Canadian-born blacksmith. He also meets the **Durbin brothers** from England and the men depart to St. Joseph, Missouri on April 28, 1864.[37]

In Missouri they look for equipment and livestock, but affordable options are hard to come by. They finally get themselves one second-hand wagon and a mixed bag of livestock: three yoke of ox, one steer-cattle yoke combo, and another of two cows. Finally, on May 22, they start their westward adventure and on May 23, **Julius** stresses in his journal, "only one pair [of ox] was broken." As a result, the outfit required all four men to be involved in the training. In theory, the two trained animals would be assigned the lead position with the other eight learning how to follow. In practice, the day's driver calls out "gee" with a lead rope tug to turn right, and "haw" to turn left, while at least two men walk on either side of the stock with prods or short whips to keep the untrained cattle in line. A fourth man might also ride or walk at the front to assist cuing the lead animals.

**Julius** also mentions having one pony and, for exactly one day, the team has a dog. The dog fights its leash and cannot stay with the group. By the end of the day, **Julius** cuts it loose. The **Merrill Team** remains unmolested during their journey through Wyoming, but **Julius'**

---

[37] Julius Merrill, *Bound for Idaho: The 1864 Trail Journal,* ed. Irving R. Merrill, (Moscow: University of Idaho Press), 1998, April 28.

observations prove valuable for confirming several facts of the Platte River Raids.

When the Raids begin, the team is fifty miles south of where the **Kelly-Larimer** and **Morris-Hastings Trains** are attacked. **Julius** learns about the associated murders on July 13 from the telegraph operator at Elkhorn Station. The next day, an emergency response detachment of one hundred soldiers from Fort Laramie reaches the **Merrill Team's** camp. By military order, one hundred and forty wagons of emigrants are detained in place until safe travel can be assured. Rather than sit around, **Julius** volunteers with a military-led search party "in pursuit of the Indians."[38] His unit marches on foot for half a day with no sightings.

**Julius's** journal validates claims from the **Granger Company** of having discovered the body of **Mary Hurley Kelly** some distance from the main road. Specifically, he says one wagon took a wrong turn, then cut across a hill to rejoin their train. In the process, they found the body. **Julius** makes gruesome observations of the body's defensive positioning at time of death, the points of entry and exit of all arrows, and the length of a tomahawk gash across her scalped-clean skull. This entry is likely supported with comments from **James Logan**, the undertaker with the **Granger Company**. **Julius** concludes with: "Leaving several to bury the body, we moved on."[39]

After the week of Raids, the **Merrill Team** continues traveling in a party of eleven wagons–one having traveled with the **Team** from as far back as in Kansas. In mid-August, the trains split at a fork in the road near Parting of the Ways.[40] Some continue towards Idaho while others turn south to Utah.

Readers should note that **Julius** touches up the contents of his journal before his passing. In 1998, a descendant revises the material again before publishing it.

---

[38] Ibid., July 16.

[39] Ibid., July 17.

[40] Julius Merrill, *Bound for Idaho*, August 21-22. He counts: "eleven wagons, thirty-three men and two women," then, a "balance" of seven wagons, before more trains leave. Then, the Merrill Team is down to three wagons.

**Primary Sources:**

Merrill, Julius. *Bound for Idaho: The 1864 Trail Journal of Julius Merrill.*
Edited by Irving R. Merrill. Moscow: University of Idaho Press,
1998.

# Merrill Team Roster

### Party 1: Milwaukee, WI to Boise City, ID

| Full Name | Birth Year, Approx. Age |
| --- | --- |
| Julius Caesar Merrill<br>*Diarist, Mining team* | 1840, 24 |
| Charles Carey<br>*Mining team* | 1827, 38 |
| Henry Durbin<br>*Mining team* | 1827, 37 |
| Steven J. Durbin<br>*Mining team* | 1829, 35 |

# Morris-Hastings Train

Surnames: Morris - Hastings - Wright - Northrop

**Two wagons, nineteen souls**
**From Davis County, IA to Walla Walla, WA**

The **Morris** and **Hastings** families from Davis County, Iowa departed separately in the Spring of 1864, but during the course of their eventful Summer, they develop a kinship that lasts for generations to come. Ella Hastings Long,[41] the daughter of **Enoch Hastings** and **Alice Morris**, shares her family story with Washington historian, Martha Scoggin in a 1973 text, *Pioneer Days on Scoggin Ridge and Pataha Prairie.* In her account, she claims her parents and grandparents are all from the same "big train of covered wagons."[42]

The family of the small town farmer, **Nelson Morris,** comes from Grove Township, which is about twenty miles south of where the **Hastings** lived on Lick Creek. Secondary sources for the **Morris'** family suggest their original wagon train departure began about 1863 from Floris which aligns with empirical evidence for **Nelson** mustering out of the Union Army as an invalid. The lag can be credited to the family staying to see their eldest son married in Iowa on March 6, 1864.[43] Once the **Morris** family reaches the North Platte River, they connect with the **Pella Company** and travel with them to Fort Laramie. Also with them by this time is **Mr. Arthur Wright** from Hennepin County, Minnesota. **Arthur** is believed to be either a teamster employed by **Nelson**, or a lone packer-miner who is only linked with them temporarily. Family stories do not preserve the context of that relationship.

---

[41] Ella Hastings Long, 1884-1972.

[42] Martha Scoggin, *Pioneer Days on Scoggin Ridge and Pataha Prairie.* (Spokane: Scoggin, 1973), 94

[43] See Iowa, U.S., Select Marriages Index, 1758-1996 for Harvey Milton Morris and Sarah Ann Shadle, FHL Film No. 968466. (The newlyweds do not join the Westward migration.)

Similarly, discrepancies in secondary sources records for **Jacob Hastings** family in Lick Creek suggest a departure directly from Putnam County, Missouri as early as 1862. More accurately, the Iowa family crossed the state border by 1860 and lived near **Jacob's** in-laws for a couple of years, but the tensions of the Civil War prompted a retreat back into the Union State.[44] From 1862 to 1864, they may have been preparing for the journey ahead. **Jacob,** who is a Christian minister by trade, opts for an ox-drawn wagon for the cross country trip. **Jacob** also has a employed teamster with him, though this individual is never named.

In the Black Hills, the **Morris** and **Hastings** families get swept up into the immediate chaos of the attacks on the **Kelly** and **Larimer families** due to their proximity to Little Box Elder Creek on July 12.[45] That day, they are approximately a mile behind the **Kelly-Larimer Train** on the same trail and witness the destruction of their camp and see the fallen emigrants. In source texts, their experiences can appear disjointed since the **Morrises** and **Hastings** are separated during the attack and chased in different directions. **Jacob's** wagon passes by the remains of a camp where "occupants had been murdered and left lying about," **Ella Long** recalled.[46] The wagons were burned, and "the ashes were still hot."

After passing the tragic scene, the employee in **Jacob's** outfit runs up a hill to better see what was going on. "He was shot by the Indians," **Ella** shared.[47] First-person accounts by other emigrants state he was approximately two miles west of the creek, on the side of the road when he fell. After being shot, he was assaulted and scalped.[48] The Northern Plains Indians chase off the **Hastings**, who must leave the employee

---

[44] See the 1860 U.S. Census for York, Putnam County, Missouri: Roll: M653_641; Pages 581-582 (Jac. Hastings Family in Dwelling No. 1656 and William Graham Family in No. 1657).

[45] Both the Kelly and Larimer memoirs place the Morris and Hastings parties about a mile behind them, which would have held them back from the scene for just under two hours.

[46] Ella Long in Scoggin, *Pioneer Days*, 1973, 94.

[47] Ibid.

[48] The details of this death were reviewed with Randy Brown, a local trail preservationist and co-author of the reference text, *Graves and Sites on the Oregon and California Trails*. At that time, he had no useful information to offer regarding the man's identity or grave location. (Personal communication to the author, November 17, 2022.)

behind, unburied. The **Hastings** are likely the first to report the tragedy to soldiers at the Deer Creek garrison.

Between the **Hastings** and **Morris** wagons is **Arthur Wright,** who made a habit of riding ahead of the covered wagon. This leaves him overexposed to danger. He was also shot, **Ella** recalled, "leaving the train to watch."[49] On July 21, a **Mr. Northrop** (who was with the **Morris** family during this event) would recount to **Sarah Rousseau** in the **Pella Company**: "They surrounded **Wright** and fired three shots at him[,] one through his heart, another in his back and one in his leg. Meanwhile, **Morse's** [sic] **wife** took the lines[,] turned as quick as thought and went back as hard as she could…"[50]

**Nelson Morris** (or his wife) turns the wagon around to race back east to the safety of an emigrant camp down the road. In the chase, Indians pelt the wagon with arrows, one passing through the shirt sleeve of baby **Ulysses**, who is in his frantic mother's arms. That night, the women and children place sacks of flour against the inner sides of the wagon box so they can hide behind them, should there be another attack. After surviving the Platte River Raids, it's possible the two Washington-bound families create a pact to travel together from then on for mutual safety.

A journal or travel log has not yet been located for this train, so their tale is woven from published pioneer histories, obituaries, corroborating first-person accounts and secondary accounts from relatives. **Martha Scoggin's** research and oral history from **Ella Long** is not widely available, as it was privately published, but there are concerns about the reliability of information in the book, including there being no references to source material or other evidence to support claims made.[51] Because factual contradictions are pervasive in the secondary sources, primary accounts (**Kelly, Larimer, Rousseau, Northrop**, etc.) are given narrative authority.

---

[49] Ella Long in Scoggin, *Pioneer Days,* 1973, 94.

[50] Sarah Rousseau, *The 1864 Diary of Mrs. Sarah Jane Rousseau*, (Phoenix: M Press Publishing, 2023).

[51] The full, transcribed oral history interview from Ella Long is also missing from the book so future researchers are unable to review her words objectively.

**Primary Sources:**

None available.

**Secondary Sources:**

"H. M. Morris." *An Illustrated History of Southeastern Washington,* Edited By Frederic A. Shafer. Spokane: Western Historical, 1906, 602.

"Enoch G. Hastings." *An Illustrated History of Southeastern Washington,* Edited by Frederic A. Shafer. Spokane: Western Historical, 1906, 606.

Scoggin, Martha L. *Pioneer days on Scoggin Ridge and Pataha Prairie.* Spokane: Scoggin, 1973. Central Washington Univ. Library accession: F897.G3 S3.

# Morris-Hastings Train Roster

### Party 1: Grove, Davis Co. IA to Walla Walla, WA

| Full Name | Birth Year, Approx. Age |
| --- | --- |
| Nelson S. Morris | 1815, 49 |
| *Head of Household* | |
| Sarah Jane Nation Morris | 1835, 29 |
| *2nd Wife* | |
| Mary Saralinda Morris | 1849, 15 |
| *Daughter of Nelson and 1st wife* | |
| Clara Cortilda Morris | 1850, 14 |
| *Daughter of Nelson and 1st wife* | |
| William Waterman Morris | 1852, 12 |
| *Son of Nelson and 1st wife, marries Nancy Hastings* | |
| Alice Suffina Morris | 1856, 8 |
| *Daughter of Nelson and 1st wife, marries Enoch Hastings* | |

Charles O. Morris                    1856, 8
*Son of Nelson and 2nd wife*

Elmer E. Morris                      1861, 3
*Son of Nelson and 2nd wife*

Ulysses S. Grant "Tum" Morris        1863, 1
*Son of Nelson and 2nd wife*

## Party 2: Lick Creek, Davis Co., IA to Walla Walla, WA

Rev. Jacob Peoples Hastings          1826, 38
*Head of Household*

Martha A. Graham Hastings            1843, 37
*Wife, pregnant*

Enoch Graham Hastings                1815, 14
*Son, marries Alice Morris*

Ephraim Daniel Hastings              1854, 10
*Son, blind*

Nancy Jane Hastings                  1856, 8
*Daughter, marries William Morris*

Judith A. Hastings                   1858, 6
*Daughter*

Amanda Elizabeth Hastings            1860, 4
*Daughter*

Martha Catherine Hastings            1861, 3
*Daughter*

Emaline Alice Hastings               Born Dec. 1864
*Daughter, unborn*

Unnamed Man                          N/A
*Teamster for the Hastings family*

## Named Individuals: Minnesota to Idaho Territory

Arthur "Buckskin" Wright               1835, 29
*Single rider, also see the Pella Company*

Mr. Northrop                           N/A
*Single rider, also see the Pella Company*

# Ringo Company

Surnames: Ringo - Forbis - Lucas - Davenport - Edwards - Beauvais - Morrice - Kirby - Guthrie - Davis - Hodge

**Seven wagons, forty-four souls**
**From Liberty, MO to California, Idaho and Montana**

In 1864, **Martin Ringo**, Missourian and former soldier in the Mexican-American War, is suffering from the wasting effects of tuberculosis and this journey West is a desperate attempt to find relief in California's dryer climate. He packs up two wagons with heavier furniture items and books that most emigrants would toss out along the way. Even though he and wife **Mary**, have a fourteen-year-old son, **John ("Johnny")**, who can help with some of the men's responsibilities, **Martin** hires a driver, **Owen**, to assist with driving the second wagon. **Mary** is about three months pregnant with her sixth child and must be increasingly careful about the workload and stress she takes on. She keeps a daily diary that is later transcribed and published by her daughter, **Mattie Bell**.

By May 18, **Martin** organizes seven wagons belonging to neighboring Missouri families who are originally destined for Oregon and Montana Territory:[52]

The **Forbis family (AKA Mr. Irvine's Train)** from Platte Co. with two wagons; the **Lucas family** from Buchanan Co. with another two wagons; and one wagon that supports **William Davenport**[53] and his gold mining team of **James Reed** and **the Martin Brothers** from Clay Co.

The **Forbis family** are originally plantation owners from Kentucky who moved to Missouri in 1841. At that time, Missouri was considered the

---

[52] Montana Territory is defined as separate from Idaho Territory starting on May 26, 1864.
[53] William Davenport is the brother of Robert H. Miller who is the editor of the *Liberty Tribune* and the brother-in-law to Mary Peters Ringo by marrying her sister Enfield "Enna" Peters.

"Far West," and **America Forbis** recalls "carving out of the wilderness" to create a new farm in Platte County. [54] Her travel experience is preserved in a biographical sketch about pioneer women, as presented at the World's Fair in 1893. When the Civil War erupts, their efforts to establish a peaceful, forever home in Missouri are destroyed by both Union and Confederate soldiers who trample on, steal from, and abuse civilian resources. Though considered Southern Sympathizers, they are fed up with the situation. Corroborating **Mary Ringo's** date of departure, **America** writes, "May 18, 1864, we started with ox-teams for Oregon via Idaho."[55]

Joining the **Forbis family** are their in-laws, led by **Thomas Irvine** with his son **Edwin** (married to **Anna Forbis**) and nephew **David** (married to **Sarah "Fannie" Forbis**). While the **Forbises** look forward to finding good soil to rebuild, the **Irvines** are set on finding gold. **Anna Forbis Irvine's** sketch about her journey is included in the same World's Fair presentation as her mother's.

In the **Lucas Train, or "Lucas & Co."** as it is sometimes referenced, former Captain in the Confederate Army, **George J. Lucas**, leads his family away from Rush Township on the border of Missouri and Kansas.[56] Because of his involvement in the War, Kansans and other pro-Unionists in the area express a constant bitterness against the family. "It was not exactly a pleasant place to live, under the circumstances," writes **William Lucas**, who is only fourteen on the journey.[57] Though originally tobacco dealers, the **Lucas family** plans to start a cattle ranch in Montana Territory, so in addition to their horse and mule-drawn wagons, they are herding cattle across the Plains.

Even though the **Ringo Train** is not present in the Black Hills during the exact week of the Platte River Raids, their account is thoughtfully included as a follow-up to expound on, confirm, or clarify prior claims.

---

[54] America Forbis, Autobiographical sketch for the World's Fair of 1893 in, "Women Pioneers," *The Anaconda Standard*, February 17, 1895, 12.

[55] Ibid.

[56] Presently Rushville, Missouri.

[57] William Lucas, Oral history, "Fifty Years and More in Santa Barbara," transcription by Michael Phillips, *Santa Barbara News-Press*, May 1, 1926, 4.

Before continuing, please note that the original families associated with the **Ringo Train** are joined by numerous others prior to reaching Fort Laramie. When this occurs, the "**Ringo Train**" reference is adjusted to the collective **"Ringo Company."**

Days before entering the Black Hills, **Mary** records the train growing in size to sixty-two wagons.[58] Named travelers who join them near Fort Laramie include: **Dr. Addison T. Guthrie's Train** from Platte Co.;[59] **Reverend Hodge**, reportedly from Clay Co.;[60] and the **Edwards Team** from Hamilton.[61] When **William Davenport** sends an August 1 letter to the *Liberty Tribune* newspaper, he includes eight more wagons in the count (totaling seventy).[62] Later additions include: the **Morrice Team** led by **Calon Morrice** of Clay Co.,[63] the **Beauvais Company** hauling trade goods from St. Joseph, [64] and **Mathias Ferris'** freighting operation (the one that **George Forman** abandons early on in his journey).

The **Ringo Company** starts into the Black Hills on July 21 and follows the Mormon Trail on the south side of the North Platte River. This path brings them past fresh graves and roadside wreckage from the Raids. At least ten writers are with the **Ringo Company** when they pass through the Laramie mountains. Compared to the confident remarks made at Fort Laramie by those who came through before them, these writers reveal a great consternation over becoming the next victims to be buried on the wayside. On July 27, near Little Box Elder Creek, **Mary** learns about the

---

[58] Mary Ringo, *Trip Across the Great Plains in 1864,* transcription by Mattie Bell Ringo Cushing (Santa Ana: Cushing, 1942), July 15.

[59] This train may include other named individuals: Dr. and Mrs. Davis (or Davies) from Kansas, as well as Mr. and Mrs. Kirby from Leavenworth, also in Kansas.

[60] Mary Ringo calls him the "preacher in our outfit," though Mr. Rushville gives him the title of "Captain."

[61] The Edwards Team joins on July 15. Haywood Edwards (b. 1842) keeps a diary of his mining team's journey to Idaho. Coincidentally, Haywood is a fourth cousin to Elijah Oliver (see the families on the North Bank Trails), and a first cousin (three times removed) to Col. Daniel Boone.

[62] William Davenport, "From the Plains, August 1, 1864," in *Liberty Tribune,* September 16, 1864.

[63] The Morrice Team joins on July 19, just east of Fort Laramie. Named individuals are Calon, David, William and John, though their exact identities require additional research.

[64] Mary Ringo spells this train's name as "Bovey." This train is carrying a supply shipment for the company run by Pierre Geminian Beauvais and his eleven sons.

many murders that have occurred, as well as a recent fight with the Indians. Her anxiety spikes and she writes: "I do hope and pray [to] God that we may get through safely, it keeps me so uneasy..."

A few days later, the **Ringo Company** is robbed and one man shot in the process (though not fatally). Accusations are made about Indians, though **Mary** is skeptical; allowing readers to wonder if a desperate victim of the prior Raids might have been trying to acquire horses so they can get out of the area. After this, the **Ringo Company** posts more guard shifts. The extra fatigue on the men is blamed for an early morning accident causing **Martin's** unexpected death. After this tragedy, **Johnny** must bear the full weight of his father's workload. **Mary** reroutes the family course from Sacramento to San Jose to be with her sister **Augusta** and brother-in-law **Colonel Coleman P. Younger**.

Readers will find that the **Ringo Company** is fortunate to have passed through the Hills at the time they did and to leave the perceived safety of Deer Creek behind on June 30, because on August 1, this soldier station becomes the target of an attack by Northern Plains Indians within forty-eight hours of their departure.


**Primary Sources:**

Davenport, William. "From the Plains, August 1, 1864." *Liberty Tribune*, September 16, 1864. (See Appendix)

Edwards, Haywood. *The Diary of Haywood Edwards, May 30, 1864 to October 31, 1864.* Typescript by A.W.D. in the Missouri Collection, Historical Society of Missouri (f-238; box #SUNP-2507; C3982). (See Appendix)

Forbis, America A. "Women Pioneers." Autobiographical sketch for the World's Fair of 1893, in *The Anaconda Standard*, February 17, 1895, 12. (See Appendix for America's submission.)[65]

---

[65] The full article also includes statements from Mrs. Brownlee/ Myra Forbis, Mrs. E. H. Irvine/Anna Forbis, and Mrs. J. R. Russel/Sarah Forbis.

Forbis Irvine Russel, Fannie. *Reminiscences.* Manuscript collection, Montana Historical Society, [SC 165].

Forbis, Jr., Jonathan. *Recollection of 1864 Trek from Missouri to Virginia City, Montana.* Typescript in John F. Forbis Papers, 1886–1901, Montana Historical Society, [SC 54].

Lucas, William T. "Fifty Years and More in Santa Barbara." Oral History Transcription by Michael Phillips, *Santa Barbara News-Press*, May 1, 1926, 4. (See Appendix)

Ringo, Mary. *Trip Across the Great Plains in 1864.* Transcribed by Mattie Bell Ringo Cushing. Santa Ana: Cushing, 1942.

Rushville. "Crossing the Plains, July 29, 1864." *The Morning Herald*, August 9, 1864, 2. (See Appendix)

Rushville. "En Route for Idaho, August 2, 1864." *The Weekly Herald and Tribune*, September 8, 1864. (See Appendix)

## Secondary Sources:

"Hon. John F. Forbis." *Progressive Men of Montana.* Chicago: A. W. Bowen & Co, ca. 1903, 159-160.

Brown, Randy. "A Special Section of Emigrant Graves: Martin Ringo." *Overland Journal* 7, no. 1 (1989): 19-22

Johnson, David. *John Ringo: King of the Cowboys.* Denton: University of North Texas, 2008.

Kemp, Annabelle. "George Johnson Lucas." *Lucas Genealogy.* Hollywood: Kemp, 1964, 145.

"Mrs. Sarah T. Lucas, Aged 94, Dies" *Woodland Daily Democrat*, April 18, 1923.

Molony, Janelle. "Women of Wyoming, Then & Now: Mary Ringo." Wyoming Historical Society. Video series launching 2024. https://youtu.be/A6eAB0ctguo?si=ifHqsUB8BuRZ-hcL

"Mrs. A. A. Forbis Taken by Death." Obituary in *The Butte Miner,* July 13, 1903, 5.

Sanders, James Upton. "John Franklin Forbis." *Montana Pioneers.* Silver Bow: Society of Montana Pioneers, 1899. (Also includes sketches from Mrs. J. F. Forbis, James W. Forbis, William P. Forbis, and Myra Bell Forbis.)

Schontzler, Gail. "The Hidden Bozeman Trail." *Bozeman Daily Chronicle,* July 6, 1996. (Contains mentions of Mr. Davies.)

# Ringo Company Roster

### Party 1:  From Liberty, Clay Co., MO to San Jose, CA

| Full Name | Birth Year, Approx. Age |
| --- | --- |
| Martin Ringo<br>*Captain* | 1819, 45 |
| Mary Ann Peters Ringo<br>*Wife, Diarist, pregnant* | 1826, 38 |
| John Peters "Johnny" Ringo<br>*Son* | 1850, 14 |
| Martin Albert "Allie" Ringo<br>*Son* | 1854, 10 |
| Fanny Fern Ringo<br>*Daughter* | 1857, 7 |
| Mary Emma Ringo<br>*Daughter* | 1860, 4 |

| Mattie Bell Ringo | 1862, 2 |
|---|---|
| *Daughter* | |

| Baby Boy Ringo | 1864, N/A |
|---|---|
| *Stillborn* | |

| Owen      (NLN) | N/A |
|---|---|
| *Second Wagon Driver* | |

## Party 2: From Platte Co., MO to Alder Gulch, M.T.

| Jonathan Franklin Forbis Sr. | 1816, 48 |
|---|---|
| *Head of Household* | |

| America A. Perrin Forbis | 1817, 47 |
|---|---|
| *Wife* | |

| Agnes J. Forbis Steele | 1844, 20 |
|---|---|
| *Daughter* | |

| William Perrin Forbis | 1853, 11 |
|---|---|
| *Son* | |

| John Franklin Forbis II | 1855, 9 |
|---|---|
| *Son* | |

| Myra Belle Forbis | 1857, 7 |
|---|---|
| *Daughter* | |

| James Wade Forbis | 1859, 5 |
|---|---|
| *Son* | |

## Party 3:  From Platte Co., MO to Alder Gulch, M.T.

| Thomas Howard Irvine Sr. | 1811, 53 |
|---|---|
| *Head of Household* | |

| Sarah Sally Bryan Irvine | 1816, 48 |
|---|---|
| *Wife* | |

| Nancy "Nannie" Irvine | 1842, 22 |
|---|---|
| *Daughter* | |

Margaret "Maggie" Irvine                    1844, 20
*Daughter*

Thomas H. Irvine                            1845, 19
*Son*

Bryan Irvine                                1849, 15
*Son*

Mary "Molly" Ellen Irvine                   1851, 13
*Daughter*

Elizabeth "Eliza" Irvine                    1855, 9
*Daughter*

Sallie "Bettie"      Irvine                 1856, 5
*Daughter*

## Party 4:  Mr. Irvine's Train (cont.)

David LeRoy Irvine                          1835, 29
*Head of Household, Son of Thomas and Sarah  Irvine*

Sarah F. Forbis Irvine                      1846, 18
*Wife, Daughter to Jonathan and America Forbis*

## Party 5:  Mr. Irvine's Train (cont.)

Edwin H. Irvine                             1837, 27
*Nephew of Thomas and Sarah Irvine*

Anna E. Forbis Irvine                       1840, 24
*Wife, Daughter of Jonathan and America Forbis*

Franklin Forbis Irvine                      1861, 3
*Son*

Mary Ella Irvine                            1863, 1
*Daughter*

## Party 6:  From Weston, MO to Deer Lodge, M.T.

| | |
|---|---|
| George Johnson Lucas<br>*Captain of "Lucas & Co."* | 1823, 41 |
| Sarah Sallie Thomas Lucas<br>*Wife* | 1829, 35 |
| William Thomas Lucas<br>*Son* | 1850, 14 |
| Adams James Lucas<br>*Son* | 1852, 12 |
| Ruth Lucas<br>*Daughter* | 1854, 10 |
| Nancy "Nannie" Lucas<br>*Daughter* | 1855, 9 |
| Mary Elizabeth Lucas<br>*Daughter* | 1858, 6 |
| Margaret "Maggie" Lucas<br>*Daughter* | 1860, 4 |
| Sallie Thomas Lucas<br>*Daughter, twin* | 1862, 2 |
| George Johnson Lucas Jr.<br>*Son, twin* | 1862, 2 |

## Party 7:  From Missouri to Idaho Territory

| | |
|---|---|
| William Davenport<br>*From Platte, Clay Co., MO.* | 1823, 41 |
| James "Jas." Reed<br>*From Clay Co., MO* | N/A |
| James Martin<br>*From Liberty, Clay Co., MO* | 1827, 37 |
| John Martin<br>*From Liberty, Clay Co., MO* | 1828, 36 |

# Emigrant Tales
## from the
# South Bank Trails

# "Westward Ho!"

The Oregon Trail has been made famous in almost two hundred years of literature and films as the premier Westward trail system, but this term is more conceptual than most people realize. Contemporary historians have suggested that the title is more of a literary convention than a fixed path on a map. As readers will soon see, in 1864, the title might even convey the meaning, "the popular trail."

Starting in 1848, Westward emigrants who followed a route parallel to the North Platte River on the south bank through Nebraska and Idaho Territories would been on the original Oregon Trail until they reached Fort Laramie. At or before the Fort, travelers wishing to stay on the official Oregon Trail would cross the River to the north bank, continue north to present-day Douglas, Wyoming then around the River's "big bend" to Casper, Wyoming.

By the 1860s, the lesser used Mormon Trail and Pony Express routes on the south side of the river increased in popularity. These paths cut more directly through Medicine Bow Forest which saved on travel time. In Philip Platt and Nelson Slater's 1852 *Guide to California Overland*, they write: "From the fort there are several roads leading westerly towards the South Pass. The Mormon trail is through the Black Hills nearly 100 miles before reaching the river. The one traveled most is near the river, though any part of the time in sight of it and is considered the best on account of grass and water" (15).

As more folks stayed on the south bank trail system, it became colloquially referred to as the "New" Oregon Trail. For researchers, this moving target invites confusion. Henceforth, in this book, the paths that stay on the south side of the River will be literally referred to as the "South Bank" trails. The author will also simplify the two options for South Bank travelers that Platt and Slater mention. The Mormon Trail can be simplified as the "Interior Route" that is closer to the base of the Laramie Mountains. The "New" Oregon Trail can be simplified as the "River Route" which has regular access to the River.

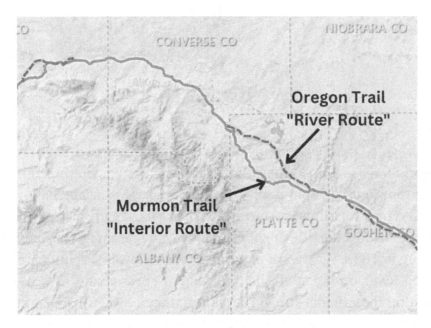

Map generated using the NPS National Trails Historic Trails Viewer, a project of the National Geographic Society. Labels added by the author.

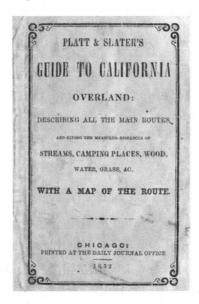

Title page from Platt & Slater's *Guide to California*. Chicago: Daily Journal. 1852.

The Interior and River Routes essentially start together at the Fort, split around some mountains, then converge again near Elkhorn Creek. The paths offer different experiences and accommodations for emigrants. There are mileage advantages on the Interior Route that could save an emigrant a full day's worth of travel, should they have enough portable water storage for themselves and their animals. If desperate, emigrants are able to adjust their course as it suits them by following any one of the intersecting creeks back to the North Platte River.[66]

The Interior Route, contains the following milestones from Fort Laramie to Deer Creek garrison, totaling 101 miles.

| Mileage | Destination |
| --- | --- |
| 9 | "Nine Mile House" |
| 12 | Cottonwood Creek |
| 15 | Horseshoe Creek (also "Horse Shoe" Creek) |
| 10 | Elkhorn Creek |
| 15 | La Bonte Creek |
| 10 | Bed Tick Creek |
| 8 | La Prele Creek |
| 10 | Box Elder & Little Box Elder Creek |
| 12 | Deer Creek |

[66] An interactive map from the National Park Services offers a filtered view of all National Historic Trails through Wyoming, including layers showing overlaps and intersections. Explore at https://nps.maps.arcgis.com

The River Route that Platt and Slater encourage travelers to use is less direct and totals 116.5 miles.

| Mileage | Destination |
| --- | --- |
| 14.5 | Lime Kiln Spring |
| 7 | Bitter Cottonwood Creek |
| 3 | Cotton Wood Creek |
| 4.5 | Dry Creek |
| 2.25 | Elk Creek |
| 2 | Rock Springs (on the right) High ledges (on the left) |
| 3.5 | Horse Shoe Creek |
| 8 | Platte River |
| 6 | Platte River (about Elkhorn Creek) |
| 16 | La Bonte Creek |
| 8.5 | Branch of La Bonte |
| 3.5 | Red Bank Creek |
| 6.75 | Small Stream |
| 8 | La Prele Creek |
| 5.75 | Spring Branch |
| 3.25 | Little Deer Creek |
| 4 | Platte River |
| 5 | Deer Creek |
| 1 | Lower Platte Ferry (Bisonette's Ferry) |
| 4 | Deer Creek |

In the forthcoming narrative, there are scenarios where an emigrant party on the Interior Route camps on a well-known creek and is attacked in broad daylight, while another emigrant party on that same creek, but further east on the River Route, is completely unaware of and immune to the event (and vice versa).[67] Beside the two main South Bank Trails, readers will soon see that detours and "offshoots" are present and some connect emigrants to the North Bank Trails via swimming or ferrying the River.

In 1861, when the Pony Express began operating its mail route through Idaho Territory (Wyoming), small horse stables and outbuildings were erected near or at regular intervals: on Horseshoe Creek, La Bonte Creek, La Prele Creek, and at Deer Creek Station. Express riders could exchange their exhausted horses with well-rested ones at these stops. The installation of telegraph lines spelled the end of the Pony Express operation and telegraph operators moved into the abandoned outbuildings. In this area, the operators were officers of the 11th Ohio Volunteer Cavalry who were charged with maintaining the lines.

A misconception about these stations is that they might offer resources or protection to emigrants. At best, they could offer watchtower-like services and share updates heard on the lines about major events or trail conditions. They were staffed with between one and four soldiers with minimal supplies for their own use. Typically bored with these outpost duties, the Union soldiers change what information they share with inquiring emigrants based on their mood and personality.

In 1922, trail preservationist, Dr. Grace Raymond Hebard and cowboy poet Earl A. Brinnstool published the book, *The Bozeman Trail*.[68] It thoroughly details an emigrant's journey over hill and plain through Wyoming. The co-authors describe the depots-turned-telegraph stations as such:

---

[67] The Interior and River Routes could be as many as six miles distant from the other at certain points.
[68] Grace Raymond Hebard and E. A. Brininstool, *The Bozeman Trail, vol 1.* (The Arthur H. Clark Company: Cleveland, OH), 1922.

Horseshoe Station:
"Thirty-six miles west of Fort Laramie; not on the North Platte, but on the [New] Oregon Trail, which from Fort Laramie to Deer Creek, did not follow the river, but went directly northwest, being several miles south of the river. In 1862 this station, also a telegraph station..." (36).

La Bonte Station (Later known as Camp Marshall):
"...A telegraph station about sixty-six miles west of Fort Laramie. Ten miles east of this old station ... had a ferry which was in operation [Bridger's Ferry]" (37).

Bridger's Ferry was an important connection point between the South and North Bank Trails that allowed emigrants access to Bozeman's new shortcut to Montana. This trail skirts the eastern side of the Bighorn Mountains through prairie lands that were not ceded for government use in the 1851 Treaty of Fort Laramie. Any wagon train risking this shortcut in 1864 would be trespassing.

La Prele Station:
"...About eighty-two miles west of Fort Laramie station; also a telegraph station" (37).

Deer Creek Station:
"...One hundred and two miles from Fort Laramie, and thirty miles east of [Upper] Platte Bridge. This fort and military station was on the largest tributary of the North Platte since leaving Fort Laramie. This was an important emigrant camping place where a ferry was in operation" (37).

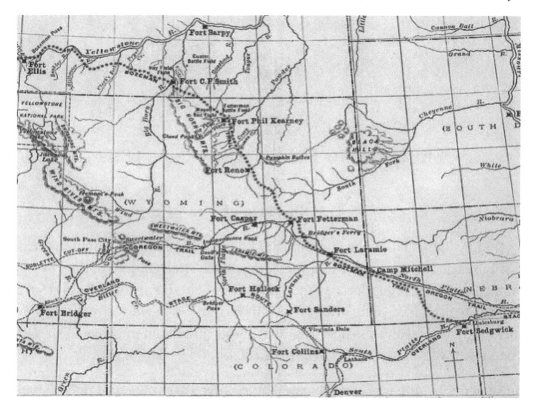

Partial view of Dr. Grace Raymond Hebard's "Map of the Bozeman Trail (from Virginia City, Montana to Fort Sedgwick, Colorado)," 1922. Permission granted by the University of Montana. Accessible online at MTMemory.org.

# Thursday to Friday, July 7–8, 1864

### Kelly-Larimer

On July 7, the five covered wagons of Kansans in the **Kelly-Larimer Train**. officially reach Fort Laramie along the South Bank Trail. On July 8, they explore what the Fort has to offer. Because the expositions of both **Fanny Kelly** and **Sarah Larimer** are produced years after the events as derivative works from one diary, readers are cautioned to consider that the stories have been informed or inflated beyond what was known to the writers in 1864.

| | |
|---|---|
| **Fanny Kelly**<br>*Kelly-Larimer* | "At Fort Laramie … we had renewed assurances of the safety of the road and friendliness of the Indians." *(20)* |
| **Sarah Larimer**<br>*Kelly-Larimer* | "This fort is one of the oldest in the country. … The fort is situated on the [Laramie] river, about two miles from where it empties into the North Platte. … At the outposts and ranches we passed[,] we had heard nothing but ridicule of pretensions to warfare..." *(34-39)* |

### Morris-Hastings

Presently on the North Bank Trails around this time are the **Morris** and **Hastings** families from Iowa. It is suspected the Washington-bound parties are not a formally united train yet but will become so in the next week. Their whereabouts from July 2 to 7 are detailed in the North Bank Trails section of the book, as they had previously been associated with the **Pella Company** (also from Iowa). They reach Fort Laramie with the **Pella Company** on July 7, then elect to cross to the South Bank Trail system, leaving their prior travel companions. **Sarah Rousseau**, diarist in the **Pella Company** writes from July 21 about this:

**Sarah Rousseau**
*Pella Company*

"There was two families that traveled in our train. One of them named **Morse [Morris]** and the other **Wright**. They left our train at Laramie to go to the South side of the river." *(July 21 - in reflection)*

The official length of time spent together is unknown, but it is long enough for **Sarah** to become familiar with their habits. Later, when she exchanges stories with survivors of the Platte River Raids, she easily recognizes which tales are about the individuals from the **Morris-Hastings Train**. While the **Pella Company** departs from Fort Laramie on July 8 (still on the North Bank Trail), the **Morrises** and **Hastings** lay over until approximately July 9.

Fort Laramie, albumen silver print from a glass negative, ca. 1866 (Public domain).

## Mahan-Moore & Merrill

Two mining teams from Missouri, the **Mahan-Moore** and **Merrill Teams** also reach Fort Laramie between July 7 and 8. Both teams take a day of rest and occupy themselves with wagon repairs or much needed self-care.

| | |
|---|---|
| **Garland Mahan**<br>*Mahan-Moore Team* | "Got to Fort Laramie … came in sight of the black hills…." *(July 7)* |
| | "Lay by to wash Etc. … I have suffered the most intense pain in the last 3 or 4 days." *(July 8)* |
| **Julius Merrill**<br>*Merrill Team* | "…the wagons needing repairing and some cattle needing to be shod… *(July 7)* |
| | "We broke one of the hounds of our wagon and were obliged to stop and fix it. … Crossed Laramie River. Good bridge. … Whisky was much in demand by the soldiers."[69] *(July 8)* |

**Julius Merrill's** mining partner **Charles Carey** tries to make the necessary repairs for the wagon but needs help from a blacksmith located about two miles west of the Fort in a civilian hamlet.

---

[69] Lieutenant Eugene Ware, stationed at the Fort, claims his troops have an inability to remain sober.

# Saturday & Sunday, July 9–10, 1864

### Kelly-Larimer

On July 9 the **Kelly-Larimer Train** with their herd of dairy cows makes a rapid departure into the Black Hills. They are noted to have some of the finest horses on the trails this summer, including a prized race horse belonging to **Josiah Kelly**. Keeping up with their pace might be daunting for parties with heavier loads or lesser horse power. By nightfall of July 10, they reach Horseshoe Creek, approximately forty miles away from Fort Laramie. Here, they rest in observance of the Sabbath.

| | |
|---|---|
| **Sarah Larimer**<br>*Kelly-Larimer* | "Forty miles from Fort Laramie is Horse-shoe Creek...." *(37)* |
| **Fanny Kelly**<br>*Kelly-Larimer* | "At Horseshoe Creek ... there was a telegraph station..." *(20)* |
| **Sarah Larimer**<br>*Kelly-Larimer* | "...in answer to our inquiries, we received similar declarations as to the quiet and peaceful state of the country through which we must pass." *(39-40)* |

### Kelly-Larimer & Morris-Hastings

The **Morris and Hastings families** from Davis County, Iowa leave Fort Laramie on the heels of the **Kelly-Larimers.** The Iowa families are believed to be traveling light and can keep up with the ambitious speed of the Kansans. In no time at all, the **Kelly-Larimer** and **Morris-Hastings** parties become familiar faces.

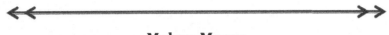

## Mahan-Moore

The **Mahan-Moore Team** with two wagons also enters the Black Hills on July 10, albeit on the Interior Route. They make it nearly to Cottonwood Creek by evening. The miners are eager to advance farther, but must be cautious because they have just repaired a broken wagon axle, replaced two tires, and are down one ox that died, "with a disease similar to the Murrain" (July 10).[70]

**Garland Mahan**
*Mahan-Moore Team*

"We are now 15 miles from the Ft. at the base of the black hills. ...the most grand and beautiful scenery bursts forth on the eye of the traveler."
*(July 10)*

## Merrill

After a three-day layover near Fort Laramie, **Julius Merrill** and his four-man mining team also depart on July 10, but don't get as far as the **Mahan-Moore Team**. They stop seven miles in to camp at "Nine Mile House." This location gets its name from being exactly nine miles from the Fort, just southeast of Register Cliff and Guernsey.

**Julius Merrill**
*Merrill Team*

"... Camped at the edge of the Black hills." *(July 10)*

Modern readers might compare this ranch setup to a small plaza with services such as the Sand Point Trading Post, an old Pony Express station, and the civilian mercantile known as Ward & Guerrier's.[71]

---

[70] The term "murrain" refers to an infectious disease, plague or other pestilence effecting livestock, though the exact affliction is unspecified.

[71] The mercantile was named for its original owners, Seth Ward and William Guerrier. Seth E. Ward is also the official sutler at the Fort's store. After the passing of his first partner (William Guerrier) Seth hired William Bullock to manage the sutlery full time, while Seth focused his attention on the mercantile.

## Forman

At this time, **George Forman**, a lone traveler with his single, gray Indian pony[72] is accompanying a widow and her children who are destined for the Fort. He offers them some degree of protection and helps drive the wagon. In exchange, the widow offers him daily meals. On July 10, he stops at "Five Mile Ranch," owned by French trader Geminien P. Beauvais.

| | |
|---|---|
| **George Forman** <br> *Lone Traveler* | "Made Beauvais Ranch 5 miles from Fort Laramie on the edge of the Fort Reservation of 10 miles square inside of which no one was allowed to camp." *(July 9-10)* |

At the ranch, **George** learns that the "Northern Sioux" are engaged in a war. He may be referring to the attacks made during Union General Alfred Sully and General Henry Sibley's expedition through Dakota Territory to push hostile Sioux away from lands now occupied by white settlers.

| | |
|---|---|
| **George Forman** <br> *Lone Traveler* | "I hesitated about going on from here on account of the Indian rumored troubles, and would have gone back to Omaha & St. Louis and gone into something there, if I could get a boat to float down the Missouri River." *(July 9 or 10)* |

**George** ultimately decides to keep going west. He pressed on to the Fort and bids farewell to the widow. He takes his time exploring all the Fort has to offer, including the sutler's store and bar, as well as the many lingering prostitutes.

---

[72] Geminen Pierre Beauvais opened the original Star Ranch in 1853 as the headquarters for his up-and-back trade operation from Missouri. In 1859, he expanded with an installation at the Old California Crossing (15 miles south of Ash Hollow, NE). Upon opening this second location, he transferred the Star Ranch title, while the initial business became known as Five Mile Ranch, or in some texts, "Beauvais' Ranch." After finishing school in St. Louis, MO, Geminen's son Edward took over the new Star Ranch. An educational sketch on the family is found in LeRoy Hafen's book, *The Mountain Men and the Fur Trade of the Far West*, Vol. 7. (Arthur H. Clark: Glendale, CA), 1965. 38-40.

**George Forman**

*Lone Traveler*

"[Fort Laramie] is a series of Barracks and Parade Grounds and Sutler's Stores & officers houses by no defensive works. It is occupied by 900 men of the Eleventh Regt. Ohio Cavalry Vols."
*(July 9-10)*

"...there are Indian camps all around the fort and hosts of Squaw Prostitutes hanging around the Barracks and soldiers quarters."
*(July 9-10)*

# Monday, July 11, 1864

### Kelly-Larimer

On July 11, the **Kelly-Larimer Train** corrals at La Bonte Creek. Nearby is the La Bonte Station (formerly a Pony Express stop). Also near the confluence of the North Platte River with La Bonte Creek is an abandoned cabin, which might have been an old stagecoach stop that ceased operation years prior. Neither memoirist mentions these sites.

**Sarah Larimer**
*Kelly-Larimer*
"Twenty-five miles farther west [of Horseshoe Creek] is another stream, that offered a pleasant place for the weary strangers' encampment." *(37-38)*

### Mahan-Moore

Stalled near Middle Bear Creek (about five miles from Horseshoe Creek), the **Mahan-Moore Team** is delayed by additional wagon repairs. Trail diarist **Garland Mahan** describes being stuck in a barren land without sufficient, clean drinking water. Fortunately, all else has been quiet in the Black Hills, "save [for] the chatter of a blackbird with white wings peculiar to these hills", and the distant laughter of coyotes at night (Mahan, July 10).

**Garland Mahan**
*Mahan-Moore Team*
"How are we to get along? ... We have to lay by all day..." *(July 11)*

## Granger

The **Granger Company**, comprising five Illinois families and at least eight wagons, is suspected to depart Fort Laramie on July 11 with a herd of horses. Details of their experience are found in two letters written by **Aaron Rockwood** and **James Logan**. In **James'** letter, he clarifies that the Company is not formally organized. Instead, the families are joined by a matter of convenience and have no loyalty bond.[73] Over the course of their journey, the California-bound families separate into the following subgroups 1) The families of **Samuel Granger** and his brother-in-law **Omar Jewell**, 2) **Aaron Rockwood** and **John Hawley's families**, and 3) **James Logan's family** (although **James** claims he usually keeps up with **Samuel** and **Omar**).

By the end of July 11, the three subgroups are suspected to be camping in the general vicinity of Cottonwood Creek, though some may go as far as Middle Bear Creek. The author has no reason to believe they camp together. Per **Aaron's** letter, there is only some accountability to have regular check-ins with **Samuel**, as he appears to set the general pace and allegedly owns "the most of the train."[74]

## Forman

On July 11, **George Forman** starts off into the Black Hills on foot, making twenty miles his first day in. Nothing exciting happens for him this day, other than reaching Cottonwood Creek and finding when pitching a tent that there are rattlesnakes underneath every bush.

**George Forman**   "My Pack and a Pick & Shovel on the Pony and I walking and
*Lone Traveler*   leading him." *(July 9 - 10)*

---

[73] James Logan, "From the Rocky Mountains," letter to the editor in *Salem Weekly Advocate,* November 10, 1864.
[74] Aaron L. Rockwood, "From the Plains," letter to the editor in *Chicago Tribune,* September 10, 1864.

**Merrill**

Also reaching cottonwood Creek on July 11, but on the Interior Route is the **Merrill Team**. They travel at a much slower pace than **Julius'** prefers, and his frustration is evident.

**Julius Merrill**
*Merrill Team*

"Road leaves the river for fifteen miles entering the Black Hills. ... To the left rises Laramie Peak towering far above all others yet clad in winter garments. ... Reached the river at sunset. ...we could go no further." *(July 10)*

# Tuesday, July 12, 1864 (part 1)

### Kelly-Larimer

The **Kelly-Larimer Train** starts from La Bonte Creek, then takes a refreshing rest at La Prele Creek, about twenty miles north (though **Sarah Larimer** only claims twelve miles).

**Sarah Larimer**
*Kelly-Larimer*

"…This stream was overshadowed by a luxuriant growth of timber…" *(38)*

"…we had already been many weeks on our toilsome journey … and with the decline of the sun[,] we looked forward to the cool of approaching night." *(39)*

"The beauty of the sunset and the scenery around filled us with admiration … without a thought of the danger that was lying like a tiger in ambush by our path." *(40)*

When at La Prele, they take in the sights and likely catch up with the **Morris-Hastings Train** who come in behind them. Considering they regularly travel up to twice this distance in a day, and that there is still sunlight, they push forward again, perhaps thinking they can reach Deer Creek garrison by dark. As **Sarah** continues to marvel at the expansive blue sky, now streaked with hues of lemon rind and juicy marmalade, hundreds of Northern Plains Indians make a sudden and ominous appearance.

| | |
|---|---|
| **Sarah Larimer**<br>*Kelly-Larimer* | "...the bluffs before us were covered with a party of about two hundred and fifty Indians, painted and equipped for the war-path, who uttered a wild cry and fired a volley from their guns into the air." *(40)* |
| **Fanny Kelly**<br>*Kelly-Larimer* | The Indians gave a "wild war whoop and fired a signal volley of guns and revolvers into the air." *(21)* |

| | |
|---|---|
| **Sarah Larimer**<br>*Kelly-Larimer* | "...We had no time to make preparations for defence [sic] before the main body halted and sent out a small force, which encircled us ... Our men immediately halted the teams and formed a corral of the wagons, and gathered their arms for defence [sic]..."" *(40-41)* |

Being encircled by Indians is recorded in multiple accounts from the Raids. This tactic terrorizes and intimidates the emigrants, while keeping them mostly trapped. In the chaos created with noise, dust, and sudden movements, any loose stock animals typically startle and take flight. Animals that escape from their owners are then chased away and taken into Indian possession (Eg. See July 12 with the **Pella Company**).

Once the dust settles, someone from the **Kelly-Larimer Train** attempts a meeting with their war chief. The war chief speaks, in English, with either **Josiah Kelly** or **William Larimer** (depending on which account one trusts)

| | |
|---|---|
| **Fanny Kelly**<br>*Kelly-Larimer* | "My husband advanced to meet the chief and demand his intentions." *(22)* |
| **Sarah Larimer**<br>*Kelly-Larimer* | "I saw my husband go out to meet the chief and demand his intentions." *(42)* |
| **Sarah Larimer**<br>*Kelly-Larimer* | "...Uttering the word[s], 'How! How!' and, placing his hand upon his breast, he [the war chief] said in English: 'Good Indian;' and pointing towards his men, he added: 'Heap good Indian – hunt buffalo, antelope, and deer...'" *(42)* |

After a reassuring handshake, the Indians act more curious than threatening. Several follow the example of the war chief and shake every emigrant's hand that they can (to which the memoirists are both amused and annoyed). Then, some peek inside the covered wagons and solicit trade interactions (which seem inequitable to **Josiah**). One asks to trade for **Josiah's** race horse. This upsets the emigrants who prize its speed and breeding potential.

**Sarah Larimer**   The others "were soon crowding around the wagons, nodding
*Kelly-Larimer*    and smiling, with very many demonstrations of good will." *(42)*

**Fanny Kelly**    "One of them laid hold of my husband's gun, but being repulsed,
*Kelly-Larimer*    desisted." *(24)*

The disapproval of **Josiah's** weapon as a trade item suggests what has since been confirmed about the Northern Plains Indians' familiarity with (and use of) modern weapons of this time. "That the hostile Indians were the Cheyennes, Arapahoes, Ogallalla Sioux, Brules, and Blackfeet, all well supplied with ammunition and the best modern firearms, were well established facts," states Hebard and Brininstool (*The Bozeman Trail,* 1922, 68).

At some point, the war chief signals the disbursement of about one hundred and fifty men who form smaller, tactical squads and canvass the trails below, on both sides of the Platte. For miles around and for multiple days, emigrants report being followed or watched by Indians from higher grounds and of seeing signal fires lit in the mountains.[75]

**Fanny Kelly**    "The chief at last intimated that he desired us to proceed ... the
*Kelly-Larimer*    Indians insisting on driving our herd." *(24)*

*To be continued...*

---

[75] See Garland Mahan, July 17 and George Forman July 15 from the South Bank trails.

## Morris-Hastings

The **Morris-Hastings Train** departs from La Prele Creek shortly after the **Kelly-Larimer Train**. Though these fast moving parties had enough consistent interaction to invite combining their wagons for the evening stretch, both **Fanny Kelly** and **Sarah Larimer's** accounts suggest they purposefully keep themselves distanced from others to remain unencumbered. This later contributes to the severity of attacks, as they are all much easier to isolate and overpower in smaller groups.

As they proceed, neither the **Morris** nor **Hastings** family stories include a mention of seeing the army of Indians ahead. This suggests the encounter with the **Kelly-Larimer Train** does not last long before the army is dispersed, and the emigrants directed to continue on.

*To be continued...*

## Mahan-Moore

On July 12, the **Mahan-Moore Team** continues to suffer the effects of having stock die off and is limited by how much travel they can endure through the more challenging Interior Route. They only cover fourteen miles from Middle Bear Creek —a disappointment compared to twenty-four miles they accomplished days prior. This evening, they camp on Elkhorn Creek.

**Garland Mahan**
*Mahan-Moore Team*
"Had a rough road and long dry hills, literally barren in our route today." *(July 12)*

## Granger

The **Granger Company's** three subgroups are suspected to reach the general vicinity of Elkhorn Creek on July 12 as well, though they are not necessarily camping together. **James Logan's** 1864 letter suggests their check-ins only happen once or twice a week. Though **James** acknowledges tthey are traveling through "hostile" territory, there is no indication that the **Granger Company** is any more concerned about their safety than usual. Similarly, in **Aaron Rockwood's** letter, he relays that a dangerous encounter with Indians is more a matter of bad luck or stupidity.

## Forman & Merrill

**George Forman** and the **Merrill Team** both start their day from Cottonwood Creek. The **Merrill Team** only travels two miles to Little Cottonwood Creek before they must stop. Their sickly ox are not faring well and need better drinking water to survive a mild alkali poisoning. **Julius Merrill** describes the alkali water and its white "crust" being found in watering holes and stuck to the low growing grasses of the surrounding area. For miles on end, emigrants report dead animals lying about, warning everyone to keep a watchful eye on their livestock. Both writers commented on this previously and are aware of the risk.

**Julius Merrill**
*Merrill Team*

"Dead cattle were to be found everywhere. No watering place or campground was free from the stench of the moldering carcasses." *(July 10)*

**George Forman**
*Lone Traveler*

"All the way from here up for hundreds of miles we passed scores of dead bloated cattle every day, killed by the heat and alkali dust and water." *(July 9 or 10)*

Though **Julius** grumbles about the minimal progress, he makes the most of his July 12 layover by prospecting in the nearest body of water. He finds nothing but a speck of color.

George Forman continues his solo journey with an additional twenty miles of walking (though he reports it being thirty). Considering an average walking speed of 2.5 to 4 miles per hour, this takes him between five and eight hours, including a noon respite.

**George Forman**
*Lone Traveler*

"Struck into the Black Hills all alone and no trains and had lunch and feed for Pony at a cool spring in a grove of bitter cottonwoods." *(July 12)*

It is unlikely **George** hauls conventional horse "feed" with him, as his pony is accustomed to eating "anything" it finds along the road–even sage brush and greasewood.[76] In the evening, **George** camps at Horseshoe Creek, near the telegraph station.

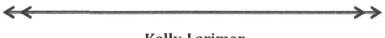

## Kelly-Larimer

While other wagon trains are calling it a day, the **Kelly-Larimer Train** is presently obligated to continue west, as directed by the war chief. He leads them along the South Bank Trail for over an hour while the sun sets and hungry bellies growl. Though the emigrants feel reluctant to have such company, the fact remains that they are currently unharmed and have been assured there is no ill intent from either the English-speaking war chief or his men.

**Sarah Larimer**
*Kelly-Larimer*

"Eight miles from [La Prele] is the memorable Little Box-Elder Creek." *(38)*

**Fanny Kelly**
*Kelly-Larimer*

"Slowly our wagons wound through the timber that skirted Little Box Elder, and, crossing the stream, we ascended the opposite bank..." *(19)*

The valley along Little Box Elder Creek runs from a canyon to the south, into the North Platte River, intersecting the South Bank Trail. When the war chief insists they follow a detour along the tributary, **Josiah Kelly** resists. He may have

---

[76] Foreman, July 12, 1864.

felt determined to reach Deer Creek garrison, just twelve miles further (less than two hours away). **Josiah** halted the team near a "rocky glen" (Fanny Kelly, 24). When the war chief insisted the wagons keep moving, **Josiah** stood his ground and corralled (Sarah Larimer, 44).

| | |
|---|---|
| **Sarah Larimer**<br>*Kelly-Larimer* | "We were approaching a deep, rocky glen, in whose gloomy depths … escape would be impossible…" *(44)* |

Once corralled in the creek's valley, the Indians pressure **Josiah** to provide them an evening meal. Outnumbered, there are few options for the wagon master other than to appease the war chief and hope he will leave after eating his fill. **Josiah** sets the men to preparing an outrageously expensive dinner from his supply of goods that should be for his new retail store. Instead of helping with the meal arrangement, **Fanny** and **Sarah** stay with their children in their respective wagons. It is suspected but unconfirmed if their husbands instructed them to stay put.

| | |
|---|---|
| **Sarah Larimer**<br>*Kelly-Larimer* | "**Mr. Larimer** was engaged in making a fire, and **Mr. Kelly**, and **two colored men** were preparing the meal…" *(44)* |
| | "**Mr. Wakefield** and **Mr. Taylor** were busy with the teams. **Mr. [Andrew] Sharp,** who was aged and almost blind, and was trembling with fear … was now distributing his store of sugar among them." *(44)* |
| **Fanny Kelly**<br>*Kelly-Larimer* | "**Mr. Larimer** and **Franklin** were tending to the fire, **Wakefield** was at the wagon getting supplies, **Mr. Taylor** was attending to the stock, **Josiah** and **Andy** were out collecting firewood, **Mr. Sharp** was passing out sugar to the Indians…" *(25)* |
| **Sarah Larimer**<br>*Kelly-Larimer* | "When all the men were busily engaged, [the Indians] threw off their mask of friendship…" *(44)* |

Right about when **Josiah** and **Andy** return, chaos breaks out. Both memoirists and **Josiah** record a play-by-play for the event, but inconsistencies are prevalent.

**Josiah Kelly**
*Kelly-Larimer*

"We were attacted [sic] by between 75 and 100 Indians who came to us about two hours before sundown and staid [sic] until we stoped [sic] for the night about sundown we had just unhetched [sic] and were going about to get supper..." *(1864)*

**Sarah Larimer**
*Kelly-Larimer*

"An Indian approached, and took a gun from near my side. To this[,] I objected in vain." *(45) (F. Kelly agrees on page 25*)

It is reasonable to conclude **Sarah's** "vain" response over having her husband's gun handled may have been overdramatic and aggressive. In fact, the next time **Sarah** lets out a wail, the chief puts a knife to her throat. If readers look back to see how **Fanny** responded to the same type of action with her husband's gun earlier, the personality extremes of these women become clear.[77]

**Sarah Larimer**
*Kelly-Larimer*

"At this instant there was a simultaneous discharge of arms, which were followed by the fearful war-whoop." *(45)*

**Fanny Kelly**
*Kelly-Larimer*

"...and when the cloud of smoke cleared ..." *(25)*

**Sarah Larimer**
*Kelly-Larimer*

"... not one of our men was in sight." *(45)*

**Sarah's** last claim is far from being true. The emigrants bear unfortunate witness to the gruesome murders of their friends and family.

**Josiah Kelly**
*Kelly-Larimer*

"I hapened [sic] to be about 20 feet from the wagons kindling a fire when they shot. ... At the report of the guns I sprung to my feet..." *(1864)*

---

[77] Their differences are also used against them in their respective narratives. Fanny makes it a point in her narrative to highlight Sarah's emotional fragility and risk-taking. In Sarah's narrative, she claims she is quick thinker and advantageous, while Fanny is somewhat thick-headed and naïve.

**Sarah Larimer**
*Kelly-Larimer*

"**Mr. Kelly** was startled by the report, and hurriedly glanced around, and saw the pale face of his wife and child in his wagon, and **Mr. [Andrew] Sharp** fall [dead] from the side of his wagon, into which he was reaching." *(49)*

**Noah Taylor** gets shot in the head right in front of **Fanny,** who hopefully shields her niece's eyes (Fanny Kelly, 29). The Indians send an arrow through **Franklin Lawrence's** legs, pinning them together so he falls near the fire. While he lays helpless on the ground, the Indians crush his skull.

In an instant, **William Larimer** flees from the camp without attempting to protect his wife or child. **Gardner Wakefield** is struck with three arrows, but is still able to run for his life and follows after **William**. Though **William's** is a cowardly response, **Sarah** excuses him in her book.

**Sarah Larimer**
*Kelly-Larimer*

"All he [**William**] could do was to make a desperate effort to save himself, and he turned and fled for his life." *(49)*

"The Attack and Capture of Our Train" illustration in Fanny Kelly's memoir, *Narrative of My Captivity Among the Sioux* (1871), page 13b.

Seeing all this, **Josiah** quickly weighs his own options, then concludes to make a desperate escape with **Andy** in tow.

**Josiah Kelly**
*Kelly-Larimer*

"[Indians were] shooting at me with bowes [sic] and arrows and I had not a thing to fight with, my gun being in the wagon." *(1864)*

In an unpublished manuscript from 1866, **Fanny** corroborates **Josiah's** feelings of inadequacy under life-or-death circumstances. Notes such as these represent the internal conflict the former Union soldier must have had regarding the inability to protect his family and the necessity of entering survival mode.

**Fanny Kelly**
*Kelly-Larimer*

"...my husband seeing no chance to get to me & they were shooting at him fast as possible, so he broke for the bushes in a ravine close by & they did not follow him." *(1866)*[78]

While fleeing, "barbed arrows whizzed past [**Josiah** and **Andy**], some passing through [their] clothing ... **Mr. [William] Larimer** passed [**Josiah**] in his flight for life toward some neighboring timber" *(29)*

The men on the run will need the protective cover of night if they are going to survive being caught and killed by the Indians. **William** and **Gardner** head for the forested hills, but their injuries stall them. **Gardner** has three arrows lodged his body and **William** receives an arrow in the thigh while running. If neither **William** nor **Gardener** can out run their enemy, their next best option is to hide.

When **Josiah** looks around to see where his companions are, he sees them fall and interprets their disappearances as death and keeps running on his own, losing track of **Andy** in the process.

---

[78] Fanny Kelly, untitled and unpublished manuscript from 1866, as found in the National Archives, Record Group 233 of the U.S. House of Representatives, 40th Congress. The transcription comes from Randy Brown in "The Kelly Story," 1986 (see Bibliography).

**Josiah Kelly**
*Kelly-Larimer*

"I ran for a ravine close by which I ran down a ways and got into a thicket of brush and concealed myself until it was dark..." *(1864)*

**Sarah Larimer**
*Kelly-Larimer*

"...After falling, [**William**] had arisen and proceeded a little farther, where he was overtaken by **Mr. Wakefield,** who said, 'I am mortally wounded; you will find my body among these bushes.' **Mr. Larimer** proceeded to a secluded place..." *(52)*

Though the warning sounds of local snakes can keep even the bravest Indians from skulking around dense shrubs and through tall grass, one Indian crawls right up to **William**. When the Indian gets close enough to pounce, **William** allegedly shoots the man in his chest. This sound alerts others to his position, so " [for] the remainder of that night he spent in endeavoring to elude his savage pursuers" (Larimer, 53).

Readers should be aware that **Sarah's** claim about her husband shooting the Indian does not align with prior claims that **William** was defenseless during the attack (his gun being with **Sarah** in the wagon). Some researchers have tossed out **Sarah's** words entirely, saying, "**Mrs. Larimer's** account of her husband's experiences that night seem highly imaginary."[79]

(Maybe)

---

[79] Randy Brown, "The Kelly Story," 1986. 13, fn 37. Kansas Historical Society, digital collection item #303250, DaRT ID: 303250. Accessed 12/01/2022 at http://www.kansasmemory.org/item/303250/page/1

**S**

# Tuesday, July 12, 1864 (part 2)

### Kelly-Larimer

Once **Fanny Kelly** and **Sarah Larimer's** husbands are out of sight, all attention returns to plundering the spoils of camp. the women their two young children, **Mary Hurley Kelly** and **Frank Larimer** are held hostage at the murder scene while the war chief watches his comrades freely explore the wagon contents.

**Sarah Larimer**
*Kelly-Larimer*

"[I] commenced to assist them to unload the wagon I was in … the Indians had mounted into the wagons and commenced the work of distributing and destroying the contents, using their tomahawks to pry open trunks and boxes…" *(45)*

**Fanny Kelly**
*Kelly-Larimer*

"They robbed us of every thing we had with us."[80] *(1865)*

**Sarah Larimer**
*Kelly-Larimer*

"**Mrs. Kelly,** kept her seat in the wagon until her presence was regarded as irksome, when the chief threw her violently to the ground and dragged her some distance, while the terrified child [**Mary**] was left to climb from the wagon…" *(45)*

**Fanny's** memoir records this part of the evening differently depending on who she is writing for. She agrees on being forcefully pulled from her wagon, but claims she is able to reach up and safely collect her niece (Kelly, 29). In an alternate narrative provided to the U.S. Government when petitioning for

---

[80] Fannie Kelly, "letter to Rezin Wells Kelly, March 10th, 1865," in *Genealogy of the John A. Kelly Family,* transcribed by Mrs. Henry Pelton and Dwight Yates (Ohio: Private Publication), 1950.

compensation for injuries and lost property, **Fanny's** story is more inclusive of abuses such as her seven-year-old niece being dragged out of the wagon. Readers might conclude **Fanny** being motivated to exaggerate the violence when there are monetary gains to collect. Readers might also bear in mind a socially appropriate censorship of violence toward a child in **Fanny's** mass market version.

The following quote has been transcribed from **Fanny's** 1866 unpublished manuscript, as submitted with her petition (original spelling intact):

**Fanny Kelly**      "In a moment two fierce looking savages stepped up in front of the
*Kelly-Larimer*      waggon that I was in[.] they seazed [sic] me by the hands & draged
me roughly out of the wagon nearly brakeing one of my limbs from
which I suffered intensly for months & will always bear the marks.
my Niece Mary Hurley 7 years of age was also caught & dragged
out." *(1866)*[81]

After the **Kellys** are removed out of their wagon, **Sarah** is instructed to take her son **Frank** to join the other captives.

**Sarah Larimer**    "I was told that my services were not required..." *(46)*
*Kelly-Larimer*

In the next moment, **Sarah** looks up to the dark hills where her husband had disappeared. She grips her son's hand and starts to run for the timber with him. The war chief must have predicted her move. He calls for her to stop and immediately return. **Sarah** doesn't mention being physically caught, but something about the warning must have been threatening enough for her to see the futility of escape.

---

[81] Fanny Kelly, untitled and unpublished manuscript from 1866, as found in the National Archives, Record Group 233 of the U.S. House of Representatives, 40th Congress. The transcription comes from Randy Brown in "The Kelly Story," 1986.

| | |
|---|---|
| **Sarah Larimer**<br>*Kelly-Larimer* | "In an authoritative manner he called, in English, saying, 'Come back!'" *(46)* |
| **Fanny Kelly**<br>*Kelly-Larimer* | "**Mrs. Larimer,** with her boy, came to us, trembling with fear, saying, 'The men have all escaped, and left us to the mercy of the savages.' ... Her agitation was extreme. ...I did not tell her what my eyes had seen, fearing that she could not endure it." *(38-40)* |

The chief then presents **Fanny** with a wreath, allegedly signifying protection (Larimer, 46). Because of the competing narratives, it is unclear if this symbolic gesture is extended generally to all the captives, or exclusively to **Fanny**. An Indian boy, whom Fanny calls "Wechla," then presents both women with a few articles of clothing, shoes, and a package of letters. At this point, readers might question the plausibility of anyone giving captives a random bundle of mail and what purpose it would serve the captors to allow this. In any case, both women claim they hatch a plan to create a paper trail with the letters.

| | |
|---|---|
| **Sarah Larimer**<br>*Kelly-Larimer* | "Among the confused mass ... was a package of letters that the young Indian brought ... which suggested to me a plan ... to strew upon the way if we should be taken ... hoping they would be a guide for our pursuing friends, or for us, if we should escape." *(47)* |
| **Fanny Kelly**<br>*Kelly-Larimer* | "...he also brought me some books and letters ... I readily conceived a plan to make good use of them. ... I said to **Mrs. Larimer** ... I shall drop them at intervals along the way ... and trust God that our friends may find and follow them to our rescue" *(41)* |

After ransacking five wagons and dumping out the every bag of flour onto the ground like snow, the Indians set the wagons ablaze. Later, researchers would also recognize this behavior as another signature tactic. In 1922, Hebard and Brininstool concluded: "These depredations along the highway of the Platte were principally made by warring tribes of Sioux and Northern Cheyennes, who scalped the white men, destroyed coaches, killed the stage drivers, burned ranches, captured whole wagon trains, took into captivity women and children, destroying, rather than utilizing the merchandise which filled the wagons."[82]

**Sarah Larimer**     "Many things which the Indians could not carry with them[,]
*Kelly-Larimer*      they gathered into a pile and lighted." *(47)*

**Fanny Kelly**      "[**Sarah's**] grief seemed to have reached its climax when she saw
*Kelly-Larimer*      the Indians destroying her property, which consisted principally
                     of such articles as belong to the Daguerrean art.[83] ... As she saw
                     her chemicals, picture cases, and other property pertaining to
                     her calling, being destroyed, she uttered such a wild, despairing
                     cry as brought the chief of the band to us, who, with gleaming
                     knife, threatened to end all her further troubles in this world."
                     *(41)*

*To be continued...*

## Morris-Hastings

While the wagon fire ahead grows hotter and hotter, the **Morris-Hastings Train** approaches the trail crossing over Little Box Elder. Passing by first, those in **Jacob Hastings** wagon look on with horror. This party's account is preserved in the oral history of **Ella Long**,[84] and through **Martha Scoggin**, a pioneer historian who compiled additional research on the family.[85] Though neither historian is a direct eyewitness, the reminiscence and compiled details align with first-person observations.

**Fanny Kelly**      "A short distance in the rear of our train [a] wagon was in
*Kelly-Larimer*      sight." *(27)*

---

[82] Grace Raymond Hebard and E. A. Brininstool, *The Bozeman Trail, vol 1.* (The Arthur H. Clark Company: Cleveland, OH), 1922, 63.
[83] Daguerreotyping is an early form of photography using mercury.
[84] Ella Long (1884-1972) is the daughter of Enoch Hastings (1850-1933) and Alice Morris (1856-1920), who both made this overland trip when young.
[85] See Ella Long in Martha Scoggin's *Pioneer Days on Scoggin Ridge and Pataha Prairie*, (1973), a 152-page spiral-bound soft cover family genealogy and Pomeroy, Washington-area history.

| | |
|---|---|
| **Ella Long**<br>*Morris-Hastings* | "**Jacob Hastings' wagon train** had just passed a few miles back, where a wagon train had been attacked by the Indians. The occupants had been murdered and left lying about and the wagons were burned. It had been but a short while before, for the ashes were still hot." *(Long in Scoggin, 1973)* |
| **Fanny Kelly**<br>*Kelly-Larimer* | When spotted, "The chief immediately dispatched a detachment in pursuit..." *(27)* |
| **Ella Long**<br>*Morris-Hastings* | "After they had passed this tragedy, the Indians attacked and tried to drive their cattle away and the driver [in the **Hastings'** party] was shot[,] leaving the train to watch."*(Long in Scoggin, 1973)* |
| **Martha Scoggin**<br>*Morris-Hastings* | "...the driver ... became excited after the Indians withdrew from attacking the men, and ran out on a hillside from the wagons to watch. He was shot by the Indians." *(1973)* |

The details of this unnamed driver's death are expounded on by other travelers who later find his corpse, study his injuries, then bury him in an expedient fashion. A week later, the driver's body is exhumed by wild animals and becomes a disturbing sight for those in the **Ringo Train.**

While the **Hastings** race to Deer Creek garrison, the **Morris** family behind them has a more difficult escape. Again, the memoirists present contradictory details, but the big picture is harmonious.

| | |
|---|---|
| **Fanny Kelly**<br>*Kelly-Larimer* | The detachment of Indians continued, "in pursuit of the small party, which consisted of only one family and a man [**Arthur Wright**] who rode in advance of the single wagon."*(27)* |
| | The horseman [**Arthur**] was almost instantly surrounded and killed by a volley of arrows. *(27)* |

"The husband of the family [**Nelson Morris**] quickly turned his team around and started them at full speed, gave the whip and lines to his wife [**Sarah Jane**], who held close in her arms her youngest child [**Ulysses**]. He then … threw out boxes, trunks, everything that he possessed." *(27)*

"The Indians … riddled the wagon-cover [sic] with bullets and arrows, one passing through the sleeve of the child's dress. … [**Nelson**] kept the Indians at bay with his revolver…" *(27)*

**Sarah Larimer**
*Kelly-Larimer*

"…while the driver encouraged the horses with all his might, his wife [**Sarah Jane**] threw out everything she could to lighten the load: they succeeded in making their escape uninjured, though an arrow passed through the sleeve of their infant child's dress. But a horseman that was riding a few yards in advance was killed." *(50-51)*

**Fanny Kelly**
*Kelly-Larimer*

"…and finally, they [the Indians] left him and rode furiously back to the scene of the murder…" *(27)*

The attack on July 12 is only one of several frightful encounters the **Morris-Hastings Train** has with Indians while on their way to Washington. Pioneer historians have noted that the journey is "beset with much trouble and hardships. [And that] Many times they were forced to fight back the hostile savages."[86] That being said, no empirical evidence supports repeated difficulties.

*To be continued…*

---

[86] Shaver, Steel & Rose. "Enoch G. Hastings" in *An Illustrated History of Southeastern Washington.* 1906 (Western Historical Publishing Co., Spokane, Wash.) Public domain (not in copyright). Their second incident occurs with different tribes, closer to Lander's Cutoff, after leaving South Pass.

## Kelly-Larimer

Back at Little Box Elder Creek, the war chief signals for all his men to clear out. They must know that if anyone from the **Hastings** party makes it to the Army post, they'd be informed on.

**Sarah Larimer**
*Kelly-Larimer*

"...they [the Indians] came to us and signified that they were ready to go, and that we must accompany them. ... We were about to be carried into captivity. ... My son, little **Frank**, caught my hand and murmured, 'Oh, mother, I don't want to go'..."" *(47)*

"The smoldering ruins of much of our property had fallen into ashes, the smoke had faded away, and night had covered the traces of confusion and death." *(48)*

**Fanny** and **Mary Hurley Kelly** are placed on horseback together. Then, **Sarah** is also placed on horseback, but her son **Frank** is not brought to her. She pleads with the Indians for him, unsure of what plans they might have for a young boy. They eventually lift him up to sit with her.

**Fanny Kelly**
*Kelly-Larimer*

"They had taken paths inaccessible to white men, and made their crossing [of the North Platte] at a point where it would be impossible for trains to pass ... having reached the opposite bank, they separated into squads, and started in every direction, except southward..." *(50)*

**Josiah Kelly**
*Kelly-Larimer*

"My **wife** and **her niece** a little girl about eight years old [were] carried off prisoners." *(1864)*

"They took a **Mrs. Lariner** [sic] and her son about eight years of age prisoners [sic] ... She [**Sarah**] says that when they started from the wagons they put **Fannie** on a horse and **Mary Herly [Hurley]**, her niece on behind her and soon after they started, close to the road **Fannie** sliped [sic] **Mary** off in the brush and told her to go hide and stay there until she would see some wagons going long the road and go to it." *(1864)*

After successfully eluding the Indians by hiding in a ravine, **Josiah Kelly** checks for the coast to be clear, then takes off again. Nothing is mentioned about what happens to **Andy**, the young boy who had escaped with him.

| | |
|---|---|
| **Sarah Larimer**<br>*Kelly-Larimer* | "Cautiously he [**Josiah**] crawled from the weeds and grass, and gaining his feet, started swiftly in an eastern direction..." *(50)* |
| **Fanny Kelly**<br>*Kelly-Larimer* | **Josiah** continued going "far out into the hills to avoid being spotted." *(31)* |

**Josiah** hopes to find safety and protection from other emigrants which he believes are back at La Prele Creek. He plans to muster a posse to help him track down his wife and niece. Instead, he gets lost.

| | |
|---|---|
| **Josiah Kelly**<br>*Kelly-Larimer* | "...when I tried to make my way back to a creek about 7 or eight miles back [at La Prele Creek] where I expected to find some trains camped. But finding the road picketed I took through the hills and got lost..." *(1864)* |

### Morris-Hastings

After being chased for five miles, the **Morrises** do reach their prior camp at La Prele Creek and hunker down. They prepare for a possible second attack by lining the wagon with sacks of flour and making the small children lay down behind the barriers.[87] In the meantime, **Jacob Hastings** arrives at Deer Creek garrison and alerts the military about the crimes he witnessed.

### Forman

Word about the incident spreads rapidly through the night. Before long, **George Forman** hears the news as far back as the telegraph station on Horseshoe Creek (approximately fifty miles from Little Box Elder Creek, or sixty from Deer

---

[87] Similar emigrant stories involve leaning feather bed ticks (mattresses) against wagon canvases so arrows stick and bind in the feathers.

Creek garrison). In addition, George notes musical announcements being heard in the area.

**George Forman**  "Indian runners or scouts (white) had come in that night with
*Lone Traveler*  news of Indian outbreaks, and were singing Indian war songs
and chants all night." *(July 12)*

## Particulars of a Recent Massacre on the Plains of Emigrants by Indians.

The Reese River *Reveille*, of 22d September, says:

L. Morse and family arrived in this city a few days ago and from him we learn some of the particulars of a terrible Indian massacre that took place the 11th of July last, at Box Elder creek, seventy miles this side of Fort Laramie. Seventy-five Indians attacked a train of five wagons, containing several families, from Jackson county, Missouri, and among them were two negro men. Sharp and three other white men, whose names we could not ascertain, and a negro man, were instantly killed, as was also a little girl, the daughter of Kelly, aged about ten years. Another man was wounded and two women were captured. After robbing the train of everything except the naked wagons, they proceeded on and met Morse's wagon, killing a young man named Arthur Wright, from Hennipen county, Minnesota, who was somewhat in advance of the wagon. Morse, with his family, escaped the blood-thirsty savages by putting back towards Laramie as fast as his horses could travel, the Indians pursuing him for five miles, keeping up a running fire and only giving up the chase when they came in sight of a large train. During the chase, Morse threw away his provisions to lighten the wagon, and his little boy received a slight wound in the arm. The two women made their escape five days after, and returned to their friends who escaped the massacre. They stated that they were well treated by the savages, and no indignities were offered them by their captors.

"Particulars of a Recent Massacre on the Plains of Emigrants by Indians," *Daily Missouri Republican* (St. Louis, MO) October 27, 1864.

# Wednesday, July 13, 1864

### Kelly-Larimer & Union Army

When the Indians notice **Mary Hurley Kelly's** absence, three or four men are sent back to reclaim her. Little **Mary** eludes discovery all night. Although neither memoirists sees what happens next, they offer an idea for readers using conjecture. **Fanny Kelly's** "motherly" version of this story casts **Mary** as a brave and capable child, while **Sarah Larimer's** version is full of pity for a child left behind by her mother.

According to **Sarah**, **Mary** finds her way back to the site of smoldering wagons at Little Box Elder Creek on the morning of July 13. She sits on a nearby hill where she can overlook the scene and flag down passer-byers who might come to her aid. **Mary** is unaware that she is being tracked down.

| | |
|---|---|
| **Fanny Kelly**<br>*Kelly-Larimer* | "The child, whose judgment was remarkable for her age, readily acceded to [the] plan..." *(46)* |
| **Sarah Larimer**<br>*Kelly-Larimer* | Something "guided the feeble steps of the child back on the trail to a bluff overlooking the road, where she sat with little folded hands, awaited the oncoming of friends. Rescue was seemingly near, now that she had reached the great road in safety, and experience must have taught her that there would be some passing trains, if not one day, perhaps the next. It was in this situation, she was seen by some soldiers ... calling them to deliver her..." *(60)* |
| **Fanny Kelly**<br>*Kelly-Larimer* | "It was a party of but three or four soldiers returning from Fort Laramie, where they had been to meet the paymaster." *(218)* |

The soldiers who first see **Mary** are not who **Fanny** believes them to be. **Corporal Hervey Johnson,** in Company G stationed at Deer Creek's garrison, clarifies in a letter that **Captain Levi M. Reinhart** (his commander) had left for Fort Laramie on or before July 10 to "go get our money."[88] **Cpl. Hervey** expects his commander to be gone at least a week. His account states, "The **Captain** and another man were on the road somewhere coming up from the fort with our money," but the men who spot **Mary** are actually supply runners who had barely just left the garrison on horseback.

| **Cpl. Hervey Johnson** Union Army, Co. G | "Three of our boys started down the road last week [reflecting back from July 18] with ammunition for some recruits that were on their way to this place. They [the three soldiers] were driven back by the Indians … They said the road was strewn for miles with arrows clothing beds flour bacon salt and other plunder, six dead men …. were seen by them scattered along the road, all of them had been killed by arrows. … Those three boys that went down the road said the first thing they saw when they come to where the indians were was the little girl." *(1864)* |

**Mary** recognizes her opportunity to be rescued and either cries out to them or waves for them to come get her.

| **Fanny Kelly** Kelly-Larimer | "…holding out her little trembling hands with eager joy and hope, imploring them to save her." *(218)* |
| **Cpl. Hervey Johnson** Union Army, Co. G | "They started off the road to go to her … [but] **one of the boys** thought she had been placed there to draw them into an ambush, so they took a circuit off some distance around…" *(1864)* |

---

[88] Hervey Johnson, "letter to Sister Sybil, July 18, 1864," in William E. Unrau, ed. *Tending the Talking Wire: A Buck Soldier's View of Indian Country 1863-1866,* (University of Utah Press: Salt Lake City), 1979.

**Fanny Kelly**
*Kelly-Larimer*

"...fearing the little figure upon the distant bluff might be a decoy to lead them into ambush, [they] hesitated to approach." *(218)*

**Fanny's** account suggests the soldiers had been harassed by Indians on the day prior and they felt especially "aroused" with fear. This emotional response is not supported in **Cpl. Hervey's** letter.

**Fanny Kelly**
*Kelly-Larimer*

"...they [the soldiers] were about crossing to the relief of the little girl, when a party of Indians came in sight, and they became convinced it was a decoy, and turned and fled." *(219)*

**Cpl. Hervey Johnson**
*Union Army, Co. G*

"...four indians dashed up towards them from behind the hill and were surrounding them[.] ... The boys dismounted[,] leveled their pieces and fired[.] they were at a distance of two hundred yards and running at full speed.  one old fellow the boys took to be the chief threw up his arms[,] dropped his spear and reeled on his horse[,] but was carried out of sight before he fell[.] ... the rest ran behind the hill but soon reappeared, they saw the boys were ready for them however ... and finally disappeared altogether." *(1864)*

At the soldiers' readiness to engage, the Indians retreat, but **Cpl. Hervey** claims the soldiers feared re-enforcements coming. They hightail back to the soldier station, fully convinced that **Mary** had tricked them. **Fanny** and **Sarah** can only hypothesize what happens to **Mary** next.

**Fanny Kelly**
*Kelly-Larimer*

"...fierce Indians stood before her, stringing their bows to take her life, thus to win another trophy, marking the Indian murderer." *(219)*

**Sarah Larimer**
*Kelly-Larimer*
"...whizzing arrows were sent into the helpless child." *(60)*

**Fanny Kelly**
*Kelly-Larimer*
"...and with the twang of the bow-strings, the delicate form of the heroic child lay stretched upon the ground..." *(220)*

After **Mary** falls, the Indians crack her skull with a tomahawk, then slice off her scalp.[89] In August, **Fanny** learns the true fate of her niece and adopted daughter, when she recognizes items being brought into the place of her captivity.

**Fanny Kelly**
*Kelly-Larimer*
"One day, as I was pursuing what seemed to me an endless journey, an Indian rode up beside me, whom I did not remember to have seen before. At his saddle[,] hung a bright and well-known little shawl, and from the other side was suspended a child's scalp of long, fair hair. ... As my eyes rested on the frightful sight, I trembled in my saddle and grasped the air for support. ... The torture was too great to be endured... I dropped from the saddle as if dead, and rolled upon the ground at the horse's feet." *(120)*

Also on July 13, though the timing is unclear, **William Larimer** comes out from his hiding place in the forest.

**Sarah Larimer**
*Kelly-Larimer*
"When morning dawned, he [**William**] was urged ... to return to the wagons to exame [sic] the ruins ... He had proceeded but a short distance, when he discovered Indians lurking among the hills ... he hastened to the place, ascertained the number of the dead and absence of his family: he then sought the cover of a projecting rock, to await the arrival of travellers that were in the area the previous day [the **Morris family**]." *(53)*

---

[89] On July 17, Julius Merrill, George Forman, and one member of the Granger Company provide additional yet disturbing details for Mary's death.

At this point, **William** does not find **Mary's** body, which lies some distance from the burned down camp. Strangely lacking from both memoirs is any mention of the soldier's skirmish with Indians. If **William** can get close enough to see the Indians lurking, he might also hear the gunshots from the foray.

### Kelly-Larimer & Morris-Hastings

Farther east, **Josiah Kelly** finally reaches the **Morris Train**, corralled at La Prele Creek.

| | |
|---|---|
| **Josiah Kelly**<br>*Kelly-Larimer* | "...[I] did not reach the trains until day light next morning." *(1864)* |
| **Sarah Larimer**<br>*Kelly-Larimer* | "...after travelling eight miles, **[Josiah]** came to a large emigrant train that had camped without knowing of the Indian troubles ahead, but had learned of it through the report of a family that had arrived **[Morris]** on the opposite side of the creek overlooking the timber, and at about a mile's distance ... and had immediately turned back..." *(50-51)* |
| **Fanny Kelly**<br>*Kelly-Larimer* | **Josiah** reached "the large train, with which the small party I had seen pursued **[the Morrises]** had previously taken refuge. They were already consolidating with other trains for defense, and would not venture to join **Mr. Kelly**."[90] *(July 13)* |

**Josiah** is offended by **Nelson Morris'** reluctance to help. The emigrants gathered at La Prele Creek will not move from the safety of camp to chase after a battle-ready army of Indians, as they have been told about. Unarmed and exhausted, **Josiah** has no reasonable option but to remain in their protection until the situation changes.

Not long after **Josiah's** arrival, **Andy Lawrence** arrives at the La Prele Creek gathering. During the prior night, he is believed to have found his way to the Deer Creek garrison, rallied support and, in the morning, rides out with a handful of cavalry to see what became of his friends and family. This plan is foiled when three

---

[90] The others camped here besides the Morris family are presently unidentified.

unknown men on horseback are seen in the distance. [91] When these men realize they have been spotted, they turn their horses around and race off in the opposite direction. The cavalry initiates a chase after the men they now believe to be criminals. **Andy** diverges and continues to search for his friends alone.

He reaches La Prele Creek midmorning and reports a devastating loss of the entire **Kelly-Larimer Train**. The inflated death toll would be ten (excluding himself and the those in the **Morris-Hastings Train**).

| | |
|---|---|
| **Sarah Larimer**<br>*Kelly-Larimer* | "The colored man, **Andy**, soon arrived; and not knowing of the escape of his companion, reported all his company killed, and he only left to tell."*(51)* |
| **Fanny Kelly**<br>*Kelly-Larimer* | "[**Andy**] was about to report all the company killed, when he joyfully discovered **Mr. Kelly**." *(31, July 13)* |

**Josiah** makes himself known and tells **Andy** about the kidnappings and the death of **Arthur Wright.** The updated death toll might now be six (**Noah Taylor, Reverend Sharp, Arthur Wright, William Larimer, and Gardner Wakefield**). **Andy** likely shares that soldiers are coming to help, but he doesn't know when.

| | |
|---|---|
| **Fanny Kelly**<br>*Kelly-Larimer* | They did not move forward "until re-inforced [sic] by many others." *(31, July 13)* |

### Granger & Union Army

On July 13, members of the **Granger Company** travel from near or at Elkhorn Creek to La Bonte Creek and beyond. The testimonies of **Aaron Rockwood** and **James Logan**, clearly show that the subgroups of the **Granger Company** are spread several miles apart during the day. By evening, **Aaron** is ahead of the other two parties near Bed Tick Creek (eight miles north of La Bonte Creek). **Samuel Granger** might be at the rear of the Company, preferring to stay

---

[91] These men are identified as Isaac DeVries, Barend "Ten" Broek and Teunis Burgraff from the Jongewaard Train. (*For more on their experience, see the events of July 13 on the North Bank Trails.*)

at La Bonte, a well-known respite point. And **James**, "preferring to be alone," camps with his family somewhere between the others, in the mountains (1864).

During the very late night hours, **Aaron** hears about the tragedy that befell the **Kelly-Larimer Train**. Word of the attack reaches him via soldiers passing by. These may be the same soldiers who were with **Andy Lawrence** in the morning, or they might be scouts who have come up with a company originally stationed at Fort Laramie.

**Aaron Rockwood**
*Granger Company*

"The first we heard of any trouble among the Indians, was about midnight of the 13th, **some soldiers** were passing, and said that the Indians had attacked and captured a train above, the day before and murdered six men, and were all about us. We had seen no sign of them, but never the less we gathered in our stock and guarded it well." *(1864)*

The death toll matches the most recent count provided by **Josiah Kelly** in the **Kelly-Larimer Train**, but it not madeclear how that new reached the soldiers. One possibility is that the passing soldiers are a response team dispatched after the three ammunition soldiers reported back to Deer Creek about the so-called ambush. These soldiers are immediately sent back out with a posse of twelve to meet and guard **Cpt. Levi M. Reinhart** (who is discreetly carrying four months of wages with him). More evidence for this comes from the writings of **Cpl. Hervey Johnson**.

**Cpl. Hervey Johnson**
*Union Army, Co. G*

"Twelve men then mounted and started down. ... we were afraid [**Capt. Levi M. Reinhart**] might be attacked. The men went on down[,] met the **Captain** all safe[,] all turned and came back with the **Capt** except two who were sent on with the ammunition..." *(1864)*

If these are the soldiers who inform **Aaron**, then at an easy trot, they could cover the thirty miles between Deer Creek and Bed Tick Creek in about three and one-half hours and would have not only spoken with the emigrants at Le Prele, but passed Bed Tick Creek much earlier in the day.[92] It is plausible, then, that the

___

92 Or, if the cavalry rides at a canter, they might pass this location in about two hours.

posse has already found the **Captain** farther down the trails and the midnight encounter is from their return trip.  Further research is encouraged.

## Mahan-Moore

On July 13, the **Mahan-Moore Team** of two wagons lays over on Elkhorn Creek (about forty-five miles southeast of Little Box Elder). **Garland Mahan's** diary entry contains no acknowledgement of any incidents, the excitement, or worry expressed by others who reach this creek along the River Route. The Interior and River Routes do not converge for another few miles, near Spring Creek.

**Garland Mahan**  "Four or five head of cattle died out of the train last night.
*Mahan-Moore Team*  There has been no grass and very little water for 40 miles. Lay by." *(July 13)*

## Forman

**George Forman** spends this Wednesday morning at Horseshoe Creek and continues to document what he hears reports and rumors from the telegraph lines passing travelers. Again, the reported number of murders depends on who saw what and when.

**George Forman**  "I had hints that 300 Indians had crossed at Deer Creek 60
*Lone Traveler*  miles ahead and had stolen stock and killing four people and robbing a train only 16 miles ahead of me, but I doubted the rumor there had been so many of them." *(July 13)*

**George** asks the **telegraph operator** about the accuracy of the rumors and whether it was safe to continue or not.

**George Forman**  "He gave me a rough answer and no information." *(July 13)*
*Lone Traveler*

With nothing else to go on, **George** proceeds ten miles to Elkhorn Creek. There, he joins a camp full of emigrants, including **the Mahan-Moore Team**. There, **George** hears what others were told by the same telegraph operator. They learned that soldiers from Company E at Fort Laramie are coming up the road to investigate the depredations and to escort covered wagon trains through the Black Hills.

**George Forman**
*Lone Traveler*

They were told "not to move[,] but to wait for other trains and soldiers as the Indians had attacked a train only a few miles ahead and stolen their stock and burnt their wagons and killed four men and captured women..." *(July 13)*

George questions why others received different information than he did.

**George Forman**
*Lone Traveler*

"I staid [sic] with this Train consisting of 23 wagons. I still doubted the rumors and would have gone on still alone but they prevented me." *(July 13)*

### Forman & Merrill

Coming up behind **George Forman** is the **Merrill Team**. When passing Horseshoe Creek on July 13, **Julius Merrill** hears a strong warning about the Indians.

**Julius Merrill**
*Merrill Team*

"Coming to a telegraph station, we were informed that the Indians had murdered a small train fifty miles ahead. ...it caused some commotion in camp." *(July 13)*

The **Merrill Team** travels late into the night and seeks safety in numbers at the increasingly populated Elkhorn Creek camp.[93]

**Julius Merrill**
*Merrill Team*

"At night, an extra guard was posted and all prepared for the worst, yet hoping for the best." *(July 13)*

---

[93] George Forman records on July 14 that after he arrived, forty-five more trains joined the twenty-three he originally counted.

**Union Army**

**Sargent Lewis Hull**, a newly enlisted soldier in Company K, writes in his July 13 diary from Fort Laramie:

**Sgt. Lewis Hull**
*Union Army, Co. K*

"Dispatches received from up the road that the Indians are killing the emigrants at different places. Company E and some men from Company I, and twelve men from Company K and two pieces of artillery sent up. **General [Robert B.] Mitchell** is expected in a few days.[94] … Considerable excitement. Sitting up late writing and waiting for news." *(1864)* [95]

**Sgt. Lewis'** remarks verify that the Union Army responds as quickly as possible to the incident. Also at the Fort, **Lieutenant Eugene Ware**, of Company F, [96] writes in his journal that the soldiers resent the responsibility of guarding emigrants in the Hills. He claims that on some days, up to half his post is pulled from the Fort to escort "ignorant" travelers from post to post.[97]

The general attitude towards escort duty was that Indians were always around and travelers should know better than to fall prey to their petty thefts and attempts at stampeding stock animals away. The initial reports of a few dead men and a claim that hundreds of Indians are swarming trail is perceived as a wild exaggeration. Unfortunately for the emigrants, bored telegraph operators and soldiers out on the Plains sometimes invented such rumors themselves to scare passing travelers as a form of entertainment.

---

[94] Brigadier General Robert B. Mitchell is presently at Fort Kearny, in Nebraska.

[95] Lewis Byram Hull, "Soldiering on the High Plains: The diary of Lewis Byram Hull, 1864-1866," Ed. Myra E. Hull, *in Kansas Historical Quarterly,* vol. VII, No. 1, pages 3-53, February, 1938.

[96] Eugene Fitch Ware (1841-1911) was commissioned in 1863 as a lieutenant with Company F of the 7th Iowa Cavalry Regiment. He is promoted to a captain due to his involvement in the Powder River Expedition.

[97] Eugene Ware, *The Indian War of 1864: Being a Fragment of the Early History of Kansas, Nebraska, Colorado, and Wyoming.* (Topeka: Crane & Co, 1911), ch. 15.

Even though multiple companies have already been assigned and sent north, the soldiers stationed at Fort Laramie have never yet seen such a hostile act from the Northern Plains tribes and have no reason to believe the claims.

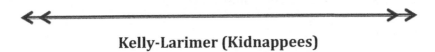

## Kelly-Larimer (Kidnappees)

After a long night of scattering this way and that, on July 13, the Northern Plains Indians continue driving their three remaining kidnappees from the **Kelly-Larimer Train** over dry, rolling lands heading north. They pass sand dunes and follow along the eastern side of accordion-fold hills leading toward the Powder River (near present-day Sussex, Wyoming).[98] By the end of the day, they reach Pine Gulch Ravine, on the north fork of the Cheyenne River. There are still about forty-three miles between there and Powder River. At Pine Gulch, the **war chief** tells **Sarah Larimer** that when they leave in the morning, he wishes to leave her seven-year-old son behind. He explains that **Frank Larimer** is of little use to them and will not be able to keep up.

| | |
|---|---|
| **Sarah Larimer**<br>*Kelly-Larimer* | "...it was a great distance to the Indian village, and over dry, sandy country ... it would be impossible for the child to endure the journey in safety." *(64)* |

**Sarah** fears that by leaving her son, he will get lost and die in the wilderness. She begs the chief to adopt **Frank** into the tribe and frames the idea as a gift. The chief accepts the offer and decides he will make **Frank** one of his own children. That evening, however, **Sarah's** decides neither she, nor her son, will be taken any farther.

| | |
|---|---|
| **Sarah Larimer**<br>*Kelly-Larimer* | In the middle of the night, "...all being still, I arose noiselessly and looked out on the scene. ... snatching the child, he awoke, and I lifted him ... Pressing him to my bosom in unspoken assurance ... I stepped noiselessly but rapidly, across the camp..." *(85-86)* |

---

[98] Powder River headwaters from the Bighorn Mountains and flows in a northerly direction until it joins with the Yellowstone River in Montana. If followed towards the eastern base of the Bighorns, the River intersects with the Bozeman Trail.

**Sarah** explains that she cannot reasonably include **Fanny** with her in the escape attempt because it is too risky. Since **Fanny's** suspicious dropping of **Mary**, the Indians guard her separately of **Sarah** and **Frank**. Golda Pelton and Dwight Yates, **Kelly family** historians and the grandniece and grandnephew of **Josiah Kelly**, conclude that **Sarah** is not misjudging the severity of her situation. The co-authors provide in their book, *Genealogy of The John A. Kelly Family*, that, "The first night after [**Fanny's**] capture, she was commanded to lie down next to a wounded Indian. A circle of Indians surrounded her and three fierce warriors sat near her with drawn tomahawks."[99]

After collecting her son, **Sarah** checks the moon's position in the sky, then she and **Frank** make a run for the hills. (*Sarah and Frank's story picks up on July 14 in the Emigrant Tales from the North Bank Trails.*)

**Sarah Larimer**   "...we travelled in a southwesterly direction until morning." *(86)*
*Kelly-Larimer*

---

[99] Mrs. Henry Pelton & Dwight Yates, *Genealogy...*, (Ohio: Private Publication), 1950, 11.

# Thursday, July 14, 1864

### Kelly-Larimer (Kidnappees)

First thing on the morning of July 14, **Fanny Kelly** and her captors discover **Sarah** and **Frank Larimer** are missing. Without understanding the choice **Sarah** had to make, **Fanny** perceives being left out of the plan as a betrayal. While some Indians begin a search for the escapees, Fanny is taken north where she is treated as a slave.

### Mahan-Moore

This morning is rather quiet for the **Mahan-Moore Team** who enjoys a partial layover at Elkhorn Creek before taking an easy half-day journey; carefully minding their sick animals.

**Garland Mahan**
*Mahan-Moore Team*
"This is truly a wild and romantic place. Here grows the gooseberry, currant, the wild plum, red haw, sarves berry and the straw berry. ...here on the edge of this creek, which forms from the spring is nearly every variety of growth." *(July 14)*

**Garland Mahan** records progressing only ten miles in the afternoon. His team ends their day at Spring Creek, where the Interior and River Routes become one, but the mining team is still about six miles distant from the other travelers who are gathering for protection.

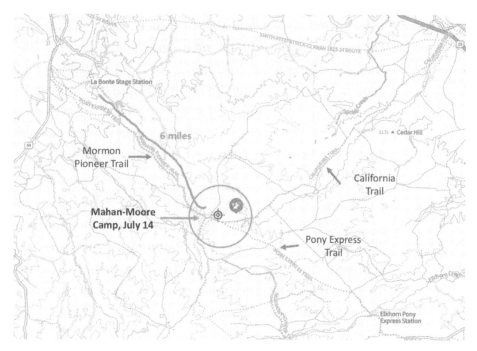

NaturalAtlas.com, Map of Converse County, WY. Accessed Aug. 11, 2023. Modified by author.

## Granger

Spread apart at three different points between La Bonte Creek and Bed Tick Creek, members of the **Granger Company** have had a trying night. Ahead of everyone, at Bed Tick Creek, **Aaron Rockwood, John Hawley,** and at least two other teamsters kept guard shifts through the night because of the midnight warnings about Indians murdering emigrants. Even with their precautions, the Indians' stealth and strategy outwitted the tired travelers.

**Aaron Rockwood**
*Granger Company*

"...about 6 o'clock we turned [the stock] out to grass, and about 7 a.m. the Indians came out of the hills near by and got within a few feet of the men on guard before they were discovered." *(1864)* [100]

---

[100]Rockwood, A. L. "From the Plains" letter to the editor in *Chicago Tribune* (Chicago, Illinois) September 10, 1864. In the Appendix.

**Aaron Rockwood**
*Granger Company*

"Henry [NLN] was out with my stock, and also the other man that was with me. I had been on guard all night, and had laid down by the wagons to sleep. ... He had but just got on the feeding ground ... when he heard a horse galloping in the direction of our camp. He looked up, and there was an Indian within a few feet of him. The Indian yelled and scared the mare; she broke the rope, and away she went with the rest." *(1864)*

"The boys that went out forgot to take the revolvers, and there was but one revolver out at the time. The man who had it emptied it at them, but does not know as he done any damage. The other boys ran into the herd, and tried to head them to the camp, and one of the teamsters got an arrow into his hip pretty badly..." *(1864)*

The blindsiding theft leaves **Aaron** and **John's** families completely stranded. In his letter, **Aaron** claims he could have saved the day if only he'd been closer.

**Aaron Rockwood**
*Granger Company*

"On July 14th the Indians stampeded about sixty head of stock from our train, while they were feeding about one and a half miles from our camp. ... They got every animal I had [about sixty], except the two Jacks [mules][101] and Jimny...""
*(1864)*

"If I could have got them there, with her[102] and my rifle I could have recovered the whole of the stock in a few hours, as there were only about ten or twelve Indians in the gang." *(1864)*

---

[101] A "Jack Mule" is the offspring of a male donkey (the "Jack") and a female horse (called a mare). When breeding the opposite combination of a male horse (a stallion) and a female donkey (called a "Jenny"), the offspring is called a "Hinny."
[102] The "her" might be his horse Jimny.

Somewhere in the mountains, ahead of **Samuel Granger's** family, **James Logan**, an undertaker by trade, boasts of his luck by being in the right place at the right time. He believes his mountain camp made him an unattractive target compared to those who were down by water sources. **James** implies that **Aaron**, a former Captain in the Union Army, should have known better than to be caught off guard.

**James Logan**
*Granger Company*

"[**John**] **Hawley** and [**Aaron**] **Rockwood** of Centralia lost all which was mostly the result of carelessness having no armed men with the stock." *(1864)*

"They [**the Indians**] happened to miss me[,] which was the only train that escaped for many miles." *(1864)*

Down closer to La Bonte Creek, **Samuel's** camp is also attacked at first light. Details of his and **Omar Jewell's** experience are preserved in **James'** letter.

**James Logan**
*Granger Company*

"The train I was mostly traveling with [**Samuel and Omar**], lost fifty-two head of stock at one time…" *(1864)*

"…the Indians watched like an eagle, and finding [**Samuel's**] stock out without the proper guard (always in the night) they come out of the mountains with a whoop and yell [at] our trains and drove them off[.]" *(1864)*

The combined result of the raids on the **Granger Company** totals more than one hundred heads of horses. Even though **James** does not see any of the action, he boldly declares, "we was ready and anxious to learn them a lesson" (1864). Despite this grandiose plan, retaliating is insensible. The challenging terrain when factored in with the Indians' riding speed, perfectly timed execution, and flawless escape choreography, only shows off how truly skilled and united the war party is at horse thievery. The Sioux, Cheyenne, and Arapahoe had the every advantage and years of practice.

In the 2006 *Atlas of the Sioux Wars*, Colonel Timothy Reese, the former director of the Combat Studies Institute at Fort Leavenworth, Kansas acknowledged that the Guerrilla warfare techniques used during the Sioux Wars of the 1850s through 1890s are "operationally and tactically complex," citing that "unfamiliar terrain and logistics dramatically affected the multiphase engagements..."[103]

## Forman & Merrill

Moving up from Elkhorn Creek on July 14 are **George Forman** and the **Merrill Team** along with sixty-seven other wagons who joined them in the night before. **George's** opinion that he might safely proceed alone, has since vanished and he resolves to stay with this group for the time being.

Today, the two soldiers who are still tasked with delivering ammunition from Deer Creek to Fort Laramie pass through this large gathering. As they do, they share about their ambush at Little Box Elder Creek, in addition to a second attack when they resumed their journey south with a twelve-man posse.

| | |
|---|---|
| **Julius Merrill**<br>*Merrill Team* | "As we were starting on we met two soldiers 'right from the troubles.'" *(July 14)* |
| **Cpl. Hervey Johnson**<br>*Union Army, Co. G* | "These two [ammunition soldiers] fell in with a squad of Indians and fought them for some time firing as many as eight balls at them. The rapid firing was what saved the boys for they did not give an Indian time to get within bowshot of them... They fought their way through and arrived safe with the supplies.[104] *(1864)* |

---

[103] Col. Timothy Reese, Foreword, in Charles Collins Jr.'s *Atlas of the Sioux Wars*, 2 ed. (Combat Studies Institute Press: Fort Leavenworth, Kansas), 2006. Col. Reese is the former director of the Combat Studies Institute at Fort Leavenworth, Kansas.

[104] The two soldiers arrive at Fort Laramie with ammunition for the new recruits on July 16, per Cpl. Hervey Johnson's letter.

**Julius Merrill**
*Merrill Team*

"Never did human beings tell more or greater falsehoods than they. ... Such hairbreadth escapes as they had had while fighting the Indians. ... The road was said to be strewn with dead bodies and ruins of wagons for miles." *(July 14)*

On the twenty-mile journey from Elkhorn to La Bonte Creek, number of wagons increases to an estimated one hundred. By banning together, emigrants hope to avoid being taken by surprise.

**George Forman**
*Lone Traveler*

"[Indians] only attack by surprise where they have the advantage over weak trains." *(July 15)*

Designated scouts ride both ahead and along the sides of the long procession to provide advance warning, should there be any appearance of Indians. For ease of readership, moving forward, this temporary collective will be referred to as the "**Hundred Wagon Train**."

### Forman, Granger, Merrill & Union Army

During the day, the **Hundred Wagon Train** is passed on the trail by a regiment of one hundred soldiers marching north in response to the distress call from Deer Creek. Based on **Sgt. Lewis Hull's** diary entry from July 13, this "regiment" is comprised mostly of Company E (under the command of **Levi G. Marshall**), a portion of Company I, and exactly twelve men from Company K, along with the two cannons. **George Forman** also specifies them as being from the 11th Regiment of the Ohio Cavalry, but most are on foot today.

**George Forman**
*Lone Traveler*

The soldiers, "passed us, and camped near us that evening. They had been attacked that morning and lost 50 mules and one man wounded." *(July 14)*

As it turns out, the assailants behind the Platte River Raids are not targeting only small or "weak" parties, as **George** previously thought. It is unclear where this attack on the cavalry occurred other than in the vicinity of Horseshoe Creek. As stories are exchanged amongst travelers, it seems no one knows what to expect from the Indians, from where, or when. Looking back at the methods of attacks featured in this book, readers can see that the stealthy morning blindsiding of the **Granger Company** is distinct from the **Kelly-Larimer Train** being overpowered and struck down. Different yet is the **Morris family's** five miles chase. Over on the North Side Trails, the onset of attacks also differ from day-to-day and location-to-location.

Up ahead, La Bonte Creek becomes the next major rallying point for emigrants to combine forces, strategize defenses, and to (begrudgingly) loan soldiers their horses on demand. While everyone rests and regroups, the commanding officer orders the cessation of travel until safety can be assured. In the afternoon or early evening, tales of the **Kelly-Larimer** incident circulate again, but with exaggerated details.

**George Forman**
*Lone Traveler*

"...Two trains had been attacked and 14 men killed and two women and three children taken captive." *(July 14)*

### Union Army

On their journey north, small squadrons of the 11th Ohio Volunteer Cavalry are sent ahead to scout the trails for Indians. Some soldiers, particularly in the case of the newly mustered soldiers of Company E, find that carving into the red rocks above La Bonte Creek is a better or more entertaining use of their time.

Rock carving at Wagon Hound Creek, about 5 miles north La Bonte Creek on Y-Knot Ranch. Inscription reads: "Co E 11 – OVC 1864." Interpretive sketch by photographer. Credit: Peter Faris (2001) Used with permission.

## Kelly-Larimer & Morris-Hastings

Finally, on July 14, the **Morris family** with **Josiah Kelly** and **Andy Lawrence** leaves their defensive corral at La Prele Creek to revisit the haunted detour at Little Box Elder Creek. It is unclear who else, if any, joins them in this departure, as they had specifically waited for reinforcements and prior references include other traveling parties consolidating with them.

**Sarah Larimer**   "This train did not move forward until late the next morning …
*Kelly-Larimer*   Women, in many instances, drove the teams," while the men
were at arms, ready for any sort of conflict. *(51)*

**Fanny Kelly** specifies that the first stop they make is at an "encampment a mile distant from the sad place" (35). The one mile mark matches the details for where the attack on the **Morris family** occurred on July 12.

**Sarah Larimer**
*Kelly-Larimer*

"At noon they stopped for refreshment and found the body of the horseman **[Arthur Wright],** which, when viewed at a little distance, resembled a clump of brushwood, from the feathered arrow-tops sticking from it-ninety arrows having entered it." *(52)*

**Fanny Kelly**
*Kelly-Larimer*

"...they found the dead body of the companion of the man who was so narrowly escaped with his family." *(32)*

The **Morrises** load **Arthur's** body into the back of their wagon then proceed down the trail leading into the valley of death. As they get closer, they find the campsite splattered with blood, powdered with flour and dusted with ashes. Most of the horrified emigrants look on with trepidation while **Josiah** takes an inventory of losses.

**Josiah Kelly**
*Kelly-Larimer*

"My load and 4 head of horses taken and destroyed." *(1864)*

**Fanny Kelly**
*Kelly-Larimer*

"All horses were taken, but **Mr. [Josiah] Kelly** found part of his cattle herd grazing nearby; **Mr. [Andrew] Sharp's** were still tied to the stake[s]." *(31)*

"They [Indians] shot some of them, and left them to decay upon the plain." *(34)*

**Sarah Larimer**
*Kelly-Larimer*

They "found the bodies of three of our company, **Mr. Taylor, Mr. Sharp,** and **Franklin,** one of the colored men." *(52)*

**Fanny Kelly**
*Kelly-Larimer*

"Both **Mr. Sharp** and **Mr. Taylor** left large families at home to mourn their loss." *(32)*

**Josiah** and **Andy** count the losses then pick through the rubble. **Josiah** searches for items of sentimental value and evidence to help identify their attackers. He specifically collects arrows off the ground as well as his wife's travel diary. **Fanny** later claims he prized that book, "more than he did his life" (33).

| | |
|---|---|
| **Sarah Larimer**<br>*Kelly-Larimer* | "Very many arrows were found strewn upon the ground, their owners having belonged to the Sioux family, though of various bands." *(55)* |

Those in the **Morris family** do not offer assistance with anything beyond collecting and burying the bodies, which causes feelings of resentment in **Josiah.**

| | |
|---|---|
| **Josiah Kelly**<br>*Kelly-Larimer* | "I could get no help from them except to bury the dead and haul the wounded to deer creek station distant about 13 miles." *(1864)* |

With all the commotion, **William Larimer** comes out from the projecting rock he'd been hiding by. He limps into camp.

| | |
|---|---|
| **Sarah Larimer**<br>*Kelly-Larimer* | "**Mr. Larimer** was found living, but wounded, an arrow having passed through his thigh near the body." *(52)* |

**Josiah** is surprised to see his travel companion alive after witnessing him fall and believing him to be dead. **William** directs his friends to search for **Gardner Wakefield**. At first, **Gardner** was "nowhere to be seen," and the search party grew confused (Fanny Kelly, 31). Based on what **William** shared about his last encounter with **Gardner's**, everyone expected to find him lying dead under a bush.

| | |
|---|---|
| **Sarah Larimer**<br>*Kelly-Larimer* | "After searching the neighborhood for a quarter of a mile from where last seen, **Mr. Wakefield** was discovered alive, but pierced by three arrows, that he had vainly endeavored to extricate, succeeding only in withdrawing the shafts, leaving the steel points imbedded in the flesh." *(53)* |
| **Fanny Kelly**<br>*Kelly-Larimer* | He was found, "pierced by three arrows that he vainly endeavored to extract, succeeding only in withdrawing the shafts, but leaving the steel points still deeply embedded." *(31)*[105] |

---

[105] Readers can see why Fanny Kelly and Sarah Larimer later entered a legal battle regarding plagiarism in their memoirs which were intended to be published in one book. Sarah Larimer jumped the gun and published her content separately–cutting Fanny Kelly out of her share in the profits.

Once the search ends, the wounded are loaded into **Nelson Morris'** wagon and the deceased are buried near the creek's crossing.[106] The burial is contentious. Only one large grave is dug to accommodate all four individuals: **Arthur Wright, Noah Taylor, Andrew Sharp,** and **Franklin Lawrence.** Source records do not identify who, but someone witnessing this event argues that it is improper to allow **Franklin** to be buried next to the other men because of his skin color. This opinion is rejected by a member of the **Kelly-Larimer Train** and all deceased are given equal funerary rites.

| | |
|---|---|
| **Ella Long**<br>*Morris-Hastings* | "Presumably they buried the dead that were left after the massacre of the ill fated immigrant train. *(Long in Scoggin, 1973)* |
| **Fanny Kelly**<br>*Kelly-Larimer* | They dug a common grave for four bodies and buried the dead in the valley of Little Box Elder." *(33)* |
| **Martha Scoggin**<br>*Morris-Hastings* | "The bodies were buried by the roadside and camouflaged so they would not be noticed by the Indians, and they had to drive off and leave their dead and journey on." *(1973)* |

As a reminder to the reader, **Mary Hurley Kelly** is still presumed alive and missing, even though her body now lies concealed by the landscape, just beyond the camp. In addition, the soldiers who first found her dismissed her as being a victim needing rescue after they felt convinced she was part of the Indian's planned ambush. They might not have communicated a need to return for her.

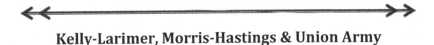

## Kelly-Larimer, Morris-Hastings & Union Army

The **Kelly-Larimer** incident survivors, with the **Morrises** and others, continue to "Fort Deer Creek," as **Sarah Larimer** calls it (1870, 54). There, they are met by **Captain Levi M. Reinhart**, the commanding officer of Company G in the 11th Ohio Volunteer Cavalry. Since the **Captain** had successfully been

---

[106] The spot selected is not far enough away from the creek to protect the graves from flooding once the creek is dammed in the 1950s. In later preservation efforts, the remains are carefully exhumed and reburied next to where Mary Hurley Kelly's grave.

escorted to the garrison the night prior, he was well informed of the tragic situation.

**Fanny Kelly**
*Kelly-Larimer*

"...soldiers returning from Fort Laramie heard the account of the attack and already glimpsed the disaster." *(35)*

Since **Capt. Levi's** arrival, multiple communications have been exchanged over the telegraph lines with **Lt. Col. William O. Collins** at Fort Laramie, including requests for additional horses and reinforcements.

**Josiah Kelly**
*Kelly-Larimer*

"Telegraffed to Fort Laramee and in one week two hundred and fifty soldiers arrived." *(1864)*

At this time, only one regiment is making their way north. Due to being robbed of horses and mules, their progress is slowed and additional horses must be acquired somehow. **Sarah Larimer** claims **Josiah** urged the soldiers at Deer Creek to join him, "to pursue and rescue the prisoners, and chastise the savages in case of resistance" (1870, 119). At present, there is relatively little that can be done safely and effectively until more help arrives. This makes **Josiah** irate.

**Josiah Kelly**
*Kelly-Larimer*

"I cam to this station and tried to get help to rescue the priseners but they could not spare a man. 50 men stationed here to gard the post." *(1864)*

The military's delay is not unreasonable considering the limited provisions they have for defending even themselves, should the Northern Plains Indians chose to descend on their location. For context, Deer Creek's military housing situation is merely a fortified stage stop with a telegraph operation. In 1864, the "fort" can house between twenty and fifty soldiers along with their wives (but only if they were employed as a cook or laundress). Outside the premise is a pleasant camping area for emigrants and friendly Indians (and/or the unemployed wives and children of soldiers). Platt & Slater's 1850 trail guide describes the local camp as being on a, "small but beautiful stream of water," with plenty of grass to allow weary emigrants to layover and recruit their animals (*Guide to California Overland,* 17).

A quarter-mile south of the garrison is an abandoned coal mine and east of the garrison is the Lower Platte Ferry (previously known as Bissonnette's Ferry).

In some accounts, it has been recorded that the ferry is constructed of eight dugout canoes lashed together, that are brought across the river by three to four men pulling on an attached rope.[107] The cost to cross a wagon on the ferry is around $5.00 ($95.00, presently), though women are typically allowed to cross for free, as recorded in some earlier accounts.[108]

**Sarah Larimer**     At Deer Creek, "The wounded men [**William** and **Gardner**] were
*Kelly-Larimer*     taken from the wagon in which they had been brought, and laid upon the burning sand … they were unwelcome guests, seeming to have no legal claims upon the garrison, and only permitted to enter by act of charity. Finally, a small tent was procured of a mountaineer, which was graciously accepted…" *(56)* [109]

The lack of hospitality shown to the injured parties might factor in there being sufficient camping conditions available to emigrants outside the walls of the garrison. Besides being materially ill-equipped, the soldiers stationed at Deer Creek (and at Fort Laramie) are notoriously dysfunctional, lazy and otherwise useless in any war effort.[110] Illustrating this point, despite the reports of danger and impending battles, the soldiers here do not sacrifice their long anticipated payday celebration. With freshly lined pockets, the soldiers relax, imbibe on whisky and host a "ball" that passing emigrants are invited to join–especially females. Though neither memoirist can judge this situation fairly, both criticize **Sarah Jane Morris** for participating in the poorly timed party:

---

[107] Joseph Goldsborough Bruff, *Journal and Drawings of J. Goldsborough Bruff: 1849-1853.* (The Huntington Library: San Marino, California), July 16.

[108] Agnes Stewart, *Diary of Agnes Stewart, letter of Elizabeth Stewart Warner: 1853 Lost Wagon Train.* (Eugene, OR: Lane Co. Historical Society, 1959) July 4-5.

[109] The identity of the generous mountaineer has not yet been established.

[110] Soldiers that are sent to the Plains at this time are predisposed to disobey Union leadership, abandon their post, or get themselves court martialed to avoid going into battle. Lieutenant Eugene Ware's journal from the Plains claims this year's outfit comprises of converted turncoats from the 1863 capture of General John H. Morgan's troops, and newly mustered Confederate sympathizers. Eugene Ware, *The Indian War of 1864: Being a Fragment of the Early History of Kansas, Nebraska, Colorado, and Wyoming.* (Topeka: Crane & Co, 1911).

| | |
|---|---|
| **Sarah Larimer**<br>*Kelly-Larimer* | "The night of their arrival in the fort, many emigrant women being camped in the neighborhood, who could be induced to dance, a ball was given; and the lady who so narrowly escaped death or abduction [**Sarah Jane Morris**], by riding with her family for their lives, having lost her wardrobe with her trunks, borrowed a dress of Mrs. Holbrook,[111] the wife of a non-commissioned officer residing in the fort." *(56)* |
| **Fanny Kelly**<br>*Kelly-Larimer* | "The mother of the child; who had so narrowly escaped death … attended the entertainment." *(38)* |
| **Sarah Larimer**<br>*Kelly-Larimer* | "[She] joined in the festivities, regardless of the sorrow and the gloom…" *(56)* |

## Morris-Hastings Epilogue

When **Nelson Morris** reaches Salt Lake City, either his or **Mr. Northrop's** recollection (who escaped with the **Hastings**) is printed in an August 13 issue of the *Union Vedette*. The account comes from "one of the emigrants who fortunately escaped and is in this city in destitute circumstances." Though the editor does not mention the name of who shared the story, the details are remarkably accurate, as only an eyewitness can provide. On the informant's survival, the paper reports: "[He] only escaped by belaboring his horse into a gallop and eluding the savages." A full transcription is provided in the Appendix. A near-identical version appears in a California paper the following month, which is also transcribed in the Appendix, as well as shown here.

After five months on the trail, the **Morrises** and **Hastings** settle in Walla Walla, Washington, only two parcels away from each other. Both families become well-known pioneers in Garfield County. **Nelson Morris** immediately throws a backyard wedding for his fifteen-year-old daughter, **Mary**, to a man twice her age. In time, **Nelson** becomes a wealthy and influential farmer. **Jacob Hastings** begins circuit-riding as a Christian minister before his sixth child, **Emaline**, arrives in

---

[111] Mrs. Ellander Brumfield Holbrook (1825-1877) is married to Calvin B. Holbrook, Quartermaster Sergeant (Q.M.S.) of Company G.

December. In 1872, **Enoch Hastings** and **Alice Morris** marry. And in 1875, their younger siblings **William Morris** and **Nancy Hastings,** also marry.

MASSACRES ON THE PLAINS.—The Salt Lake Vedette gives the following account of an Indian massacre, on the Plains, east of that city:

It will be remembered that early in July we briefly chronicled the fact that emigrants had been attacked by Indians on Deer Creek, one hundred miles west of Fort Larimie. From one of the emigrants, who fortunately escaped, and is in this city in destitute circumstances, we have learned the following particulars, with the names of the killed and wounded. The attack was made on the 12th of July last by a band of Sioux and Cheyenes at Box Elder, above the mouth of Dry Creek, on the North Platte. The following were killed: N. Taylor, from Coffee county, Kansas; Mrs. Sharp, from Woodman county, Kansas; Arthur Wright, Minneapolis, Hennepin county, Minhsota; colored boy Frank, Kansas; Mr. Wakefield, Woodson county, Kansas, formerly from Maine; William L. Larrimer, of Allen county, Kansas, was wounded in the thigh. His wife and child were taken prisoners by the savages, and were in durance two days. On the fifth day they came into deer creek all right. Mrs. Fanny Kelly and niece were taken prisoners. The former is supposed to have escaped, but the niece (a child) was found murdered and scalped. Our informant only escaped by belaboring his horse into a gallop and eluding the savages.

"Massacres on the Plains," editorial in, *Chico Weekly Chronical-Record*, September 3, 1864.

**Forman**

While those at Deer Creek drink and dance the night away, soldiers and emigrants back at La Bonte Creek are startled this evening by the rumbling of hooves in the distance.

**George Forman**
*Lone Traveler*

"Our company was on the Le Bonte Creek … when a fearful stampede came down the Road and passed us like a Regiment of Horse. Our soldiers were camped a mile away. The cry was raised of 'The Indians.'" *(July 14)*

"I was in bed, and with the others, rushed to the mouth of the corral, where all was excitement, and some women were there with frying pan handles, etc., ready to fight with the men. Other women rushed across the corral to their own wagons crying out 'Oh My Baby' etc. and things were lively…" *(July 14)*

"It turned out that a party of Indians had really passed us, but saw no chance for attack. Signal guns were fired to our herders and answered. These trains were all emigrants and Missourians and brave men and women, too." *(July 14)*

This stampede might be the same one seen from the North Bank Trails midmorning of July 14, near the North Douglas Bend located opposite the confluence of La Prele Creek with the North Platte River. (*See the story of the Pella Company in Emigrant Tales from the North Bank Trails.*)

# Friday, July 15, 1864

### Kelly-Larimer

On July 15, **Josiah Kelly** is still denied his request for a rescue team. By now, he has likely learned that a young girl matching the description of his niece, **Mary Hurley Kelly**, was seen near the attack site, alive. Being unable to search for his family continues to be a source of frustration for **Josiah**. It is possible that **Cpt. Levi Reinhart** or other soldiers assure him that reinforcements are on the way and will surely find **Mary** in the process, assuming she is still around.

### Forman, Merrill & Union Army

Since being awakened in the dark of night, the **Hundred Wagon Train** at La Bonte Creek is on high alert this morning. The one-hundred-man regiment of the 11th Ohio Cavalry (turned Infantry) tries to organize the fearful emigrants into a united force. Despite his parents urging to stay out of any fighting, **Julius Merrill** is ready and willing to offer his support to **Captain Levi G. Marshall** and the defense mission.

**Julius Merrill**
*Merrill Team*

"At daybreak our military commander called out an extra guard for the stock. This was the first and last time it was done and really[,] a more sensible precaution could not have been taken as the Indians generally stampede stock about sunrise." *(July 15)*

## Mahan-Moore

On July 15, the **Mahan-Moore Team** finally gets a late move on after a morning hunt in the mountains. **Garland Mahan** logs twenty miles in his diary, which includes joining the **Hundred Wagon Train** at La Bonte Creek.

## Forman, Granger, Mahan-Moore, Merrill & Union Army

While **Julius Merrill** continues to speculate on how and when the Northern Plains Indians will plan their next attack, those who consolidate with the **Hundred Wagon Train** share more testimonies from the Platte River Raids.

**George Forman**
*Lone Traveler*

"We hear of a train attacked ten miles behind us by the same party of Sioux who passed us last night." *(July 15)*

It is unclear who shared this story, who might have been the victim, or in what capacity. Further research is needed to find a traveler account with a July 14 robbery (or attempt), preceded by a stampede, somewhere between Elkhorn and La Bonte Creeks. There are strong links to a robbery on the North Bank Trail, on the **Pella Company**, but more definitive evidence is needed to confirm the connection.

When the Captain releases the **Hundred Wagon Train** to move forward, **Julius** starts looking forward to seeing the remains at Little Box Elder Creek that he's heard so much about, but first, they find **Aaron Rockwood** and **John Hawley** (from the **Granger Train)** stranded at Bed Tick Creek.

| | |
|---|---|
| **Julius Merrill**<br>*Merrill Team* | "After much delay… We travelled until noon but saw no bodies along the road … we came to a train from which 52 mules and horses had been taken. They were left with not enough to draw their wagons. The Indians had wounded but one man in getting the stock." *(July 15)* |
| **George Forman**<br>*Lone Traveler* | "We moved on to where the 50 mules were stolen and find 2 wagons unhurt and unloaded." *(July 15)* |
| **Garland Mahan**<br>*Mahan-Moore Team* | "a no. of wagons on 10 miles to Luparill [La Prele] creek. They had been robbed by the Indians…" *(July 15)* |
| **George Forman**<br>*Lone Traveler* | " The captain of the Troops pressed four yoke of Oxen from our train to haul them on." *(July 15)* |
| **Julius Merrill**<br>*Merrill Team* | "We divided our teams and hauled their wagons to Laparall [La Prele] Creek " *(July 15)* |

After redistributing livestock and other resources, the **Hundred Wagon Train** and its military escort continues to La Prele Creek, in the afternoon. **Julius** continues to be on the lookout for the macabre.

| | |
|---|---|
| **Julius Merrill**<br>*Merrill Team* | "We started again, nearly all dreading to see the victims of the arrow and tomahawk…" *(July 15)* |
| **James Logan**<br>*Granger Company* | "With two pieces of artillery[,] move on…." *(1864)* |
| **Aaron Rockwood**<br>*Granger Company* | "On the 15th we moved up to a creek about ten miles, where we could get plenty of water…"*(1864)* |

At La Prele Creek, **Capt. Levi G. Marshall** calls the **Hundred Wagon Train** and his soldiers to a halt. Once again, he sends detachments of soldiers and volunteers to scout the trails ahead for potential threats.

| | |
|---|---|
| **George Forman**<br>*Lone Traveler* | "We go into camp all day waiting for our men to return. They came back that night, had found a number of whites killed and buried their bodies…" *(July 15)* |

The returning scouts also report that just as many attacks are occurring on the North Bank Trail.

**Garland Mahan**
*Mahan-Moore Team*

"The Indians are committing horrible acts along here, robbing and murdering emigrants." *(July 15)*

**George Forman**
*Lone Traveler*

"A freight train on the North side of the river just opposite us a few miles [was] attacked and some of our soldiers went out and had a skirmish with them,[112] and they came back for reinforcements and pressed some of our horses (my pony among them) and men and went some 15 [miles] North of the Platte where another train had been robbed." *(July 15)*

The "just opposite" location points to the North Douglas Bend where unsuspecting folks on the North Bank Trails have been targeted for at least three consecutive days. The robbery from fifteen miles north could either be referring to travelers taking a northward detour in on Bozeman's Trail, or it could indicate an incident happening on the stretch of trail between the Floodplains and the Ferry of the Platte near Deer Creek (the more likely of the two possibilities).[113] More details are needed to support the soldiers' report and draw any specific conclusions.

While camped, the **Hundred Wagon Train** doubles in numbers by the end of the day.

**Garland Mahan**
*Mahan-Moore Team*

"That night we and some soldiers camped on La Parelle [La Prele] Creek and was joined by 50 more wagons making 200 wagons in all. Indians are now all around us making signals from the Hills with large fires to each other." *(July 15)*

---

[112] The "skirmish" might be a reference to the Jongewaard Train's experience where the emigrants attempt to recruit help from soldiers in the area, but in a misunderstanding, they are chased down and arrested. (*For more on this, please see the Emigrants Tales from the North Bank Trails.*)
[113] In the window of time provided, this may be a reference to the Oliver or Shoemaker Trains. Those attacked left messages staked to the ground with warnings and details of their losses.

As more scouts return, there continues to be excitement in camp, lasting through the night. Oddly, the following events, as shared by **Julius,** are not supported by any other first-person accounts.

| | |
|---|---|
| **Julius Merrill**<br>*Merrill Team* | "Towards night a party of soldiers returned to camp having discovered some Indians and stock. All was commotion. The soldiers with two mountain howitzers started in pursuit..." *(July 15)* |

**Julius** provides no directional insight for where the Indians are keeping the stolen animals, nor are there any hints for how many are spotted in the area. Despite the possibility of a battle with nearby Indians this evening, some emigrants in the very crowded camp try to take their minds off the day's stress.

| | |
|---|---|
| **Julius Merrill**<br>*Merrill Team* | "A dance was started in a Missouri train[114] in which some soldiers [who were] left to guard their camp participated. Some, having too much whisky, began to be quarrelsome, and one or two skirmishes occurred." *(July 15)* |

When the partying ends and the camp quiets down, somebody imagines hearing a gunshot. Though **Julius** derides the idea, saying that, "those calm enough to use their own ears were not disturbed," several men respond to the signal by rushing off for a mid-night battle.

| | |
|---|---|
| **Julius Merrill**<br>*Merrill Team* | "They soon came back saying all was quiet, and we were allowed to rest in peace the remainder of the night." *(July 15)* |

---

[114] The "Missouri Train" mentioned here is not yet identified.

# Saturday, July 16, 1864

### Kelly-Larimer & Union Army

On July 16, at Deer Creek garrison, the wounded and distressed survivors from the **Kelly-Larimer** and **Morris-Hastings Trains** continue to rest after their traumatic experience–all, that is, except **Josiah Kelly**. He continues to press **Capt. Levi Reinhart** to take more immediate action against his attackers and to rescue the captives. **Josiah** might not know that that additional troops under the command of **General Robert B. Mitchell** have been called out all the way from Fort Kearny in Nebraska (a four hundred miles distance). This number of deployments is verified in a news report appearing in the *Chicago Tribune.*

> An emigrant train of thirteen wagons was attacked by 600 Sioux Indians a short distance above Fort Laramie, and after a desperate fight the emigrants were overpowered, thirteen of their number having been killed. The Indians burned the wagons, after robbing them of what they wanted, and carried off all the stock. Six companies of troops were met between Fort Kearney and Laramie, and went in pursuit of the Indians.

"FROM ST. LOUIS: Highly Interesting Military and Border News – From Idaho and the Gold Regions," *Chicago Tribune*, July 22, 1864, 1.

This sensationalized wording is reflective of yellow journalism techniques to increase newspaper sales, similar to how zingy clickbait terms and SEO strategies are employed in modern online publications.

## Forman, Granger, Merrill, Mahan-Moore & Union Army

On July 16, the (**Two**) **Hundred Wagon Train** remains detained at La Prele Creek either by military order or by a vote (depending on the diary one believes).

**Julius Merrill**
Merrill Team

"Having good feed, the train voted to lay over."
(July 16)

**Garland Mahan**
Mahan-Moore Team

"Lay by." (July 16)

Those in the **Granger Company** are under the impression that no one is allowed to travel and that even if the (**Two**) **Hundred Wagon Train** wanted to or voted to move forward, **the commander [Capt. Levi G. Marshall]** would stop them because of various military initiatives to secure the area.

**Aaron Rockwood**
Granger Company

"...[We] lay there two days for the military to fool around and do nothing. They could have had two hundred volunteers,[115] and there were over one hundred of them, and two mounted howitzers, and the trail perfectly plain to follow, but they would not go." (1864)

Despite **Aaron Rockwood's** "do nothing" comment about the 11th Ohio, **Julius Merrill's** accounts claims the troops are fully engaged in preparations to advance. He also verifies that emigrants are invited (again) to participate in volunteer assignments. Some detachments provide damage control, others look for stolen horses, and some are tracking if Indians are still in the area. As much as **Aaron** believes the average man would take up this mantle, few actually do.

**Julius Merrill**
Merrill Team

"About noon, the soldiers not returning[,] who had gone in pursuit of the Indians last night, volunteers were called for by the lieutenant in charge of the camp. I, in company with twelve others, volunteered." (July 16)

---

[115] This is likely a broad guess of the available and able-bodied men with guns in the emigrant camp.

**George Forman**
*Lone Traveler*

"They looked very warlike going out with two Mountain Cannon and some shells."[116]  *(July 16)*

**Julius Merrill**
*Merrill Team*

"Having gone about half a mile, we met the **soldiers** returning. ... The **troops** followed the [Indians'] trail to the river and gave up further pursuit. ... Upon being discovered the night before, the Indians had broken camp and retired across the Platte." *(July 16)*

**Julius** claims the failed capture results in his volunteer detachment being dissolved and ordered back to camp. In the evening, the **(Two) Hundred Wagon Train** is met by Company H, led by **Captain Jacob S. Schuman**, in a late arrival from Fort Laramie.

**Aaron Rockwood**
*Granger Company*

"...there were near five hundred wagons come up, and about one hundred and ten soldiers." *(1864)*

**James Logan**
*Granger Company*

"The **soldiers** ordered us to halt and keep all back until there was near five hundred wagons together then two hundred soldiers[.]" *(1864)*

According to **Sarah Larimer's** memoir, at least a portion of the soldiers pass by and go up to Deer Creek garrison this same evening (1870, 111).

---

[116] Mountain Cannon and Howitzer are two names for the same weapon.

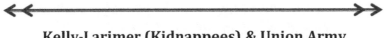

## Kelly-Larimer (Kidnappees) & Union Army

After dark, word arrives at Deer Creek garrison that one of the kidnapped women and a child have returned from captivity and are in the care of emigrants on the North Bank Trail. They are attended by several women and their presence stirs up a commotion with "hundreds" of people trying to see the survivors for themselves (Larimer, 112).

**Sarah Larimer**
*Kelly-Larimer Train*

"As the waters were too high for us to cross that night, a soldier, by the name of [**William**] **Sparks**,[117] who happened to be there, kindly offered to cross the river and inform my husband of our safe arrival…" *(113)*

Because **William Larimer** is wounded, **Josiah Kelly** responds to **Sarah's** arrival. After crossing the North Platte River, he barrages **Sarah** with questions about his wife and niece's condition and whereabouts.

**Sarah Larimer**
*Kelly-Larimer Train*

"**Mr. Kelley** immediately came over to inquire the fate of his family, but I was able to give him no very encouraging information." *(113)*

It is unclear if **Josiah** returns to the garrison that night, or if he waits until the morning to cross back over. First-person accounts only say that **Sarah Larimer** and her son, **Frank,** stay all night with members of the **Roe Train**.

---

[117] William Sparks is mentioned in Martha Roe's journal on July 16 (on the North Bank Trail).

# Sunday, July 17, 1864

### Kelly-Larimer (Kidnappees)

First thing on the morning of July 17, **Sarah Larimer** and her son ferry over the North Platte River to Deer Creek garrison with associates of the **Roe Train**, whom **Sarah** now considers to be friends.

| **Sarah Larimer** | "It was the 17th of July, and five days since our capture, that |
|---|---|
| *Kelly-Larimer Train* | we crossed the broad bosom of the North Platte, on our way |

| | to Fort Deer-Creek. The waters had fallen so as to allow us to go over in a wagon…" *(116)* |
|---|---|

"...Heaven in mercy sent an easier crossing, among friends who, though yesterday strangers, were already much interested in our welfare." *(117)*

**Sarah** reconnects with her husband, while **Josiah Kelly** relays the details of the kidnapping and escape to anyone who might listen. He finally convinces **Capt. Levi M. Reinhart** to provide him a military escort to join in his search for **Mary Hurley Kelly**.

### Forman, Granger, Mahan-Moore, Merrill & Union Army

The **(Five) Hundred Wagon Train** now has well over one-hundred soldiers with them at La Prele Creek. After being told in so many ways that the wagon trains must stay put. But with the late arrival of Company H, emigrants might believe that conditions for their safety have been met, so they should be allowed to move on. After yesterday scouting, the 11th Ohio is confident no surprises await between La Prele and Deer Creek and the commander finally releases the (**Five**) **Hundred Wagon Train** to proceed with caution. The **Granger Company** remains dependent on the (compulsory) generosity of others in the procession of wagons that stretches out for miles on end.

**Aaron Rockwood**
*Granger Company*

"After waiting two days on the creek, we moved up to Deer Creek, twenty miles, between military station and telegraph office. The emigrants volunteered their teams to move our wagons to that point, thinking we would be safer there than on the road..." *(1864)*

Before reaching Deer Creek, however, there is a long delay at Little Box Elder Creek.

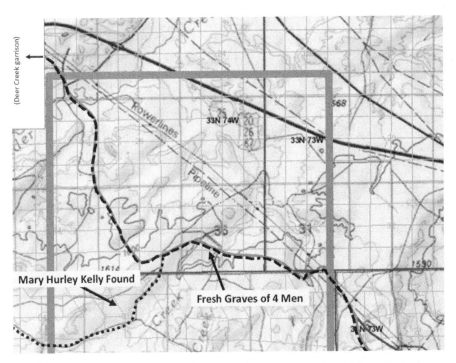

Map showing the Oregon Trail (dashed) on the South Bank Trail System, passing over Box Elder and Little Box Elder Creeks in Douglas, Wyoming. Map generated using the NPS National Trails Historic Trails Viewer. Modified by the author.

| **James Logan**<br>*Granger Company* | "We move on … passing many horrid sights of burnt trains, destroys goods &c.." *(1864)* |
| **George Forman**<br>*Lone Traveler* | "Noon camp at Box Alder [sic] Creek where the 14 were killed and the two women and children had been captured, a **Mrs. Kelly** and a **Mrs. Larimer**. … Burnt wagons and new graves were at all those camping grounds." *(July 17)* |

It should also be noted, again, that **George's** published journal is informed beyond his personal observations. He embellishes his writing prior to publication using news reports and the women's dramatized memoirs of the 1870s.

| **Julius Merrill**<br>*Merrill Team* | "One of our train, being behind had taken the road to the left instead … He soon saw his mistake and started across to the road we were upon." *(July 17)* |
| **Aaron Rockwood**<br>*Granger Company* | "…as we were moving up, we [including **John Hawley**] took another road which passed about two miles to the right of the scene." *(1864)* |
| **Julius Merrill**<br>*Merrill Team* | "…About midway[,] he discovered the body of a child which had been murdered by the Indians. The train was halted." *(July 17)* |
| **Aaron Rockwood**<br>*Granger Company* | "Near the road we were on, was found one of the children, a little girl six years old, with several arrows in her body and scalped." *(1864)* |
| **James Logan**<br>*Granger Company* | "We found a little girl and man shot through with two arrows[.] each, scalped and tomahawked and we buried them." *(1864)* |

The little girl is **Mary Hurley Kelly** and the man is likely the driver employed by **Jacob Hastings** (both of whom are discovered after crossing the Creek). According to later Union Army reports, the bodies are found by accidental means and credited to the curiosity of dogs (or wolves).

| **Cpl. Hervey Johnson**<br>*Union Army, Co. G* | "A party of our company were out yesterday and found the body of a little girl with several arrows sticking in it[.] A large gray wolf was eating the child..." *(July 18, 1864)* |
| --- | --- |
| **George Forman**<br>*Lone Traveler* | "On the hill near the creek to the East[,] one of our dogs found the body of a little girl about 5 years old." *(July 17)* |

The discovery soon draws a crowd. **Julius Merrill** acknowledges "the wolves had gnawed the flesh from one of it[s] legs," but this could just as likely have been a wound inflicted by the domestic dogs running ahead of the **Granger Company,** as **George Forman** claims.

| **George Forman**<br>*Lone Traveler* | "...the dog was tearing its limbs. It had been tomahawked and scalped and had lain there in the hot sun four or five days and full of maggots and flies. There were two steel painted arrows in its body...." *(July 17)* |
| --- | --- |
| **Julius Merrill**<br>*Merrill Team* | "...The body was that of a little girl about six years of age... one arrow had entered the left hip and... another had entered the side... across the top of her head was the gash of a tomahawk about four inches in length..." *(July 17)* |

### Merrill

| **Julius Merrill**<br>*Merrill Team* | "Leaving several to bury the body, we moved on." *(July 17)* |
| --- | --- |

The **Merrill Team** may be some of the first people to deliver the sad news of **Mary Hurley Kelly's** demise to those waiting at Deer Creek garrison, or to the squad **Josiah Kelly** is coming east with. One can only hope that **Julius** keeps the gorier details to himself during that interaction.

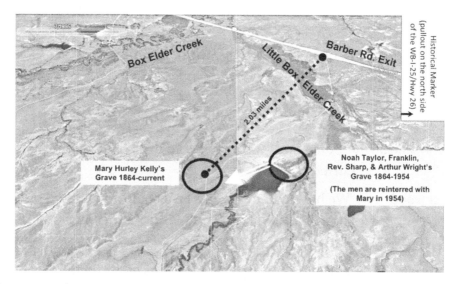

Grave locations, relative to I-25/US-26. 1985 satellite image from the U.S Geological Survey, marked by author.

Mary Hurley Kelly's grave identified and marked in 1945 by William Wayne Morrison. Mr. Morrison was a historian of emigrant trails and pioneer graves from Cheyenne, Wyoming. His research, photos, essays, and collection of source items are archived with the American Heritage Center. *Photo credit:* W.W. Morrison Collection.

## Forman, Granger, Mahan-Moore & Union Army

**Sarah Larimer** records that before burying **Mary**, someone tears off a piece of her white dress to help identify the remains (115).

| | |
|---|---|
| **Cpl. Hervey Johnson**<br>*Union Army, Co. G* | "...some tools were procured of a train and the body was buried..." *(July 18, 1864)* |
| **Aaron Rockwood**<br>*Granger Company* | "We buried her as well as we could and passed on. That happened about fifteen miles from the Deer Creek Station..." *(1864)* |
| **George Forman**<br>*Lone Traveler* | "We buried it[,] about 18 inches of dirt being thrown over it where it lay, and no coffin, mountain fashion." *(July 17)* |

"Mountain fashion" is a practical above-ground method of protecting a body when one has inadequate digging tools, or time to prepare a more traditional resting place. The body can be covered with dirt, then piled with river rock or other heavy stones collected from the area. The rock pile is supposed to deter scavenger animals from being able to disturb the remains as they decompose.

In 2019, Richard Rieck, a trail history enthusiast, conducted a survey of behaviors and trends from emigrants burying their deceased along the Oregon and Overland-California Trails. He suggests that preventive measures such as these rock piles may only have provided short-term emotional reassurance to those performing burial rites but were ultimately ineffective.[118] He found in his survey of trail diaries that, "Wolves were hated by emigrants for digging into burials and toppling markers. Numerous diarists reported seeing body parts, clothing, and long tresses of women's hair scattered by canines around graves. Covering a tomb with stones ... was no guarantee that it was safe."[119]

---

[118] Richard Rieck, "Trail Deaths, Trail Graves, and Cenotaphs; Here? There? Where?" in *Overland Journal,* 37, no.1 (Spring 2019). Richard's research is supported by the oversight and assistance of Randy Brown.
[119] Ibid., 22.

## Kelly-Larimer & Union Army

Upon leaving the garrison, **Josiah Kelly** steels himself to find his niece.

**Sarah Larimer**
*Kelly-Larimer Train*

"In accordance with his plan, **Mr. Kelly** procured a squad of men, it being unsafe to go alone, and proceeded in search of the lost child. ... The squad of soldiers, in their search, came up to a company of emigrants standing a little back from the road; but, alas, too late! The body of little **Mary** had been found pierced by three arrows, and she had been scalped by the ruthless knife..." *(114)*

**Josiah Kelly**
*Kelly-Larimer Train*

"We have since found **Mary** shot with two arrows, scalped and tomahawked. What I have suffered since that time no press of tongue can express." *(1864)*

**Sarah Larimer**
*Kelly-Larimer Train*

"To the travellers, who found her, she was only the mutilated corpse of a murdered child. ...but with humane feelings gave her a resting-place in the earth, and, with the usual precaution in such cases, secured a piece of her dress by which the body might possibly be identified." *(114-115)*

After the burial rites are complete, the **(Five) Hundred Wagon Train** proceeds west but **Josiah** stays in the area to mourn, shore up the rock pile, and create a grave marker similar to those made for the adults who were buried on the other side of the creek.[120] At a later date, **Cpl. Hervey Johnson** visits Little Box Elder and tries to find all the graves he'd heard about, but cannot find **Mary's**. Perhaps over the next couple of weeks, it had fallen down.

**Cpl. Hervey Johnson**
*Union Army, Co. G*

"...we stopped ... to look at and read the inscriptions on some graves that were near. There were four headboards and but one broad grave. The names of the men were

---

[120] Randy Brown, "Attack on the Kelly-Larimer Wagon Train," *WyoHistory.org* (Wyoming Historical Society; Wheatfield, WY), 2016.

given and the inscription was 'Killed by indians on the 12th of July.' There is a grave of a little girl somewhere there but we couldn't find it." *(August 11, 1864 to Sybil)*

By the re-discovery of **Mary's** grave by W. M. Morrison in 1945, there was no marker left standing, so Mr. Morrison adds a new one, as shown in the prior closeup grave image.

In 1954, the remains of the four adults were exhumed and moved to the location of Mary Hurley Kelly with the assistance of W. W. Morrison and state engineer, L.C. Bishop. Randy Brown, 2016. Permission granted.

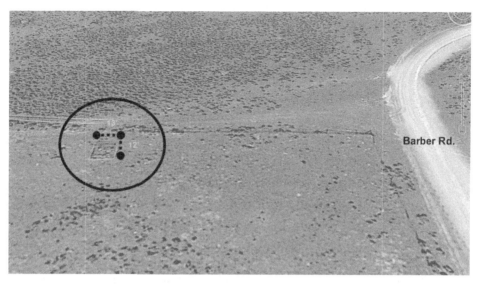

In 1966, members of the Wyoming Historical Society erected a fence around the ad-hoc cemetery on the corner of privately-owned land. Map created using a 2013 satellite image provided by Google Earth Pro, marked by author.

## Forman, Granger, Kelly-Larimer, Mahan-Moore & Union Army

**George Forman**
*Lone Traveler*

"We moved out in grand style, **our train** 3 miles long."
*(July 17)*

After a short procession, the lengthy **(Five) Hundred Wagon Train** spies another grim sight—a second body. It appears that if **Julius Merrill** had spotted it on his way out, he left it to be dealt with by others, just as he did with **Mary Hurley Kelly's** body.

**Aaron Rockwood**
*Granger Company*

"...within about six miles of the station, we found a man beside the road shot with arrows and stripped of all but his pants. He had been dead, I should think, about four days, but we cannot find out anything about him." *(1864)*

**Cpl. Hervey Johnson**
*Union Army, Co. G*

"...the body of a man was also found ... stripped of the clothing except pants and boots and hats." *(July 18)*

**George Forman**
*Lone Traveler*

"Beside the side of the road was a dead man, his body full of arrows, looking like a brush heap with the feather end of the arrows out. He was stripped and scalped and was black with the sun and the maggots rolling in billows from his mouth and nose. He had been there about 5 days and had strayed from his train[,] hunting probably[,] and been killed by the Indians. ... the dried blood was all over the ground and shreds of clothing on the bushes showing his struggles before death." *(July 17)*

This body is suspected to be **Jacob Hastings'** unnamed employee. Referring back to the night of July 12, after being chased down the road, this teamster-driver left the safety of the wagon train to run up a hill. Descendant stories suggest he was trying to get a better look at what happened.[121] From the descriptions given, his body was found about two miles west of Little Box Elder. Further research on his identity is encouraged.

Considering how **Josiah** and his search party had just come through the area, it is odd that they did not find (or at least mention) this man's body lying so close to the road. It was also not found when the **Morris** family initially scoured the scene on July 14. Perhaps, once again, the dogs in the **Granger Company** are to credit for the odorous discovery.

**Aaron Rockwood**
*Granger Company*

"He was buried [where] he lay." *(1864)*

**Garland Mahan**
*Mahan-Moore Team*

"Our train buried a man and a child (little girl 9 years old) found on the road..." *(July 17, written from Deer Creek)*

**George Forman**
*Lone Traveler*

"About a foot of dirt was thrown over him where he lay and we moved on." *(July 17)*

---

[121] Ella Long, in Martha Scoggin's *Pioneer days on Scoggin Ridge…* 1973.

**Forman, Granger, Mahan-Moore, Merrill, Morris-Hastings & Union Army**

After one more burial (less formal than the last), the **(Five) Hundred Wagon Train** arrives at Deer Creek garrison in present-day Glenrock, Wyoming. The **Merrill Team** is presumed to have arrived ahead of the rest.

**George Forman**
*Lone Traveler*

"Six miles further we came to Deer Creek[,] a sma post and Telegraph Station[,] 100 miles west of L camped one mile beyond, now fully 500 wagons.'

On arrival, the emigrants hear the full story of the **Kelly-Larimer** incident. Depending on who spoke with whom at the sprawling camp outside the station's grounds, there are variations on the tales diarists preserve. They do not agree on facts such as **Frank Larimer's** age, or details from the escape.

**Aaron Rockwood**
*Granger Company*

"We learned when we came to Deer Creek[,] back on the 13th, the Indians, about 30 in number, had surrounded a train of three or four wagons, six men and their families, professing to be friendly Indians, and kept on with them for a few miles, and then demanded their supper." *(1864)*

"The emigrants were in their [the Indian's] power and therefore stopped to comply with their demand, and, as they were making a fire to cook it, the Indians commenced the attack and killed or wounded all but one white man [**Josiah Kelly**] and a negro [**Andy Lawrence**]." *(1864)*

**Garland Mahan**
*Mahan-Moore Team*

"They were killed by Indians a day or two ago. They have taken little squads that have passed along for 35 miles along the road. Captured a train of 6 wagons, killed six men out of 11 and took the women prisoners." *(July 17)*

**Aaron Rockwood**
*Granger Company*

"They [**Josiah** and **Andy**] both commenced to run on the first alarm, and made their escape to some willows on the bank of the stream, and it be night, they got to the station."[122] *(1864)*

**James Logan**
*Granger Company*

"When we arrived at the Deer Creek Post, we found several wounded men, one of whom will die..." *(1864)*

**Julius Merrill**
*Merrill Team*

"At the station lay two men of the same party [**William Larimer** and **Gardner Wakefield**], both badly wounded." *(July 17)*

"The women were taken across the Platte and travelled northward two days. The aunt of the girl took a pony. The other [**Sarah Larimer**] with **her little boy** [**Frank**] four years old started on foot. She took off her skirts and bound them around her feet so as to leave no trail. ...The second day after leaving the camp of the Indians, the woman and child reached the river opposite Deer Creek Station about ten miles above where the massacre occurred." *(July 17)*

**Garland Mahan**
*Mahan-Moore Team*

"One woman got away at night ... She got to the Ft. today.[123] ... The woman is an intelligent person." *(July 17)*

**Aaron Rockwood**
*Granger Company*

"...one of the women came in the night before we got there, bringing her little boy with her. She had made her escape in the night, and had travelled two nights and part of the last day and came in safe." *(1864)*

**James Logan**
*Granger Company*

"...and a lady that had been captured with her little boy six years old had escaped and just returned faint[,] on foot[,] sore[,] carrying her boy four days and nights..." *(1864)*

---

[122] This mention of an arrival confirms prior questions about Andy Lawrence's whereabouts on the evening of July 12.

[123] This reference of "today" (July 17) aligns with Sarah Larimer's account.

**George Forman**
*Lone Traveler*

"She [**Sarah**] had escaped and with her little boy[,] walked over 40 miles barefoot over Prickly Pears … and was now safe with her husband." *(July 17)*

**Aaron Rockwood**
*Granger Company*

"Her husband was one of the wounded and is likely to recover. The other wounded man [**Gardner Wakefield**] was a single man and is probably dead before this [letter gets read]." *(1864)*

**George Forman**
*Lone Traveler*

"But **Mrs. [Fanny] Kelly** is still a captive…" *(July 17)*

**James Logan**
*Granger Company*

"…another lady that was carried off[,] who tried to escape[,] has not yet returned[,] perhaps recaptured and killed." *(1864)*

By the end of the day, several hundreds of emigrants camp near the military post, crowding in on both sides of the North Platte River. Those who incurred losses expect the 11th Ohio to act on the depredations, but no one seems to trust their efficacy in carrying this task out. The number of horses and mules reported stolen is exceedingly high and recovering this large of a herd, plus arranging a hostage recovery is now a much more serious undertaking than the emergency responders initially prepared for.

**Garland Mahan**
*Mahan-Moore Team*

"The Military, who are pursuing them [the Indians] say they have several 1000 head of stock that they have run off…" *(July 17)*

## Granger & Wood

Fear and desperation provoke some emigrants to find an alternative means of restoring their losses and getting out of the tortured Black Hills as soon as possible. For those who can jump on the opportunity, they press their luck with the **Wood Freight Train.**[124] These eastbound Mormon travelers have been

---

[124] The full identity of those in the Wood Freight Train has not yet been established. The freighting operation has six-wagons pulled by mules.

leading a large number of mules from Salt Lake City to "Kanesville" and "Winter Quarters," AKA Council Bluffs, Iowa and Florence, Nebraska (respectively). Because of the Platte River Raids, this freighter is forced to turn back from Deer Creek to wait out the situation near the Platte Bridge Station in Casper, Wyoming.

Amongst those willing to do whatever it takes to move ahead, and at whatever the cost, are those in the **Granger Company**. When these families learn that the **Wood Train** helped other families, they are convinced this is their best chance at getting to safety.

| | |
|---|---|
| **James Logan**<br>*Granger Company* | "Fortunate for these families who had lost their stock[,] there came in a large drove of mules from Salt Lake City going to the Missouri River for Freight[,] which could not proceed with safety ... conducted by Capt. Wood who kindly took some twenty wagons with families on to Salt Lake City." *(1864)* |
| **Aaron Rockwood**<br>*Granger Company* | "On reaching [Deer Creek,] **Captain [Samuel] Granger** and myself learned there had been a train of six wagons and sixty loose mules left there that morning for Salt Lake. ... We mounted a couple of mules and started after them. We overtook them at Platte bridge, twenty-eight miles; stayed over night with them..." *(1864)* |

**Samuel Granger** and **Aaron Rockwood's** chase on horseback after the **Wood Train** is reckless, especially without the (perceived) protection of any military or other travelers riding with them. By leaving the camp, the men are also violating the stay-in-place order that was issued to the locals.

# Monday, July 18, 1864

### Forman, Granger, Mahan-Moore, Merrill & Union Army

On the morning of July 18, those camped around Deer Creek garrison continue to hear story after story from folks who endured threats, attacks, robberies, and lost lives on nearly every inch of trail between Fort Laramie and Deer Creek. The emigrants try to consolidate facts, compare evidence, narrow down suspects, and grieve from the traumatic experience.

**James Logan**
*Granger Company*
"There are several tribes who have declared war against the emigrants and are stealing everything they can lay hands on and killing all who they find defenseless. In Idaho from Laperell and Deer Creek to Port Bridges,[125] they have made a general and almost simultaneous descent on the emigrant." *(1864)*

With these testimonies and evidence collected from the attacks (saddles, arrows, etc.), the responsible tribal bands can be narrowed down. **Cpt. Levi Reinhart**, the commanding officer at Deer Creek garrison, prepares for a formal military response. His preparations are backed by **Brigadier General Robert B. Mitchell,** who is still on his way from Nebraska with two more regiments, although the **Brigadier** plans to hold a peace council when he arrives to attempt a negotiation prior to any escalation. [126] In the meantime, **Cpt. Levi** welcomes in the two regiments that were organized at Fort Laramie.

---

[125] This is a reference to Fort Bridger in Utah Territory (on the territorial border), which is now in Uinta Co., Wyoming.
[126] Brigadier General Robert B. Mitchell is the senior commander of the District of Nebraska, an area spanning from Omaha, NE to South Pass, WY.

**Cpl. Hervey Johnson**
*Union Army, Co. G*

"Two hundred men and two pieces of artillery arrived here yesterday from the fort. They are awaiting orders this morning." *(July 18)*

"The men who came up yesterday have received orders, about one hundred and sixty of us start to night [sic] or tomorrow morning to hunt the indian village. ... a good many of the emigrants are going with us, we want to get one hundred of them if they will volunteer, if they wont then we will 'press them into service.'" *(July 18)*

While attempting to muster additional volunteers and keep the area secure, the detainment order is reinstated.

**Julius Merrill**
*Merrill Team*

"We were ordered not to move by the military."
*(July 18)*

**George Forman**
*Lone Traveler*

"We had been ordered to not move on and all emigration was stopped." *(July 18)*

**Garland Mahan**
*Mahan-Moore Team*

"Lay by." *(July 18)*

**Julius Merrill**
*Merrill Team*

"Volunteers were called for to go to the Powder River, there to fight the Indians and destroy their villages."
*(July 18)*

It is unclear if the Army offered compensation for volunteering. Even if an emigrant feels compassion in this situation, they must still weigh the pros and cons of going.

**George Forman**
*Lone Traveler*

"...an expedition is organized to go and rescue [**Fanny Kelly**], and our trains are ordered to furnish a number of men and horses with 12 days cooked rations to go with the soldiers to Tongue and Powder Rivers 200 miles north, but we refuse as we have a long way to go yet..."
*(July 18-20)*

**Julius Merrill**　　　　"Three-fourths of our train volunteered." *(July 18)*
*Merrill Team*

Various reports suggest between one hundred and one-hundred-sixty soldiers are organized into squads to be sent across the North Platte River to take action. The present intent is to scout for signs of the kidnappees and stolen horses and interrogate Indians for any useful information that might lead them to either. Some will be sent due north to Tongue and Powder River and others will head west to Wind River. **Cpl. Hervey Johnson** is amongst those gearing up for battle. His deployment leaves at one o'clock in the morning and does not return until July 24. He sends a list of the soldiers going on this expedition to his sister Sybil.

**Cpl. Hervey Johnson**　　"...there were about one hundred and sixty of us, thirty
*Union Army, Co. G*　　　　of co G [under **Cpt. Levi Reinhart**], a detachment of Co E
　　　　　　　　　　　　[under **Cpt. Levi Marshall**], the whole of Co H [under
　　　　　　　　　　　　**Cpt. Jacob Schuman**], detachments of Cos I and K, and
　　　　　　　　　　　　two pieces of artillery" *(July 25, 1864)*

It is unclear how many emigrants joined (or were pressured into) the mission. From the testimonies presented in this book, only the participation of **Julius Merrill** and **Josiah Kelly** can be confirmed.

**George Forman**　　　　"So 150 Soldiers start north." *(July 18)*
*Lone Traveler*

**Wm. Boardman**　　　　"The Expedition went as far as Wind River." *(Aug. 6)*
*Union Army, Co. G*

### Granger & Wood

Midday, **Aaron Rockwood** and **Samuel Granger** return from Platte Bridge Station with thirty-one mules from the **Wood Train** (AKA the **"Salt Lake Train"**). It is unknown if the captain of this train, **Mr. Wood**, charges a fee for the use of his mules, or if he lends them generously.

**Aaron Rockwood**
*Granger Company*

"We got the mules from the **Salt Lake Train**. ...they sent back thirty-one mules to help us. ...they only had that many animals to spare." *(1864)*

The fact that the **Granger Train** is now able to replace the stock that was stolen during the Platte River Raids and haul their wagons on does not negate the standing military order to cease all travel.

### Forman, Merrill & Union Army

Besides **George Forman's** refusal to contribute of volunteer, several civilian revolt against the Union today. With all the military activity, emigrants feel anxious to leave. Many fear if they stay too long, the Indians will retaliate on anyone and everyone near the garrison. There is also the reality that if emigrants essential resources are being pillaged by the 11th Ohio (in the name of war), then there is a greater urgency to either reach their intended destination, or to get to a place where they can replace what is taken.

**Aaron Rockwood**
*Granger Company*

"When we got back to Deer Creek Station, we found they had started out with one hundred soldiers and ten days' rations, to try to recapture the stock. ... **Granger** and **myself** started our wagons." *(1864)*

According to North Bank Trail emigrant, **Sarah Rousseau**, when a wagon train bolts from the camp, two cavalrymen jump on their horses and chase after the wagon train to stop them (July 18). She never identifies who was chased down, nor on which trail.

By the end of the day, the unit that **Julius Merrill** volunteered with disbands and returns to Deer Creek because the emigrant-volunteers develop "hard feelings" against the military (July 18). **George Forman** records the emigrants in camp deploy a group of strong minded and outspoken representatives to convince the post commander that they should not be held back any longer.

**George Forman**
*Lone Traveler*

"After a day's rest we send a delegation to the **Col. Marshall** of the Post that we are strong enough to protect ourselves and need no troops and that we will move on in the morning." *(July 18)*

**S**

# Tuesday, July 19, 1864 (part 1)

### Kelly-Larimer & Union Army

Having left Deer Creek in the wee hours of the night, **Josiah Kelly** and the ad-hoc regiment of the 11th Ohio Volunteer Cavalry, under the command of **Cpt. Levi Marshall** have already found the paper trail **Sarah Larimer** told them to look for.

**Josiah Kelly**

*Kelly-Larimer Train*

"I started with them to go to Powder River village... The first day out[,] I in co. with three soldiers struck the trail that they went with the priseners[.] we know from papers dropped along it." *(August 15)*"

It is unclear how many pages **Josiah** found and which direction they truly led him. As a reminder to the reader, after **Fanny Kelly** and **Sarah Larimer** were abducted, their captors split up and leave in different directions to fool anyone who might attempt to follow. Any trail left behind could be highly misleading.

The account of **Private. William Boardman** provides a different lead that determines Wind River to be the ultimate destination for **Josiah's** squad, regardless of *any* hard evidence.[127] He also claims **Josiah** is in a squad of five men, under the immediate direction of **2nd Lieutenant John Brown**.

---

[127] William F. Boardman, "Letter from the 11th O.V.C." letter to the editor dated August 6, 1864, in *The Highland Weekly*, October 20, 1864. Also see the Appendix.

## Forman, Granger, Mahan-Moore, Merrill & Union Army

On July 19, having made a strong case for lifting the travel ban, **George Forman** and many others pack out from Deer Creek, knowing full well that if there is another incident with Indians, they would not have the protection of the Union Army. It is a price that emigrants are not only willing to pay but believe they have already paid. The weak military presence on the trail and lazy attitudes rendered their obligatory trail protection services entirely ineffectual. Also, as evidenced in the Platte River Raids, the cavalry regiment sent from Fort Laramie in response to the depredations could not even prevent the theft of their own mules. For the emigrants leaving Deer Creek, today is no different, in terms of safety, than leaving Fort Laramie last week. These sentiments are made abundantly clear in **Aaron Rockwood's** letter:

**Aaron Rockwood**
*Granger Company*

"I had seen enough to satisfy me there was no hope, and I came to the conclusion that we could expect no help from any man, or the Indians receive any damage from one who is keeping from one to three squaws to sleep with and raise families by, and therefore thought it best to take the first chance to go on." *(1864)*

Those leaving today include **George Forman**, the **Merrill Team,** the **Mahan-Moore Team** and a portion of the **Granger Company.**

**Aaron Rockwood**
*Granger Company*

"We offered to the families that were with us enough [mules] to move two of the three families, but they preferred to stay and await the return of the expedition, thinking to recover their stock, or part of it...." *(1864)*

**James Logan**
*Granger Company*

"**Hawley** and **Rockwood** of Centralia were both left behind and what has become of them I can't say it..." *(1864)*

**Julius Merrill**
*Merrill Team*

"We were glad to move again, still in large trains. ... no one had been troubled above Deer Creek Station." *(July 19)*

**Garland Mahan**
*Mahan-Moore Team*

"Formed a train of 44 wagons and started again." *(July 19)*

**George Forman**
*Lone Traveler*

"We move on up the Platte valley following the River to the Lower Platte Bridge..." *(July 18-20)*

There is about a twenty-two mile journey to the Lower Platte Bridge, AKA "Richard's Bridge," in present-day Evansville, Wyoming, which is reasonably achieved in one day's travel.

## Forman & Wood

After leaving the Black Hills, **George Forman**, the lone packer from Canada, expresses his relief.

**George Forman**
*Lone Traveler*

"...our main danger from the Indians is pas

**George** walks six miles past the Lower Platte Bridge to the Platte Bridge Station where he meets the **Wood Train**. **Mr. Wood** may be waiting in the area for the **Granger Company** to return with their thirty-one borrowed mules.

**George Forman**
*Lone Traveler*

"One **Mormon train** on their way back East had fought the Indians three days in the Black Hills and had turned back for Salt Lake again." *(July 21)*

Details on this series of attacks on the **Wood Train** have not yet been found.

## Granger - Epilogue

Most of the **Granger Train** also express their appreciation for putting some distance between themselves and the Black Hills. Those who depart immediately are the families of **Samuel Granger, Omar Jewell, and James Logan.**

| | |
|---|---|
| **James Logan**<br>*Granger Company* | "Since these troubles we have traveled in large trains and had no trouble. ...my face is set for the setting sun until stopped by the Pacific ocean in some quiet valley home, with fruits and flowers, rippling streams and humming bees for me to make a final rest; to spend my days in peace, away from the noise and bustle of business, annoyed no more by glistening bayonets and clamoring for spoils." *(1864)* |

Shortly after departing, **James Logan** breaks away from the **Grangers and Jewells** to stay through the winter in Carson Valley, Nevada where he envisions his idyllic future in California. In 1865, he continues to St. Helena in Napa County and helps incorporate the town. He becomes a renowned coroner and embalmer – his methods of handling the deceased being unparalleled.

The **Logans** are recognized pioneers in Northern California, however, the new arrivals suffer terribly by the turn of the century. After the Great San Francisco Earthquake in 1906, **James'** daughter **Daisy** contracts tuberculosis and seeks treatment in a Los Angeles sanitarium.[128] She dies in June of 1909 and her obituary states she "was never well after the San Francisco disaster."[129] Two months later, one of **James'** grandsons falls off a cliff in Yosemite National Park. Afterward, **James'** son, **Milburn,** buries himself in medical studies so intensely that he has a mental breakdown. News reports claim he has an "unbalanced mind"[130] and is "over-taxed"[131] to the point of causing a stroke. This results in a

---

[128] Possibly at the Barlow Sanitarium which opened in 1902.
[129] "Daisy Logan Keeny," obituary in *St. Helena Star*, June 11, 1909.
[130] "Dr. Logan Dies From Exposure," in *San Francisco Call*, December 27, 1905.
[131] "Old Friend Writes of the Late Dr. Milburn Hill Logan," in *St. Helena Star*, January 5, 1906.

committal to Agnews Insane Asylum in Santa Clara.[132] By December of that year, **Milburn** wanders outside in the middle of the night and dies from exposure to cold.

The **Grangers** and **Jewells** continue through to Northern California where **Samuel Granger** picks up work as a carpenter in Hollister. Within five years, they are joined by **Mary Granger's** brother, Adolphus, and in the 1870s, **Mary's** parents and another brother come out and start a ranch in Sonoma County. **Samuel** helps run the ranch with his brother-in-law for at least a decade. In 1899, **Mary** dies after a long battle with cancer and **Samuel** moves in with his daughter, Cora, who lives in Lane County, Oregon. His mental health deteriorates until a judge rules him insane in 1917. His daughter is simultaneously reported to be "mildly insane," per the hospital's evaluation, though she is not committed.[133] **Samuel** dies at the Oregon State Insane Asylum[134] Sadly, his "creamains" (cremated remains) are never claimed by a relative. To this day, he resides in canister #81 in the Hospital's mausoleum.

**Omar Jewell** becomes a dairyman in the Olema Valley of Marin County. In 1864, he purchases a tract of land on Lagunitas Creek. According to the 1870 U.S. Census Agricultural Schedule, the Jewell Ranch boasts forty milk cows, forty pigs, a herd of horses, and ranch cattle which affords the family a comfortable lifestyle. After battling an illness at length, **Omar** dies in 1875, leaving the dairy operation to his wife, **Vienna**, and two sons who carry on diligently.

**Aaron Rockwood**
*Granger Company*

"...for a week after they commenced they were stealing the stock and attacking the trains all up and down the Platte River for fifty miles, and no one to stop them, and the Emigrant had to rely on his own protection. ...there were a great many wounded and different trains, and as I near as I can find out they have captured above 2,000 head of horses and mules from the emigrants. *(1864)*

---

[132] Later renamed the Agnews State Hospital.
[133] Lane County Court Records of March 20, 1917, in the matter of "Sam'l Granger," courtesy of Oregon State Archives.
[134] Later renamed the Oregon State Hospital.

Aaron Rockwood's letter does not specifically mention when his and John Hawley's families finally leave Deer Creek, only that, "we lay by a while before we moved on" (1864). Aaron mentions that he continues the journey with cattle now hauling his wagon. It believed he purchased the cattle, but it is unclear from whom. He claims that for him to reach Salt Lake, "will take all the money I have and my watch" (1864). Based on a mention of the Sweetwater Station near Independence Rock on July 23, it is likely that Aaron and John departed on July 20.[135]

Aaron initially heads to Monterey, California, then moves inland to the city of Hollister. On October 21, 1868, his wife, Anna, is terrified by the largest earthquake in state history to date.[136] The 6.8 magnitude shocks ripped through the Hayward and Calaveras Fault, flinging the Rockwood house off its foundation, resulting in a narrow escape. Anna does not recover from the trauma and as a result, Aaron brings her before an Alameda physician and judge to be committed to the Insane Asylum of California.[137] Evidence for her insanity includes her belief that earthquakes are the result of torpedoes planted in the ground by the Chinese. After eleven months, Anna is released back to her husband and within a year of being released, she vanishes, and Aaron remarries. He eventually becomes a short line engineer for the San Francisco Belt Railroad that serves the waterfront ports presently in the Embarcadero District.

It is believed John Hawley's family stays in either Utah or Nevada for the winter, then continues to Los Angeles, California in 1865. It is unknown if John resumes a career in hotel management.[138] His daughter's obituary appears to contain the only clear evidence of their journey, stating: "In Wyoming the train was attacked by Indians who drove off all the stock and burned the wagons, but members of the party were rescued by soldiers."[139]

---

[135] The seventy-plus miles between Deer Creek and Independence Rock would average out to between 17-25 miles traveled per day.

[136] This earthquake is also called the "Great San Francisco Earthquake," until the 1906 event surpassed it in severity and claimed the title.

[137] Later renamed the Stockton State Hospital.

[138] An info search with the city's historical society has not turned up any helpful information.

[139] "Jennie B. Wildermuth obituary," in Los Angeles Times, May 29, 1924. The claim that the Hawley wagons were burned is unsubstantiated.

### Mahan-Moore - Epilogue

The large train that the **Mahan Team** joins with upon leaving Deer Creek travels rather slow over the next week. After spending one night near a small lake twelve miles out, they reach the Platte Bridge Station on July 20. The miners continue steadily towards the Sweetwater Route where **Garland Mahan** complains of being riddled with delays and inconveniences such as being "compelled" to travel on Sabbaths and not having any decent grass for the oxen. After crossing the Green River, they take Sublette's Cutoff going northwest into "high mountains, wild and romantic" (Mahan, August 10). Nothing exciting occurs from there on, other than verbose descriptions of grand scenery that "our eyes feasted on," (Mahan, September 3). They arrive in Virginia City on September 6.

**Garland** and his brother **Augustus** stay in Helena, Montana for the next two years and "engaged in ranching and mining," per a biographical sketch on **"Gus"** in *History of Cole, Moniteau, Morgan, Benton, Miller, Maries, and Osage Counties* (Goodspeed Publishing, 1889, 871). While there, **Garland** produces a second diary detailing his mining experience, though this item could not be preserved and transcribed, according to his daughter.[140] In 1866, **Garland** and **Gus** return to Cole County, Missouri on a nineteen-day boat ride down the Missouri River. **Garland** mentions in his return diary that the mining boom was extreme profitable, though he does not specify his personal earnings. Back home, **Garland** (now twenty-seven) marries and begins a quiet life as a schoolteacher. **Gus** (twenty-three) goes back to living with his parents on the family farm.

Their mining partners, **John Moore** and **William Mayger**, remain in Helena permanently; first gold panning in the gulch mines, then transferring to pit mining for quartz. **William** eventually becomes the superintendent of a quartz mine near Helena and continues working in this industry for nearly fifty years.

---

[140] Carrie Barker, "Introduction" in *Garland Jefferson Mahan's Diary, 1864…*, 1965.

S

# Tuesday, July 19, 1864 (part 2)

## Ringo Company

At this point, it is important to acknowledge that while severe depredations are occurring in the Black Hills this week, droves of families and freighters are still coming in from the east and the west. Some are entirely unaware of the danger and destruction ahead of them. Both Army posts at the north and south ends of the Black Hills restrict entry to the fated area until July 19th. Because of this, there is quite a crowd waiting to start all at once.

Of those coming into from Missouri are the **Ringo Train** of five households and one mining team, who have been growing in numbers as they approach Fort Laramie. Before reaching this milepost, however, the **Ringo Company** (presently including one freight team from the **Beauvais Company**[141]) faces two unpleasant interactions with Indians. Back on July 15, at a telegraph office in Melbeta, Nebraska, **Martin and Mary Ringo** are warned about serious attacks being made on emigrants ahead. "We did not think much of it," **Mary** claims but this attitude does not serve them well.[142] Only two miles west, two parties who had been loosely associated with the **Ringo Company** are attacked.

---

[141] This is a supply shipment to one of the Beauvais family ranches and trading posts along the trails. One is Star Ranch near the Old California Crossing in Nebraska where the trader Pierre Geminian Beauvais lives. The other is Lone Star Ranch, AKA "Five-Mile Ranch," just east of Fort Laramie. Starting in the late 1850s, Pierre's eleven sons join the transport business and haul trade goods from St. Joseph to various stage stops, ranches, military and trading forts along the Oregon Trail. They return to Missouri with hides, furs and other goods from Plains Indians to be re-sold as far away as New York. Some historical records claim the Beauvais family kept fifteen to twenty freighting wagons in the trail rotation at all times.

[142] Mary Ringo, *Trip Across the Great Plains in 1864*, transcription by Mattie Bell Ringo Cushing (Santa Ana: Cushing, 1942), July 15.

**Mary Ringo**
*Ringo Company*

"...they attacted two of our wagons ... we saw the Indians manouvering around them and then rode close enough to shoot the arrows through their wagon sheet just missing their heads." *(July 15)*

The parties attacked belong to a **Mr. Gouly**[143] and **Haywood Edwards** from Missouri who, after passing the telegraph station, turn down a wrong path, and become separated from the group. Singled out, as they are, the emigrants shoot back at the Indians, but their attackers pivot and escape by crossing the North Platte River. Once on the North Bank Trail, this band of Indians proceeds to attack another emigrant party and leave one man wounded and another one dead. The victims' identity has yet to be established.

**Haywood Edwards**
*Edwards Team (Ringo)*

"Got alarmed at the Indians and got with a large train [**Ringo Company**] & camped at Gricklin's Ranch[144] 5 miles east of Scots Bluff." *(July 15)*

**Mary Ringo**
*Ringo Company*

"...we went back to the ranch, correlled, and prepared for a fight... " *(July 15)*

There, the **Ringo Company** is joined by even more Missourians including **Calon Morrice's** mining team. That night, **Mary** "could not sleep a wink."

---

[143] Possibly a transcription error for Dr. Guthrie.
[144] The owner and exact location of a "Gricklin's Ranch" has not been identified. It is possible this is a reference to Ficklin Springs Pony Express Station in Melbeta which is twelve miles from Scotts Bluff Station.

| | |
|---|---|
| **Mr. Rushville**<br>*Ringo Company* | "Our train is composed of our own, **Capt. Hodges**, **Doctor [Addison] Gutherie's**, of Platte County, and **[Calon] Morris**, of Clay County. We all get along smoothly... I forgot to mention that **Floyd** and **[Mathias] Farris** of Buchanan, are travelling with us with their trains." *(July 29, 1864)* |

When the **Ringo Company** proceeds the next day, **Mary's** carefree attitude is replaced with anxiety. The **Ringo Company** faces their second ordeal on July 19. There are numerous commentaries on this encounter. As **William Davenport** and **Mr. Rushville's** letters are written after the event, their iterations contain perspectives **Mary** and **Haywood's** diary entries do not have.[145]

| | |
|---|---|
| **Mr. Rushville**<br>*Ringo Company* | "This morning we had a false alarm and made ready for a fight, but no Indians appeared, and our boys through mistake fired on two friendly Indians..." *(July 29, 1864 re: July 19)*[146] |
| **Mary Ringo**<br>*Ringo Company* | "We have quite an exciting time, corralled [sic] twice thinking the Indians were going to attack us but we mistook friendly Indians and one of our train fired at them, we are fearful that it will cause us more trouble as the Indian has gone to the Fort to inform against us." *(July 19)* |
| **Haywood Edwards**<br>*Edwards Team (Ringo)* | "Travelled till noon and camped at a ranch 9 miles east of Fort Laramie." *(July 19)* |

| | |
|---|---|
| **Wm. Davenport**<br>*Ringo Company* | "Owing to some difficulties we had with the Indians below Fort Laramie[,] at Scott's Bluff[,] the emigration formed themselves into large companies." *(1864)* |

---

[145] Both editorials are included in the Appendix of this book.
[146] Rushville. "Crossing the Plains, July 29, 1864" in *The Morning Herald*, August 9, 1864, 2.

On July 19, the **Ringo Company** convenes near the Bordeaux Ranch, approximately seven miles east of Fort Laramie. While camped, **Mr. Rushville** hears about the Platte River Raids.

| | |
|---|---|
| **Mr. Rushville**<br>*Ringo Company* | "They are doing considerable mischief along the route of travel from here to Deer Creek, one hundred miles above Fort Laramie. ... Men are collecting in large trains for the purpose of travelling with greater safety."" *(July 29)* |

Again, the **Ringo Company** grows in numbers. **Mr. Rushville** acknowledges that a larger group, though it will be slow and more difficult to coordinate movement, "is as small a train as can get along safe" (July 29, 1864).

| | |
|---|---|
| **Wm. Davenport**<br>*Ringo Company* | "Our company, consisting of the **Martin brothers** and **Jas. Reed** of Clay county, **Forbes**, **Irvin**, **Lucas & Co.**, from the Platte and Buchanan counties, – **Beauvais & Co.**, from St. Joseph, with **Mr. Ringo and family**, and others, making in all about 70 wagons, have been traveling together for mutual protection." *(1864)* |
| **Mr. Rushville**<br>*Ringo Company* | "Our train is composed of about seventy wagons, owned by a number of different men. **Mr. Beauvais**, formerly of your city [St. Joseph]; **Mr. Milette**, of Deer Lodge Valley, Idaho [Montana]; The **Morrises**, of Clay County; **Davenport**, of Clay, and many other families of small trains." *(Aug. 2)*[147] |

**William Lucas**, who is fourteen at this time, says the wagon train grows in numbers far beyond what can be honestly counted.

| | |
|---|---|
| **William Lucas**<br>*Lucas & Co. (Ringo)* | "In our particular train there were sixty to seventy wagons, occupied by our friends and neighbors." *(1926)* |

---

[147] Rushville, "En Route for Idaho," letter to the editor in *The Weekly Herald and Tribune*, Sept. 8, 1864. (The original letter is dated August 2, mailed from Fort Caspar. See the fully transcribed item in the Appendix.)

# Wednesday, July 20, 1864

### Ringo Company

On July 20, the seventy-wagon **Ringo Company** reaches Fort Laramie. As anticipated by **Mary Ringo**, they face consequences for their mistaken actions against two innocent men from a friendly tribal band. Fort commander **Lieutenant Colonel William O. Collins** determines the remedy.

| | |
|---|---|
| **Mary Ringo**<br>*Ringo Company* | "...detained at the Fort on account of having shot at that friendly Indian and had to recompence them by paying them some flour, bacon, sugar and coffee and were glad to get off on those terms." *(July 20)* |
| **Mr. Rushville**<br>*Ringo Company* | "...happily the thing will pass by without any serious difficulty." *(July 29, 1864 re: July 20)* |

Though they are warned to be more cautious moving forward, **Mr. Rushville** continues to communicate a sense of superiority in this situation.

| | |
|---|---|
| **Mr. Rushville**<br>*Ringo Company* | "I think we are plenty able for the Indians, although they fight under many advantages. The troops along the route do all they can to favor the emigrants." *(July 29, 1864 re: July 20)* |
| **William Lucas**<br>*Lucas & Co. (Ringo)* | "...when we passed through country where it was known that the Indians were hostile, we doubled up until there were from two hundred to three hundred wagons— |

formidable array for anything short of a good-sized army of Indians to tackle." *(1926)*

**America Forbis**
*Forbis & Irvine (Ringo)*

"Our train was so long that one end could not be seen from the other." *(1893)*

Before they can leave, however, Union soldiers request the use of their horses. Most emigrants find refusing the pressure difficult, but **America** explains that her family had been so mistreated by both Union and Confederate armies while in Missouri that they are now intolerant to abuses of civilian resources.

**America Forbis**
*Forbis & Irvine (Ringo)*

"[Missouri] was the common battleground of the rebellion, harassed by both sides, protected by neither, and the theatre of the most appalling scenes of fratricidal warfare. Our farm horses were taken for Calvary uses, our produce for the commissary, our lambs devastated..." *(1893)*

**William Lucas**
*Lucas & Co. (Ringo)*

"You know, I rather imagine the union army wanted that stock of ours pretty badly. I shouldn't wonder but what a force had been sent out to pick it up, but my father had learned his strategy as a captain in the confederate army, and they didn't get it." *(1926)*

**George Lucas'** response to the request is paired with a display of his experience protecting his company during the Civil War.

**William Lucas**
*Lucas & Co. (Ringo)*

"Father organized a sort of flying squadron, a horseback brigade, which attended the slow moving train on either flank, scouted far in advance along our line of march, and also acted as rearguard." *(1926)*

From that day on, **George** is considered the captain of the **Ringo Company**.

**Haywood Edwards**
*Edwards Team (Ringo)*

"Past Lorina [Laramie] and camped 5 miles west of the fort." *(July 20)*

## Merrill - Epilogue

Out by the Platte Bridge Station in present-day Casper, Wyoming, July 20 is remarkably mundane for **Julius Merrill** and his mining team, who have managed to stay unharmed throughout the week.

**Julius Merrill**        "Indian excitement [is] nearly subsided." *(July 20)*
*Merrill Team*

**Julius** documents the scramble of other wagon teams trying to repair damaged equipment and redistribute resources in order to get free from the tragedy behind them. In the evening, he camps near the Upper Platte Ferry & Ford, approximately two miles from the soldier station. In the days ahead, he mentions the trails being "clogged with wagons,"[148] getting blisters on his feet and taking the Lander Cutoff after South Pass. He rants about how unreliable the mileage markers in J. L. Campbell's 1864 guidebook are. On his way to Boise City, his mind never appears to return to the conflicts in the Black Hills. In his last diary entry of September 19, he shares: "No sooner is the journey ended than all is forgotten and every one is happy."

In Idaho, the mining team is successful finding gold. **Julius** spends his gold dust on a comfortable piece of land in Iowa. **Henry Durbin** invests his treasure in a local farm, but his wife and children never join him. He returns to Wisconsin in 1866. **Steven Durbin** spends his gold earnings on a vacation before putting down roots in Wisconsin as a rancher and horse breeder. **Charles Carey** makes a fortune in blacksmithing for the mining boomtown before returning home to his family in 1867.

## Kelly-Larimer, Merrill & Union Army

About thirty miles north of Deer Creek, a regiment of the Union Army is on day two of their mission to look for signs of stolen horses, search Indian villages

---

[148] July 21.

and interrogate residents for information about **Fanny Kelly** and, if necessary, capture a politically important hostage to hold until the safer return of **Fanny**. Besides going due north along the east side of the Bighorn Mountains, as **Fanny Kelly** and **Sarah Larimer** have recorded their kidnappers taking them, the Army may also be following anecdotal evidence supplied by soldiers at Fort Laramie. This alternative lead, shared in a letter by **Pvt. William Boardman**, directs another portion of the Army toward Wind River, which is due west from the garrison.

| | |
|---|---|
| **Pvt. Wm Boardman**<br>*Union Army, Co. G* | "During the latter part of May last, **'Old Grass,'** one of the Platte Sioux Chiefs, with a party of seventy-five warriors, started up the road from Fort Laramie, ostensibly for the purpose of fighting the *Utes*, a (war-like tribe some 200 miles above[149] here)..." *(August 6)*[150] |
| | "It was not more than two weeks after [this interaction] we began to hear of depredations on the other side of the Platte. It was thought by many at that time, that he [**Old Grass**] was going for the purpose of disturbing emigration." *(August 6)* |

**Fanny's** husband **Josiah Kelly** is with regiment heading north into the Powder River Basin as an emigrant volunteer. He is assigned to a squad of four men from Company E, presently captained by **2nd Lt. John R. Brown.** On the Powder River Expedition, the **2nd Lieutenant** leads his squad away from the main body of soldiers to go "prospecting" for Indians.[151] When his squad is between four and nine miles distant from their commander and morning camp on a creek (later named for him), he finds exactly what he was looking for: a fight.

---

[149] The use of "above" here is not a reference to a cardinal direction (ie. north), rather is it applied similar to the expressions "further along the road," "beyond here," or "ahead." In comparison, a mention of something being "below" is be back in the direction one came from or "behind."

[150] William F. Boardman, "Letter from the 11th O.V.C." letter to the editor dated August 6, 1864, in *The Highland Weekly*, October 20, 1864. Also see the Appendix.

[151] Fanny Kelly, *Narrative of My Captivity...*, 1871, 223-224.

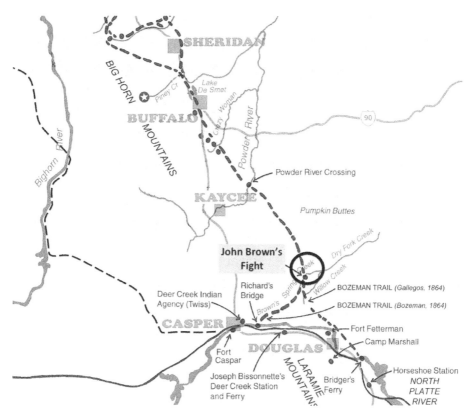

Partial view of the Bozeman Trail showing the location of Brown's Spring Creek and the approximate location of where 2nd Lt. John Brown from Co. E was attacked and killed. Reprint permission granted by Sylvia Bruner, Jim Gatchell Memorial Museum. Modified by author.

**Cpl. Hervey Johnson**
*Union Army, Co. G*

"A small squad of Co E ran into a band of indians forty or fifty, in the afternoon and attacked them..." *(July 25)*

**Pvt. Wm Boardman**
*Union Army, Co. G*

"**Lieut. John Brown**, of co. E, with a party of five men ... came suddenly upon a party of about seventy-five Indians, herding about 150 head of stock, which they were taking to their villages. **Lieut. Brown** and party immediately attacked them." *(August 6)*

**Josiah Kelly**
*Kelly-Larimer Train*

"We ran onto[sic] about 50 Indians with a large drove of horses[.] we got close onto them before we saw them, just as we saw them they started for us ... We broke for the command which we supposed was about three miles to our right but found it to be about seven miles distant. The Indians ran us about four miles..." *(August 15)*

Every account points to **2nd Lt. John** issuing the order to fight and, probably, taking the shot first.

**Pvt. Wm Boardman**
*Union Army, Co. G*

"...the Indians closed in on the small party, who bravely stood their ground as long as possible, but were soon compelled to retreat..." *(August 6, 1864)*

**Josiah Kelly**
*Kelly-Larimer Train*

"We made several stands but they were trying to out flank us on both sides and surrounded us so that we dare not stand longer than to make one shot. ... All that saved us was our horses out winded theirs." *(August 15)*

"One of our party **Lieut. Brown** was killed by them. He fell ten feet from me." *(August 15)*

**Cpl. Hervey Johnson**
*Union Army, Co. G*

"The **second Lieutenant** who was in command of the squad was shot off his horse[,] the arrow going in near the spine at the small of his back." *(July 25)*

**Pvt. Wm Boardman**
*Union Army, Co. G*

"...the **Lieutenant** was pierced by two arrows. ... The rest of the party, supposing the **Lieutenant** to be killed, retreated to the main command..." *(August 6, 1864)*

The four retreating men leave **2nd Lt. John** at the scene and report back to their commander that if he is not actually dead, then he is as good as dead. George C. Underhill, the post surgeon of Fort Laramie, records the cause of death as an "Arrow Shot," and logs July 20 as the official date of death.

**S**

# Thursday-Saturday, July 21-23, 1864

### Kelly-Larimer & Union Army

On July 21, word arrives at Deer Creek garrison that **2nd Lt. John Brown** has been mortally wounded. A runner may have delivered the news to the garrison where it was passed along via telegraph. The news reaches **Sgt. Lewis B. Hull** at Fort Laramie on July 23, as evidenced in his diary.[152]

**Sgt. Lewis Hull**
*Union Army, Co. K*

"Dispatch received that **Lieut. Brown**, Co. E. was killed in a charge on the Indians over near Powder river; his body shot full of arrows and scalped." *(July 23)*

**Cpt. Levi Marshall,** commander of the ad-hoc regiment, sends a team out in the morning to recover the body of the downed soldier. When this team arrives, they are surprised to find the **2nd Lt.** alive.

**Cpl. Hervey Johnson**
*Union Army, Co. G*

"...an ambulance was sent, to bring in his body ... he was still alive ... two arrows in his body ..." *(July 25)*

**Pvt. Wm Boardman**
*Union Army, Co. G*

"One arrow struck him in the small of the back and only lacked an inch or two of penetrating his body. Another arrow went in at the back of this neck, and came through his throat." *(Aug. 6)*

---

[152] Lewis B. Hull, *The Diary of Lewis Byram Hull, 1864-1866.* Ed. Myra Hull. Topeka: Kansas State Historical Society, 1938.

**Cpl. Hervey Johnson**
*Union Army, Co. G*

"...the feather was cut off the one through his neck and it was drawn through. They gave him some water to drink and it ran out at the wound..." *(July 25)*

**Sgt. Lewis Hull**
*Union Army, Co. K*

"**Lieut. Brown**, dead; shot with two arrows, one in the back and one in the neck. Lived till morning." *(July 30)*

**Pvt. Wm Boardman**
*Union Army, Co. G*

"[He] breathed his last a short time after he was taken to camp." *(Aug. 6)*

After breathing his last, Company E does what they can to preserve the **2nd Lt.'s** body until they can lay him to rest in a more appropriate location.

**Cpl. Hervey Johnson**
*Union Army, Co. G*

"His entrails were taken out and the place filled with salt[.] He was buried in a shallow sandy grave." *(July 25)*

After the burial, a portion of the regiment continues to Powder River, reaching it on July 22.

**Cpl. Hervey Johnson**
*Union Army, Co. G*

"No Indians there[.] Scouts were sent out in three different directions but found nothing, camped on wind river[153] for the night... " *(July 25)*

**Josiah Kelly** writes that he believes the Union Army may have chased or scared the Indians away, though this is only hearsay.

**Josiah Kelly**
*Kelly-Larimer Train*

"the command went for them ... don't know as they killed any of them." *(August 15)*

On July 23, after a failed mission, **Cpl. Hervey Johnson** reports that the regiment exhumes the salt-preserved remains of the **2nd Lt.** to be brought back to Deer Creek garrison.

---

[153] This location might be an error.

| **Cpl. Hervey Johnson**<br>*Union Army, Co. G* | "Came back by the place where the **[2nd] Lieutenant** was left[.] staid all night, took up his body and started for Deer Creek before daylight [on July 24]." *(July 25)* |

## Ringo Company

From July 21 to 23, "Nothing of importance transpires," for the **Ringo Company** other than several cattle dying off, requiring some of the travelers to slow down and take longer respites.[154]

| **Mary Ringo**<br>*Ringo Company* | "We get into what is called the Black Hills and no one ever saw such bad roads… [at Horseshoe Creek,] Our stock gave out and two belonging to the outfit died." *(July 22)* |
| **America Forbis**<br>*Forbis & Irvine (Ringo)* | "Work animals died in great numbers from drinking alkali water, and carcasses fairly indicated the way to the bewildered pilgrims. But we became so accustomed to carnage, that we could detect a stench of the decaying human body from that of the beast." *(1893)* |
| **Mary Ringo**<br>*Ringo Company* | "We remain in camp … they drive the cattle over the river where they get good grass." *(July 23)* |
| **Haywood Edwards**<br>*Edwards Team (Ringo)* | "Remained on the same place and rested our cattle and gathered kearns [cow chips]." *(July 23)* |

**Martin and Mary Ringo** have two wagons, yolked with different animals: one with mules, the other with oxen. If their stock dies off, they might become stranded. According to **Mary's** mileage log, they travel an average of fourteen miles per day. If the average speed of an ox is two miles per hour, then mathematically speaking, her animals are being pushed to their limit on a daily basis.

---

[154] Mary Ringo, *Trip Across…, 1864*, July 21-23.

## Forman - Epilogue

Near the Platte Bridge Station, **George Forman** considers taking the Bozeman or Bridger shortcut to Virginia City, Montana, but decides against it because, though "it saves many miles … it is too dangerous from the Indians" (July 20). While there, he learns that the regiment of soldiers from Deer Creek were attacked and one man killed. He calls the soldiers who fled (including **Josiah Kelly**), "Poltroons" (cowards) who are "no good whatever against the Indians" (July 20).

So, rather than taking the shortcut "through the heart of the Hostile Indian Country," **George** walks his grey pony south along the Sweetwater Trail towards South Pass. (July 21). As he does, he references an old song about how slow wagon trains move and touts his remarkable fitness which allows him to pass them all by on foot, "making 25 to 30 miles a day" (July 21). At an average walking pace of fifteen to twenty minutes per mile, this means he walks at least ten hours per day, every day. If weather and road conditions are favorable, he hangs his boots across his pack and goes barefoot.

**George Forman**
*Lone Traveler*

"I pass many trains and 'The Packer with the Grey Pony' was well known on the Plains that year." *(July 21)*

On July 22, **George** meets a group of Northern Plains Indians he identifies as being Arapahoe. He actually meets **Chief Bill Grass (Wacanka yapi)**, a Sihasapa Blackfoot-Sioux Chief who is coming west from Nebraska.[155] Owing to his accomplishments in various battles, **Chief Bill** also has the warrior name of Charging Bear.[156] **Chief Bill** warns **George** that farther down on the road are "Heap Utes" who are enemies of their nation. He advises **George** to go back north with his men. **George** claims the Chief and his army of fifty warriors are planning

---

[155] Chief Bill Grass is referenced by Pvt. William Boardman as the possible culprit behind the Raids (see July 20).
[156] LaDonna Brave Bull Allard, "John Grass biographical sketch," *American-Tribes.com*, 2020. https://american-tribes.com/Lakota/BIO/JohnGrass.htm. His son John Grass (Mato Watakpe) is Jumping Bear (or the younger Charging Bear). John Grass is accused by Fanny Kelly of being involved in the attack and kidnapping.

to gather at Red Buttes (south of the Platte Bridge Station) with the intent, "to assist the whites." **George** heeds the warning and follows them up. Details of **Chief Bill's** interaction with the nearby soldiers are shared in the narrative of the Union Army.

| | |
|---|---|
| **Cpl. Hervey Johnson**<br>*Union Army, Co. G* | "Night before last [July 23] two of the boys from Platte Bridge came down and told us that the Indians were coming in there and wanted to go down to the fort to get something to eat. They said they saw a heap of bad Indians with a heap of ponies…" *(July 25)* |

At Red Buttes, **George** meets up with and joins the **Wood Train** and three families of the **Granger Company**. He joins them when they continue down the Sweetwater Trail towards Salt Lake City, Utah. On July 26, this collective encounters "Mounted Indians all around," who are believed to be the Utes that **Chief Bill** warned **George** about. Fortunately, the Utes leave them alone. **George** stays with this collective until he turns west at Lander's Cutoff.

On his own again, **George** catches what he calls, "mountain fever," and begs for help from a passing widow and her children. "I saw many widows on the Road travelling this way and found them the only Good Samaritans on the Route" (July 28-29). After recouping, he offers to repay the widow's kindness by driving the wagon for her (and presumably taking care of the stock animals). On July 30, they pass by fresh emigrant graves marked as being killed Indians ten days prior, which lines up with the attacks that, "the Arapahoes [**Chief Bill**] had told me of."

After passing through Star Valley on the Wyoming-Idaho border, **George** utilizes Goodale's Cutoff from Fort Hall. This shortcut routes him through lava beds presently protected at Craters of the Moon National Monument and Preserve. He writes that the road conditions are torturous. About a week later, the **Merrill Team's** wagon wheels grind through the crunchy geological hell. **Julius Merrill** writes, "As far as the eye can reach, there is nothing but this black volcanic rock. … It was a desolate, dismal, scenery" (September 1-4).

**George** reaches the Boise Basin in mid-August, a full month before the **Merrill Team** can start their digging. After trying his luck in the crowded mines, **George** becomes homesick. He the hardships endured on this journey are worse than other mining adventures in his past. He believes the soggy 6-weeks spent on a steam clipper to the gold fields in Australia in 1852 were better in comparison.[157] In the late Spring of 1865, **George** returns to Canada West (Ontario), arriving towards the end of the year. In his retirement, **George** and his wife compile the loose pages of his journal and in 1883, they create a memoir that he titles, "Biographical Sketch of the Life and Ancestry of Geo. Forman of Stratford, Ontario, Canada." Portions of his memoir have appeared in various academic journals, though the full manuscript has never been made public.

---

[157] Australia's initial gold rush began in 1851. Many California "49ers" sailed across choppy oceans to reach those goldfields after they had had enough of California. If departing from Ontario, George may have sailed first to the United Kingdom, then south around the Cape of Africa (a British colony from 1806-1870), before heading due east to Victoria, Australia.

# Sunday, July 24, 1864

### Kelly-Larimer & Union Army

**Josiah Kelly**
*Kelly-Larimer Train*

"Got back here on Sunday." *(August 15)*

    **Cpt. Levi Marshall's** regiment returns from the Powder River Expedition to Deer Creek garrison late on July 24. Coming in with them is **Lt. Cpt. Henry C. Bretney**, post commander of Platte Bridge Station. On arrival, they are told that the Platte Bridge Station is under threat of attack by Indians. This report comes after **Chief "Old Grass"**[158] or **"Bill Grass"**[159] and his band of warriors gathered at Red Buttes.

**Pvt. Wm Boardman**
*Union Army, Co. G*

"'**Old Grass**' and his party were there, asking permission to pass down to Fort Laramie." *(August 6)*

    **Cpt. Levi** assumes the worst and sends part of Company E back out with a howitzer and violent intent.

**Pvt. Wm Boardman**
*Union Army, Co. G*

"**Capt. Marshall**, commanding [the] expedition, sent word to the troops stationed there to hold them [the Indians] until his command could come up and take them prisoner, acting on the suspicion..." *(August 6)*

---

[158] Per William Boardman's letter from August 6, 1864.
[159] Per Hervey Johnson's letter from July 25-26, 1864.

**Cpl. Hervey Johnson**
*Union Army, Co. G*

"…and if they would not tell[,]to kill them and their [wives] and papooses[,] burn their lodges and take their ponies." *(July 25)*

When Company E returns to the Platte Bridge Station that night, **Lt. Cpt. Henry C. Bretney**, is noticeably upset at the man he left in charge during his absence. Prior to the unsubstantiated accusation of **Chief Bill**, the **Lt. Cpt.** had issued orders to **1st Sgt. Henry Merwin** to kill all Indians on sight.

**Cpl. Hervey Johnson**
*Union Army, Co. G*

"he gave the Sergt. whom he left in charge[160] imperative orders to shoot any Indians who came about. … I hope he will be courtmartialed because he acted contrary to express orders…" *(July 25)*

### Ringo Company

Still working their way through the Black Hills on July 24, the **Ringo Company** passes a ranch where more travelers bow out from the collective. The **Ringos,** and others who are ready and able, abandon their brief companions at Horseshoe Creek and move ahead.

**Mr. Rushville**
*Ringo Company*

"We left **Mr. [Mathias] Farris**[161] and **Capt. Hodge**[162] back on Horse Shoe Creek, trying to recuperate and rest their cattle."*(Sept. 8)*

The seventy wagon company that banded together at Fort Laramie continues to fall apart as the rugged terrain and lack of water weakens every man, wagon and beast.

**Haywood Edwards**
*Edwards Team (Ringo)*

"Nooned on the hill west of Horse Shoo Creek and camped on Elkhorn Creek. Went 16 miles. *(July 24)*

---

[160] 1st Sargent Henry D. Merwin.
[161] Mathias Ferris' Shipping Company is mentioned in George Forman's journal as the first employer he hired on with, then abandoned one day later.
[162] Mary Ringo calls Mr. Hodge a reverend.

**Mary Ringo**
*Ringo Company*

"We leave the train that we have been traveling with and join **Calon Morrice[']s**. ... **Mr. [Addison] Guthrie** advised us to go on. Their cattle are dying off so fast..." *(July 24)*

In addition to the endurance challenge that **Martin Ringo** puts his cattle through, it is likely the cattle are being weakened from alkali poisoning. Several other journals contain mentions of the alkali "dust" clinging to the grass around the poisonous water sources.

**Mary Ringo**
*Ringo Company*

"...the road is strewn with dead cattle." *(July 24)*

# Monday, July 25, 1864

### Kelly-Larimer & Union Army

On the morning of July 25, **Cpl. Hervey Johnson** records a second burial for **2nd Lt. John Brown** at Deer Creek garrison, five days after his reported death, "with military honors."[163] Despite the ceremony, there is no record of his internment at or near the garrison. A quick look at the former grounds in Glenrock, Wyoming reveals that the property has since been cemented over and turned into a recreational center.

| **Sarah Larimer** | "His remains were taken to Fort Deer-Creek for |
|---|---|
| *Kelly-Larimer Train* | internment, and thence to his friends in Ohio." *(120)* |

This singular remark from **Sarah Larimer** provides a clue on the case, though the third reburial is still a mystery. In the 1970s, A. W. Judge, then director of the Fort Caspar Museum, requested a commemorative headstone to be erected for the **2nd Lt.** at Fort Caspar (Platte Bridge Station). To date, this request has not been fulfilled.

---

[163] Letter dated July 25, 1864 from Deer Creek.

Interpretive panel installed at the former site of "Deer Creek Station," at the corner of 4th and Cedar Streets in Glenrock, Wyoming. Image from Google Earth Street View, 2023.

U.S. Headstone Application for Military Veterans, 1925-1970 for John Brown.

After the funeral, **Cpt. Levi Marshall** departs from Deer Creek, with a squad heading back to Platte Bridge Station. **Josiah Kelly** joins this mission, determined to get justice.

**Josiah Kelly**
*Kelly-Larimer Train*

"Monday went up to Platte Bridge 25 miles from here."
*(Aug. 15)*

From Platte Bridge Station, **1ˢᵗ Sgt. Henry Merwin** leads an Army unit down to where **Chief Bill Grass** and his men are camped, despite his conviction that these Indians are entirely innocent.

| | |
|---|---|
| **Josiah Kelly**<br>*Kelly-Larimer Train* | "Met a party of Indians coming down…" *(Aug.15)* |
| **Pvt. Wm Boardman**<br>*Union Army, Co. G* | "**Serg't Meriom** … went to the camp of **'Old Grass'** with 12 men, to have a talk with him … **'Old Grass,'** however, probably 'smelling a mice,'[164] raised the war-whoop, down came their wigwams, and in a few minutes the whole Indian party were on their way to the hills." *(Aug. 6)* |

It is possible, though unverifiable, that the **1st Sgt.** may have signaled to the **Chief** that something was amiss in order to give him a head start.

| | |
|---|---|
| **Pvt. Wm Boardman**<br>*Union Army, Co. G* | "**Serg't Meriom** and a party immediately pursued, and the Indians made a stand near the foot of the bluffs, and a sharp skirmish of about three-quarters of an hour ensued, resulting in the Indians being dispersed." *(Aug. 6)* |
| **Josiah Kelly**<br>*Kelly-Larimer Train* | "…wounded one Indian[,] took one man and 22 squaws and children priseners." *(Aug. 15)* |

In this Battle of Platte Bridge, at least ten of **Chief Bill's** men are killed or wounded. One soldier, Chavil St. Clair from Company G., receives a minor wound. **Chief Bill** is shot twice but escapes the foray and seeks asylum at the ranch of former Indian Agent and retired Union Major, Thomas Twiss.[165] **Cpt. Levi** ensures

---

[164] This expression holds the same meaning as "smelling a rat," or figuring out there is a ploy, trap or other scheme.

[165] From 1857 to 1861, Thomas Twiss served as an agent between the U.S. Government and the Northern Plains Indian Tribes. He lived and conducted his business about four miles from Deer Creek

the unit destroys the remaining wigwams, captures as many of the Indians' horses as possible, then takes sixteen or seventeen of their wives and five or six children as hostages.

**Josiah Kelly**
*Kelly-Larimer Train*

"They claimed to be innocent and friendly but said they knew that the Indians at Powder River village had a white woman prisoner. They sent the Indian after her and told him if he brought her in fifteen days they would all be set free and if not[,] they would all be shot." *(Aug. 15)*

### Ringo Company

Undisturbed in the Black Hills, those in the **Ringo Company** finally hear about the troubles ahead when they are camped near the La Bonte telegraph station.

**Haywood Edwards**
*Edwards Team (Ringo)*

"Traveled over hills & camped on a creek called Labonta." *(July 25)*

Remarkably, not one writer in this **Company** mentions being warned about the gruesome scenes along the trail while they were at Fort Laramie. There is also no notice received from the telegraph station at Horseshoe Creek. Surely, with the launch of several military initiatives, elusive criminals at large and people dead and missing, updates and warnings would still be spreading on a daily basis.

**Mr. Rushville**
*Ringo Company*

"A telegraph dispatch came to Platte Bridge, yesterday evening, that Deer Creek station had been attacked. *(Aug. 2, referring to July 25)*

---

stage station; then occupied by Joseph Bissonette, Lutheran missionaries, and various land surveyors. This site was called the Upper Platte Agency. After Twiss resigned from the position, he was still considered a trusted friend of the Indians. See James Nottage, "Indian Agent Thomas Twiss, Man of Two Worlds," *WyoHistory.org*, July 5, 2022. https://www.wyohistory.org/encyclopedia/indian-agent-thomas-twiss-man-two-worlds.

**America Forbis**
*Forbis & Irvine (Ringo)*

"…travel through the country, infested by the war-like Sioux… But still we made merry. Men and women, old and young, would gather round the campfires and sing familiar songs to the accompanying notes of the guitar." *(1893)*

It appears **Mr. Rushville** has his place names reversed and that **America Forbs** is not quite understanding the gravity of the situation. In camp, **Mary Ringo** hears more bad news from a southbound traveling party.

**Mary Ringo**
*Ringo Company*

"Some emigrants came to camp who had a man killed by the Indians last night [July 24], they report some sad times ahead…" *(July 25)*

This emigrant party has been identified as that of William Barkley, Joseph Aspling, Thomas Soler, Henry Schaefar, and Charles Long. They are traveling east from Salt Lake City, Utah to Kansas City, Missouri. Henry Schafer is the man killed while camped at La Bonte Creek, per the testimony of Charles Long. When this wagon train returns to Missouri in September, Charles' story is shared in the Courier-Journal. In it, he claims the remains of Henry are carried only as far as Fort Laramie, but family descendants believe they are transported all the way back to Johnson County, where he is allegedly interred.

The mules and stock had to be well herded and guarded on account of the troubles with the redskins. Mr. Schaefor, being very cautious about his stock, left camp about ten o'clock to see whether the guard and mules were all right, which seemed to be, and was on his return to the camp again; when all at once a report of a rifle was heard, and the same time the loud cries of Mr. Schaefor for Charles Long; whereupon Charles Long hurried to the spot, and arrived just in time enough to hear from his own lips that he was shot mortally. Charles Long took him to the camp, and did all for his comfort that he could do. He died in about fifteen minutes and a half past ten o'clock. The train started immediately and drove on for two days and nights with the corpse to get to Fort Laramie.

Excerpt from Charles Long, "Further Indian Atrocities," *Courier-Journal*, September 8, 1864, 1.

Despite the imminent danger reported, the **Ringo Company** remains confident in their own strength.

**Mr. Rushville**
*Ringo Company*

"You can at once appreciate the danger we might be in. But our train feel confident that we will not be attacked, and that if nothing else will satisfy [the Indians] but a fight with us, we can whip them very easily. *(Aug. 2)*

# Tuesday, July 26, 1864

### Ringo Company

The next day, the **Ringo Company** covers only a short distance, camping near Wagon Hound Creek.

**Mary Ringo**
*Ringo Company*

"...get a very late start - we only travel some 5 miles and correll and send the cattle some 2 miles where they get good grass." *(July 26)*

**Haywood Edwards**
*Edwards Team (Ringo)*

"Crossed a ridge of 6 miles in the forenoon and camped on a small creek. Laid by in the evening." *(July 26)*

### Union Army

**Sgt. Lewis Hull**
*Union Army, Co. K*

"Dispatch Reported fight on Upper Platte bridge. Several Indians killed." *(July 26)*

By July 26, telegraph relays have informed **Lt. Col. William O. Collins** and others at Fort Laramie about the Battle of Platte Bridge.[166] While **Cpt. Levi Marshall's** squad continues to look for **Chief Bill**, the **Lt. Col.** requests that the wives and children who were taken hostage be brought down to Fort Laramie along with the thirty Indian ponies that were taken from **Chief Bill**.

---

[166] This is distinctly different from the Battle of Platte Bridge on July 26, 1865 in which Lt. Caspar Collins is killed (along with four other soldiers).

# Wednesday, July 27, 1864

### Ringo Company

On July 27, the **Ringo Company** noons at La Prele Creek, where they first learn about the depredations on the **Kelly-Larimer** and **Morris-Hastings** trains.

**Mary Ringo**
*Ringo Company*
"...travel some 15 miles and stop on a creek ... We find posted on a tree a notice that the Indians have killed six men near here. We hear they have had a fight ahead of us." *(July 27)*

The "fight ahead" reference might be about the Battle of Platte Bridge.

**Mary Ringo**
*Ringo Company*
"I do hope and pray God that we may get through safely, it keeps me so uneasy and anxious." *(July 27)*

While the **Edwards Team** had been keeping up with the **Ringo Family**, on July 27, they fall slightly behind. They won't reach La Prele until the next day.

**Haywood Edwards**
*Edwards Team (Ringo)*
"Went 10 miles & camped on a small creek." *(July 25)*

### Union Army

Thirteen days after **Brig. Gen. Robert Mitchell** left from Fort Kearny, he finally arrives at Fort Laramie and takes stock of what has occurred on the Plains under the command of **Lt. Col. William Collins**.

**Sgt. Lewis Hull**  "**Gen. Mitchell** came in from Kearney with an escort of 7th
*Union Army, Co. K*  Iowa. Salute of seven guns heard in honor of his arrival. Agent
in." *(July 26)*

The agent who arrives is unclear, though he apparently chastises the post for crimes against innocent Indians. When word gets out that the **Lt. Col.** has arranged for the women and children to be held hostage at the Fort, another visitor confronts them on this as yet another example of how they have wronged the Indians. This man then demands the release of the hostages.

**Josiah Kelly**  "...a french man came and claimed all but one [woman] and
*Kelly-Larimer Train*  her children as his family[.]" *(Aug. 15)*

Whether this claim is true or not, most of the hostages are released to him, as well as every pony.[167] When the soldiers hear about this release, they consider it to be a reflection of the **Lt. Col.** going soft.

---

[167] Douglas McChristian, *Fort Laramie and the U.S. Army on the High Plains 1849-1890*, National Park Service, Feb. 2003, 243.

# Thursday, July 28, 1864

### Ringo Company

On July 28, the **Ringo Company** camps three miles east of Little Box Elder Creek crossing (suspected to be at Spring Canyon Creek).

**Mary Ringo**  "Nothing of importance transpires today." *(July 28)*
*Ringo Company*

### Kelly-Larimer & Union Army

After two weeks of rest at Deer Creek, **William Larimer** has recovered from his arrow wound to the thigh and hopes to take his wife and son to a more suitable place of refuge where they can make a plan to recover their losses. Today, the **Larimers** join a group of southbound soldiers who can escort them back to Fort Laramie.

**Sarah Larimer**  "The soldiers returned to Deer Creek, on the 27th, and
*Kelly-Larimer Train*  the following day we set out with them en route for Fort
  Laramie." *(Larimer, 123)*

**Cpl. Hervey Johnson**  "The woman who was captured and made her escape,
*Union Army, Co. G*  has gone to the fort with her boy and husband who has
  recovered from his wounds." *(August 11, 1864 to Sybil)*

## Chief Bill Grass - Epilogue

On or around July 28, **Cpt. Levi Reinhart** learns that **Chief Bill Grass** has been recovering from his wounds at a ranch just four miles away from the garrison.

**Pvt. Wm Boardman**
*Union Army, Co. G*

"**Capt. Rinehart** wished to place a guard over him [the chief], but Maj. Twiss promised to be responsible for his safe keeping..." *(August 6)*

Extra watchmen are posted outside the ranch, regardless of the former Indian Agent's good word. Six days later, a small party of Indians comes to the ranch, shoots at the posted guard and scares them off, then runs in to collect **Chief Bill** and carry him off the premise. It is unclear how much involvement Thomas Twiss had in orchestrating this escape or if he turned a blind eye to the event.

Chief Bill Grass, AKA "Uses Him as a Shield," father of John Grass. From Col. Alfred Burton Welch Archives (ca. 1972). https://www.welchdakotapapers.com/2011/11/chief-john-grass-2/

**Chief Bill's** next moves are recorded in an Oral History provided by his son and subchief, **John Grass**, as told to his adopted grandson, Alfred Welch in 1915.[168] After escaping, the **Chief** heads north to rejoins his family by heading due north to the Cheyenne River, then east into Dakota Territory. At some point, near Moreau River (north of Cheyenne Creek in present-day northwest South Dakota), the **Chief** and his son **John Grass** are approached by a band of Hunkpapa.

**John Grass**
*Sihasapa Tribe*

"We saw a woman standing apart. She had light skin ... She talked white talk. ... The Hunkpapa had attacked a wagon train to the west of the Black Hills and killed all the people but two white women. ... She had been with them for about one summertime." *(1915)*

The woman in captivity is **Fanny Kelly. Chief Bill** offers the Hunkpapa a deal to exchange horses for the woman. When the "headman," Brings Plenty (who previously purchased **Fanny** from a band of Sioux Oglala), disagrees with the exchange, **Chief Bill** offers him an alternative.

**John Grass**
*Sihasapa Tribe*

"There is one other thing you can do. You can keep the white woman and we will bury you today." *(1915)*

The "headman" wisely accepts the first offer and receives sixteen horses for **Fanny**. More on her release is found in the **Kelly family** epilogue.

**John Grass**
*Sihasapa Tribe*

"After a long time we took the white woman to Fort Sully and gave her to the white people there. ... My father and I did this thing. I am glad about it. Men know of it." *(1915)*

At the adoption ceremony for Alfred Welch into the Grass family and Yanktonai Sioux Nation in 1913, (then) **Chief John Grass** spoke about his father, saying that **Chief Bill** advised him years ago, "not to fight the white man, but to help with the white man, to give to him honor and respect..."[169]

---

[168] John Grass, "Fanny Kelly Story," Oral History to Col. Alfred Burton Welch in 1915. Transcribed by Everett Cox, *Welch Dakota Papers*, 2011. https://www.welch dakotapapers.com/2011/11/chief-john-grass-2/. (Also see the Appendix)
[169] Everett Cox, "Adoption of Welch as His Son," Welch Dakota Papers, 2011. https://www.welchdakotapapers.com/2011/11/chief-john-grass-2/.

## Union Army

The day after **Brig. Gen. Robert Mitchell** arrived at Fort Laramie, **Lt. Col. William O. Collins,** "was relieved from the command of the post at Fort Laramie and given general supervision of all post and detachments west of Julesburg in the District of Nebraska," reports Collins family historian Agnes Wright Spring.[170] The **Brig. Gen.** establishes his new headquarters at Fort Laramie and installs his escorts from Companies D and F of the Seventh Iowa Cavalry Volunteers as the new occupants.

The **Brig. Gen.** reassigns the **Lt. Col.,** to inactive field operations mostly related to protecting the telegraph lines.[171] The demotion results from the **Lt. Col.** being considered ineffective in his role as a leader of men. Replacing him as fort commander is Major John S. Wood from the Seventh Iowa Cavalry Volunteers. **Sgt. Lewis Hull** records the change being officially announced the next day.

| | |
|---|---|
| **Sgt. Lewis Hull**<br>*Union Army, Co. K* | "Change reported in this department; Maj. Wood to command the post. Lieut. Reeves to be inspector general in the department." *(July 29)* |

An anonymous correspondent with the *Indianapolis Star* writes of this change of command that, "The force at the fort is inadequate to the task," and that the **Brig. Gen.** "is now busy in instituting measures to punish the Indians."[172] This writer is believed to be a member of the Seventh I. V. C. Not all news about the demoted **Lt. Col.** is as slanted against him, however. Some imply he remains as helpful as possible in his new role.

---

[170] Agnes Wright Spring, *Caspar Collins: The Life and Exploits of an Indian Fighter of the Sixties*, New York: Columbia University Press, 1927, 59.

[171] Per *General Orders No.* [blank], District of Nebraska, issued July 28, 1864, Letter No. 80, William O. Collins.

[172] See citation with following image. The author only signs his name as "Far West."

Ft. Laramie is a military post of no strength, but pleasantly situated, kept cleanly, and consists of a collection of wooden and adobe buildings, used for military purposes. The site is in the angle of junction of the Platte and Laramie rivers, and a chain of hills on the north and south overlook it. The 11th Ohio volunteers, commanded by Lt. Col. Collins, have been stationed here for over two years past, but will be relieved by a detachment of the 7th Iowa in a few days. Lt. Col. Collins was superseded a few days since by Maj. Wood, of the 7th Iowa.

Loud complaints have been made against Lieut. Col. Collins for his neglect to furnish proper protection to emigrants from Indian depredations. He is reported to have said that the emigration this year was composed of d—d cop perheads, fleeing from a draft and not entitled to any protection. Likely this charge is untrue. But the feeling against him among emigrants and settlers is universal.

"An Overland Trip to California," Anonymous correspondence from July 30, 1864, *Indianapolis Star*, September 9, 1864, 2. (Excerpt)

## Correspondence,

### FORT LARAMIE, July 31, 1864.

EDITORS CHAMPION :—I find reports of troubles with Indians west of here, very rife, and are informed by Gen. Mitchell, who is personally looking after matters, that thirty-two Indians have recently been killed by the troops, and one soldier killed and several wounded in return. Troops are now stationed at various points between here and South Pass, which is some 300 miles west of here, and two companies start out to-morrow to patrol the road.— Both Gen. Mitchell, and Col. Collins, the commander of the post, are determined that the Indians shall have enough of war, and that as far as possible, with the force at their command, the emigration shall receive efficient protection. It would be well for all parties going west of here, however, to go well armed, and in large numbers, and always be vigilant.

"Correspondence from Fort Laramie July 31 1864," *Freedom's Champion*, August 25, 1864, 2. (Excerpt)

**S**

# Friday, July 29, 1864

### Ringo Company

When the **Ringo Company** moves forward the on July 29, the **Edwards Team** catches up with them from five miles behind. Midday, they pass a mass marked grave: a testament to the tragedies befalling those at Little Box Elder Creek.

| | |
|---|---|
| **Haywood Edwards**<br>*Edwards Team (Ringo)* | "Nooned at Deer [Little Box Elder] Creek."<br>*(July 29)* |
| **Mr. Rushville**<br>*Ringo Company* | "Since my last to you from near Fort Laramie, we have passed through an exciting period. We are now one hundred and twenty miles above Laramie, near where the Indians, a short time since, burnt five wagons, and killed several men and children, and took some women prisoners." *(Aug. 2)* |
| **Mary Ringo**<br>*Ringo Company* | "...After traveling some 5 miles we see the corpse of a man lying by the side of the road, scalped, had been buried on top of the ground and the wolves had scratched it up. I think we ought to have buried him." *(July 29)* |

The body **Mary Ringo** sees is **Jacob Hastings'** unnamed driver, who was previously buried on July 17 by **George Forman** and others. The eighteen inches of dirt do not prevent his corpse from being revealed. The **Ringo Company** leaves the body to (hopefully) be reburied by someone else.

**Wm. Davenport**
*Ringo Company*

"We passed through the Black Hills[,] where the Indians have committed most of their depredations this season[,] without being molested, and camped the night of the 29th of July, about three miles this side of Deer Creek..." *(1864)*

Between July 29-30, the anonymous correspondent from the Seventh I.V.C. heads up through the Black Hills, sees the same sight, but does nothing about it.

If we die, we will be buried somehow in or oh the ground, and a rude board will tell to those who come *shortly* after us who fell there and when. Or, more probably, wolves will resurrect us for a hungry meal. Such was the fate of the tenement of one grave we passed a few days since. He had been buried about two weeks. The wolves had dug him up, and nothing remained but the bones, hair and clothing about the grave. Carcasses of dead animals line the roadside and taint the air, while the scorching rays of a dog-day's sun reflected from limestone hillsides and sand bars as fiery as a "burning marl," give us a foretaste of the trials of eastern pilgrims. But flickering hope bids us to the Eden beyond the Rocky Mountains, where seasons are reversed, sea breeze and mountain winds meet in "sweet embrace," in grassy valleys watered by ice-cold mountain rills, with a never ending spring; and we rush on over the fallen. FAR WEST.

"An Overland Trip to California," Anonymous correspondence from July 30, 1864, *Indianapolis Star*, September 9, 1864, 2. (Excerpt shown)

That evening, the **Ringo Company** camps between Deer Creek and Little Box Elder Creek. There, their luck finally runs out and they are attacked by an unknown assailant. Details such as who exactly is shot and where they are at the time are also inconclusive.

**Mr. Rushville**
*Ringo Company*

"Night before last [July 29] one of our men, well near the Corral, was fired upon by an Indian, and badly wounded, but not fatally; his name was **D. C. Davis**, from Kansas." *(Aug. 2)*

**America Forbis**
*Forbis & Irvine (Ringo)*

"...one of our party was shot by an Indian that had crept almost into the circle without being discovered by the guards." *(1893)*

**Wm. Davenport**
*Ringo Company*

"Shortly after dark[,] a gentleman by the name of **Davis**, from Kansas, went out about fifty yards from the camp to look after his horses that were picketed out, and an Indian shot and wounded him in the right arm and side, making a painful tho' not dangerous wound." *(1864)*

**Mary Ringo**
*Ringo Company*

"...About dark[,] **Mr. Ravel** went out to bring in his horses when a man shot him through the arm, in a short time all lights were extinguished and every man to his post expecting to be attacked by the Indians but we do not think it was the Indians but a band of robbers." *(July 29)*

**William Lucas**
*Lucas & Co. (Ringo)*

"We had two or three little scrap[e]s with the Indians and some other mishaps, but nothing really serious." *(1926)*

**Wm. Davenport**
*Ringo Company*

"The shooting of **Mr. Davis** created considerable excitement in camp, as we expected to be attacked by Indians in force." *(1864)*

In the "excitement," there is no mention of returning fire, nor do the emigrants make a plan to pursue the horses that are stolen (or frightened off).

| | |
|---|---|
| **Mr. Rushville**<br>*Ringo Company* | "During the excitement that followed, before we could get our horses inside the Corral they managed to steal three of them." *(Aug. 2)* |
| **Wm. Davenport**<br>*Ringo Company* | "The Indian succeeded in stealing three horses **Mr. Davis**, one from **Mr. Irvin**, and one from **Da** There was only one Indian seen, and I think his was to steal horses." *(1864)* |
| **Haywood Edwards**<br>*Edwards Team (Ringo)* | "Had 3 horses stolen & one more wounded by the Indians." *(July 29)* |

## Kelly-Larimer & Ringo Company

During their travels, the **Ringo Company** passes the Army escort with the **Larimer family**, though no mention is made of this. This evening, however, the emigrants heading in opposite directions appear to exchange shots with each other unknowingly.

| | |
|---|---|
| **Sarah Larimer**<br>*Kelly-Larimer Train* | "When en route to Fort Laramie, the second afternoon [July 29], our encampment was in an extensive grove; and while some of our men were rambling about, several shots were fired at them. Supposing this an attack by savages, they returned the fire, causing quite a sensation in camp. ... Fortunately[,] the timber proved a shield, and no one was injured. ... The invaders were travellers belonging to an emigrant train that was corralled just beyond the woods. This company was en route for the Pacific coast, and with it were some aged persons and many children." *(Larimer, 127)* |

**S**

# Saturday to Sunday, July 30–31, 1864

### Kelly-Larimer

When the **Larimers** continue south on July 30, **Sarah Larimer** notes the same roadside corpse that no one is willing to rebury.

**Sarah Larimer**
*Kelly-Larimer Train*

"As we travelled, the following day [July 30], we saw the body of a man who had been killed by Indians and buried by kind travelers, but not, exhumed by wolves, it lay by the roadside." (*Larimer, 127*)

Eighteen days after **Jacob Hastings' driver** died at the hands of Northern Plains Indians, his remains lay decomposing under the sun. Because of his exposure to the elements (including the summer heat), any remaining soft tissues and internal organs are likely diminished and/or are eaten off by wildlife, while hair, bones, and cartilage settle to the ground in the general outline of what used to be. Soon, any marker left by those who initially buried him will also become lost to time and weather.

### Ringo Company

Fearing another robbery or other attack, **Martin Ringo** and all other men in the **Ringo Company** are exhausted this morning from their double guard shifts though the night.

**Wm. Davenport**
*Ringo Company*

"The whole company stood guard during the night so as to be prepared in case we were attacked." *(1864)*

**America Forbis**
*Forbis & Irvine (Ringo)*

"Males, young and old, had guard duty to perform." *(1893)*

The fatigue takes an unfortunate toll on the **Ringo family**.

**Mr. Rushville**
*Ringo Company*

"Most of us had been up the entire night, watching for an Indian attack. We were close to some brush near North Platte, and could not tell how many of our foes were lying in the brush, waiting for day to dawn when they begin the attack. ... Just as day dawn began to streak the East, myself with others were standing against our wagons, listening at the crack of every Bush around us, and, every now and then, could hear **Davis**, the wounded man, groan most piteously." *(Aug. 2)*

**Mary Ringo**
*Ringo Company*

"And now Oh God comes the saddest record of my life for this day my husband accidentally shot himself..." *(July 30)*

**Mr. Rushville**
*Ringo Company*

"All at once, a loud report of a shot gun was heard a few wagons passed [past] us." *(Aug. 2)*

**Wm. Davenport**
*Ringo Company*

"Just after daylight on the morning of the 30th ult., **Mr. Ringo** stepped outside of the wagons, as I suppose, for the purpose of looking around to see if Indians were in sight and his shot gun went off accidentally in his own hands, the load entering at his right eye and coming up out at the top of his head. ... At the report of his gun[,] I saw his hat blown up twenty feet in the air, and his brains were scattered in all directions." *(1864)*

**Haywood Edwards**
*Edwards Team (Ringo)*

"**Mr. Ringo** shot himself." *(July 30)*

**Mr. Rushville**
*Ringo Company*

"...a man belonging to our train, from Gallatin, Daviess County–**Martin Ringo**– discharged his shot-gun accidentally, and blew the top of his head off. He leaves a large and helpless family, on their way to California." *(Aug. 2)*

Because **Martin Ringo** dies in an accidental, self-inflicted event, it is not counted in the toll of losses for the Platte River Raids.

**Mary Ringo**
*Ringo Company*

"[Martin] was buried by the wayside and oh, my heart is breaking. ...my little children are crying all the time and I - oh what am I to do." *(July 30)*

**Mr. Rushville**
*Ringo Company*

"...We spent part of the day in digging a grave up on the hill close by,[173] and left [**Martin**] to rest until the resurrection morn." *(Aug. 2)*

**Haywood Edwards**
*Edwards Team (Ringo)*

"We buried him and went 5 miles. Camped." *(July 30)*

## Ringo - Epilogue

In light of the loss, **Mary Ringo's** fourteen-year-old, **Johnny,** takes over as a guard and learns how to drive the wagon on-the-go with the guidance of other men who step in to help.

**America Forbis**
*Forbis & Irvine (Ringo)*

"I recall an instance when a mere boy [**Johnny Ringo**] was standing night guard at the wagon next to mine. He was so exhausted by the heat and fatigue of the day's travel that he would fall asleep at his post, and at intervals through the night his watchful mother [**Mary Ringo**] would arouse him by a gentle call from her wagon. ... She did not sleep that night, but kept watch in place of her boy, and awakened and only when she feared he would be discovered neglecting his duty. His father was killed only a few nights previous while on guard duty at the same wagon." *(1864)*

On July 31, the **Ringo, Forbis, and Lucas** families leave Deer Creek and the Black Hills behind for good. **Mattie Bell Ringo Cushing**, who is only two years old

---

[173] Martin Ringo's grave is located just west of present-day Glenrock, Wyoming.

on this journey, later writes of her mother **Mary's** character in the introduction of **Mary's** published diary: "I think she was the bravest woman I ever heard of—left as she was with five children to look after." **Mattie Bell's** children, Frank and Zana Cushing, attribute the **Ringo family's** recovery from a grief stricken state to her "amazing fortitude and complete wisdom."[174]

The family's October climb through mountainous areas in Nevada are quite difficult on **Mary**, who is late in her pregnancy. She detours the family to Austin where a relative lives. There, she delivers her sixth child: a stillborn son who is disfigured.[175] At this point, **Mary** ceases to write in her diary and falls into a depression. According to **Mattie Bell**, **Mary** blames herself for mangling the unborn with her emotional distress. **Mattie Bell** finishes the tale for her mother in the conclusion of the book:

> "We took the mules and one wagon to San Jose ... we finally reached San Jose where Mother's sister lived. My aunt [Augusta] and her husband [Col. Colman Younger] had a very large place and Mr. Younger raised blooded cattle. They had a small house on the place that had formerly been a carriage house and had been made into a house. We lived there a year as mother was not able to do anything for some time..."

In 1870, **Mary's** younger son, **Martin Albert Ringo,** shows signs of tuberculosis—the same bacterial infection that **Martin** struggled with. While **Johnny Ringo** takes up the burden of earning money to support the family, **Mary** tends to **Martin** until he passes away in 1873, at nineteen. As a consequence, **Mary** contracts the deadly disease and dies three years later.

Around this time, **Johnny's** anger leads to him making poor life choices and getting caught in vigilante schemes, including a murder. He is imprisoned several times in Texas before moving to Arizona Territory. The fresh start doesn't last long and **Johnny's** anger continues to get the best of him. After murdering two more men, he removes himself to Tombstone, but his reputation is ruined. Whether driven by Post-Traumatic Stress Disorder (PTSD) or Depression, **Johnny** begins drinking heavily and once again gets mixed up with illegal activities.

---

[174] Mary Ringo's grandchildren compose the published diary's dedication.

[175] It is possible this child is given the name Austin Ringo.

Starting in 1879, any criminals in Tombstone would be answering to the new Sherriff, **Wyatt Earp** (son of the wagon master in the **Pella Company**[176]). In December of 1881, **Wyatt's** brother **Virgil** takes a mysterious blow from a shotgun and **Wyatt** automatically assumes the man behind the crime is **Johnny**. **Johnny** denies any involvement and challenges **Wyatt** and Doc Holliday to a showdown in the street but **Wyatt** tosses him in jail instead. A month later, **Wyatt's** other brother, **Morgan,** is killed. Again, **Johnny** is accused but he denies responsibility and **Wyatt** doesn't have enough evidence to actually pin the murder on him.

As is his habit, **Johnny** disappears for a while (this time to Mexico), but when he comes back in July of 1882, he goes on an extended drinking binge and rides out into the Sonoran Desert with a couple of other no-gooders. On July 13, **Johnny** wanders off on his own and allegedly commits suicide but those who find him also notice that his hands feet are tied and items of clothing torn from his body. The evidence never adds up and theorists continue to debate the matter to this day.

## Forbis & Irvine - Epilogue

The **Forbis** and **Irvine** families separate from the **Ringo Company** after South Pass and head to Montana Territory through Lander's Cutoff. They arrive in Virginia City on September 27 after a "long and trying" journey, according to a biographical sketch found in the book, *Progressive Men of Montana*.[177] They spend their first winter tent camping in the mining town with unchecked crimes and loose governance which tests their mettle. **America Forbis** reflects on the dichotomy of the miners who are "rolling in wealth [but] destitute of the necessities of life."[178]

In the Spring of 1865, **Jonathan Forbis** moves his family away from the lawless "spectacle," as **America** calls it, and starts farming just outside of Helena. **Jonathan** becomes a commissioner for Lewis and Clark County and gets highly

---

[176] For the Pella Company's 1864 journey across the Plains, see the North Bank Trails.
[177] "Jonathan Forbis," (A. W. Bowen & Co., Chicago), 159.
[178] America Forbis. See her autobiographical sketch from "Women Pioneers" in the Appendix.

involved in Territorial legislature. Unfortunately he dies within a few years from a stroke. **America** never remarries, but alternates spending time in the homes of her daughters. She becomes "one of the most highly esteemed and beloved pioneer women of Montana" and "a woman of sterling character and many attractive qualities," according to her obituary.[179]

Their five younger children do extraordinarily well in their endeavors, whether it be in mining or in law. **William** devotes himself to his mining work a bit too much, though, and the strain on his body leads to an early death. He leaves a considerable fortune to his wife and children. **John Jr**. and **James** become attorneys and establish the firm Forbis & Forbis. Daughters **Agnes** and **Myra** marry well to a local doctor and banker.

The **Irvines** move to Butte, Montana where cousins **Edwin** and **David** begin placer mining. **David** is so skilled at this that he becomes a well-known authority in the industry as a whole. With his success, he contributes substantially to the establishment of the Deer Lodge College.

Not to be outdone by their male counterparts, the **Forbis** and **Irvine** women make it a point to be noticed for their contributions to Montana's history. In 1893, **America** and three of her daughters chronicle their journey west and the personal sacrifices they make to turn the wildness of transient mining settlements into sociable and productive places of permanence.

---

[179] "Mrs. A. A. Forbis Taken by Death," obituary in *The Butte Miner*, July 13, 1903, 5.

trace of their lives or identity. There were, however, in those wild and furious times, women of staunch and honest womanhood, and Montana's pioneer history, if not the history of these women, is principally the history of the men who were sustained and encouraged by these brave souls. Of these women, a very few have been found, and have submitted a few facts of what must have been busy and eventful lives.

"Women Pioneers." Autobiographical sketches for the World's Fair of 1893, in *The Anaconda Standard*, February 17, 1895, 12. (Excerpt)

## Lucas - Epilogue

The **Lucas family** also takes Landers Cutoff to Montana Territory. Though they have every intention of being boomtown cattle ranchers, they can only put up with the rough lifestyle for a short time. In 1868, **George Lucas** opens The Pacific House, a hotel and restaurant initially designed to meet the needs of weary travelers, though it receives excellent reviews and quickly becomes an attractive venue for weddings and other classy events. Despite his success as a hotelier, **George** abandons this venture within the year and in the Fall of 1868 relocates the family to Woodland, California (outside of Sacramento).

In California, they are considered highly respected citizens and are popular in many ways. After **George** passes away in 1898, his obituary writer claims, "Everyone now living occupies an honored position in the community of which he or she is a representative."[180] For the next twenty years, "**Mrs. [Sarah] Lucas** was the head of one of the first families in Yolo county, there being none that ranks higher in the esteem of all."[181]

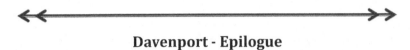

### Davenport - Epilogue

**William Davenport** and his mining team depart to Bannack and Virginia City via Bridger's Trail near Casper, Wyoming. He hopes to beat other miners to the placer mines that are calling his names.

### Edwards & Morrice Teams - Epilogue

**Haywood Edwards** and **Calon Morrice's** mining teams take the longer, but presumably safer route to Montana via Landers Cutoff. Once in Star Valley, they follow the Salt River north into Idaho (state), then west to the Boise Basin where **Haywood** ceases to mention the **Morrice Team**. **Haywood** builds himself a rudimentary log cabin then starts prospecting in the Boise River by mid-October.

**Haywood** continues to journal about his experience with brief comments such as: "Worked at our mining," "Still worked," and "Miner it is." In 1867, he makes the long journey back to Missouri where he settles into farming, marries and starts a family.

---

[180] "G. J. Lucas Dead," Obituary in the *Woodland Daily Democrat*, October 21, 1898.
[181] "Mrs. Sarah T. Lucas, Aged 94, Dies," Obituary in the *Woodland Daily Democrat*, April 18, 1923.

Mr. Edwards was born at Hillsville, Carroll county, Va., November 27th, 1842, and came with his parents to Caldwell county in 1849. He went west in 1864 and spent two and a half years in the mines of Idaho and then returned here, where he has resided ever since. He was married January 4, 1870, to Miss Elizabeth J. Diddle, who survives, together with two children—Aaron B. Edwards and Mrs. W. A. Railsback.

"Haywood Edwards Dead." Obituary in *The Hamilton Farmer's Advocate*, June 6, 1912, 4.

## Kelly Family - Epilogue

Long after others have dispersed and left the Black Hills of Idaho far behind, **Josiah Kelly, Andy Lawrence** and **Gardner Wakefield** remain at the Deer Creek garrison. They are left with little to nothing to live on and are at the mercy of government or family aid, or on the generosity of passing families. In the meantime, **Josiah** continues to aid the Army in their efforts to recoup stolen animals and track down **Fanny Kelly**.

**Andy** returns to Kansas and by 1865 and enlists with the U.S. Colored Troops. By then, Civil War activities are diminishing, and it is unclear where his regiment serves. In the 1880 U.S. Census, **Andy** is found living in Mound City, Kansas near Fort Scott. He marries, has five children and supports them all with a career in stone masonry.

After eight months of medical attention from the post surgeon, **Gardner** dies from internal damage caused by his arrow wounds. His body is sent to Maine for burial. Though his death is delayed, it is still attributed to the Platte River Raids and considered in the toll of losses.

**Fanny Kelly** is taken deeper into the Powder River Basin, or "Chahalee Wacapolah," as she believes her captors call it. She specifically details her time in captivity being "east of the Big Horn Mountains," in a country "scarred by countless trails of buffalo" (62-64). Despite the repeated efforts of **Josiah** and the Army to rescue her,

**Fanny** endures months of being sold and resold, treated as a slave, and she struggles to maintain any hope for her family's survival. She later writes to her brother-in-law, "The Indians told me that they had killed all but me..."[182] During her captivity, her life is threatened on multiple occasions, including by burning on a stake. She is oddly counseled by the tribe she is held by that the death she is expecting is not out of cruelty, but simply a matter of evening the score in a "You kill my people, I kill yours" type of transaction.

In the Fall of 1864, **Fanny** is traded for (or purchased) from a tribal band of Hunkpapa by **Chief Bill Grass** and his son **John Grass (Mato Watakpe),** whom she calls in her memoir, "**Jumping Bear.**" In addition to the memoir and **Chief John's** oral history with Alfred Welch, there is an additional oral history interview from **Chief John's** wife, **Mary** that supports this exchange and subsequent captivity.

| | |
|---|---|
| **Mary Grass**<br>*Sihasapa Tribe*<br>*(Mrs. John Grass)* | "When the warriors captured the two women in the wagons, **John Grass** got one of them for a lot of horses..."<br>*(1921)*[183] |

**Fanny** singles **Chief John** out as being one of the guilty parties involved in the **Kelly-Larimer** incident of July 12, though she equally credits him with saving her life from the abuses of her other captors.

---

[182] Fannie Kelly, "letter to Rezin Wells Kelly, March 10th, 1865," in *Genealogy of the John A. Kelly Family,* transcribed by Mrs. Henry Pelton and Dwight Yates (Ohio: Private Publication), 1950.
[183] Mary Grass (Kampeskaimanipiwin, AKA Walking on the Shell Woman) is Chief John Grass' second wife and the adoptive mother of Alfred B. Welch.

**Fanny Kelly**
*Kelly-Larimer Train*

"...a young Blackfoot, whose name was Jumping Bear, saved me from the approaching doom... His activity in the attack on our train, and the energy he displayed in killing and pillaging on that occasion, notwithstanding his efforts to make me believe the contrary, forbade me to think there was any sympathy in his interference in my behalf." *(67)*

**Chief John** assures **Fanny** that he does not intend to cause her harm and has found sympathy for her cause. She capitalizes on his sentiment and requests that he deliver a letter to Fort Sully on her behalf. What he doesn't know is that she has carefully added in details about her circumstances that become integral to her ultimate rescue.

**Mary Grass**
*Sihasapa Tribe*
*(Mrs. John Grass)*

"**John Grass** had the Indians when they fought those soldiers between the forks of the Cannon Ball [south of Fort Rice in present-day North Dakota]. He had the white woman there. She wrote a letter. They sent it with Porcupine as the messenger. **John Grass** wanted to give her to the soldiers to take home. She cried about that. I had that letter. I had other things she wrote when she was with the Indians. ... I put them all into the fire. *(1921)*[184]

It isn't until December when the Army lands a negotiation for **Fanny's** release. She is immediately hospitalized at Fort Sully for several serious injuries, including broken bones. **Fanny** and **Josiah** reunited in February of 1865 and returned to Kansas.

---

[184] Mary Grass, "Mrs. John Grass talks to Welch," Oral History to Col. Alfred Burton Welch, April 28, 1921. Transcribed by Everett Cox, *Welch Dakota Papers*, 2011. https://www.welchdakotapapers.com/2011/11/chief-john-grass-2/.)

Jumping Bear Promising by the Moon, to Carry My Letter to the
White Chief at Fort Sully.

Illustration of Fanny Kelly with the twenty-four-year-old, future Sihasapa Blackfoot-Sioux Chief, John Grass. Found in Fanny Kelly's 1871 memoir, *Narrative of My Captivity,* 198-199.

Unfortunately, **Fanny's** reunion with her husband is short lived. In 1867, just one week before their first biological child is due to be born, **Josiah** dies from cholera. **Fanny** names her son after him and moves in with the **Larimers** in Wyoming (state) temporarily, squeaking out a living as a laundress while working on her memoir. When **Sarah Larimer** publishes a duplicative book in 1870, **Fanny** leaves her "false friend" and heads to Washington, D.C. to petition the government for restitution for the Plains Indians' crimes against her family (250).

| **Fanny Kelly**<br>*Kelly-Larimer Train* | "During my stay in Washington, Red Cloud and a delegation of chiefs and head warriors from the different tribes of the Dakota or Sioux Nation, arrived. They all recognized me as once having been with their people…" *(252)* |
| **Mary Grass**<br>*Sihasapa Tribe*<br>*(Mrs. John Grass)* | "When he [**Chief John**] and Swan went to see the Ate Itancan [Father Leader] at Washington, once, this woman came and shook hands with him and called in Kola Mitawa ["My Friend"] and was glad to see him. He was not bad to her[,] but the other Indian men had been bad to her and she cried much." *(1921)* |

**Fanny** is awarded a sizable sum for her list of losses, to be docked from the government's annuities to the tribes found guilty of involvement. In 1880, **Fanny** marries a man from Washington D.C. and lives a modest life with him. Eventually, her only son, Josiah Jr., names three of his four children Josiah, Fanny, and Mary.

## Larimer Family - Epilogue

For the next ten years, **William**, **Sarah** and **Frank Larimer** bounce around, opening a photography studio first at Fort Laramie, then in Julesburg, Colorado from 1866-1867, and for a short time at Sherman Station, Wyoming in 1867. While at Sherman Station, **William** takes on a Star Postal Route contract to deliver mail from there to Point of Rocks in Sweetwater County. **Fanny Kelly** takes refuge with them there after her husband dies.

By 1870, the **Larimer family** lives in Sweetwater County and their thirteen-year-old son is working as a teamster for **William**, who is listed as a "Stage Proprietor" in the U.S. Census.[185] **Sarah** takes break from photography to write her memoir and publishes it in 1870. Four years later, the family returns to

---

[185] 1870 United States Federal Census of Sweetwater County, Wyoming Territory. Frank is shown living separately of his parents in Point of Rocks, while William and Sarah reside farther west at Anthony's Saw Mill.

Kansas and banks on **Sarah's** photography business while both **William** and son **Frank** study law.

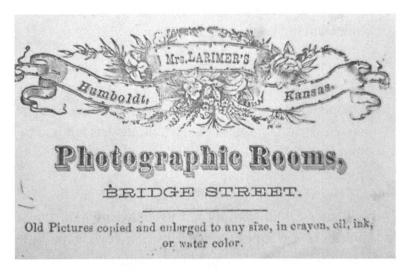

Sarah Larimer's business card for "Photographic Rooms," from Humbolt, Kansas, ca. 1874.

Returning to where **William's** asthma was terrible in the first place drives him to leave again, but **Sarah** is comfortable with her business and the profit it brings in. The couple separates, amiably, and **William** moves to Lead, South Dakota, just outside of Deadwood. While he develops a successful law practice and accrues land, **Sarah** dabbles in journalism, fiction writing and painting. She continues to write about the West and various Plains cultures and becomes a regular contributor to *The Bohemian* literary journal. In her obituary in the Fort Worth *Record*, there is a claim that Sarah wrote "several novels, but these have never been submitted for publication."[186]

In 1891, their son **Frank** dies for unknown reasons and leaves no heir. Then, by 1895, **William** removes to the Oil City Sanitarium in Little Rock, Arkansas for treatment of "consumption" (tuberculosis), then dies there, leaving his estate to his wife.[187]  **Sarah** manages the funds well. She invests in commercial real estate

---

[186] "Photograph Gallery Nucleus of $30,000 Fortune Built Up By Fort Worth Woman," Obituary of Sarah Larimer, *Record*, August 24, 1913, 1.
[187] Loretta L. Evans, "Sarah Luse Larimer 1836-1913: Indian Captive, Photographer, and Business Woman," in *Pegasus* (Dallas: Dallas Genealogical Society, vol.1, no. 1, 2013) 21-37.

and lives comfortably and quietly until her passing in 1913. Upon her death, her net worth is a reported $30,000,[188] or approximately $941 thousand dollars by today's standard.

---

[188] "Photograph Gallery…" Obituary, *Record*, August 24, 1913, 1.

# Meet the People
## on the
# North Bank Trails

(in alphabetical order)

# "Bachelor" Shoemaker

Surnames: Shoemaker

**One wagon, at least one soul**
**Omaha, Nebraska to Idaho or Montana**

**Mr. Shoemaker** (or "**Old Bachelor Shoemaker**," as South Bank Trail traveler **George Forman** calls him), is believed to be **Daniel Shoemaker Jr.**, a second-generation German American, born about 1805 in Preble, Ohio as the third oldest of nine children from Pennsylvania Quakers. With the Land Act of 1820, the United States government made tracts in the Northwest Territory available for settlement on a credit-based system.[189] The **Shoemakers** likely take advantage of this opportunity and relocate thirty miles across the Ohio state border to Wayne Township in Indiana where they establish a farm.[190]

In 1829, **Daniel Jr.** marries Miss Phebe Marine and by 1843, they have one daughter together. **Daniel Jr.** may have worked in carpentry, as his father encouraged his sons to do, though there is no record of his early employment. **Daniel Jr.'s** marriage does not last long and after his divorce in 1847, Phebe takes their only child with her into her second marriage. By 1860, both his ex-wife and daughter die, leaving the fifty-six-year-old with no reason to stay in the area.

Though there have been extensive searches for material to craft the backstory for **Daniel**, and numerous relative-descendants contacted for assistance with this request, a lack of specific mentions in empirical evidence

---

[189] The Northwest Territory included land north of the Ohio River, from the western border of Pennsylvania to the Mississippi River (presently Ohio, Indiana, Illinois, Michigan, Wisconsin, and parts of Minnesota).
[190] The 1820 U.S. Federal Census shows his father, Daniel Shoemaker Sr. living with seven children under the age of sixteen and two adults over the age of twenty-five. One daughter, Maria, may have married of died young, while the ninth child, Jesse, is not born until 1821.

makes this a challenge. Telling his story from within the Black Hills of Idaho, is made easier by first introducing his younger brother, Jesse Shoemaker.

Jesse is a well-known tourism and hospitality entrepreneur in Hall and Merrick counties in Nebraska. In 1859, Jesse and a business partner establish the Lone Tree Ranche next to a primitive stagecoach station, three miles outside of present-day Central City. At that time, there were no provisions available for weary travelers heading west until they reached far off settlements such as Denver or Salt Lake City. Starting in the Fall of '59, Jesse began transporting resources from Omaha to the Ranche. According to J. L. Campbell's emigrant guidebook, this roadside stop provided groceries, hay, and corn.[191]

Area historian, Alfred Andreas records in his 1882 book, *History of the State of Nebraska: Merrick County*, that, after only a few months, Jesse knew the business was profitable enough to warrant him bringing his whole family out.[192] Of those invited were Jesse's wife and children, siblings (both older and younger), and his mother-in-law.

In 1860, Jesse opens Shoemaker's Point, a family-run business, where his in-laws and siblings can contribute. It is located approximately eight to eleven miles west of the first, on the banks of Wood River. An 1861 newspaper advertisement for this place claims that the new "Ranche & Emigrant Station ... Keeps Hay, Grain, and Supplies. Good stables and Hotel accommodations. First-rate places to CAMP. Wood, water and grass, abundant."[193]

**Martha Roe**, Iowan in the **Roe Train**, mentions camping at this exact location during her journey. She writes about her Sabbath activities on June 5, 1864, "...writing a letter to Father   then singing and then supper and then gassing [or "chatting"] a while and then a good sing and prayrs and bead [bed] shoe makers Point."

Five days later, **Sarah Rousseau**, diarist in the **Pella Company**, comes by and comments: "We passed the Lone Tree Ranche this morning, we are now

---

[191] John L. Campbell, *Idaho, Six Months in the New Gold Regions: The Emigrant's Guide* (New York: Sinclair Tousey. 1864), 47.

[192] (The Western Historical Company: Chicago), 1882.

[193] "Jesse Shoemaker's Ranche & Emigrant Station: Shoemaker's Point," advertisement in *The Huntsman's Echo*, August 1, 1861.

about 130 miles from Omaha. Went a few miles and camped for the night."[194] Modern readers might guess that those "few miles" brought the **Pella Company** to the "Good accommodations" that Campbell's guidebook says can be found at Shoemaker's Point.[195]

In addition to the two resupply and respite businesses, Jesse purchases land south of Wood River on one of the riverine islands of the North Platte that the area is known for.[196] He names this business, "Shoemaker Island," and uses the water-locked property to raise horses and cattle. With this, Jesse posts herder-for-hire services.[197] Evidence shows Jesse employing his children and nephews, and most likely his older brother, **Daniel Jr.,** as teamsters for this shipping and herding task. The teamster position is comparable to a modern-day truck driver making long distance pick-ups and deliveries.

It is at this point, descendants believe **Daniel Shoemaker Jr.** becomes the "Old Bachelor" that **George Forman** meets along the South Bank Trail, with a load of leather, food and herd of horses. [198] In 1864, **Daniel Jr.** is fifty-nine and single. **George** claims that this man is "bound for Idaho," though no further details clarify if he is headed to the Boise Basin or to East Bannack and Alder Gulch in Montana Territory. **George** never mentions anyone else with the bachelor, though it would be expected to have assistants to manage all the animals.

Presently, no 1864 travel record has been found for *any* **Shoemaker** party, though alternate primary and secondary accounts help track the elusive man's movements and distances traveled through Nebraska and Idaho

---

[194] Sarah Rousseau, *The 1864 Diary of Mrs. Sarah Jane Rousseau* (Phoenix: M Press Publishing, 2023), June 10, 1864.
[195] J. L. Campbell, *Idaho, Six Months…*, 1864, 47.
[196] Eg., "Grand Island City."
[197] See the advertisement posted in *Grand Island Times* (Grand Island, NE) April 8, 1874, page 3: "NOTICE! We the undersigned wish to inform the public that we will make up a herd of cattle and horses on Shoemaker Island Hall county Neb to commence on the 1st day of May 1874. Persons wishing to have stock herded can deliver them at -Grand Island or at Shoemaker Island, in Platte River. For further particulars fee the undersigned Jesse & C. Shoemaker 8apr-3t."
[198] George Forman, "Biographical Sketch of the Life and Ancestry of Geo Forman of Stratford, Ontario, Canada", (unpublished manuscript), July 6, 1864. On the south side of the North Platte River, he may have been at Ficklin's Station, named after the superintendent of the Pony Express route, Benjamin F. Ficklin, which was approximately one mile west of present-day Melbeta, Nebraska.

Territories. From the entries, it appears **Daniel Jr.** travels at an impressive clip through the Black Hills, making more than twenty-five miles per day through the (presumably) familiar territory. He is reportedly robbed after rounding the "Big Bend" in the North Platte River and coming into the lowlands between the North Douglas Bend and Deer Creek garrison.[199]

In the **Pella Company, Sarah Rousseau** records on July 13: "...another train that they call the **Batcheler** [sic] had 28 head of horses taken the day after we lost ours."[200] Parties who are attacked on this same stretch of the trail that day retreat back to join a larger party for protection, **Daniel, Jr.** included. **Martha Roe** confirms this retreat on July 13 entry from the North Douglas Bend:

"the first thing we know[,] a man came up and gave the alarm of an attack of the Indians ahead ... we drove as fast as we could and drove on a huddle with the rest[.] learned that they [Indians] had stampeded and took 28 horses."[201]

The balance of **Daniel Jr.'s** trip is unclear. Neither the author nor the descendants know where he goes from there, or when he returns. It is unknown if he can even fulfill his leather and food delivery, or if he must return to Shoemaker Island to replace the stolen horses. Though an 1870 city directory for Omaha, Nebraska lists **Daniel Jr.** renting an apartment and working as a teamster, there is a considerable lack of specific empirical evidence to support the observed **"Bachelor Shoemaker"** being **Daniel Jr.** (as opposed to a different brother, son, nephew, or in-law). Ryan Shoemaker, a 3rd great-grandson of Jesse, explains, "**Daniel Shoemaker** is a bit of a mystery to our side of the family."[202] Kathy Lay, another 3rd great-grandchild agrees, "He is difficult to find information on," however, after reviewing every possibility, she believes **Daniel Jr.** to be "the best suspect so far."[203] As a caution, the author has decidedly eliminated the use of a first name from the forthcoming narrative.

---

[199] The author has coined this place opposite of Box Elder Creek, "Bixby Point."
[200] Sarah Rousseau, *1864 Diary,* July 17 (from the north bank emigrant camp near Deer Creek Garrison).
[201] See the Roe Train.
[202] Ryan Shoemaker, personal communication to author, April 16, 2023.
[203] Kathy Lay, personal communication to author, February 7, 2023.

**Primary Sources:**

None found.

**Secondary Sources:**

Molony, Janelle. "Jesse Shoemaker: Pioneer of Merrick County's
    Hospitality Tourism Industry." *History Nebraska* vol. 105, no.2, (Summer,
    2024).

# Shoemaker Roster

### Party 1: Unconfirmed to Idaho Territory

| Full Name | Birth Year, Approx. Age |
| --- | --- |
| NFN Shoemaker | Unknown |
| *Lone Traveler* | |

# Brown Train

Surnames: Brown

**Three wagons, ten souls**
**From Decorah, Iowa to Red Bluff, California**

In the **Brown Train** are surviving family members of pre-Civil War abolitionist John Brown, who was sentenced to death in 1859. In addition to being a conductor for the Underground Railroad,[204] JOhn is well known for his organization and leadership in two significant and provocative historical events:

1) The Pottawatomie Massacre of 1856 in Kansas Territory, in which John led five of his sons, including **Salmon Brown**, and three other radicals to murder pro-slavery voters in Kansas Territory. The effect of these deaths triggered additional guerilla violence between pro-slavery and anti-slavery supporters, including the Battle of Osawatomie and the Battle of Black Jack. One son died from the engagement. From then until Kansas joined the Union in 1861, the Territory was nicknamed "Bleeding Kansas."

2) Harpers Ferry Seize of 1859 in West Virginia, in which John would take more of his sons and associates with him to the Harpers Ferry Armory and Arsenal with the plan to seize the assets, funnel them through the Underground Railroad, then deliver them to slaves who could then emancipate themselves by either force or fall. While **Salmon** refused to participate in this, as did John's second wife, **Mary Brown**, one daughter was heavily involved as an accessory.

---

[204] Conductors helped physically guide slaves ("passengers") to freedom. Harriet Tubman is arguably the most famous conductor.

**Annie Brown**, who was only fifteen at the time, was fully aware of the plans and aided her father in the concealment of men who were gathering at the Kennedy Farm, a safe house located five miles from the target. She and a sister-in-law tended house and managed a social front to keep nosy neighbors away while the men stockpiled guns and supplies.

The seize was unsuccessful and ended much like the Battle of Alamo with every last man inside being given no escape. Ten men died in the event, including two more of John's sons. After being captured, John and a third son receive the death penalty. One son, Owen, escaped by virtue of being a guard and lookout still stationed at the Kennedy Farm on the day of the attack. He fled for his life. **Annie** and her sister-in-law were sent back to New York days prior, but the anguish and guilt drove **Annie's** sister-in-law insane and some believe that after delivering her (now) fatherless baby, she willed herself to die. In later years, **Annie** admitted that she never fully recovered from the consequences of the Siege.

After these traumatic events, and the fall of John Brown, the **Brown family** needs to get away from the persecution they experience while in their North Elba, New York home. The surviving family members became destitute celebrities. Supporters petitioned to make a relief fund for the widows and fatherless. Encouraging letters and donations from sympathizers pile in, but **Mary** has widows, grandchildren, and three daughters to care for and only one son able to earn an income.

**Salmon** helps how he can, but by 1863, he has a wife and two small children to provide for and the pressure on him increases. He repeatedly loses job opportunities due to his and his father's reputation. In one of the family's lowest moments, supporters offer to adopt **Mary's** children from her. **Mary**, a native New Yorker, daughter of a hard-working blacksmith, and mother of eighteen,[205] refuses to cave under the pressure, but seeing her children suffer is too high a cost. She sends her eldest daughters away to school and hopes they can find employment. **Annie** and **Sarah,** attend school in Concord, Massachusetts and board at an Underground Railroad stop: the home of Louisa May Alcott, famed author of the *Little Women* series.

Years later, excitement over John Brown's role in delivering the first shot of the Civil War has still not simmered down. In 1861, Union soldiers start marching to the tune of the old folk song, "Glory Hallelujah," and singing new lyrics:

> *John Brown's body lies a-mouldering in the grave,*
> *John Brown's body lies a-mouldering in the grave,*
> *John Brown's body lies a-mouldering in the grave,*
> *His soul goes marching on![206]*

In early 1862, twenty-six year-old **Salmon** enlists with Company K of the New York Regiment as a commissioned lieutenant. He travels with the regiment as far as Albany, "but when the officers found that a son [of] John Brown was among them they demanded his resignation...," according to his wife.[207] This rejection stings. In his own words, **Salmon** reports, "I felt hurt and humiliated that I should be unwelcome in a regiment which was ready enough to sing that my father's body lay a mouldering in the grave..."[208]

Not long after, an uncle of **Abbie's** visits the **Browns** in upstate New York, "and told such glowing tales of [California] ... that we felt impelled to emigrate to that land of golden opportunities."[209] The decision is easy for **Salmon** who claims he just wants to "go away."[210] When **Salmon**

---

[205] Mary Brown bore John thirteen children of her own, as well as raising five of seven children from his first wife.

[206] Lyrics by James E. Greenleef, C. S. Hall, and C. B. Marsh, 1861.

[207] Abbie C. Hinckley Brown, "Across the Plains in the Early 60's as Told by One Who Participated in the Stirring Events of That Adventureous Western Era," *Lake Placid News,* September 29, 1916, 5-7.

[208] Salmon Brown, 1914 communications and 1916 Interview with Fred Lockley, quoted in Bonnie Laughlin-Schultz, *The Tie That Bound Us: The Women of John Brown's Family and The Legacy of Radical Abolitionism* (New York: Cornell University Press, 2013), 93.

[209] Abbie Brown, "Across the Plains..." *Lake Placid News,* Sept. 29, 1916.

[210] Salmon Brown, 1914 and 1916, quoted in *The Tie That Bound Us* (2013), 96.

approaches his mother with this idea, she is favorable and the family makes arrangements to leave New York as soon as possible.

In September of 1863, "**Salmon's** family, **Mary**, and **Ellen** first took a train out..." [to Ohio, to visit Owen, then,] "they continued west, arriving in the early Winter of 1863-1864 in Decorah, Iowa where **Sarah** and **Annie** were to meet them."[211] At this time, **Annie** is teaching at a school for free African-American children.

Though various sources conclude that **Salmon** felt swayed by a piece of farm land that was too good to pass up, perhaps he also felt a degree of security in this state. Decorah may have been a safe haven along the route where John Brown had once escorted a group fugitive slaves through the state on the way to Canada, with the aid of "Railroad Agent," Josiah Grinnell.[212]

After an exceptionally cold Winter, the **Brown** women complain. Iowa is no substitute for the sunshine they were promised. So, **Salmon** sells the farm and in April of 1864, they begin West again. He packs up three covered wagons: one for his immediate family, one for his mother and sisters, and a third to haul six Spanish Merino sheep that he intended to breed and sell the wool. With the family as teamsters are two young men who are also dazzled by the California dream.[213]

**Salmon's** wife **Abbie** records that their trip may have been doomed from the start. "Before we started from Decarah [Decorah], in Iowa ... a man who was going from that town ... arrived at Council Bluffs and told them [the newspapers] that the family of John Brown was going to cross the Plains. From there[,] the news preceeded us... That was how the rebels ... found out that we were on the way."[214]

---

[211] Bonnie Laughlin-Schultz, *The Tie That Bound Us: The Women of John Brown's Family and The Legacy of Radical Abolitionism* (New York: Cornell University Press, 2013), 97-98.

[212] This occurred in February of 1859, months before the Harpers Ferry Siege. A local church allegedly purchased six-shooters and Josiah Grinnell (of Grinnell, Iowa) allowed the use of his parlor room to stockpile the arms and host the "passengers."

[213] In Daniel Rosenberg's 1975 essay, "Mary Brown: From Harpers Ferry to California," a reference is made to these men being a George (NLN) and Mr. (NFN) Smith. In Abbie Brown's memoir, she calls them "two young men who wished to go to California and drive the team for their board."

[214] Abbie Brown, "Across the Plains…" *Lake Placid News*, Sept. 29, 1916.

The **Browns** took rumors of Indian depredations seriously from the start and as early as in Nebraska, they begin looking for other families to join with to increase their chances of crossing the Plains unharmed. At different points along the way, they make friendly, though reserved, connections with other Iowans passing by.

**Salmon** strives to keep their identities anonymous, just in case a Confederate or Southern Sympathizer should feel the need to express their ongoing hatred toward the family, though **Martha Roe** identifies the family members by name from the very beginning of their meeting.[215] This may have something to do with their shared connections to Grinnell history.

From July 10-11, the **Browns** and **Roes** camp with the **Pella Company** after being alarmed by a close encounter with Indians. **Sarah Rousseau** in the **Pella Company** only ever refers to the **Browns** as the "**New York Train.**" In time, the **Browns** create a special bond with the **Olivers,** who prove themselves trustworthy companions and seem to already know who the **Browns** are, regardless of any false identity **Salmon** may have tried to pass off on them.

Two days later, after another close call, the **Browns** and their new friends in the **Oliver Train** gather with a larger group of travelers consisting of the **Howard Train** (aka the "Tennessee Train" full of Sympathizers) and another wagon train full of **Missourians** (who are Confederate "Rebels," per **Abbie's** memoir). "Only hours after this amalgamation[,] the wagon train was harassed by several hundred Sioux."[216] **Abbie** remembers the Indians being "armed to the teeth with guns and lances," encircling them and making a grab at her sister-in-law, **Annie's,** long hair. [217] The almost nineteen-year-old screams in terror, which elicits laughter amongst their harassers.

With some smooth talking by the leaders in this traveling group, and with a not-so-subtle show of arms, the Indians ride off. The **Brown's** gratitude towards their protectors quickly fades when their true identities

---

[215] Martha Roe uses a conventional spelling of "Broun."

[216] Daniel Rosenberg, "Mary Brown: From Harpers Ferry to California" (Occasional Paper Series No. 7, The American Institute for Marxist Studies, 1975), 21.

[217] Abbie Brown, "Across the Plains…" *Lake Placid News*, Sept. 29, 1916.

are figured out. They feel pressured to remain in company with the **Howards** and **Missourians**, especially when another attack could happen any day, but their time together only provides time for the Southerners to form a plot to rape and murder the **Browns**.

When a couple of men defect from the Southerners and confirm the plans to **Salmon**, the **Browns** flee with every ounce of energy they can squeeze out of their stock animals. They charge forward, day and night being chased by people who promise that if they catch up, blood will be spilled. The **Browns** reach safety at Camp Conner in Idaho, where they inform Camp Commander, Captain David Black, about their pursuers. Three hours later, the **Howards** and **Missourians** roll in and face an Army intervention that sends both parties packing in opposite directions, displacing each by sending them hundreds of miles out of their way.

The primary narrative for the **Brown Train's** 1864 journey comes from the 1914 memoirs of **Abbie Brown**, which were originally published in a 1916 issue of New York's *Lake Placid News.* Unfortunately, the details are lacking powerful anchor points characteristic of journals or diaries: dates and locations. This makes conjecture (connecting the dots) more necessary than is ideal. Fortunately, the first-person accounts of **Martha Roe** and **Sarah Rousseau** and the descendant research on the **Oliver** and **Howard Trains** make this process easier. In addition to these eyewitness and descendant-vetted reports, there are innumerable news articles from 1864 reporting facts and details that corroborate the movements of the **Brown** family, and the subsequent chase after the Platte River Raids.


**Primary Sources:**

Brown, Abbie C. Hinckley. "Across the Plains in the Early 60's as Told by one who Participated in the Stirring Events of That Adventureous Western Era." *Lake Placid News*, September 29, 1916, 5-7.[218]

---

[218] Note: This item has been edited by Will Bagley and reprinted in the *Overland Journal, 37,* no. 2 (Summer 2019), 68-76.

Brown, Salmon. 1914 communications and 1916 Interview with Fred Lockley, quoted in Bonnie Laughlin-Schultz, *The Tie That Bound Us: The Women of John Brown's Family and The Legacy of Radical Abolitionism.* New York: Cornell University Press, 2013.

**Secondary Sources:**

Bennet, Addison. "Son of John Brown, Noted Raider, Lives in Portland." *Oregonian.* February 25, 1917.

"John Brown's Son in Portland," *The Daily Journal.* April 20, 1901, 5.

Laughlin-Schultz, Bonnie. *The Tie That Bound Us: The Women of John Brown's Family and The Legacy of Radical Abolitionism.* New York: Cornell University Press, 2013.

Lockley, Fred. "Observations and Impressions of the Journal Man." *Oregon Daily Journal.* May 29, 1919, 8.

M.H.F. "A Brave Life." *Overland Monthly and Out West Magazine,* 6, no. 34, October 1885, 360-367.

Reck, Al. "John Brown's Family Comes West: Chapter 1—John Brown's Family Comes West." *Oakland Tribune.* January 8, 1961, 4-M.

Reck, Al. "John Brown's Family Comes West: Chapter 2—John Brown's Family Comes West." *Oakland Tribune.* January 15, 1961, 4-M.

Reck, Al. "John Brown's Family Comes West: Chapter 3—Indians Terrorize John Brown Party." *Oakland Tribune.* January 22, 1961, 4-M.

Rosenberg, Daniel. "Mary Brown: From Harpers Ferry to California." Occasional Paper Series No. 7, The American Institute for Marxist Studies, 1975.

"The Brown Family." *Gold Hill Daily News.* September 29, 1864. (Transcribed in the Appendix.)

Webster, Sandra. "Mary Ann Day Brown, Widow of John Brown." *The Adirondack Almanack*. March 26, 2016.

# Brown Train Roster

## Party 1: Decorah, IA to Red Bluff, CA

| Full Name | Birth Year, Approx. Age |
| --- | --- |
| Salmon Brown | 1836, 28 |
| *Wagon Master, Son of John and Mary Brown* | |
| Abigail "Abbie" C. Hinckley Brown | 1839, 25 |
| *Wife, Memoirist* | |
| Cora A. Brown | 1860, 4 |
| *Daughter* | |
| Minnie Eliza Brown | 1863, 1 |
| *Daughter* | |

## Party 2: Decorah, IA to Red Bluff, CA

| | |
| --- | --- |
| Mary Ann Day Brown | 1816, 48 |
| *Head of Household, Widow of John Brown* | |
| Anne "Annie" Brown | 1843, 19 |
| *Daughter* | |
| Sarah Sadie Brown | 1846, 16 |
| *Daughter* | |
| Ellen Brown | 1854, 10 |
| *Daughter* | |

*[Continued]*

## Other Individuals: Iowa to California

George (NLN)                          N/A
*Teamster/Driver*

(NFN) Smith                           N/A
*Teamster/Driver*

# Howard Train, AKA "Howard Caravan"

Surnames: Howard - Scroggin - Birks

**At least seventeen wagons, at least seventy-six souls
From Marshall Co., Iowa to the Pacific Northwest**

The **Howard Train** is captained by the most senior traveler featured in this book. **Charles Howard** is seventy years old and his wife **Mary** is sixty-six when they embark on their journey across the Plains. **Charles** and **Mary** travel with at least seventy-six souls (plus four additional hired drivers). Those known to be traveling with them are as follows: three of **Charles'** siblings, including the widow and family of his deceased brother **Allen**; three of their adult children with grandchildren and some great-grandchildren; plus five other nieces and nephews who were more or less adopted by the **Howards**.

Though **Charles** was born in North Carolina but he and his siblings grow up in Haywood, Tennessee. By 1851, the **Howards** move en masse to Marshall County, Iowa. Over the years, neighboring families (**Birks** and **Carpenters**) intermarry with the **Howards.** With the sheer size and age ranges of children in the family, there are some overlapping relationships such as **Lucetta** and **Elizabeth Carpenter** marrying **Martin Van Buren Howard** and his nephew **Charles,** respectively, causing the sisters to become an aunt and niece to each other. There is also an occasional marriage between first cousins.[219]

By 1860, many of the **Howard** and **Birks** families live in the Timber Creek area of Marshall County, but to use an old adage, you can take the **Howards** out of the South, but you can't take the South out of the **Howards**.

---

[219] In Council Bluffs, Iowa, on May 29, 1864, Harry Greene Hill (son of Elizabeth Ann Howard) marries Martha "Mattie" Virginia Howard (daughter of James W. Howard, brother to both Elizabeth and Charles).

During the Civil War, young men begrudgingly serve in the Union Army (though some enroll with the Confederates, pitting cousin against cousin).[220] Between 1862 and 1864, bachelors end up marrying the nearest eligible bride–one way to avoid or delay one's conscription to the Union. In another case, **Charles'** firstborn son **William** paid a deferral fee of $200.00 to delay the service demand on his son **Martin**–a modern-day equivalent of $4,600. [221]

Their departure from Iowa is said to be prompted by social conflicts. Though the family is anti-slavery in principle, they openly support the Confederacy, which makes them "unwelcome" everywhere they go (first in Tennessee, then in Iowa).[222] Early in 1864, **Charles** attends a town meeting where at the mention of a Confederate battle win, "**Charles** tosses his hat into the air and says, 'Hurrah for Jeff Davis.'"[223] This flippant remark brings the crowd surging to their feet to silence the Southern Sympathizer. A lawyer in attendance settles the crowd, but the townspeople ostracize the **Howards** and their leaving becomes imperative.

Some family historians speculate **Charles** does not assume full leadership of the hegira,[224] suggesting instead that he delegates this authority to his eldest son **William**, a forty-year-old clergyman.[225] In Mid-April, the massive caravan sets a course from Saint Joseph, Missouri (where they outfitted) to Northern California, "well-armed and well provisioned."[226] They head out with mostly ox-drawn prairie schooners, but **William** had also

---

[220] In the Brown Train, memoirist Abbie Brown elaborates, "Many of that train were deserters from [General Sterling] Prices' army" (1916).

[221] Randall Lovejoy, "The Howard Wagon Train", *The Genie* 22, no. 4. (1988), 201.

[222] Richard C. Smith, public forum communication, 2005. "The Ancestry and Family History of Louise Anna (Kielley) Booth of Grand Forks ND," http://kielle.ancestryregister.com/00005Kielley_web/KIELLEBIBLIO00005.htm

[223] Lovejoy, *The Howard Wagon Train* (1998), 201. Jefferson Davis served as the president of the Confederate States from 1861 until 1865.

[224] A hegira is a group escaping persecution by seeking freedom or asylum in a new country.

[225] Randall Lovejoy, great-grandson of the newlyweds Jeremiah and Mary Birks, proposes the younger generation as the wagon master, while Charles is the leader in name only, but other researchers have maintained that Charles represented the Howards in both name and deed. See Roberta Everett, "Mary Elizabeth Henderson Howard (23 June 1798-19 Dec 1879), *Find a Grave.com* [Memorial ID 34496072], last modified January 3, 2023, https://www.findagrave.com/memorial/34496072/mary-elizabeth-howard.

[226] Lovejoy, "The Howard Wagon Train" (1998), 201.

gifted his newlywed daughter, **Mary Birks (Howard),** with a handsome span of horses which may have enticed the Northern Plains Indians to approach the large caravan in the Black Hills.[227]

During one evening camp, while women were preparing dinner, "a large band of painted warriors circled on their horses around the **Howard** camp. The men quietly got their guns ... [but] **William Henry Howard** advised them not to make the first move," writes Randall Lovejoy, great-grandson of **Jeremiah and Mary (Howard) Birks** (*The Howard Wagon Train,* 1998, 202). After a show of friendly intentions, the Indians "began taking seats and helping themselves to the meal."[228] At some point, the leader of this band makes it known that he wants to buy (or trade for) **William's** daughter. At fourteen-years-old, **Nancy** is an attractive youth with long blonde hair.

Tensions run high and the **Howard men** feel threatened by the tribal band's behaviors. While the **Howards** keep their weapons close and ready, **William** approaches the leader and explains to him that what they are doing and asking for is rude. After this conversation, "the chief gave a low whistle" and "his warriors hastily arose and followed him out of camp."[229] On that occasion, the **Howard Train** remains unmolested, though **William** hides **Nancy** away, inside a wagon, for the rest of the journey.[230]

Later, however, while the members of the train are asleep, a thundering sound pulls them from their dreams. "The very earth seemed [to be] trembling," but this earthquake is actually the stampeding away of their stock animals.[231] Someone loosed the animals from their corral and picket lines under cover of darkness. The **Howard men** mount their few remaining horses and chase after the scattering animals. The cattle had not gone far and are easy to round up, but it takes an entire day to locate and wrangle the

---

[227] Mary and Jeremiah Birks married before the journey in Marengo, Iowa. Pleasant Scroggin and Sarah Howard Scroggin also travel with eight heads of horses.
[228] Lovejoy, "The Howard Wagon Train" (1998), 202.
[229] Ibid., 201.
[230] From the Brown Train, there is a remarkably similar story of the youthful Abbie Brown being harassed by Indians because of her beautiful hair.
[231] Ibid., 202.

horses. "They felt certain that the Indians had caused the stampede, although they never knew for sure" (Lovejoy, 202).

During close encounters with the **Brown Train**, someone in the **Howard Train** recognizes their association with John Brown, leader of the 1859 siege on Harpers Ferry armory in West Virginia. Someone with the **Howard Train** allegedly threatens to finish delivering justice to the family of the abolitionist, with particular comments made about **Abbie** becoming pregnant with a Confederate's baby.

After the Union Army releases emigrant families from an imposed travel ban at Deer Creek, the **Browns** make a fearful dash to stay far ahead of the **Howards**. At Camp Conner in Soda Springs, Idaho,[232] the commander Captain David Black apprehends **Charles** and his nephew **Oliver**, because of accusations made by the **Browns**. The commander demands these men recite the Oath of Allegiance in an impromptu naturalization ceremony.[233] This process walks the oath-taker through renouncing their loyalty to their former country and making a commitment to uphold the constitution of the United States.

**Charles** feels humiliated by the patriotic demand. Besides noting that his family had been living north of the Mason-Dixie line for over a decade, he responds by reciting his military accomplishments in the War of 1812 as a Tennessee Mounted Gunman. Then, he rattles off his ancestral lineage from the **Howard's** arrival on the Mayflower ship through to their contributions in the Revolutionary War. His long-winded answer appeases the post commander, but as a peacekeeping measure, the commander assigns military

---

[232] Randall Lovejoy cites that this impromptu mitigation occurs at Fort Hall but it is likely a typo error. Stronger evidence for Soda Springs and Camp Conner come from Abbie Brown's mention of the Morrisite colony: "We traveled nearly a week before we reached Soda Springs where a colony of Morrisites, who had seceded from the Mormons, were living and being protected by soldiers" (Abbie Brown's Memoir, 1916).

[233] An 1860's Oath of Allegiance signature page with a space for notarization is viewable through the Library of Congress. It reads: "I do solemnly ___ that I will support, protect, and defend the Constitution and Government of the United States against all enemies, whether domestic or foreign, and that I will bear true faith, allegiance, and loyalty to the same, any ordinance, resolution, or law of any State Convention or Legislature to the contrary notwithstanding; and further, that I will do this with a full determination, pledge, and purpose, without any mental reservation or evasion whatsoever; and, further, that I will well and faithfully perform all the duties which may be required of me by law. So help me God."

escorts to start the **Browns** and **Howards** out from the fort in different directions: the **Browns** to California; the **Howards** to Oregon.

**Charles'** nephew and adopted son, **Alfred Kennedy**, is twenty-one when crossing the Plains. He keeps a daily journal of the trip, along with a full roster of those who came along (though this item has since become lost). [234] Without this source document, facts about the journey come from descendant reminiscences, published obituaries and pioneer biographies, and from the extensive research of family historian, Randall Lovejoy.

Supporting facts also come from **Gerrit Roorda**, a trail diarist from the **Jongewaard Train,** who captures multiple interactions with the **Howard Train**. In addition, the recollections of **Abbie Brown** place the **Howards** behind them near the North Douglas Bend. There, they gather nearly eighty wagons in response to hearing reports of treacherous Sioux tribes in the area. This explains why both **Howard** and **Brown** accounts describe the emigrants as already on the defensive when the Indians arrive.

**Primary Sources:**

Kennedy, Alfred H. *The Howard Trek Across the Plains: 1864 Diary,* (unpublished).

**Secondary Sources:**

"Former Linn "Pioneer Dies." Obituary of Rachel Anne Gillespie Howard. *Albany Democrat* (Oregon), December 10, 1920, 1.

Lovejoy, Randall. *The House of Howard: A compilation of the genealogy of the Howard Family*, with Richard C. Smith (unpublished, undated).

Lovejoy, Randall. "The Howard Wagon Train." *The Genie*, 22, no. 4. (1988): 201-206.

---

[234] The location of this item is presently unknown. The last known owner, was Marjorie Wakefield (born Helen Zumker) who is the adopted granddaughter of Martha "Mattie" Howard Hill and a third cousin, once removed to Randall Lovejoy. Marjorie had no descendants upon her death in 1999.

Stoller, Ruth. "Sheridan – A.B. Faulconer's Town." *Old Yamhill: The Early History of its Towns and Cities*, (Yamhill: Yamhill Co. Historical Society, 1976): 72-73.

Whitley, Edythe R. "Family Histories: Howard." *Red River Settlers* (Baltimore: Clearfield Company, 1980), 33.

# Howard Train Roster

## Party 1: Marshall Co., IA to Le Grande or Yamhill, OR

| Full Name | Birth Year, Approx. Age |
| --- | --- |
| Charles Murphy Howard
*Captain* | 1794, 70 |
| Mary Elizabeth H. R. Howard
*Wife* | 1798, 66 |
| Andrew Jackson Myers
*Charles Howard's nephew and farmhand* | 1834, 30 |

## Party 2: Marshall Co., IA to Umatilla, OR

| | |
| --- | --- |
| Rev. William Henry Howard
*First-born Son of Charles and Mary* | 1824, 40 |
| Margaret Wilson Howard
*Wife* | 1824, 40 |
| Nancy Eugenia Arabella Howard
*Daughter* | 1850, 14 |
| Sarah Jane Lee Howard
*Daughter* | 1855, 9 |
| John Robert Howard
*Son* | 1859, 5 |
| William Howard
*Son* | 1861, 3 |
| James Ashley Howard
*Son* | 1863, 1 |

## Party 3: Marshall Co., IA to Yamhill, OR (then to CA)

Charles Augustus Howard                    1834, 30
*Sixt-hborn Son of Charles and Mary*

Elizabeth Jane Carpenter Howard            1836, 28
*Wife, sister of Lucetta Carpenter Howard*

## Party 4: Marshall Co., IA to Albany, OR

James Lawrence Howard                      1838, 26
*Eighth-born Son of Charles and Mary*

Rachael Anne Gillespie Howard              1846, 18
*Wife*

William Franklin "Frank" Howard            1863, 1
*Son*

## Party 5: Marshall Co., IA to Umatilla, OR

Jeremiah Birks                             1844, 20
*Head of Household, brother of John T. Birks*

Mary Henderson Howard Birks                1846, 18
*Wife, Daughter of Rev. Wm. Howard, Granddaughter of Charles and Mary*

Phoebe Ellen Birks                         Due Feb. 1865
*Daughter, unborn*

## Party 6: Marshall Co., IA to Yamhill, OR

Martin Van Buren Howard                    1842, 22
*Son of Rev. Wm. Howard, Grandson of Charles and Mary*

Lucetta Larue Carpenter Howard             1843, 21
*Wife, sister of Elizabeth Carpenter Howard*

## Party 7: Marshall Co., IA to Yamhill, OR

Pleasant Marion Scroggin                   1833, 35
*Head of Household, widower to John Birk's sister*

Sarah Elizabeth Howard Scroggin            1836, 32
*Second wife, daughter of Charles and Mary*

| Charles Carter Scroggin | 1858, 6 |
|---|---|
| *Son* | |

| Mary Frances Scroggin | 1859, 5 |
|---|---|
| *Daughter* | |

| Stephen Leonard Scroggin | 1860, 4 |
|---|---|
| *Son* | |

| Martha Alice Scroggin | 1864, 0 |
|---|---|
| *Daughter* | |

## Party 8: Marshall Co., IA to Yamhill, OR

John T. Birks          1839, 25
*Head of Household, Brother of Jeremiah Birks*

Virginia Ann Howard Birks      1840, 24
*Wife, Daughter of Charles and Elizabeth, Granddaughter of Charles and Mary*

William Robert Riley Birks      1862, 2
*Son*

## Party 9: Marshall Co., IA to Yamhill, OR

Elizabeth W. Shropshire Howard    1800, 64
*Sister-in-Law to Charles and Mary, Widow of Charles' brother Allen*

Calvin Baston Howard        1837, 27
*Son*

Nancy Emily Howard         1814, 51
*Sister to Charles, Widowed by James Wilkinson*

## Party 10: Johnson Co., IA to Solano Co., CA

James Webster Howard       1816, 48
*Brother to Charles*

Mary Jane Justus Howard      1822, 42
*Second wife*

Elizabeth Boyd Howard       1840, 24
*Daughter of James and first wife, Sarah*

Edward Charles Howard                          1850, 14
*Son, firstborn from second wife, Mary*

Henry Clay Howard                              1852, 12
*Son*

Jasper Howard                                  1854, 10
*Son*

Lucinda Howard                                 1855, 9
*Daughter*

James Webster Howard Jr.                       1858, 6
*Son*

Emily Ann Howard                               1861, 3
*Daughter*

Helen Edmondson Howard                         1863, 1
*Daughter*

## Party 11: Marshall Co., IA to Yamhill, OR

William Albert Howard                          1818, 46
*Son of Allen and Elizabeth Howard, Nephew to Charles and Mary*

Mary Hannah Howard                             1821, 43
*Wife*

Oliver Perry Howard                            1842, 22
*Son*

Mary Jane Howard                               1844, 20
*Daughter*

Allen Hardy Howard                             1846, 18
*Son*

Samuel Filmore Howard                          1849, 15
*Son*

William "Willie" Albert Howard                 1859, 5
*Son*

## Party 12: Johnson Co., IA to Walla Walla, WA

Oliver Perry Howard                    1822, 42
*Son of Allen and Elizabeth Howard, Nephew to Charles and Mary*

Rosanna "Rosa" Smith Howard            1833, 31
*Wife*

Dallas Howard                          1852, 12
*Daughter*

Silas Howard                           1854, 10
*Son*

Alphaeus Howard                        1856, 8
*Son*

Emerita "Emma" Camille Howard          1858, 6
*Daughter*

Jasper Howard                          1861, 3
*Son*

## Party 13: Johnson Co., IA to Walla Walla, WA

Thomas Hill Howard                     1824, 40
*Son of Allen and Elizabeth Howard, Widower, Nephew to Charles and Mary*

Theodore Frelinghugsen Howard          1853, 10
*Son*

Joshua Allen Howard                    1854, 9
*Son*

Clarence Edwards Howard                1856, 8
*Son*

Sarah Elizabeth Howard                 1858, 6
*Daughter*

## Party 14: Linn Co., IA to Astoria, OR

"Dr." Wyatt Alonzo Wherry                    1818, 46
*Head of Household, the "doctor" on the trip, farmer by occupation*

Roenna Josephine Hill Wherry              1829, 35
*Wife, daughter to Dabney and Elizabeth Hill, Niece to Charles and Mary*

William Wyatt Wherry                          1850, 14
*Son*

Elizabeth Suzannah Wherry                 1851, 13
*Daughter*

Charles May Wherry                             1853, 11
*Son*

Samuel Alonzo Wherry                         1855, 9
*Son*

Andrew Jackson Wherry                       1857, 7
*Son*

Thomas Jefferson Wherry                     1860, 4
*Son*

John Robert Wherry                             1862, 2
*Son*

## Party 15: Johnson Co., IA to Union Co., OR

Lucinda Kennedy[235]                            1837, 27
*Niece and adopted daughter of Charles and Mary*

Alfred Harrison Kennedy                      1843, 21
*Nephew and adopted son of Charles and Mary, trail diarist*

## Other Individuals:

4 Unnamed Teamster/Drivers          N/A

---

[235] Parents are John and Edna (Howard) Kennedy, both deceased.

**Mentions Only (they do not complete the journey):**

Dabney Pettis Hill                        1790, 74
*Head of Household*

Elizabeth Ann Howard[236]                 1798, 66
*Wife, sister to Charles Howard*

Dr. Harry Greene Hill                     1839, 25
*Son, Nephew to Charles and Mary*

Martha "Mattie" Virginia Howard Hill   1838, 26
*Daughter-in-law, Daughter of James and Sarah Howard, Niece to Charles and Mary*

---

[236] The eldest daughter of James Weber Howard, Martha marries Harry Hill in Council Bluffs, IA on May 29, 1864 then remains behind.

# Jongewaard Train

Surnames: Jongewaard - Jot - Mars - Van der Meer - DeVries - Ellerbroek - Roorda - van Rossum.

**At least 7 wagons, 49-50 souls**
**From Pella, Iowa to Grande Ronde Valley, Oregon**

The **Jongewaard** and **Rysdams** families are Iowa pioneers who left the Netherlands in the 1840s and '50s to escape disagreeable religious and political conditions. The initial wave of Dutch immigrants settle in Pella, Iowa with the Reformist Reverend Hendrick Scholte who named the city.

Some of the emigrants leaving Iowa for Oregon in 1864 are not naturalized due to their age upon immigration from Europe and are still considered aliens in the country. They feel forced to leave Iowa, in part, because Governor Sam Kirkwood makes a demand that they either leave the country or become citizens (and consequently eligible for conscription).[237] The ultimatum discounts the fact that Marion County residents consistently met volunteer quotas for war service.

It is unclear if the families and neighbors intended to stay together as one unit while traveling, but in truth, the train is divided from the get-go. Members of the **Rysdam Train** depart May 1, five days in advance of the **Jongewaard Train**. The delay is caused by one man, **Gerrit Roorda,** who has a terrible throat infection requiring a last minute doctor's visit. Further, some suspicion has been made into whether or not the two leaders could get along for the duration of the trip. While this is a valid excuse for splitting even the best of friends on an endurance-based journey, conclusive evidence is unavailable.

The Dutch families remain divided until after the Platte River Raids, where they will meet near Casper, Wyoming and compare stories of survival. The narrative in this book primarily follows the **Jongewaard Train**. The **Jongewaards** have several

---

[237] Samuel J. Kirkwood (Term: 1860-1064). In January of 1864, he is replaced by William M. Stone (Term: 1864-1868), whose policies, in turn, offend the Earp family of the Pella Company.

friendly interactions with familiar Iowa names featured in this book. Particularly clear entries in **Gerrit's** log of meeting others are:

> On June 7, **Gerrit** writes that two men from the **Jongewaard Train** are sent back to look for the "Curtis Company" (AKA **Pella Company**) who were with the **Oliver Train** at that time (also referenced on June 5 in Columbus, NE).

> On June 11, **Gerrit** writes he met back up with the Curtis Company at Wood River. He specifically names Israel Curtis, "Th." (Tom) Ellis, and "another man" from the **Pella Company**.

> On June 15, **Gerrit** claims the train, "caught up with," the **Howard Train**, and later "joined" them (temporarily) on June 17.

In the early hours of July 13, those in the **Jongewaard Train** wake up near the North Platte River's northernmost bend through the mountains, just past McKinstry Ridge. Their morning attackers use a double-team strategy to maximize impact. Some sneak amid the livestock and silently cut them free from picket lines and tethers. Then, when the others appear and startle the emigrant camp, the loose animals are easily stampeded away. With the major loss, only a few men can pursue the Indians on the three remaining horseback: **Isaac DeVries**, **Teunis Burgraff,** and **Barend "Ten" Broek**. In the small battle that breaks out, it seems more horses are harmed than people.

**Jana Jongewaard**, who was a toddler at the time, later recalls for historian Charles Dyke that the fearful mothers, "lined up the canvas wagon covers with their feather beds so as to protect the women and children, and while the arrows penetrated the canvas, they sank harmlessly in the feathers."[238] When the attack comes to a lull, the men on horseback make a dash to find help but are mistaken for being the horse thieves they wish to report on. Union soldiers on the trail shoot at and arrest two of them until they can explain their way free. The third man, **Isaac**, hides until he can find his way back to the train. Fortunately, no person is reported killed or maimed in the military skirmish, but every last horse is killed or injured.

The primary source document for the **Jongewaard's** story is **Gerrit Roorda's** daily log book. He is a wagon driver for **Lutje Mars**. Unfortunately, during the transcription of his log, the incorrect date of 1861 was recorded in the title. Certainly

---

[238] As told by Mary Ellerbroek-Hornstra, "The Oregon Trail," in Charles Dyke's *The Story of Sioux County*, (Orange City: n.p., 1942), 411.

with careful evaluation of the overlaid stories presented in this book, readers will see the undeniable connection to the year of 1864 and any doubt can be put to rest. A small portion of supporting material also comes from Allie Brunia. She writes a recollection of her own journey west through the "Panama Route" by boat to San Francisco. In her story, she confirms, "some relatives and friends had preceded by wagon-train, as Uncle **Gerrit E. Roorda** did" (*Roorda Family History*, 61-62).

Charles Dyke, author of 1942 book, *The Story of Sioux City,* also captured detailed recollections of three children from **Lutje Mars** and **Cornelius Jongewaard,** though the original interviews he held with them are not available to modern researchers. An account of the **Rysdam Train's** journey, as well as an in-depth backstory of the Dutch emigration from the Netherlands into Iowa can be found in Toni Rysdam-Shorre's 1985 book, *Gerrit… A Dutchman in Oregon.*

Of interest to many western historians is marital link between the **Rysdams** and the **Earp family** (in the **Pella Company**). After **Magdelena Rysdam** elopes with **Virgil Earp** in 1860, patriarchs **Gerrit Rysdam** and **Nicholas Earp** coordinate an annulment by crafting a tale about **Virgil's** death while fighting in the Civil War. Though there is no evidence to suggest the ex-in-laws hold animosity towards one another, there is certainly a motivating factor to limit any time spent together on the trail: **Virgil** is very much alive and well.[239] If a casual word were to pass to **Magdelena** (who is traveling with her toddler-aged daughter from **Virgil**), the betrayal could cause a terrible scene.

**Primary Sources:**

Brunia, Allie. "A Trip to Oregon in 1864." *Roorda Family History,* Private publishing by William Frans Brunia, 1984, 61-62.

Ellerbroek, John. "The Oregon Trail," in Charles L. Dyke's *The Story of Sioux County*, 2nd ed. (Orange City: n.p., 1942): 402-412.

Ellerbroek-Hornstra, Mary. "The Oregon Trail," in Charles L. Dyke's *The Story of Sioux County*, 2nd ed. (Orange City: n.p., 1942): 411-412.

---

[239] Virgil and older half-brother Newton Earp are currently serving in the Union Army.

Jongewaard-Bogaard, Janna C. "The Oregon Trail," in Charles L. Dyke's *The Story of Sioux County*, 2nd ed. (Orange City: n.p., 1942): 404-412.

Roorda, Gerrit. "Day Book of Gerrit E. Roorda, 1861 [sic, 1864]." *Roorda Family History*. Private publishing by William Frans Brunia, 1984, 37-34. (Copy held in Geisler Library Archives of Central College in Pella, IA.)

**Secondary Sources:**

Beltman, Brian W. "Civil War Reverberations: Exodus and Return Among the Pella Dutch During the 1860s." In *The Dutch-American Experience: Essays in Honor of Robert P. Swierenga*, Edited by Hans Krabbendam and Larry J. Wagenaar (Amsterdam: VU Uitgeverij, 2000).

Beltman, Brian W. *Nineteenth-Century Dutch Migrants Extraordinaire on the Prairie-Plans*, 1997. Paper presented at the 11th Biennial Conference. (Holland: Hope College, 1997). (Available through Hope.edu.)

Rysdam-Shorre, Toni. *Gerrit… A Dutchman in Oregon.* (1985, Bend, OR: South Forty Publications).

# Jongewaard Train Roster

## Party 1: Pella, IA to La Grande, OR

| Full Name | Birth Year, Approx. Age |
| --- | --- |
| Cornelius Jongewaard<br>*Captain, Head of Household* | 1828, 36 |
| Helena "Ellen" S. Jongewaard<br>*Wife, pregnant* | 1833, 31 |
| Elizabeth Jongewaard<br>*Daughter* | 1856, 8 |
| Ariaantje Jane Jongewaard<br>*Daughter* | 1858, 6 |
| Ringert C. Jongewaard<br>*Son* | 1859, 4 |

Katherine Jongewaard                      1860, 3-4
*Daughter*

Jane Cornelia Jongewaard                  1863, 1
*Daughter*

Trijntje "Tryna" Jongewaard               Born Nov. '64, N/A
*Daughter, unborn*

## Party 2: Pella, IA to Portland, OR

Arie Jongewaard                           1835, 29
*Cornelius' brother, Head of Household*

Dirkie Van Rossum Jongewaard              1838, 26
*Wife, pregnant, sister to John van Rossum*

Ringert A. Jongewaard                     1857, 7
*Son*

Hendrika Jongewaard                       1859, 5
*Daughter*

Jannetje Jongewaard                       1861, 3
*Daughter*

Gysbert Jongewaard                        1863, 1
*Son*

## Party 3: Pella, IA to Portland, OR

Albert John "J" Jongewaard                1825, 39
*Cornelius' brother*

Nicholas Klaus "K" Jongewaard             1830, 34
*Cornelius' brother*

## Party 4: Lake Prairie Township, IA to Grand Ronde, OR

Geert Dirk "George" Jot                   1818, 46
*Head of Household*

| | |
|---|---|
| Setske "Sarah" Jot<br>*Wife* | 1826, 38 |
| John Jot<br>*Son* | 1858, 6 |
| Dirk Jot<br>*Son* | 1860, 4 |
| (Infant) Jot<br>*Child, unborn* | Born 1864, 0 |

## Party 5: Pella, IA to Portland, OR

| | |
|---|---|
| Lutje Mars<br>*Head of Household* | 1821, 43 |
| Jannetje Van der Meer DeVries<br>Ellerbroek Mars<br>*Second Wife* | 1825, 39 |
| Alida Van der Meer<br>*Jennetje's sister* | 1846, 18 |
| Isaac "Ike" DeVries<br>*Son of Issak and Jannetje DeVries, Teamster* | 1845, 19 |
| Peter Ellerbroek<br>*Son of Gerrit and Jannetje Ellerbroek* | 1851, 13 |
| John Ellerbroek<br>*Son of Gerrit and Jannetje Ellerbroek, memoirist* | 1853, 10 |
| Maria "Mary" Ellerbroek<br>*Daughter of Gerrit and Jannetje Ellerbroek* | 1858, 6 |
| Pieter Mars<br>*Son of Lutje and Jannetje Mars* | Abt. 1860, Abt. 3 |
| Alida "Adeline" Mars<br>*(Twin) Daughter of Lutje and Jannetje Mars* | 1863, 1 |
| Simon Mars<br>*(Twin) Son of Lutje and Jannetje Mars* | 1863, 1 |

Gerrit Epke Roorda                          1841, 23
*Teamster, diarist*

## Named Individuals: Pella, IA to Portland, OR
Teunis Burgraff                             1842, 24
*Teamster*

Mrs. Burgraff                               N/A
*Wife*

Barend "Ten" Broek                          1830, 34
*Teamster*

John "J." Bohland                           1807, 57
*Unknown role*

# Rysdam Train Roster

## Party 1: Pella, IA to Portland, OR

| Full Name | Birth Year, Approx. Age |
|---|---|
| Gerrit Rysdam | 1806, 58 |

*Captain, Head of Household*

| | |
|---|---|
| Arie Albert Rysdam | 1849, 15 |

*Son*

## Party 2: Pella, IA to Portland, OR

| | |
|---|---|
| John van Rossum | 1824, 22 |

*Head of Household, disappears mid-trip*

| | |
|---|---|
| Magdalena "Ellen" Catherine Rysdam Earp van Rossum[240] | 1842, 22 |

*Wife, daughter of Gerrit Rysdam*

| | |
|---|---|
| Nellie Jane Earp | 1860, 4 |

*Daughter of Virgil and Magdalena Earp*

| | |
|---|---|
| Arie Gerrit van Rossum | Born Jan. '65, N/A |

*Son, unborn*

## Party 3: Lake Prairie Township, IA to La Grande, OR

| | |
|---|---|
| Jan "John" Van Blockland | 1834, 30 |

*Head of Household*

| | |
|---|---|
| Adrianna Johanna "Jane" Magdalena Rysdam Van Blockland | 1840, 24 |

*Wife, daughter of Gerrit*

| | |
|---|---|
| Cornelius Van Blockland | 1843, 23 |

*Relative to Jan*

---

[240] She will remarry in Oregon to a Mr. Thomas J. Eaton (1844-1891).

## Party 4: Pella, IA to La Grande, OR

Bonne E. van der Meulen 1803, 61
*Head of Household*

Engeltje A. Noorman van der Meulen 1809, 55
*Wife*

Egbert Bonnes Vander Meulen 1833, 33
*Son*

Antje Roelsma Vander Meulen 1845, 19
*Daughter-in-law, wife of Egbert*

Aartje Bonnes Vander Meulen[241] 1835, 31
*Son*

Jacob Vander Meulen 1841, 23
*Son*

Arie "Arjen" Bonnes Vander Meulen 1846, 17
*Son*

---

[241] Alternative spellings or nicknames used: "Ate" or "Otte."

# Oliver Train, AKA "Indiana Train"

Surnames: Oliver - Boone – Lower - Shonkwiler - Johnston

**At least seven wagons, thirty-four souls**
**From Dalles, Iowa to Grande Ronde Valley, Oregon**

    **Elijah Turner Oliver** and **Catherine Boone Oder Oliver**, the heads of the **Oliver** family, are originally Quakers from Kentucky. **Catherine** is related to the celebrity frontiersman and Revolutionary War hero, Colonel Daniel Boone. After her mother passed away, **Catherine** was raised by her grandparents, George Ovid Boone Sr. and Catherine Yocum.[242] George's father is a first cousin to Daniel and **Catherine** is a first cousin, three times removed.

    **Elijah** and **Catherine** move to Indiana in their early adulthood, marry in 1823, and raise five sons together. Between 1850 and 1853, three of their sons join them for their next move West: to the town of Dallas on the southern outskirts of Marion County, Iowa.[243] There, two of their sons, **Joseph** and **Elial** marry daughters from the neighboring **Lower** family, who also maintain a conservative Quaker lifestyle.

    What motivated the departure of these two families to Oregon is not documented in any family records, though historically speaking, Quakers were pacifists, opposed to war. Ultimately, this meant they did what they could to avoid the drafts and conscriptions that started in 1862. In 2002, Emery Oliver, a great-grandson of **Elijah**, shared that the **Oliver** family "moved around a lot for some reason."[244]

---

[242] Ann Flower, personal communication to author, November 7, 2023. Ann is a 2nd great-granddaughter of Elijah and Catherine.
[243] County Land Office Records show a purchase of 80 acres on May 1, 1855. May 15, 1855 shows another 40 acres. Then, another purchase is made on June 3, 1856 for 40 more acres.
[244] Emery Oliver, "Oral History interview, 2002," by Marshall Kilby and Eugene Smith for the Oregon History Project, (La Grande: Eastern Oregon University, 2004). Accessed August 28, 2022, https://library.eou.edu/ohgr/oliver_transcript.pdf

A brief first-hand account of the **Oliver Train's** journey is found in a 1918 story by **Mary Jane Lower Oliver**, as composed from a Portland, Oregon nursing home prior to her death. The handwritten text reads:

"I was married to Joseph Elcana Oliver in 1849 in Pulaskey County, indiana on the Bank of the Tippecanou River. started the next thursday to Illenoys in Scot County lived there til the sumer of 53 moved to Iowa lived there til in 64 started acros the plains in an ox team the 11 of may arived in Eastern Oregon near summersvill in September crosed the cascades Mountains in a wagon...was on the road 2 weeks went to washington county lived there 2 years moved to Portland in 67 in kings addision on the west side lived there several years moved on east side in 1898. Lived there til 1910 went to California in September stayed there til the first of July 1911. came to the Paton Home in September the 13 1912. husband died 1904 aged 79 years. riten by Mrs. Mary J. Oliver in the year 1918. Mary J. Oliver's hand and pen."[245]

Secondhand sources that are available contain travel date discrepancies and no tracking information, but these details can be confirmed with direct cross references found in other wagon train diarist accounts such as **Pella Company** diarist, **Sarah Rousseau's** entry from July 17 that mentions the **Olivers** by name, and **Brown Train's** memoirist, **Abbie Brown's** references to them as the **"Indiana Train."** Family historian, Emery Oliver, confirmed additional details in a 1992 speech for the Union County Historical Society. He is quoted: "In 1864 my Grandparents and Great-grandparents arrived [in Union County, OR]. Among these settlers were **John van Blockland** [in the Rysdam Train], W .H. Patten, C. L. Blakeslee, and John McKinnis."[246]

The **Oliver, AKA "Indiana Train"** leaves Iowa on May 11, 1864 and arrives in Oregon mid-September. The wagon master is **Elijah's** eldest son, **Hiram**. While

---

[245] This item was transcribed and shared publicly in 2008 on Ancestry.com by user-descendant Pearsey. Mary Jane's original spelling is left intact.
[246] Emery Oliver, "Oliver Wagon Train," Speech at Meeting of Union County Historical Society, March 14, 1992. Further research into John McKinnis from Knoxville, Iowa and his association with the Jongewwaards is encouraged.

the **Olivers** have their hearts set on the Grande Ronde Valley of Oregon, the **Lowers** look forward to life in other parts of the Pacific Northwest.[247] One train member's obituary states the travelers overland in ox-drawn covered wagons, though evidence proves horses are employed as well. [248]

Of those on the North Bank Trail system through the Black Hills, the **Olivers** are among the first emigrants to be attacked during the Platte River Raids. Their losses are noted by others who pass the warning note **Hiram** erects in the area of their attack. The note, documented by **Sarah Rousseau** in the **Pella Company**, reads: "...we saw a paper staked to the ground. ... It stated that the **Oliver Train** had lost 8 head of horses[.] no lives lost, but had a very narrow escape."[249] From the **Pella Company's** impeccable distance records, researchers can ascertain the attack on the **Oliver Train** occurred approximately twelve miles to the east of Deer Creek Garrison, on the opposite side of the North Platte River from where Box Elder Creek joins it. The emigrants retreated east, to the nearest place of perceived safety.

From the **Brown Train**, **Abbie Brown** identifies the date of the attack on the **Olivers** as July 12. She wrote in her 1916 memoir, "as several emigrants were killed in the night before we joined them[,] we felt that we ought to get in a larger train."[250]

When the **Roe Train** descends from McKinstry Ridge on July 13, they are met by a gathering of wagons, initially totaling 28. In this gathering is the **Brown Train**. In **Abbie Brown's** memoir, she described those in the **Oliver Train** as being sympathetic to their story. She writes: "They seemed to know who we were and were very friendly..."[251] In addition, she mentions that some in the train were "tinctured" (marked by) African American blood.[252] Not once did she say that

[247] "George W. Johnston," obituary in *The Dallas Chronicle*, October [day unknown], 1910. The writeup states: "They crossed the plains to California in 1864. From that state they removed to Oregon in 1868, and lived in various cities in Oregon and Washington..."
[248] "John R. Oliver," obituary in *The La Grande Evening Observer*, 1 May 1950.
[249] Sarah Rousseau, *The 1864 Diary of Mrs. Sarah Jane Rousseau* (Phoenix: M Press Publishing, 2023), July 17, 1864.
[250] Abbie Brown, "Across the Plains...," in *Lake Placid News*, September 29, 1916.
[251] Abbie Brown, "Across the Plains..." *Lake Placid News*, Sept. 29, 1916.
[252] The full quote reads: "We went with a small train from Indiana, some of whom were tinctured with colored blood. They seemed to know who we were and were very friendly..."

anyone in the train was Black, though for more than one-hundred-fifty years, historian-biographers have interpreted this singular remark as such.

Clarity on this matter comes from **Catherine Oliver's** relationship to the Boones (who had since moved to Greene Co., Missouri). Daniel Boone's son, Nathan, took one of his own slaves as a mistress.[253] This resulted in one illegitimate child, a biracial daughter named Caroline Boone. She married a neighboring African American, and their children (**Catherine's** fourth cousins) continued marrying into the Black community for several generations. Coincidentally, **Catherine** is also a fourth cousin to **Haywood Edwards** (*see the Ringo Company on the South Bank Trails*).

After recovering from the loss during the Platte River Raids, the **Oliver Train** stays with the **Roe and Brown Trains** temporarily, then continues West to Oregon and Washington without them.

Though a first-person diary from someone within the **Oliver Train** is not presently available, readers might find the authoritative accounts by Emery Oliver, grandson of Hiram to be particularly helpful.

**Primary Sources:**

Oliver, Mary Jane L. "Story of Trip to Oregon." Handwritten note. (Portland: n.p., 1918). (Shared on Ancestry.com in 2008 by user "Pearsey.")

**Secondary Sources:**

"Elijah Warren Oliver." Obituary in *La Grande Observer,* November 24, 1919.

"Family Relics Given to Museum." *Daily Gazette-Times*, January 7, 1985.

Gaston, Joseph. "James A. Stephens." Biographical sketch in *The Centennial History of Oregon, 1811-1912*, vol. 4, 60-63. (Chicago: S. J. Clarke, 1912).

---

[253] Some historians claim Mariah Boone (born 1819 in Kentucky, also seen spelled "Maria") had previously partnered with another slave named Quinn, with whom she had one son. It is unclear when Mariah was displaced to the Boones' farm in Missouri, but subsequent census records continue to show Quinn and their son in Kentucky, without her.

Gekeler, W. R. "Do You Remember?" Biographical sketch of Hiram W.
     Oliver. *Eastern Oregon Newspaper*, January 24, 1963.

"Hiram Wesley Oliver." Obituary in *La Grande Observer,* January 16,
     1908.

"Jack R. Oliver in Business in City Since 1888." Biographical sketch. *La
     Grande Observer*, July 20, 1945.

"John R. Oliver." Obituary in *La Grande Observer,* May 1, 1950.

Oliver, Emery. "Oliver Wagon Train," Speech at Meeting of Union County
     Historical Society. March 14, 1992. (Also included with the Emery Oliver
     Oral History Interview resource.)

Oliver, Emery. Oral History interview, 2002, by Marshall Kilby and
     Eugene Smith for the Oregon History Project. (La Grande:
     Eastern Oregon University, 2004). https://library.eou.edu
     /ohgr/oliver_transcript.pdf

"Pioneer of Oregon Gone: H.W. Oliver Passed Away Last Evening"
     obituary in *TheLa Grande Evening Observer*, January 16, 1908.


Shaver, F., Steele, R., and Rose, A. "Eliel Oliver." Biographical sketch in
     *An Illustrated History of Southeastern Washington,* (Spokane: Western
     Historical Publishing, 1906).

# Oliver Train Roster

## Party 1: Dalles, IA to La Grande, OR

| Full Name | Birth Year, Approx. Age |
|---|---|
| Elijah Turner Oliver *Head of Household* | 1803, 61 |
| Catherine Boone Oder Oliver *Wife, Relative to Col. Daniel Boone* | 1806, 58 |

## Party 2: Dalles, IA to La Grande, OR

| | |
|---|---|
| Hiram Wesley "Wes" Oliver | 1827, 37 |

*Wagon master, Son of Elijah and Catherine Oliver*

| | |
|---|---|
| Julia Ann McCaleb Oliver | 1829, 35 |

*Wife*

| | |
|---|---|
| Elijah Warren Oliver | 1857, 7 |

*Son*

| | |
|---|---|
| Turner Oliver | 1860, 4 |

*Son*

| | |
|---|---|
| John "Jack" Robert Oliver | 1862, 2 |

*Son*

| | |
|---|---|
| Albert Marshall Oliver | 1864, 0 |

*Son*

## Party 3: Pulaski Co., IN to Portland, OR / Pomeroy, WA

| | |
|---|---|
| Joseph Elkanah Oliver | 1825, 39 |

*Head of Household, Son of Elijah and Catherine Oliver*

| | |
|---|---|
| Mary Jane Lower Oliver | 1830, 34 |

*Wife, pregnant, Daughter of William and Rebecca Lower*

| | |
|---|---|
| Charles E. Oliver | 1856, 8 |

*Son*

| | |
|---|---|
| Emery Oliver | 1863, 1 |

*Son*

| | |
|---|---|
| James "Jay" Oliver | Due Jan. 1865 |

*Son, unborn*

*[Continued]*

## Party 4: Scott Co., IN to Portland, OR / Pomeroy, WA

J. Elial "Eli" Oliver                    1830, 34
*Head of Household, Son of Elijah and Catherine Oliver*

Nancy Lower Oliver                    1833, 31
*Wife, pregnant, Daughter of William and Rebecca Lower*

Mary Ellen Oliver                    1850, 14
*Daughter*

Naomi Catherine Oliver                    1852, 12
*Daughter*

John Wesley Oliver                    1855, 9
*Son*

Rebecca Jane Oliver                    1857, 7
*Daughter*

James Hiram "Biff" Oliver                    1859, 5
*Son*

Asbury Oliver                    1862, 2
*Son*

Idaho May "Ida" Oliver                    Born July 29
*Daughter*

## Party 5: Dalles, IA to Portland, OR

William Lower                    1808, 56
*Head of Household*

Rebecca Gooding Lower                    1812, 52
*Wife*

Rebecca Ann Lower                    1849, 15
*Daughter, unmarried*

## Party 6: Dalles, IA to Portland, OR

Benjamin Franklin Shonkwiler     1827, 37
*Head of Household*

Phoebe Lower Shonkwiler     1840, 24
*Wife, daughter of William and Rebecca Lower*

Elizabeth Jane Shonkwiler     1857, 7
*Daughter*

Mary Alice Shonkwiler     1860, 4
*Daughter*

William F. Shonkwiler     1863, 1
*Son*

## Party 7: Dalles, IA to Portland, OR

George William Johnston     1837, 27
*Head of Household*

Elizabeth Jane Lower Johnston     1843, 21
*Wife, daughter of William and Rebecca Lower*

John William Johnston     1861, 3
*Son*

George Elsberry Johnston     Jan. 1864, 0
*Son*

# Pella Company, AKA "Curtis Company"

Surnames: Earp - Rousseau - Curtis – Hays - Hamilton - Parker - Clark

**At least nine wagons, thirty-eight souls**
**From Pella, Iowa to San Bernardino, California**

The **Pella Company** is primarily composed of four families from Marion County, Iowa who have known and worked with each other for many years. For some, such as the **Curtis** and **Rousseau** families, their relationship has been built over the course of twenty years where the area pioneers and patriarchs are colleagues in county work and familiar faces in the Freemasons society. Both have lengthy relationships with the **Hamilton** family, as **John Hamilton Jr.** and his father (not on the journey) both worked as county clerks who would be interacting frequently with **Israel Curtis**, District Attorney and **Dr. James Rousseau**, county land surveyor. Compared to these connections, the **Earp family** is the newest addition to the crowd, having only lived in Iowa for the last fifteen years, and loosely at that.[254]

**Nicholas Earp** is elected the wagon master of the **Pella Company** by reason of being to California once before during his military service. He is a former Sargent who served in the Black Hawk War of 1832, the Mexican-American War of 1846-48, and, due to a disability making it difficult to be on the field, he served as a Union Provost Marshal for Marion County during the Civil War (1861-retirement in 1863). During the Mexican-American War, his regiment traveled through Southern California and **Nicholas** came back home with grand ideas for farming on the Pacific Coast.

In 1863, **Nicholas'** son, **James** returns as a "cripple" from his Civil War service, while two other sons, Virgil and Newton continue to fight. When teen son, **Wyatt**, attempts to run away and enlist twice, both times, **Nicholas** intervenes. Having seen enough, and being wounded himself, **Nicholas**,

---

[254] Nicholas Earp went back and forth to his old residence in Monmouth, Illinois for several years, conducting shady property deals and bootlegging liquor (for which he was tried and convicted of twice).

retires from the Army, as he'd loathed the burden of recruiting young, bright-eyed boys to be lost on the battlefield. For this reason, he might be considered a "Copperhead," or a "Peace Democrat," that opposed the War for reasons outside the issue of slavery. He also has lawsuits from questionable land sales catching up to him. More and more, 1864 becomes his year to get out of town.

During the Platte River Raids, **Nicholas** seems to overlook sixteen year old **Wyatt** as a young man capable of fighting alongside him during the repeated attacks on the **Pella Company**. Instead, **Nicholas** calls on **James** to ride with him in the engagements, leaving **Wyatt** (who is arguably the best shot and least emotionally volatile of the family) to stand guard over the women and children. **Wyatt** and his younger brothers are frequently emasculated by **Nicholas'** forceful leadership and physical discipline and the residue of this formative experience can be seen in their future careers as all three become lawmen, sworn to protect the weak and keep the peace.

The **Curtis family** is led by Baptist Reverend, **Israel Curtis**, but those who know him, call him "I. C." **Israel** also opposes the war as a religious pacifist and may fall into the same political category as **Nicholas**. **Israel** is an outspoken Democrat and active in local government affairs. He is also one of the founders of Central College, where his eldest son, **William Jesse** graduates with a law degree. For a few years, he and **William Jesse**, work together at the firm, Curtis & Curtis, but **Israel** eventually steps into the role of District Attorney for Marion County and his son assumes the case load at their lucrative practice. On the journey, **William Jesse** is responsible for herding cattle, a skill that he doesn't appear to be any good at, considering he loses control of them regularly.

**Israel's** wife, **Lucy**, is the epitome of social grace and sacrificial love. She delivers her ninth child days just before the **Pella Company** plans their departure, causing the **Curtises** to be late for their scheduled launch. Seven months later, she delivers her tenth baby, conceived while on the Overland-California Trail. In addition to her new babies, the **Curtises'** daughter, **Mary Curtis Hays** is also pregnant en route and delivers a child in August, while daughter-in-law, **Frances Curtis** becomes pregnant in late October.

The **Rousseau family** is perhaps the most well-to-do and it is generally believed that upfront trip expenses and **Nicholas'** guide fees are covered between **Dr. James Rousseau** and **Israel Curtis** (though **Israel's** cash is funneled into cattle). **Dr. James Rousseau** is a "Renaissance Man," who not only worked as a land surveyor for Marion County (including laying out a city bearing his name), but he is also a practicing country physician. His work is comparable to modern day naturopathy, as opposed to conventional allopathic (prescription-oriented care) and surgical practices. As if those workloads are not enough, **Dr. James** also serves as the first postmaster for Liberty Township.

**James'** wife, **Sarah Rousseau**, is a gentrified lady and classical pianist from New Castle Upon Tyne. She catches his eye after immigrating to the United States in the 1830s. While teaching music at a Ladies' finishing school in Michigan, they meet serendipitously when **James'** cousin **Lovell Harrison Rousseau** calls on **Sarah's** sister at the school.[255] After a few years living on the Rousseau Plantation in Kentucky, the **Rousseau's** relocate to the unincorporated Elm Grove Forest in Iowa, west of a ferry depot on the Des Moines River. There, **Sarah** continues tutoring piano until her rheumatoid arthritis becomes more debilitating than her husband's medical expertise can manage. They are motivated to move by the possibility of a climate cure. **Sarah** is confined to a wheelchair for nearly the duration of this journey and requires a personal assistant: **Matilda Field**, a spinster who becomes romantically entangled first with the **Rousseau's** teamster, then later with a stranger from Utah.

The **Hamilton family** comes from one of the earliest pioneer settlers in Lake Prairie Township (where Pella, Iowa is established by Dutch Reformist, Hendrick Scholte). **John Jr.'s** family built the first permanent home in the area in 1843, planted the first fruit orchard in 1847, then sold their property to the Dutch who settled in the area that same year. In Dutch historian Kommer Van Stigt's *History of Pella, Iowa and Vicinity*, both the

---

[255] Coincidentally, in 1864, **James'** cousin is now a Brigadier General in the Union Army and on the vice presidential ticket, running against Andrew Jackson.

**Hamiltons** and the **Curtises** are identified as being some of the few Americans who welcomed the Dutch settlers to the area.[256]

The **Hamiltons** temporarily move back to Ohio, where **John Jr.** was originally born, but return to Iowa by 1854. At that time, they bring a **Miss Sarah Jane Auten,** who is listed in census records as being a **Hamilton,** though county marriage records don't show their union until December 31, 1860. **John Jr.** and **Sarah** travel with one young boy identified in an eyewitness account as "Little Oscar Hamilton," though there appears to be no empirical record of his existence. Right after the **Pella Company's** attacks in the Black Hills, **Sarah** delivers a "fine son,"[257] as recorded by **Sarah Rousseau. Nicholas Earp** also writes about this, saying: "**Mrs. Hamilton** brought forth a fine boy a few days after we war attacked by the Indians."[258] Outside of these remarks, however, there is no record of this child, and it is presumed he dies before 1868.

At some point near Council Bluffs, Iowa, the **Clark family** joins the **Pella Company**. They are a Mormon couple being led by their son-in-law, **Robert Parker**, from Illinois to Provo, Utah, where two of the **Clark's** daughters live as next door neighbors. Daughter Mary (**Robert's** wife) is expecting her second child in August of 1864. Family stories suggest **Robert,** age twenty-eight, has made long distance wagon trips innumerable times, having first gone from Kanesville (Council Bluffs) to Provo in 1852. Then, while still a teen, **Robert** began serving as an escort or guard along the Sweetwater Trail. He spends his summer months helping Mormon families reach Salt Lake City in safety.[259] Other sources say he also provides a similar service from Salt Lake City to a Mormon settlement in San Bernardino. During the 1864 journey, **Robert** becomes a dear friend to **Dr. James Rousseau** through acts of selfless giving and bravery.

---

[256] Kommer Van Stigt, *History of Pella, Iowa and Vicinity,* (Pella: Central College, 1981).

[257] Sarah Rousseau, *The 1864 Diary of Mrs. Sarah Jane Rousseau* (Phoenix: M Press Publishing, 2023), July 15, 1864.

[258] Nicholas Earp, personal communication to James Coplea, April 2, 1865.

[259] This work may have been contract work, as opposed to Robert being part of the Mormon Militia, as no military record exists for him.

Authoritative accounts for the **Pella Company's** trip are plentiful as descendants have spent countless years investing in research, writing stories, and coordinating efforts to preserve their shared history. In particular, the work of Linda Kay Ford and Ella Parker Ogden (descendants of the Parker family), Pamela Greenwood (descendant of the Curtis family), and Richard Molony and Evalyn Anderson (descendants of the Rousseau family) have provided biographical material that is rich for further study. San Bernardino historian, Nicholas Cataldo, has also produced a veritable library of articles on the **Pella Company** as well as publishing a book specifically on the **Earp family's** experience.

Though these are wonderful resources, the primary source material used in the forthcoming narrative is straight from the eyewitness accounts of **Sarah Jane Rousseau's** 1864 trail diary and **Nicholas Earp's** 1865 letter.

## Primary Sources:

Earp, Nicholas. "Copy of a Handwritten Letter From Nicholas Earp to James Coplea," Pella Community Memory Database, Pella Public Library [Identifier: 2019.1.62.11], April 2, 1865. (In Appendix.)

Rousseau, Sarah J., *The 1864 Diary of Mrs. Sarah Jane Rousseau,* (Phoenix: M Press Publishing, 2023).

## Secondary Sources:

Anderson, Evalyn. "Anderson History." Essay, Grinnell: Marion-Linn D.A.R. Chapter of Iowa, 1934.

Cataldo, Nicholas R. "Curtis Family Legacy Began on a Wagon Train." *Pioneer Tales, 4*, no. 3, 2020.

Cataldo, Nicholas R. "Diary of the Earp Wagon Train." *The Tombstone Epitaph*, November 27, 2019: 7.

Cataldo, Nicholas R. *Pioneers of San Bernardino 1851-1857.* San Bernardino: San Bernardino County Museum Association, 2001.

Cataldo, Nicholas R. "Sarah Jane Rousseau: Diary of the Earp Wagon Train to San Bernardino." *San Bernardino Sun,* 1999.

Cataldo, Nicholas R. *The Earp Clan: The Southern California Years.* (San Bernardino: Backroads Press, 2006).

Cataldo, Nicholas R. "The Rousseau Diary and the Earp Wagon Train t to San Bernardino, 1864." *Overland Journal,* 33, no. 3 (2015): 115-128.

Cataldo, Nicholas R. "This pioneer's diary details cross-country trip to San Bernardino." *San Bernardino Sun.* March 21, 2022.

Daglish, Steven. "Sarah Jane Daglish - Trip Across The Plains." *The Daglish Family* (Blog), June 9, 2007. http://daglishfamily. blogspot.com/2007/06/sarah-jane-daglish-trip-across-plains.html

"Diary Tells of 1864 Trek by Covered Wagons." *San Bernardino Sun-Telegram*, November 21, 1954, 26.

Gourley, Bruce. "Baptists and the American Civil War: May 12, 1864" CivilWarBaptists.com, Last modified May 12, 2014. CivilWarBaptists.com/thisdayinhistory/1864-may-12/

Greenwood, Pamela. "Biography of Lucy Mildred Holman Curtis." Unpublished manuscript, shared on Ancestry.com ["The Holman, Harvey, Greenwood, Morgan, Cashel family tree..."], April 6, 2007.

Greenwood, Pamela. "Biography of Israel Coleman Curtis." Unpublished manuscript, shared on Ancestry.com ["The Holman, Harvey, Greenwood, Morgan, Cashel family tree..."], April 6, 2007.

Greenwood, Pamela. "Some Thoughts on the Pella Expedition." Genealogical Essay, December, 2006.

Molony, Janelle. "1864: More than Massacres." *Annals of Wyoming* (Autumn 2021): 30-47.

Molony, Janelle. "A Day in the Life with Sarah Rousseau." Official Author Page. Last modified, March 31, 2020. http://janellemolony.com/category/rousseau-project/a-day-in-the-life-with-sarah-rousseau.

Molony, Janelle. "How a Victorian Immigrant Almost Became the First Lady." *The Michigan Historical Review* 48, no.1 (2022): 131-139.

Molony, Janelle. "John Hamilton, Biographical Sketch." FindAGrave.com [Memorial 69280274], Last modified Sept. 20, 2023.

Molony, Janelle. "Sarah Jane Daglish: A Case of Mistaken Identity." *The Stars In Your Family* (Burbank: Southern California Genealogical Society, 2021).

Molony, Janelle. "Victorian Sweetheart Wins Over the Wrong Michigan Suitor." *GenTales Magazine (online),* March 2020.

Molony, Janelle. "When the Earps Fought Indians," *Wild West Magazine,*" (Fall, 2024).

Molony, Richard. Oral History Interview by Joyce Hansen. *San Bernardino Oral History Project.* San Bernardino Public Library, January 14, 2003.

Muckenfuss, Mark. "Tales from the trail." *Press Enterprise,* August 2, 2014.

Nollen, Carl. "Rousseau." *Marion County Genealogical Society Newsletter,* (October, 2020).

Ogden, Ella P. *Parker-Ross Memoirs.* (Salt Lake City: n.p., 1965).

Ford, Linda K. Robert Pollack Parker Genealogy Notes. Parker Heritage.ning.com. Last modified April 6, 2010. https://parkerheritage.ning.com/profiles/requests/robert-pollock-parker-the.

# Pella Company Roster

## Party 1:  From Pella, IA to San Bernardino, CA

| Full Name | Birth Year, Approx. Age |
|---|---|
| Nicholas Porter Earp<br>*Wagon Master, Head of Household* | 1813, 51 |
| Virginia Ann Cooksey Earp<br>*Wife* | 1821, 43 |
| James Cooksey Earp<br>*Son* | 1841, 23 |
| Wyatt Barry Stapp Earp<br>*Son* | 1848, 16 |
| Morgan Seth Earp<br>*Son* | 1851, 13 |
| Warren Baxter Earp<br>*Son* | 1855, 11 |
| Adelia Douglas Earp<br>*Daughter* | 1861, 3 |
| Charles Lefterdy Copley<br>*Teamster* | 1842, 24 |

## Party 2:  From Pella, IA to San Bernardino, CA

| | |
|---|---|
| Rev. Israel Coleman Curtis<br>*Head of Household* | 1813, 51 |
| Lucy Mildred Holman Curtis<br>*Wife, becomes pregnant en route* | 1819, 45 |
| Richard Henry Holman Curtis<br>*Son* | 1843, 21 |
| Emerine Holman Curtis<br>*Daughter* | 1848, 16 |

Louis Foulk Curtis                      1852, 12
*Son*

Allen Vail Curtis                       1855, 9
*Son*

Israel Coleman Curtis Jr.               1859, 5
*Son*

Nancy E. "Lida" Curtis                  1861, 4
*Daughter*

Penelope E. Curtis                      Born May, 1864, 0
*Daughter*

Jenny Lucy Curtis                       Born Dec., 1864
*Daughter, born en route*

## Traveling Party 3:  From Pella, IA to San Bernardino, CA
Stephen Thomas Hays                     1833, 31
*Head of Household*

Mary Elizabeth "Eliza" Curtis Hays      1836, 28
*Wife, pregnant, Daughter of Israel and Lucy Curtis*

Charles Coleman Hays                    Born Aug., 1864
*Son, born en route*

## Party 4:  From Pella, IA to San Bernardino, CA
William Jesse Curtis                    1838, 26
*Head of Household, Son of Israel and Lucy Curtis*

Frances Sophia Cowles Curtis            1837, 27
*Wife, pregnant*

Holman Cowles Curtis                    1863, 1
*Son*

Mack (unknown full name)                N/A
*Hired teamster*

## Party 5:  From Liberty, IA to San Bernardino, CA

| | |
|---|---|
| Dr. James Alexander Rousseau<br>*Head of Household* | 1812, 52 |
| Sarah Jane Daglish Rousseau<br>*Wife, Diarist, Wheelchair-bound* | 1815, 49 |
| Sarah Elizabeth Rousseau<br>*Daughter* | 1849, 14 |
| John James Rousseau<br>*Son* | 1852, 12 |
| John Albert Miller Rousseau<br>*Son* | 1856, 8 |
| Matilda Field<br>*Aid to Sarah (Work-for-transport)* | 1843, 21 |
| Thomas Jefferson ("TJ") Ellis<br>*Hired teamster, Wagon driver* | 1843, 21 |

## Party 6:  From Knoxville, IA to San Bernardino, CA

| | |
|---|---|
| John Bentley Hamilton<br>*Head of Household* | Abt. 1837, 25 |
| Sarah Jane Auten Hamilton<br>*Wife, pregnant* | Abt. 1837, 25 |
| Oscar Hamilton<br>*Non-biological son or ward* | Unknown |
| Baby Hamilton<br>*Son* | Born July, 1864 |
| Levi Tucker | 1833, 29 |
| *Acquaintance from Knoxville. He is heading to Sacramento, CA.* | |

## Traveling Party 7:  From Illinois to Provo, UT

William C. Clark                    1800, 64
*Head of Household*

Mary Doyle Clark                    1804, 60
*Wife*

Robert Pollack Parker               1836, 28
*Captain/Guide, Son-in-law*

# Ridgley Party

Surnames: Ridgley - Dickson - Smith – Button - Kelley - Donovan - Colburn - Phillips

**At least six wagons, thirty-two souls
From La Crosse, Wisconsin to Ruby Valley, Montana**

Joshua and **Rebecca Ridgeley** are farm owners living six miles north of La Crosse, Wisconsin where they allegedly keep a tavern.[260] With only one child, a daughter named **Mary**, the couple must hire help to work the land. In 1857, **Joshua** takes on an apprentice: eight-year-old **Albert Jerome Dickson**. After young **Albert's** father dies, his mother "bonded him out" to the **Ridgleys** until he came of age. In exchange for his labor, he receives room and board. Though **Albert's** mother remarries twice, **Albert** reserves the use of the title "Dad" for **Joshua**.

The **Ridgleys** are early settlers of the state of Wisconsin; **Joshua** being a "well-known prominent citizen of the County," according to a biographical sketch of their daughter found in the *Biographical History of La Crosse, Trempealeau and Buffalo Counties, Wisconsin* (1892, 356-357). **Joshua** was born in Maryland and raised in Pennsylvania, where he met his wife, **Rebecca**. She was a "good companion," of Dutch or Germanic ancestry (*Biographical History,* 357). According to the diary and letters of **Albert**, **Rebecca** is a "sprightly" woman with a sense of fashion and a fantastic cook (Dickson, *Covered Wagon Days*, 1989). Dana Cahoon, the 3rd great-grand-niece of **Joshua and Rebecca** has added to this that **Rebecca** "seems to have been a woman of great fortitude."[261]

---

[260] This claim was made by Albert J. Dickinson in his book *Covered Wagon Days*, though no empirical evidence has substantiated this claim.

[261] Dana Cahoon, personal communication to author, June 13, 2023.

As **Albert** paints him, **Joshua** is somewhat of a simple man who favors wearing cowhide boots. He is described as illiterate, but Dana Cahoon has since argued that **Joshua** was at least partially literate, citing his middle class upbringing and civic activities.[262] Another descendant, Alan Ridgely Griswold, shared that when his 3rd great-grandfather was younger, he wrestled with the future President Abraham Lincoln.[263] Alan also shared that one Winter, as an adult, **Joshua** developed frostbite and sawed off his own toes. Neither claim has been substantiated, but if the latter were true, it should be factored into the hardships endured while walking thousands of miles across the American Frontier.

After seeing their daughter married off in 1860, the **Ridgelys** leave the care of the farm to **Mary** and her husband, while they prepare for an adventure of a lifetime. Enticing advertisements of gold being discovered in Idaho Territory cause **Joshua** to pack up and leave on May 5, 1864. Now, fourteen-year-old **Albert** is expected to do his share of "man's work," on the Trail instead of the farm.

In the original **Ridgley Party** are three wagons led by oxen and steer: **Joshua** drives one wagon; **Albert**, the second; and a local Baptist Deacon drives the third. **Albert** describes **Deacon Sylvester Smith** as a gray-whiskered, "roly poly" man with a good nature (*Covered Wagon Days*, 23). With **Sylvester** are his second wife and three sons, including **Alonzo** (whom **Albert** calls "**Lon**"). **Albert** remembers there being challenges in that family with the "poor woman in the back of the deacon's wagon ... with a cross baby" (63). **Albert** admired twenty-three-year-old **Lon's** scrappiness and called him "ruddy," "wholesome," and the only one who looked forward to having a fight with Indians.

On June 9, the **Ridgleys** are joined by two wagons belonging to a family allegedly from Iowa, with the surname "**Bouton**." The **Button family** is actually from Danby, Vermont, but leaves in in the Fall of 1863 and spends the winter in Iowa. The four households traveling west with **Catherine Herrick Vail Button** all descend from original Vermont colonists and most settled on what is considered "Dutch Hill," a Quaker enclave in the Danby

[262] Ibid., June 13, 2023.
[263] Ibid., May 1, 2023. (Dana is a first cousin of Alan.)

Borough between 1765 and 1794.[264] In 1858, a **Kelley** relative ventured to California and wrote back a sterling review to the New Englanders.[265] In 1859, **Alfred and Albert Kelley's** older brother George traveled to Sonoma County via what was known as the Panama Route (by ship, through the isthmus).[266]

George leaves the operation of his marble mill in Mill Brook to the twins, but in the early 1860s, the marble industry wanes and the population of Danby steadily falls due to Westward Expansion. The effect turns county settlements into ghost towns. The twins decide that there is no better time to leave, so they sell their properties to relatives and outfit themselves with two wagons: one for the **Kelley brothers** (who each married a **Button** sister) and one for the **Button brothers** (who each married a **Hulett** sister).

A week later, the growing wagon train is joined by the **Donovan Team** consisting of three young men from Iowa, hoping to find gold in Denver, Colorado. A few days after, they are joined by four miner-packers led by **George Colburn**, who is allegedly coming from "Raleigh," Missouri.[267] By the end of June, there are six identified wagons with the **Ridgley Party**, though on July 2, **Albert** claims there are twenty-seven with them.[268]

With the few geographical marks and dates provided in **Albert's** book, the author has deduced their average daily mileage of 19 to 22 miles per day. The **Ridgley Party** has very long travel days, considering the typical speed of an ox at about two miles per hour. The wagon train reaches Fort Laramie on July 3 and stays overnight for the Independence Day festivities. Days before reaching the Fort, **George** goes missing. When he returns, he has a new horse that he claims he acquired from a poor sap down the road who needed money. But when an angry emigrant later demands the return of his

---

[264] J. C. Williams, *The History and Map of Danby, Vermont,* (Rutland: McLean & Robbins, 1869).

[265] J. M. Guinn, "George F. Kelley," Biographical Sketch in *The History of the State of California and Biographical Record of the Sierras* (Chicago: Chapman Publishing, 1906), 345.

[266] This journey would take approximately eight weeks instead of the four to six months expected when traveling by trail.

[267] This location does not exist.

[268] This might be an interpretive error of the original text.

stolen animal, someone in the **Ridgley Party** intervenes and forces **George** to relinquish the horse before the situation escalates further.

When the Party strikes into the Black Hills on July 5, **George** somehow gets himself another new horse. This time, he claims he bought it fair and square from the military. He pressures young **Albert** to validate his stories, should anyone ask, but **Albert** is already suspicious of the man's "finder's keepers" reputation. That evening, **Joshua** holds a meeting and the wagon train votes to banish the thieving liar. By morning, **George** and his packers ride off and are never seen again.

When the **Ridgley Party** reaches Bridger's Ferry in Orin, Wyoming, they seriously consider taking Bozeman's new cutoff to Montana by way of Indian foot trails on the east side of the Big Horn mountains. They ultimately decide not to take the risk – a wise decision, even though to do so might save them a week's worth (or more) of travel time.[269] By July 8, the **Ridgley Party** is safely out of the "Hills" and camped across the North Platte River from Deer Creek garrison. It won't be until later that they hear about the depredations that fell upon those behind them. When stories of the **Kelly-Larimer Train** murders hit the news circuit, journalists conflate details so much that **Joshua and Rebecca's** daughter believes it was her own family that perished. **Albert** claims, "It was six months before Mrs. Ridgley's daughter and my mother learned differently" (*Covered Wagon Days*, 104).

There is one additional party introduced in the tale of the **Ridgley Party**: a father-son duo from Rock Island, Illinois. **Edward Phillips** and his sixteen-year-old son **Charles** travel light and swift. **Joshua** does not clarify exactly when or how he made their acquaintance, but he specifically tracks the movements of the **"Phillips Boys"** who seem to be a week's worth of travel ahead of him. **Joshua** scans notes staked on the sides of the trail until he finds updates on their whereabouts. A portion of the **Phillip's** story is found in the obituary of Elenor Phillips (included in the Appendix).

The story of the **Ridgley Party** comes primarily from **Albert's** daily diary kept along the way. It is reasonable to assume he logged the journey on **Joshua's** behalf, though the original item never found its way back to the

---

[269] The Townsend Train Fight of July 7, 1864 made this trail particularly dangerous.

**Ridgleys**. In 1929, **Albert's** son compiled the information from **Albert's** daily journal and produced a version of the item. His son has emphasized in the book's introduction that he "adhered strictly to the facts as presented in the original memorandums, notes, journals, and private papers" (*Covered Wagon Days*, 16).

Instead of publishing the daily journal as-is, however, **Albert's** son embellishes his father's journey with a creative narrative and adds contextual information and conclusions that would have been unknown to **Albert** at the time. Much like with the tales of **Fanny Kelly and Sarah Larimer**, this stylistic choice is problematic to the modern researcher. Several of the claims made in the book, *Covered Wagon Days*, are factually inaccurate or impossible. If there are concerns regarding the material, as it applies to the events in this book, the author will make the reader aware.

**Primary Sources:**

Dickson, Albert Jerome. *Covered Wagon Days.* Edited by Arthur Jerome Dickson (Lincoln: University of Nebraska Press, 1989).

**Secondary Sources:**

"Alfred Kelley." Obituary in *Petaluma Argus-Courier*, July 27, 1900, 4.

"Edward Phillips." Biographical sketch in *Montana Pioneers: Constitution, Members and Officers, with "Portraits and Maps,"* Edited by James Sanders (Society of Montana Pioneers, 1899), 195.

Guinn, J. M. "George F. Kelley." Biographical Sketch in *The History of the State of California and Biographical Record of the Sierras* (Chicago: Chapman Publishing, 1906), 345.

"Mrs. Mary [Ridgley] Hartley." Biographical sketch in *Biographical History of La Crosse, Trempealeau and Buffalo Counties, Wisconsin...* (Chicago: Lewis Publishing Co., 1982), 356-357.

"Phillips." Obituary of Elenor Phillips in *The Madisonian*, June 11, 1892, 2.

Williams, J. C. *The History and Map of Danby, Vermont.* (Rutland, McLean & Robbins, 1869).

# Ridgley Party Roster

## Party 1:  From La Crosse Co., WI to Virginia City, MT

| Full Name | Birth Year, Approx. Age |
|---|---|
| Joshua Ridgley | 1814, 50 |
| *Wagon Master, Head of Household* | |
| Rebecca Radebough Ridgley | 1820, 44 |
| *Wife* | |

## Party 2:  From La Crosse Co., WI to Ruby Valley, MT

| | |
|---|---|
| Albert Jerome Dickson | 1850, 14 |
| *Teamster, Diarist* | |

## Party 3:  From La Crosse Co., WI to Ruby Valley, MT

| | |
|---|---|
| Sylvester Smith | 1803, 61 |
| *Head of Household, Baptist Deacon* | |
| Mary Hildreth Smith | 1821, 43 |
| *2nd Wife* | |
| Sylvester Alonzo "Lon" Smith | 1841, 23 |
| *Son* | |
| William Hildreth Smith | 1859, 5 |
| *Son* | |
| Edwin Smith | 1861, 3 |
| *Son* | |

## Party 4:  From Danby, VT to Petaluma, CA

Catherine Herrick Vail Button            1810, 54
*Mother, Widow of Anson Button*

Joseph Button                           1833, 29
*Head of Household, Son of Catherine*

Melissa Betsey Hulett Button            1834, 30
*Wife, Sister of Ellen*

Frank Joseph Button                     1855, 9
*Grandson of Catherine*

Jessie Button                           1857, 7
*Granddaughter of Catherine*

John Button                             1860, 4
*Grandson of Catherine*

Catherine "Katie" Vail Button           1861, 3
*Granddaughter of Catherine*

## Party 4 (Continued)

Isaac Vail Button                       1836, 28
*Head of Household, Son of Catherine*

Ellen Belle Hulett Button               1839, 25
*Wife, Sister of Melissa*

## Party 4 (Continued)

Alfred Kelley                           1817, 46
*Head of Household, Twin of Albert*

Eunice Herrick Button                   1829, 35
*Wife, Daughter of Catherine, Sister to Charity*

Katie Virginia Kelley        1849, 15
*Granddaughter of Catherine*

Myron B. Kelly        1851, 13
*Nephew from Alfred's brother William*

## Party 4 (Continued)
Albert Kelley        1817, 46
*Head of Household, Twin of Alfred*

Charity Signor Button Kelley    1840, 24
*Wife, Daughter of Catherine, Sister to Eunice*

Charles Albert Kelley        1860, 4
*Grandson of Catherine*

Caroline Lydia Kelley        1863, 1
*Granddaughter of Catherine*

## Party 5:  From Iowa (Approx.) to Denver, CO
Joseph "Joe" Donovan        N/A
*Miner*

Tim Ware        N/A
*Miner*

William "Billy" Moore        N/A
*Miner*

*[Continued]*

## Party 6:  From "Raleigh," MO[270] to Unknown

George Colburn                          N/A
*Miner/Packer*

Three Other Men                       N/A
*Miners/Packers*


## Mentions Only:  From Rock Island, IL to Ruby Valley, MT

Edward Phillips                         1818, 46
*Head of Household*

Charles Phillips                        1848, 16
*Son*

---

[270] There is no city or county of "Raleigh" in Missouri.

# Roe Family

Surnames: Roe - Cathcart - Clark - Leonard - Redfern

**Three wagons, at least eight souls**
**From Grinnell, Iowa to Virginia City, Montana**

**Isaac** and **Martha Roe** exchange their wedding vows in Grinnell, Iowa just three weeks before launching out West.[271] In a letter to a cousin, **Martha** writes that she has "found her man," and that the two of them would be going to Montana "for life."[272] They start out on May 4 and aim for Bannack, Montana on Grasshopper Creek, where **Isaac's** brother William has just erected the first permanent home in the area.[273]

Twenty-year-old diarist, **Martha**, is a recent graduate of Grinnell University and has been working at a hotel in the city. Her husband **Isaac** is seeking his share of the newly discovered gold. Prior to this journey, **Isaac** had gained valuable trail experience by freighting on the Oregon and Mormon Trails to Denver, Colorado, and had recently visited Bannack in 1863. He hires a cook named **Alex Cathcart** and a team of men to accompany him (who **Martha** collectively refers to as "the Boys"). Altogether, there are at least two wagons immediately associated with the **Roes**.

There is another traveling group temporarily with the **Roes**: the **Redferns**. Starting in June, **Martha** names a **Mr. and Mrs. Redfern** and mentions children. The **Redferns** are suspected to be a father and son from Richland, Iowa, heading to Virginia City, Montana, but empirical evidence for them does not match there being a "Mrs." along. Whoever the **Redferns** are,

---

[271] Martha Freeman Roe, *Diary of Martha Roe, May 4, 1864 to September 8, 1864,* eds. Burkett and Burkett, April 16, 1864.

[272] Yvonne Freeman Rose, "Martha Freeman Roe Loughridge," in *The History of Beaverhead County,* (Beaverhead County: Beaverhead Co. History Book Assoc., 1990), 350.

[273] William Roe is one of the first prospectors to arrive in the area with teams led by John White from Denver, Colorado in 1862.

they go their separate ways in mid-August (near Parting of the Ways and Lander's Cutoff).

**Martha's** trail diary is very personal in nature. She doesn't emphasize typical sights and mileage markers along the way (compared to other records from this time frame). She spends a great deal of time writing on the relationships between members of the train, and often tracks her and **Isaac's** health. **Isaac** has a pain in his groin that the train believes he may die from. **Martha** suffers from "tremendous" headaches that frequently force her onto "the sick list."

There is no telling how torturous it may have been to endure a migraine on a non-air conditioned wagon that rocks and bounces so much over the trail that it can churn butter in a day's ride. Hardly two days can pass between her episodes, until she reaches Wyoming. Then, from July 10 to 24, her sickness is somewhat forgotten. At least, on paper.

**Martha's** diary contains repeat references to others on the trail, suggesting long-lasting connections with other survivors. Two weeks into their trip, the **Roes** become closely associated with the **Howard Train** from Iowa (starting May 13). By July, they routinely camp with the **Brown Train,** also from Iowa (starting July 8). Normally quite opinionated in her writing, **Martha** does not capture any of the very serious conflicts these two trains have with each other. Perhaps she tries to keep her nose out of trouble. Martha also records a brief association with the Dutch families in the **Jongewaard Train** who travel in proximity to the **Roes** from July 13 to at least July 20.

After the Platte River Raids, **the Roes** are one of the first families to welcome **Kelly-Larimer Train** members, **Sarah Larimer** and her son **Frank,** back from their two-day captivity and three-day escape. **Martha** writes about it on July 16 from the large emigrant camp on the north bank of the Platte, opposite of Deer Creek Garrison:

"Just after supper in came one of the womin [sic] and children that was captured by the Indians[.]  she came a long ways and were tired and faint[.]  her husband is across the river to the fort wounded[.]  she did not know anything about it  staid [sic] all night with us ..."

Future readers should be aware that **Martha's** language is representative of the times and she can be perceived as insensitive to minority cultures. There are also some suggestive entries for the honeymooner. On one occasion, **Martha** and **Isaac** run off to take a dip in the river by themselves to celebrate her twenty-first birthday (July 3). On another, after **Martha** finishes her morning chores, she washes in the river before getting into bed with **Isaac** in the middle of the day (Aug. 7). A few of the more curious finds in **Martha's** diary include meeting a swearing duck (see July 10 for an explanation), watching the cook fall in love with a friendly prairie chicken and pet it for an hour (May 20), and seeing the train play jailhouse to a mule thief who was on the run from the local sheriff (Aug. 13).

In 1979, **Martha Roe's** trail diary was transcribed by a personal acquaintance of the family, **Harold Blinn**. Then, in 1982, **Martha's** grandson, **Lester W. Burkett** published the contents under a different title. The original item is located at the Museum of the Rockies in Montana.

## Primary Sources:

Roe, Martha A. *Guide to a Trip to Idaho, 1864,* Transcription by Harold Blinn. Manuscript at Washington State Univ. Library [Special Collections], 1979.

Roe, Martha. *Diary of Martha Roe, May 4, 1864 to September 8, 1864, Grinnell, Iowa to Bannock, Montana.* Edited by Grace and Lester Burkett. Manuscript at Montana State Univ. Library [Special Collections], 1982.

## Secondary Sources:

"A Prominent Bannackite is Gone…" Obituary of Isaac Roe in *Helena Semi-Weekly Herald,* November 27, 1873, 2.

Freeman Rose, Yvonne. "Martha Freeman Roe Loughridge." *The History of Beaverhead County.* (Dillon: Beaverhead Co. History Book Assoc., 1990), 350.

"Isaac Roe." Biographical sketch in *Progressive Men of Montana.* (Chicago: A. W. Bowen & Co., ca. 1903), 1192-1193.

"Mrs. Loughridge, Pioneer, is Dead." Obituary of Martha Freeman Roe Loughridge in *The Anaconda Standard,* May 13, 1920, page 10.

"William Roe." Biographical sketch in *Progressive Men of Montana.* (Chicago: A. W. Bowen & Co., ca. 1903), 393-395.

# Roe Train Roster

## Party 1: Grinnell, IA to Bannack, MT

| Full Name | Birth Year, Approx. Age |
|---|---|
| Isaac Roe<br>*Captain* | 1835, 29 |
| Martha Ann Freeman Roe<br>*Wife, Diarist* | 1843, 21 |
| Alex T. Cathcart<br>*Cook* | 1832, 32 |

## Party 2: Grinnell, IA to Bannack, MT

| | |
|---|---|
| Rodney Clark<br>*Mining team, "The Boys"* | Unknown |
| S. Leonard<br>*Mining team* | Unknown |
| Samuel (NLN) [274]<br>*Mining team* | Unknown |
| John (NLN)<br>*Mining team* | Unknown |
| Thomas Howell<br>*Mining team* | Abt. 1841, 23 |

[274] **Author note:** I realize with great annoyance that it is entirely possible for the "S" to be "Samuel" in Samuel Leonard. That being said, without conclusive evidence, these notes will remain open to further discovery.

## Party 3: Unknown to Lander's Cutoff

Mr. Redfern       Unknown
*Temporary Associate*

Mrs. Redfern       Unknown
*Temporary Associate*

# Emigrant Tales
## from the
# North Bank Trails

# "Westward Ho!"

After crossing the Nebraska border into Idaho Territory, there is a twenty-eight mile stretch of trail to reach Fort Laramie. Depending on the wagon train outfit and health of the stock animals, this distance can be covered in one to two days' time. Emigrants on the north side of the North Platte River are using what has been considered the "Old Oregon Trail," as well as other given names such as the Council Bluffs Road, Child's Cutoff, the Overland Trail or the California Trail. Again, to simplify matters, the author will use the conventional term, "North Bank Trail(s)," moving forward.

In 1864, staying on the North Bank is the less popular choice to get through the Black Hills (compared to the South Bank Trails) due to less frequent access to water sources and an exceedingly difficult terrain. Chances are, if emigrants could have comfortably crossed from the North to the South Bank Trails at or before this point, they would have. This year, however, with a heavy snowfall and exceptional melt, the North Platte River is swollen full and, in certain places, the current could be dangerously swift to manage crossing without a bridge. Unfortunately, there is no bridge option at Fort Laramie, so those determined to cross must weigh their options.

They might try converting their wagons into boats and swimming their animals through the rough and frigid waters while risking a total loss if the wagon boat topples or is swept away. Depending on the size of the outfit and weight of the load being carried, a converted wagon could also be pulled across the river with many helping hands reeling it in by rope. This service could be arranged with local traders, ranchers or Indian bands in exchange for valuable items in the emigrant's possession. If cost and time delays are not an issue, emigrants might pay an excessive fee to have their goods ferried over.

If none of these options are feasible, there is another possible crossing point at Bridger's Ferry, approximately fifty miles north of the Fort. Between the hamlets of Orin Junction and Ammon are the remains of a ferry operation that is no longer in service, but emigrants can use what is left there at their own risk. An example of this is found in the narrative of the **Ridgley Party** where certain members intend to go south from Fort Laramie on the Bozeman Trail to Colorado, but must continue up to this crossing point, then double back down to the Fort again on the South Bank Trails.

Partial view of Ezra Meeker's "Old Oregon Trail Map" as printed in *The Ox Team: or, The Old Oregon Trail, 1852-1906*, (New York, NY: Ezra Meeker, 1907), 252-253. Public Domain.

OVERLAND ROUTE
TO
CALIFORNIA,

DESCRIPTION OF THE ROUTE, VIA

COUNCIL BLUFFS, IOWA;

KEEPING THE NORTH SIDE OF THE PLATTE RIV-
ER, FOR THE WHOLE OF THE DISTANCE,
LYING NEAR THAT STREAM;
THENCE OVER THE

SOUTH PASS,

VIA THE

GREAT SUBLETTE AND BEAR RIVER
CUT-OFFS, AND THE TRUCKIE
RIVER ROAD,

OVER THE

SIERRA NEVADA,

TO

SACRAMENTO VALLEY.

By Andrew Child, of Wisconsin.

Title page from Andrew Child's *New Guide for the Overland Route to California*. Milwaukee: Daily Sentinel Steam Power Press, 1852.

When Andrew Child, author of the 1852 guidebook, *New Guide for the Overland Route to California,* reached the Fort in 1850 and was faced with the dilemma of crossing the River or not, he noted: "The Platte is here sometimes fordable, but more often otherwise, and owing to the great rapidity of its current, it is unsafe to ford, except in very low stages of water" (20). He concludes that staying on the North Bank Trails is "incomparably better" for competitive emigrants who might lose days' worth of travel time if they go through the ordeal of a crossing attempt (21).

For those who have resolved to continue on the North Bank Trail, many weary travelers, it becomes essential to rest and recuperate one's animals before trying to navigate the difficult path ahead. While resting up, women typically wash the family laundry and prepare a large batch of ready-to-eat meal items such as crackers. For a fee, folks can cross the North Platte River on a locally operated ferry to check for any telegraphs or letters at the post office on the Fort's campus. Those wanting to enjoy leisure activities can attend a traveling musician's concert or watch a dramatic spectacle at the Fort while the fort commander, **Lt. Col. William O. Collins,** takes a cut of the ticket sales.

When emigrants feel rested and ready for the challenges ahead, they might rely on a guidebook, such as Andrew Child's, for recommendations on where to find ample grass and water and good camping spots. The *New Guide* lists the following landmarks starting from the camps opposite of Fort Laramie until reaching the Lower Platte Ferry (Bisonette's Ferry) northwest of the Deer Creek garrison:

| Mileage | Destination |
| --- | --- |
| 4 | Dry Creek & Steep Ascent |
| 4.5 | Pass Between Mountains |
| 2.5 | Good Cold Springs (on the right of the road), near Cottonwood Trees |
| 7 | Road Joins River (in Long Canyon) |
| 7.5 | Fine Bottom Between Hills (in Sawmill Canyon, on Middle Bear Creek) |
| 1.5 | Alder Clump on the left (presently, Box Elder Spring) |
| 1 | Good Road (after a steep ascent) |
| 3 | Gradual Descent to a Creek |
| 1 | Deep Creek (not bad to cross) |
| 8 | to River, rough road |
| 4 | Descend to River (outside of Orin Junction) |
| 10 | Steep and Craggy Ascent ("McKinstry Ridge") |
| 5 | Road Descends to Rolling and Barren Country |
| 15 | Low Land Bordering the River |
| 3 | Lower Ferry of the Platte (Bisonette's Ferry) |

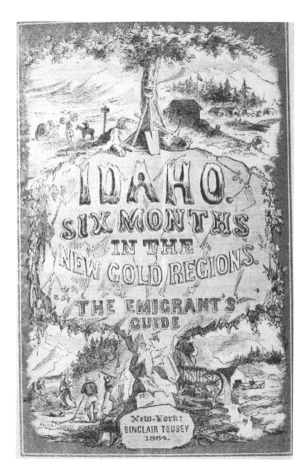

Front cover of John L. Campbell's *Idaho, Six Months in the New Gold Regions: The Emigrant's Guide*. New York: Sinclair Tousey. 1864.

In 1864, John Lyle Campbell releases a new guidebook titled, *Idaho, Six Months in the New Gold Regions: The Emigrant's Guide.* This book includes updated, no-fuss navigational notes that virtually retires the 1852 predecessor. **Sarah Rousseau**, diarist in the **Pella Company** quotes directly from this guidebook on several occasions. **Joshua Ridgley** in the **Ridgley Party** also purchases a guide for thirty-five cents before starting his journey, but it is unclear which version it is. In the newer guide, there are fewer landmarks noted from Fort Laramie on:

| Mileage | Destination |
|---------|-------------|
| 4 | Dry Creek |
| 7 | Cold Spring, Cottonwood Trees |
| 7 | Road Joins River (wood, water, grass, in Long Canyon) |
| 9 | Alder Clump on left (Box Elder Spring) |
| 9 | Road somewhat sandy |
| 9 | to River (near Lost Creek) |
| 4 | Rough Road, descends to the river again (outside of Orin Junction) |
| 10 | Steep and Craggy Ascent, Road Mountainous ("McKinstry Ridge") |
| 5 | Road descends to the River, sandy roads |
| 16 | High, Rolling, Barren Country and lowlands bordering the river |
| 3 | Lower Ferry of the Platte (Bisonette's Ferry) |

The "steep ascent" near present-day Gurnsey requires many emigrants to abandon precious furniture items on the side of the road. If their stock animals still struggle to haul their wagon loads on the uphill grade, emigrants might "double team" by combining their animals with another company's, then take turns using up nearly every ounce of their stock's strength to make the trip not only once, but twice (to bring up both sets of vehicles).

Severe downhill slopes into creek-carved valleys require brake systems to be installed on wagons (which the blacksmiths near Fort Laramie are all too happy to provide for an exorbitant fee). Alternatively, emigrants can try to "lock and bough back" their wagons by tying a rope to a sturdy object uphill, then slowly releasing slack to allow their vehicle to descend at a controlled speed (similar to rappelling).

By 1864, there are multiple bypass trails that can circumvent some of the difficult obstacles ahead and lessen the toll on bodies and equipment. As shown in the following map, a network of options is easily spotted north of the Glendo Reservoir.

Differentiating the intersecting California Trail (solid) and Oregon Trail (dashed) on the North and South Bank Trail Systems. Map generated using the NPS National Trails Historic Trails Viewer, a collaborative project of the National Geographic Society (*https://nps.maps.arcgis.com/*). Labels added by the author.

Several of the emigrants on the North Bank Trails this season have had interactions prior to reaching the Fort, which makes their collaborative story more dynamic. Some interactions are pleasant and bonds have formed between traveling parties. One example can be clearly seen with the **Pella Company** and **Jongewaard Train,** all former residents of Marion County, Iowa who have lengthy pre-existing relationships as friends, neighbors and colleagues.

Others on the North Bank Trails might not have formal relationships yet, such as with the **Brown** and **Oliver Trains,** but even chance encounters prepare the way for making life-saving bonds. Or, as seen in the case of the **Howard Train**, their time spent with the **Missouri Train** corrupts their character so much so, they become entangled in criminal activities.

# Saturday, July 2, 1864

### Roe

On July 2, the tired out, two-wagon **Roe Train** from Grinnell, Iowa passes by familiar faces in the **Jongewaard Train** before reaching Fort Laramie. The **Roes** may have waved a hand in passing or called out a, "See you there," as they have shared a similar origin and destination for quite some time.

After spying the Fort from the opposite side of the North Platte River, **Martha Roe**, wife of the wagon master, writes that they continue just past it (approximately 3 miles). When they roll into camp, "friendly" Sioux and other Plains Indians might greet them, offer to make trades, or simply observe their weekend religious practices with curiosity. For some emigrants, these interactions help to relax any previously held prejudices against Plains Indians. Others, such as those in the **Pella Company**, remain doubtful and hypervigilant.

| | |
|---|---|
| **Martha Roe**<br>*Roe Train* | "Travailed bout 8 M and that found us at ft Laramie  bout 4 oclock  camped in an Indian grave yard" *(July 2)* |

On the south side of the River, there is a Euro-American style graveyard outside the Fort's premise, where soldiers and civilians are buried in the ground.[275] However, the graveyard **Martha** describes on the north side of the River is an unusual sight for her: an aerial grave. **Martha** writes that this

---

[275] It is believed that Gardener Wakefield from the Kelly-Larimer Train is later buried at this cemetery, presently known as "Fort John Cemetery."

particular grave featured a body "stuck up on a tree to dry."[276] The burial practice employed causes viewer curiosity and, for some emigrants, superstitious fear.

This funerary practice is one example of how some Plains Indian tribes honor their loved ones. Only a basic explanation is provided here, as the nuances are beyond the scope of this book. Bodies of deceased males are wrapped in animal skins and blankets, then placed atop either a constructed or natural scaffold such as crossbeams balanced amid sturdy tree branches.[277] If a tree is unavailable or unsuitable, long poles can be raised vertically and leaned against each other (much like one would prop opposite tent poles). Additional poles or branches are set across the top of those "legs" to create an elevated surface. Similar to ancient Egyptian and Nordic practices, items of significance such as jewelry or weapons can be laid to rest with the deceased. Weather permitting, the body dries out.

"Indian burial place on Deer Creek, near Fort Laramie - From a photograph by A. Gardner." Illustration from *Harper's Weekly*, March 6, 1869, 152.

---

[276] Martha Roe, *Guide to a Trip to Idaho, 1864*, Ts. Blinn (1979), July 2.
[277] Deceased females do not typically receive this treatment. Again, the explanation for this is beyond the scope of this book.

## Brown

**Abbie Brown**, daughter-in-law of abolitionist John Brown, and memoirist from the **Brown Train,** does not record a specific date or location for most of her experiences, but her visit to Fort Laramie appears to coincide with the **Roes**.[278] Since July 2 is a Saturday, it is likely the **Browns** plan a layover at the Fort to observe their Sabbath. While there, **Abbie** describes a burial structure similar to what **Martha** writes about.

| | |
|---|---|
| **Abbie Brown**<br><br>*Brown Train* | "One day we camped for dinner [lunch] under a fine large cottonwood tree. When we were about half done eating[,] someone looked up in the tree and saw a dead Indian wrapped in a Buffalo skin[,] lying in the branches. It did not take us long to move from there as we were afraid something might drop down on us."[279] *(1916)* |

Because of the family's association with the 1856 massacre at Pottawatomie Creek[280] and the 1859 siege on Harpers Ferry in Virginia, they received persistent harassments and threats back in New York. Southern Sympathizers have threatened to take justice into their own hands and exact due punishment on **Salmon Brown** (who was directly involved in the 1856 massacre) and his younger sister **Annie** (who was directly involved in the 1859 siege). If their identity is discovered while on the journey, both siblings have everything to lose.

To try concealing their identity **Abbie** and **Salmon** use state names to identify themselves and others. For example, they are referred to as the **"New**

---

[278] Details from the Platte River Raids place the Brown Train in repeated close association with the Oliver, Pella and Roe Trains.

[279] Abbie Brown, "Across the Plains…," *Lake Placid News*, Sept. 29, 1916, 5-7.

[280] In this Kansas vigilante mission led by Salmon's father, John Brown directed the murder of five political enemies with swords. John Brown later claimed that this act was in self-defense, as those slayed were rumored to have made plans to set fire to the Browns' cabin and shoot anyone who ran out. This explanation was told to one of his supporters, E. A. Coleman, in a candid conversation. Further documentation of the 1879 Coleman conversations can be found in American sociologist, W.E.B. Dubois' 1909 biography, *John Brown* (Philadelphia: G.W. Jacobs & CO., 1909).

York Train," the **Oliver Train** is called the **"Indiana Train,"** and the **Howard Train** is the **"Tennessee Train"** who are associated with the **"Missouri Train."**[281] The one and only exception to this is found in the diary of **Martha Roe**, who names members of the **Brown Train** clearly.

## Oliver

Though there is no travel log to reference, the **Oliver Train** with six families from Indiana and Iowa camps somewhere near Fort Laramie between the dates of July 2-4. This date range is a calculated guess made by working backwards from firsthand observations of their presence further along the North Bank Trail.

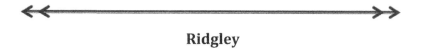

## Ridgley

On July 2, the **Ridgely Party** from La Crosse, Wisconsin on their way to Montana Territory,[282] arrives at a Plains Indian "village," about three miles northeast of Fort Laramie. Currently, six vehicles have been identified with this emigrant group, though it appears others have gathered with them up until this point and **Albert Dickson** claims they have twenty-seven wagons camped together.[283] This number probably includes the four-man packer-miner team from Missouri, led by **George Colburn**.

**Albert Dickson**
*Ridgley Party*
"The whole flat for nearly a mile between us and the river was covered with their lodges, set regularly in rows facing upon several streets. The lodges were of summer-killed elk or buffalo hides and would hold fifteen or

---

[281] Al Reck, "John Brown's Family Comes West: Chapter 3—Indians Terrorize John Brown Party," *Oakland Tribune*, January 22, 1961: 4-5M. Abbie Brown recorded two separate enemies on the trail: that of the Howards (The Southern Sympathizers) and the "Rebels" from Missouri who had upset them as far back as in Council Bluffs.
[282] Montana Territory incorporates on May 26, 1864.
[283] Ridgely-Dickson-Smith (3), Bouton Family (2) and the Donovan Team (1).

twenty persons ... They were fancifully decorated with paintings in vivid colors..." *(74)* [284]

**Albert's** description of the area is quite thoughtful coming from a fourteen-year-old. It is absent of racial criticism or fear that is common of many writers of this era. Later in the day, however, his tone shifts when his foster father hears bad news. In camp, **Joshua Ridgley** speaks with a "string of packers" heading east who share a story about a Mr. Farnham getting into a grapple with an Indian who sprang out from hiding to steal the packers' horses (78). During the hand-to-hand combat, the Indian pulled out a revolver and "blew Farnham's head off" (78). Mr. Farnham was personally known to the **Ridgleys** and to **Albert**, as he was from La Crosse. The packers cite this event happening about a hundred miles back (north), and about a week prior. Currently, no obituary or internment information has been found on the deceased.

| | |
|---|---|
| **Albert Dickson** | "Double guards with extra guns and ammunition |
| *Ridgley Party* | watched that night." *(78)* |

### Howard & Jongewaard

Also nearing Fort Laramie on July 2, is the **Jongewaard Train** from Pella, Iowa. **Gerrit Roorda**, teamster for **Lutje Mars** and diarist, records his company camping for the night a little farther east of the **Ridgleys**.

| | |
|---|---|
| **Gerrit Roorda** | "...got in sight of Laramie Peak today and stopped about |
| *Jongewaard Train* | 7 miles east of Laramie." *(July 2)* |
| **Allie Brunia** | "...relatives and friends had preceded by wagon train, as |
| *Jongewaard Train* | Uncle **Gerrit E. Roorda** did." *(61)*[285] |

---

[284] Albert Jerome Dickson, *Covered Wagon Days*, Ed. Arthur Jerome Dickson, (Lincoln: University of Nebraska Press, 1989).

[285] Allie Brunia, "A Trip to Oregon in 1864," in *Roorda Family History*, (Private publishing by William Frans Brunia, 1984), 61-62.

Where they stop, both sides of the River are camps of peaceful bands of Plains Indians in teepee and wigwam homes.[286] At this location, they are almost opposite of the Bordeaux Station (which is on the south side of the North Platte River).[287] Over at the trading station, Indians and trappers can sell animal pelts and dried meats to passing emigrants and the shop keep can sell freighted-in groceries and liquor at outrageous prices.

At this time, the **Howard Train** is presumed to be either with or ahead of the **Jongewaards.** Prior entries from **Gerrit Roorda** indicate regularly associating with the **Howards** from as early as June 2, when **Gerrit** numbers the wagons in his train: "Our train consisted of 24 wagons now[,] mostly from Marion County, Iowa." This total accounts for seven wagons in the **Jongewaard** and seventeen in the **Howard's** (though they are recently from Marshall County, Iowa).

Again, on June 15, **Gerrit** logs: "Caught up with the **Howard Train**." Additional attempts are made to stay in connection with each other through June 17, when **Gerrit** writes that they, "joined the **Howard Train**" at Skunk Creek, near Lexington, Nebraska. From June 18 to June 23, "the train was divided in two," but **Gerrit** shows a reconnection on June 24 with a near verbatim entry: "Our train consisted of 24 wagons mostly of Marion County, Iowa."

## Missourians & Virginians

Also in the vicinity of Fort Laramie are two other parties identified by **Brown family** writers simply as the **Missouri Train** (AKA, "Missouri guerellas,"[288] or "Rebels"[289]) and two young men from this group who will be referred to from now on as the **Virginians**. There is no biographical sketch for these travelers because their identities have not yet been established.

---

[286] Some of these residents remain year-round as the wives and children of soldiers at Fort Laramie.
[287] This is the location of the August 1854 Grattan Massacre between the U.S. Military and visiting Sioux and Brule tribes.
[288] "The Grave of John Brown," editorial in *The Soldiers' Journal*, October 5, 1864, 6.
[289] Al Reck, "Chapter 3," *Oakland Tribune*, January 22, 1961, 4-5M.

In a 1933 *Oakland Tribune* article about the **Brown family's** journey to California, a reference is made to the **Missouri Train** that, "had with it a number of hot-headed men... They were still in a vindictive mood over the recollection of the way **John Brown** had marshalled the free-soilers against them."[290] Having met this train near Nebraska's Chimney Rock, **Abbie Brown** writes that her family hastily excuses themselves from that camping area because of hostile comments made by the **Missourians** about the Civil War.[291]

Per historian Daniel Rosenberg, the two **Virginians** are believed to have been traveling with the **Missouri Train** from the beginning of their journey. He wrote in his 1975 research paper that they were, "members of the Confederate group,"[292] but based on their behaviors this Summer, they might be considered Unionists—those who reside in a Confederate state and either support the ideals of the Union or oppose the actions of the Confederacy.

### Morris-Hastings & Pella Company

The **Pella Company**, led by **Nicholas Earp**, though previously in close proximity to their hometown acquaintances in the **Jongewaard Train**, are presently lagging. On July 2, the **Pella Company** is still in Nebraska, camped opposite of Chimney Rock, in what is now Bayard. They still have more than sixty miles, or four days' worth of travel, to reach Fort Laramie.

**Sarah Rousseau**
*Pella Company*

"...when we stopped[,] the Indians came to us. We had quite a time with them. They had skins to sell and Moccasins. We bought 1 [Elk] skin[293] and we gave a dollar and a quarter, the other[,] one a cup of sugar and

---

[290] "After Harpers Ferry," editorial in *Oakland Tribune*, May 21, 1933. A word of caution: The quoted source is listed as Abbie Brown in a January 25, 1913 issue of *The Outlook* news magazine from New York. On further investigation, the 1913 article, "My Father, John Brown," was actually written by Salmon Brown and does not contain the detailed quote as shown.

[291] Abbie Brown, "Across the Plains...," *Lake Placid*, Sept. 29, 1916, 5-7.

[292] Daniel Rosenberg, *Mary Brown: From Harpers Ferry to California*, (The American Institute for Marxist Studies; New York), 1975, Page 21.

[293] This detail is pertinent to the events of July 14.

bought **John [Rousseau]** a pair of moccasins which we paid for in meat. They appeared very friendly..." *(July 2)*

**Sarah Rousseau**
*Pella Company*

"Our horse Charlie is still very lame. Traveled some 18 miles to-day." *(July 2)*

During this or in an upcoming interaction east of Fort Laramie, a white man offers to trade one of his horses for **Dr. James Rousseau's** favorite horse, Charlie, who is visibly suffering. When **James** does not agree to the trade, the man warns him. "He said we wouldn't be able to carry him through," **Sarah** reflects (July 14).

With the **Pella Company** at this time are at least four other emigrant groups who joined them after crossing the Missouri River at Council Bluffs:

- The **Clarks**, an older Mormon couple in a single wagon cart, led by their son-in-law, **Robert Parker**. They are going from Navoo, Illinois to Provo, Utah, just outside of Salt Lake City;

- The **Nelson Morris family**, going from Davis County, Iowa to Washington;

- The **Jacob Hastings family**, also from Davis County, Iowa and heading to Washington;[294]

- **Arthur Wright**, a Minnesota farmer and mining hopeful who is originally from Canada.[295]

## Shoemaker

Even further east is a man who goes by the last name of **Shoemaker** with his single wagon and a herd of horses. Because a first-person travel record is

---

[294] Also see the Morris–Hastings Train biographical sketch and narrative in the South Bank Trail section of this book.
[295] Arthur W. Wright, "Hennepin County, Minnesota Vital Statistics Card," (Portland: Oregon Historical Society, n.d.).

lacking for him, **Mr. Shoemaker's** location is determined by comparing the accounts of others on the trail and triangulating his position. At present, he is on the south side of the North Platte River and will not cross to the north side of the North Platte River until he reaches Fort Laramie.

Working backwards from a future sighting at Ficklin's telegraph station on July 6 leads to believing that **Mr. Shoemaker** is near Ash Hollow on July 2 (about two hundred miles from his suspected place of origin on Wood River, near Grand Island, Nebraska).[296]

---

[296] Specifically, on July 6, George Forman (who is featured in the South Bank Trail stories) sees Mr. Shoemaker at Ficklin's telegraph station, between Chimney Rock and Scotts Bluff, in Nebraska.

# Sunday, July 3, 1864

### Roe

The **Roe Train** spends their Sunday, July 3 in the same camp near the Indian graveyard. During the day, the newlyweds, **Isaac and Martha Roe** set aside time for their ritual Bible reading and hymnal singing after a special birthday bath.

**Martha Roe**
*Roe Train*

"This is Sabbath Morning and my birth day[,] that being my 21st birth day[.] after doing the ordinary work[,] **Isaac and I** went and took a bath in the river  ... then came reading of the bible[,] then sing[,] then supper" *(July 3)*

### Brown

No direct mention of visiting Fort Laramie is found in either **Salmon Brown** or his wife **Abbie's** memoirs and correspondences, however, the **Browns** are suspected to remain near the Fort until approximately July 6, based on future sightings. Moving forward, readers may notice an effort by the **Browns** to stay near or with the **Roes**, yet distant from the **Missourians**.

### Oliver

At some point during their weekend layover at Fort Laramie, it is plausible the **Oliver Train** makes a friendly connection with the **Browns**. In **Abbie Brown's** 1916 memoir, she claims no one in her family had disclosed their true identity to anyone yet but, as with the **Roes**, a special connection is formed regardless.

**Abbie Brown**
*Brown Train*

"They **[the Olivers]** seemed to know who we were and were very friendly."[297] *(1916)*

If identities were revealed, the **Olivers** would be kindred spirits to the **Brown's** cause and sympathetic to their flight. As most members of the Quaker culture did, the **Olivers** held a zero-tolerance outlook on war and human rights issues such as slavery and gender inequality. As far back as 1776, Quakers were "prohibited from owning slaves, and 14 years later [1790] they petitioned the U.S. Congress for the abolition of slavery."[298] Many were also instrumental in the operation of the Underground Railroad through Iowa (as were the **Browns**).[299]

## Ridgley Party

On July 3, the **Ridgley Party** leaves the peaceful Indian village, and stops again just one mile northwest of Fort Laramie. There, **Albert Dickson** collects valuable information on the travel season so far.

**Albert Dickson**
*Ridgley Party*

There was, "a temporary shelter of boards at the left of the road where an officer and his assistant were keeping a record of the traffic … A tally of the traffic was also kept on the south side of the river…" *(78)*

The number of wagons, carts and other outfits passing Fort Laramie on the South Bank Trails reached about four thousand so far. Comparatively, numbers from the North Bank Trails have reached a whopping six thousand.

---

[297] Abbie Brown, "Across the Plains…," *Lake Placid*, Sept. 29, 1916, 5-7.
[298] "Quaker Activism" on History Detectives, n.d., *PBS*, https://www.pbs.org/opb/historydetectives/feature/quakeractivism/#:~:text=The%20Quaker%20campaign%20to%20end.
[299] On a separate, but related note, the famous suffragette Susan B. Anthony (also a Quaker) found her life intertwined with the Browns when two of her brothers, Daniel (1824-1904) and Jacob (1834-1900), joined John and Salmon Brown in the Kansas Raids. When John was hung for his involvement in the Harpers Ferry siege, Susan held a memorial in his name. See more on this in Alma Lutz, "Susan B. Anthony and John Brown," *Rochester History*, XV, no. 3 (Rochester Public Library, 1953).

If this discrepancy is an indication of anything, it is not evidence for ease of travel, timesaving, or better food and water provisions. Instead, this could be reflective of many emigrants on the North Bank Trails being unable to safely cross (or afford to cross) the North Platte River. Readers can also speculate the heavier traffic being related to the release of J. L. Campbell's new guidebook promising gold at the end of the road.

**Joshua Ridgley** had a guide that he bought, "for thirty-five cents at La Crosse before we started," but it is unclear which trail system the guidebook is for (*Covered Wagon Days,* 52). If he had planned to follow the South Bank Trails, then (being unable to cross the river) he would need some additional advice to lead them through the Black Hills on the opposite bank. **Joshua** ferries over to the Fort to inquire about the trail ahead.

| | |
|---|---|
| **Albert Dickson**<br>*Ridgley Party* | "The road [leaves] the Platte for a time and skirted a range of hills cut by deep ravines. ...It would be well to look to our wagons and equipment before attempting it. We therefore decided to lay over the next day. It would be a pleasant place to spend the fourth." *(89)* |

During his visit to the Fort, **Joshua** meets a **Mr. Seth Bullock**, whom he claims is the sutler's store keeper.

| | |
|---|---|
| **Albert Dickson**<br>*Ridgley Party* | "While there, they made some purchases at the sutler's store kept by Seth Bullock. Many years later[,] I came to know Mr. Bullock ... in Deadwood." *(82)* |

There is a major factual error in this claim. The sutler's store was managed by Seth Ward from 1857 to 1871.[300] In addition to this military post, Seth partnered with a Cheyenne interpreter, William Guerrier, in a civilian mercantile (Ward & Guerrier at the Sand Point Trading Post located nine miles west of the Fort, on the south side of the River).[301] Seth also partnered with Robert Campbell & Co. in a mule train shipping operation that directed goods from St. Louis, Missouri straight to his principal places of business. In a

---

[300] Seth Edmund Ward (1820-1903).
[301] William Guerrier (1812- 1858).

biographical sketch from the Denver Public Library where Seth Ward's correspondences are archived, they claim, "As sutler he enjoyed a monopoly at the busiest post on the frontier."[302]

In 1858, the merchant William Guerrier passed away and Seth hired on William Bullock from St. Louis. He gave William the official position as manager of the sutler's store.[303] "Sutler Bullock," as he was called, also served as an Indian agent as needed. It is entirely possible that as a youngster, **Albert** remembered this incorrectly and blurred these details with the later well-known U.S. Marshall Seth Bullock of Deadwood, South Dakota (who would have been fifteen in 1864).

Back at camp, **Albert** mentions that after supper, a miner named **George Colburn** "struck out in the direction of La Bonte up the river, above Bridger's Ferry" (89-90). **George's** sudden, secretive and lone errand is strange to the **Ridgelys**, but **George** had previously told them that he'd spent the last seven years of his life on the Plains. If this statement is true, then they have no reason to worry about him. Even so, the plan seems fishy to **Albert** because **George** leaves his three companions behind. In any case, **the Ridgleys** expect him back by nightfall.

In the evening, **Albert** hears the sounds of regular munitions testing at the Fort from across the River.

**Albert Dickson**      "At sunset we heard the cannon booming..." *(90)*
*Ridgley Party*

As the sky turns dark, the **Ridgleys** expect **George** to return, but he does not.

**Albert Dickson**      "When he didn't show up that evening[,] we asked his
*Ridgley Party*         companions where he had gone. They said they didn't
                        know; and they showed no concern..." *(90)*

_____

[302] "Seth Edmond Ward Papers," Denver Public Library Archives, Accessed April 25, 2023. https://archives.denverlibrary.org/repositories/3/resources/8802.
[303] William Galt Bullock (1815-1896).

## Jongewaard

**Gerrit Roorda**
*Jongewaard Train*

"We laid over today and some of our men went to the Fort to look for letters but the Postoffice was not open." *(July 3)*

The fourteen mile round-trip errand from their camp located east of Fort Laramie is a disappointing, day-long excursion to a post office closure. It is likely **Cornelius Jongewaard** is expecting **Gerrit Rysdam** (who left five days before him) to have left a note at the post office with an update on their travel experience.

Unlike others who firmly designate Sunday as a non-traveling day of rest, entries in **Gerrit Roords's** logbook reveal the **Jongewaard Train** is comfortable traveling on this day of the week, as needed. It is believed, however, that **Cornelius,** a staunch Christian leader in the group, incorporated some sort of religious study on Sundays. In a reminiscence provided by **Mary Ellerbroek-Honstra** (stepdaughter of **Lutje Mars**) relates how one private prayer session by her stepfather is received by curious Indian onlookers.

**Mary Ellerbroek-Hornstra**
*Jongewaard Train*

"As **Mars** was a devout man, he was praying earnestly and long in a sonorous tone of voice with his face uplifted and his eyes closed, and the Indians were astonished and did not know what to make of it." (411)[304]

## Howard, Missourians & Virginians

Either during the visit to Fort Laramie, or early on in the Black Hills, those in the **Howard Train** make a connection with the **Missouri Train** and the **Virginians**. As the **Howards** are Southern Sympathizers and draft evaders, the

---

[304] Mary Ellerbroek-Hornstra, "The Oregon Trail," in Charles Dyke's *The Story of Sioux County* (Orange City: n.p., 1942), 402-412.

traveling parties have plenty in common to support an ongoing association that endures until (at least) Fort Hall in Idaho state. There is no indication that the **Howard Train** remains in company with the **Jongewaard Train** from Fort Laramie on. In fact, circumstances of the Raids support there being a separation by distance, as does the lack of further name mentions in **Gerrit Roorda's** day book.

## Morris-Hastings & Pella Company

Back in Nebraska, the **Pella Company,** led by **Nicholas Earp**, leaves their camp near Chimney Rock, causing **Sarah Rousseau** to complain about traveling on a Sunday.

**Sarah Rousseau**
*Pella Company*

"Oh that we may spend this Sabbath as near right as we can under present circumstances." *(July 3)*

The **Pella Company** goes twenty miles on July 3, stopping where they can see Scotts Bluff National Monument out in the distance. They usually stick to an average of twelve miles per day. This longer day is a bit too much for one of the **Rousseau's** lead horses with a lame foot. It is possible **Dr. James Rousseau** provides at least some comfort or care to the animals using his background in naturopathy.

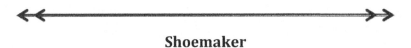

## Shoemaker

Farther east, **Mr. Shoemaker** is guesstimated to be just west of Oshkosh, Nebraska where the Nebraska Sandhills are visible for miles on end on the North Bank Trail.[305] Along the South Bank Trails, however, **Mr. Shoemaker**

---

[305] According to one geography enthusiast, the Nebraska Sandhills span upwards of 20,000 square miles, making it "the largest sand dune formation in the Western Hemisphere." (*ALandingADay*, "Lewellen, Nebraska (and the nearby Sandhills)," December 5, 2014, https://landingaday.wordpress.com/2014/12/05/lewellen-nebraska-and-the-nearby-sandhills/.

must "rise the bluffs" and travel along a hard and barren stretch of trail for several miles before dipping down into a spring valley for grass and water.[306]

---

[306] P. L. Platt & N. Slater, *Platt & Slater's Guide to California Overland* (Chicago: The Daily Journal, 1852), 13.

# Monday, July 4, 1864

### Roe

Celebrating Independence Day along the trails involves gathering with other emigrants and locals for communal festivities and feasting. Just west of Fort Laramie, **Martha Roe** prepares an elaborate dinner with plumb cake (similar to a bread pudding), rice pudding, boiled ham, beans, applesauce, fresh bread with molasses, churned butter, coffee and tea with sugar and cream, rice pies, and (if that isn't enough) she bakes cookies.

| | |
|---|---|
| **Martha Roe**<br>*Roe Train* | "This is independence day ... prepared to celebrate this day in the wash tub ... The boys was over to the fort nearly all day" *(July 4)* |

Over at the Fort, the miners accompanying the **Roe Train** attend a "negro show;" a performance that is not mentioned by other travelers featured in this book. What she is referencing may either be a traveling minstrel show, or a soldier-crafted variety show presented in blackface. **Sgt. Lewis B. Hull,** who is stationed at the Fort during this time, notes in his diary that this particular holiday production consists of "pantomime, burlesque, songs, etc." and that seats were not only sold out, but crowded in (July 4, See Appendix).

An early description of these types of events comes from a civilian artist who spent six months with the Missouri Mounted Volunteers in 1848, at what was called Fort Childs, AKA "New Fort Kearny" in Nebraska. The artist, William Tappan, wrote about a blackface production in his journal on June 24:

"...last night were serenaded by a very good band of eatheopian songsters[.] it seemed strange to hear those familiar airs which I had so often listened to in the cities of the east repeated in the midst of this vast plain where everything is savages & where our lives are guarded by the rifle & the bayonete. called to mind the many comforts of home & blessings of civilized life[.]"[307]

In the same year the Missouri Mounted Volunteers called these shows comforting, renowned abolitionist (and friend of John Brown) Frederick Douglass declared in his Rochester, New York newspaper that minstrel shows and Ethiopian serenades were produced by "filthy scum" to benefit society's corrupt.[308] Conversely, American scholar Robert Toll has argued in a 1978 article for *American Heritage* magazine that, in the years leading up to the Civil War, "no one took minstrel shows seriously; they were meant to be light, meaningless entertainment."[309]

In 1864, **Lt. Caspar Collins**, the son of the Fort's commander **Lt. Col. William O. Collins**, wrote to his mother about the entertainment options at their disposal while out on the Plains. "[Caspar] indicated that they had a circulating library, a band, amateur theatricals, and an occasional ball," shared Fort Laramie historian, David Heib.[310]

A later description is found in the testimony of Sgt. Reinhold R. Gast of the 8th Cavalry, who served from 1887-1892:

> "Small variety and minstrel shows occasionally relieve the tedium of post life. 'Once in a while,' recalled Sergeant Reinhold R. Gast, 'from the outside, a minstrel show passed through.' The frontier regular, hungry for entertainment, welcomed even the most mediocre traveling troupe. ... A stage and seats were improvised, and the entertainment-starved garrison usually turned out en masse..." When theatrical productions were

---

[307] William Tappan, *William Tappan's Diary 1848*, Eds. Ellen Tappen and Richard E. Jensen, Nebraska State Historical Society Digital Collection [RG5326.AM].
https://history.nebraska.gov/collection_section/william-henry-tappan-1821-1907-rg5326-am/
[308] Frederick Douglass, editorial in *The North Star*, October 27, 1848.
[309] "Behind the Blackface," *American Heritage*, April/May, 1978, 64, no. 1.
[310] David Hieb, "The Civil War and the Uprising of the Plains," in *Fort Laramie National Monument, Wyoming* (National Park Services: Washington D.C., 1954). Accessible at
https://www.nps.gov/parkhistory/onlinebooks/hh/20/hh20l.htm

developed in-house and performed by soldiers, "enthusiasm frequently replaced talent."[311]

In addition to exploitative theatrics at the Fort that holiday soldiers make visits to emigrant camps to recruit women for an evening dance.

**Martha Roe**
*Roe Train*

"...and a soldier came and he invited us all over to a ball [since] girles are scarce" *(July 4)*

**Martha** declines the invitation. Instead, the women in her camp (possibly including the **Browns**) visit with the Indians, socialize until dark, then go to bed. About the aerial grave, she adds sarcastically, "all this time our Indian staid sentinel," as if it were a guardian watching over them.

## Brown & Oliver

The **Brown Train** seems to be keeping a low profile for July 4. Neither **Abbie Brown** nor her husband **Salmon** remark on celebrating the holiday in any of their published accounts. It is possible that the **Olivers** use the evening to prepare for an early morning start into the Black Hills and avoid any of the festivities.

## Howard, Missourians & Virginians

The **Howard Train's** official length of stay at the Fort is unknown, though they, along with the **Missouri Train** and the two **Virginians,** are suspected to be present for the day's various entertainments.[312]

---

[311] Sgt. Reinhold R. Gast, in Don Rickey, Jr.'s *Forty Miles a Day on Beans and Hay: The Enlisted Soldier Fighting the Indian Wars* (University of Oklahoma Press: Norman, 1963), 196-197.
[312] One member of the wagon train, Alfred H. Kennedy, keeps a diary of "the Howard trek across the plains," but upon Alfred's death in 1931, the diary could not be located and has been lost to researchers since (per Randall Lovejoy's essay in *The Genie*, 1988).

**Ridgley Party**

Also among those staying near the Fort for the holiday are the **Ridgley Party.** After waking to the same booming signal of cannon fire, the men get to work on shoring up their for the increased demands of the trail ahead.

| **Albert Dickson** | "We spent the forenoon greasing the wagons, tightening |
| *Ridgley Party* | the bolts, putting leathers at the end of loose spokes ... to |
| | tighten the wheels, and getting everything ready for a |
| | rough piece of road." *(90)* |

In the meanwhile, **Rebecca Ridgley**, **Mary Smith** and the **Button women** do the family laundry. To dry out the wet and wrung clothes, the women might string ropes between covered wagons, or stretch it from a wagon bow to a nearby shrub or tree. Despite the dusty, outdoor conditions, wives are expected to provide typical home life comforts, albeit on a smaller scale.

| **Albert Dickson** | "There were baking, churning, mending, and all the |
| *Ridgley Party* | usual domestic activities of a large household." *(90)* |

For recreation, **Albert** claims the children chase around with other Indian children on stick horses. This does not seem to include **Albert**, who has been expected to perform the duties of a grown man from day one. Once his own chores are finished, **Albert** takes a walk along the trail and reads the notes staked along the sides. Some emigrants leave messages for those behind them by writing on a piece of paper or cloth then either tie or impale the note on a stick before running the base of the stick into the ground. These notes sometimes contain warnings about road conditions or Indians ahead, details of a new grave nearby, or provide a welfare check to a party that has fallen behind. **Albert** finds one such welfare check from Edward and Charles Phillips, who became acquainted with the **Ridgley Party** very early on the trip but did not remain with the wagon train. [313]

**Albert Dickson**
*Ridgley Party*

"I came upon another note from the **Phillips boys.** It was dated a week earlier [approx. June 27] and stated a man named [John] Bozeman was gathering up a train for the purpose of laying out a new road to Virginia City by way of the east side of the Big Horns, and that they were going to try to get in with them." *(90)*

The **Phillips Boys** are unable to catch up with or "get in" with the **Bozeman Caravan**, considering John Bozeman is at least two-hundred-forty-miles north of Fort Laramie (on Piney Creek near present-day Kearny, Wyoming) by the time the **Phillips Boys** even hear of their departure.

## Bozeman's Caravan (Briefly)

Mountain man John Bozeman's impact on the histories of Territorial Montana, Idaho and Wyoming is lengthy, but a brief synopsis of his recent travel experience is included here to help establish context for the Platte River Raids, especially as it relates to July 4 of 1864.

In the Winter of 1862-63, John Bozeman and John Jacobs, a fur trapper, take a trip from the mining town of Bannack, Idaho Territory (Montana) back south to St. Louis, Missouri. After they pass Virginia City into the settlement that would eventually be named after Bozeman, instead of continuing northeast to the Missouri River and ferrying down to St. Louis, they decide to follow an old Indian foot trail around the Big Horn Mountains.

The path they "discover" brings them straight through an important ecological area for the migrating Buffalo that Plains Indians greatly depend on. These Buffalo hunting grounds that have also been the subject of numerous

---

[313] Edward Phillips, born in England (1818-unknown) travels from Rock Island, Illinois to Montana Territorywith his son Charles (1848-1927). Edward's wife, Elenor (1812-1892) stays back, then joins her family in either 1865 or 1866. When she arrives, she is officially one of the first female residents of Madison County, Montana (per her obituary in *The Madisonian*, June 11, 1892). See the appendix for a transcription.

disputes between neighboring tribal bands competing for resources (especially between the Crow and Lakota-Sioux).

This southbound foot trail traces the base of the Mountains down into the Powder River Basin. Before 1862, the foot trail rarely saw the presence of white men other than a few low key hunter-packers and had not seen any wagon traffic at all. To complicate matters, an 1857 treaty agreement with the U.S. Government and representatives of various Northern Plains Indian tribes dictates that emigrants and the Union Army are limited to using only the pre-existing trails through tribal-occupied lands. This means sticking to the North and South Bank Trails and not taking any detours. Soldiers stationed along the North Platte River are expected to facilitate safe travel on the designated trails and to enforce the treaty agreement, should there be a breach.

According to these terms, the two men coming through the Basin are guilty of trespassing. Along the way, they cross a branch of the Yellowstone River, then the Tongue River, pass through present-day Buffalo, Montana, cross over Middle Fork Powder River, and come through present-day Kaycee, Wyoming. From there, they skirt around a series of accordion-fold bluffs until reaching the North Platte River between the Lower Ferry of the Platte and what the author has designated as the North Douglas Bend. When they reach Fort Laramie, they are excited about the new shortcut that shaves six weeks' off the typical travel time between points (compared to going around the Wind River Mountain Range and through the Bridger-Teton forest).

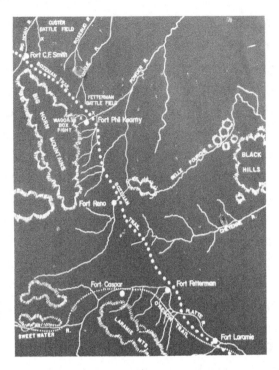

Map of the Bozeman Trail inscribed on the historical marker near Fort Fetterman. Photo and permissions granted by Jenna Thornburn, Wyoming Pioneer Museum.

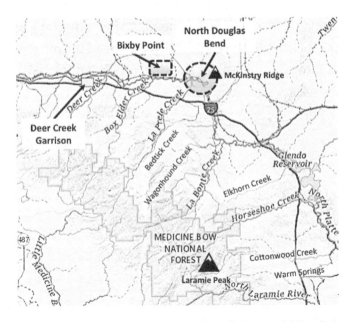

Map of Converse County, Wyoming showing the author-designated "North Douglas Bend" and "Bixby Point." U. S. Geological Survey (USGS), modified by author.

During the 1863 emigrant travel season, John Bozeman and an interpretive guide, Rafael Gallegos, attempt to capitalize on their experience by leading a small collection of wagon trains on a reverse route from the Fort, up through the Basin to Virginia City. They collect a steep fee from each party and promise to get them to the goldfields faster than anyone else. Shortly into their trip, they are intercepted by a war party of both Cheyenne and Sioux bands. The Indians tell the guides that wagons are not allowed to come through because the tracks they make in the ground can disrupt Buffalo migration. After the confrontation, the guides turn their wagon trains back down to the North Bank Trail.

Buffalo in Montana, black and white negative, ca. 1909. Library of Congress [96513773].

A year later, John Bozeman tries his luck again with the same scheme. In mid-June of 1864, John Bozeman rallies a massive caravan of eighty-three covered wagons with get-rich hopefuls from Fort Laramie. A caravan of this size might be considered more intimidating and harder to turn back, should they be confronted again. These emigrants pay him five dollars each (about $96.00 USD in 2023) to lead them through the basin. For John Bozeman, the risk of being caught is worth the price of $415 in greenbacks or gold (nearly $8,000 in 2023).

On July 4, after crossing the Bighorn River near present-day Hardin, Montana, the folks in **Bozeman's Caravan** celebrate Independence Day by shooting down a large herd of Buffalo. The result is devastating to the population. The next day, the emigrants move one, leaving one hundred corpses to rot where they lay.[314]

This Buffalo massacre is especially notable as a key inciting factor for the Platte River Raids. At either an 1867 or 1868 peace treaty meeting with several Powder River Basin tribal leaders at Fort Laramie, Crow Chief Bear Tooth expresses his grievance over the needless slaughter. He laments to the military, "Your young men … have killed my game, my buffalo. They did not kill it to eat it. They left it where it fell."[315]

Killing Cows and Spikes on the Snow. Near Cohagen, MT, B/W negative, 1880. L. A. Hoffman Collection, Montana Historical Society.

---

[314] This specific date and number killed comes from wagon train member John T. Smith. His and other wagon train member accounts are easily found in the two volume anthology published by Susan Doyle: *Journeys to the Land of Gold: Emigrant Diaries from the Bozeman Trail, 1863-1866* (Helena: Montana Historical Society Press, 2000).

[315] See Christopher W. Czajka, "There Is No Country Like the Crow Country: The Crow Indians and Montana Settlers," *PBS Thirteen: Frontier House,* accessed May 5, 2020, https://www.thirteen.org/wnet/frontierhouse/frontierlife/essay73.html.

## Jongewaard

Back on the North Bank Trails, the **Jongewaard Train** enjoys a partial day of rest before traveling seven miles and camping opposite of Fort Laramie. They still cannot receive any of the mail they'd been waiting on because of the holiday.[316]

**Gerrit Roorda**
*Jongewaard Train*

"We laid over till 4 o'clock and got to the Fort Laramie a little after sundown. Here we heard the cannon roar."
*(July 4)*

It is nice to think the soldiers sent up their own version of celebratory fireworks by way of cannon fire, but other travel accounts clarify this is part of a regular munitions test schedule.

## Morris-Hastings & Pella Company

Still in Nebraska, the **Pella Company et al.** has a setback at Spring Creek due to the **Rousseau's** lame lead horse. Because they are close enough to Scotts Bluff, several emigrants in this wagon train take advantage of the opportunity to double back and get an up close view of the scenic landmark.[317] If this includes crossing the frigid North Platte River, that might be accomplished by carefully fording on horseback from sandbar to sandbar. Sometimes, reliable crossing points are marked out by long poles stuck into the sandbars. Between these pseudo islands, the river might only be an inch or a few feet deep, but the current is strong enough to sweep people off their feet and drag them to their death.[318]

---

[316] The United States Postal Service has observed Independence Day closures since 1776.

[317] This rest stop is about four miles west of the Scotts Bluff monument, according to J. L. Campbell's 1864 Guide.

[318] On June 20, Sarah records a "sad accident" when a man from another wagon train attempts to walk out to one such "island in the river" to get firewood. His feet were swept out and he "got drowned." Nicholas Earp tried to retrieve the man's body, "but the current was too swift."

**Sarah Rousseau**

*Pella Company*

"The girls went to the Bluffs today with **Em Curtis, Richard Curtis** and **Mr. [Robert] Parker** to take a view of the surrounding country. They said it was a pretty sight." *(July 4)*

Being wheelchair bound, **Sarah** must rely the sightseeing descriptions that others relay to her. In this case, "the girls" reporting to her are **Sarah's** daughter **"Libby" Rousseau** and personal aide, **Matilda Field**.

In the evening, the **Pella Company et al.** celebrates the holiday with one speech from **Thomas Ellis,** the son of Pella, Iowa's first mayor,[319] and another from **William Jesse Curtis,** a beloved up and coming lawyer with the firm Curtis & Curtis. After the formalities, the **Pella Company, Clarks, and Morris-Hastings** kick up a dance.

View of Scotts Bluff Monument from the North Platte River near Gering, NE. Ken Lund (2005), https://www.flickr.com/photos/kenlund/69184417.

---

[319] Thomas Jefferson Ellis (1843-1895). His father is William J. Ellis (1818-1870: the first mayor of Pella, Iowa from 1856-1857, then county treasurer from 1858 to 1860.

**Shoemaker**

If **Mr. Shoemaker** is keeping on pace with his load of leather and herd of horses, then he might be camping this evening about ten miles east of the picturesque Court House Rock.[320]

---

[320] According to Platt and Slater's 1852 *Traveler's Guide…*, the Court House Rock and Jail Rock formations are "8 or 10 miles south of the road, though it appears … not more than 1 or 2 miles from it."

# Tuesday, July 5, 1864

### Union Army & Ridgley Party

After a night of celebrating past dark, hundreds of emigrants in the vicinity of Fort Laramie now have to compete to leave the overcrowded camps. Modern readers might imagine this scenario resembling the logistical mess of a parking lot after a major sporting event or sold out concert. Travelers who were once spread out now vie for their chance to get ahead of the slow train, stay away from the reckless train, and gain every inch on competing mining teams. Because of the difficult terrain ahead, there are also traffic jam situations while emigrants try to overcome the geological obstacles.

On the North Bank Trails ahead are a series of steep climbs, deeply eroded wheel ruts, and long stretches of rugged, wagon rattling ground. In between rocky bluffs that sidewind like the waters that carved them, the trail dips down and swerves into spring-carved valleys that can lead worn down travelers back to the banks of the North Platte River for refreshment. Since this trail system receives heavier traffic than the south side of the River, there is more competition for wild vegetation if emigrants do not carry their own supply of animal feed with them.

On July 5, the **Ridgley Party** is more than ready to launch their journey into the Black Hills. With all the equipment preparations completed on the day prior, they appear to have only one disruption to their departure.

**Albert Dickson**      "**George Colburn** had not come back yet." *(91)*
*Ridgley Party*

As a reminder to the reader, **George Colburn** left the Ridgley Party two days prior on a suspicious lone mission. Figuring that **George** knows what he is doing, the **Ridgley Party** strikes the trail early and fast. When ascending their first set of hills near Guernsey, **Albert Dickson** notes a surplus of heavy furniture items dumped along the waysides. The sight of a finely crafted escritoire writing desk tossed on a heap upsets **Rebecca Ridgley,** who appreciates the value of such items.

| **Albert Dickson**<br>*Ridgley Party* | "This was no new occurrence, however, as we had frequently seen chairs, bedsteads, or other articles … warped by exposure to the elements." *(91)* |
|---|---|

At a midday rest near a spring, the **Ridgley Party** is surprised to see **George** coming in to their camp. They are even more surprised by what he brings back with him.

| **Albert Dickson**<br>*Ridgley Party* | "[He] rode up from the southwest on a United States mule with a government saddle and bridle. He explained that he had bought the outfit. We knew the government wasn't selling mules or horses; they were needed too badly. And furthermore the brand on this one had not been 'vented,'[321] so that it would not have been a legal transfer anyway." *(91)* |
|---|---|

This is the second time **George** has been caught stealing. Prior to reaching Fort Laramie, he was caught lying about a newly acquired horse when the emigrant-owner he stole it from caught up with the **Ridgley Party** and confronted the thief. This suspiciously similar event causes **Joshua Ridgley** to question the wisdom of associating with **George** and his team.

In a private conversation with **Albert, George** discloses that there is a wagon train of Missourians who camped a short distance away, who recently "let" their horses stampede loose and run off, leaving them free for the taking.[322] He predicts that they will put blame on Indians, feign fear and not venture to go after the missing horses. He tells **Albert**, "I'll go out in the

---

[321] Venting a cattle brand is as simple as branding a straight bar overtop the existing brand mark. This was done to evidence a sale or transfer of ownership.

[322] These Missourians have not been formally linked to the rebels being avoided by the Brown Train.

mornin' an' git some of them hosses 'fore night" (95). **Albert** suspects this story is not entirely true.

By evening, the **Ridgley Party** covers an astounding distance up to thirty-three miles. Considering an "ox pace" of two miles per hour on level ground, this day's journey likely included over sixteen hours of hauling and hiking near to the point of exhaustion.

| | |
|---|---|
| **Albert Dickson**<br><br>*Ridgley Party* | "After a drive which taxed the endurance of the oxen and ourselves as we made camp at Alder Clump Springs [AKA Box Elder Spring], in an upland pass ... The springs bubbled up clear and cold." *(92)* |

Box Elder Spring/Alder Clump Camp on Rankin Ranch in eastern Glendo, Wyoming. Still image from Dr. Brandon J. Semler's "Larry Cundall: A Real Wyoming Cowboy," *Torrington Tales and Trails* (Eastern Wyoming College, September 23, 2023), https://www.youtube.com/watch?v=xXYFL8qyRcE.

As predicted by **George**, some men from a wagon train of Missourians come down into the **Ridgley's** camp and share a wild tale of Indians making a dash through their camp, beating drums, shaking bells, while "whooping and yelling" (95). Before the emigrants could reach their guns and defend themselves, the Indians had chased off fourteen horses into the surrounding hills.

| | |
|---|---|
| **Albert Dickson**<br>*Ridgley Party* | "As there seemed to be no use trying to recover the stolen animals out in the rough country, they had decided to rearrange the loads, throw out what they couldn't carry, and divide up the stock so all could go on." *(95)* |

After hearing this story, **Albert** consults with **Joe Donovan** and **Alonzo "Lon" Smith** about what **George** might be up to. There are enough red flags to demand a response from the wagon master.

| | |
|---|---|
| **Albert Dickson**<br>*Ridgley Party* | "That evening a meeting was held in our corral to which our friends from Raleigh, Missouri [**George Colburn** and his mining team] were not invited. **Colburn's** story was compared with the [Missouri] emigrants' account. His former suspicious behavior … mysterious absences; the horse deal; the army mule; and now - this." *(95)* |

The meeting results in a very tired **Joshua** doling out justice. Out on the Plains, horse thievery—especially from the Army—is commonly dealt with by lobbing a rope over a branch of a nearby tree, hanging the criminal and posting a sign stating their alleged crime. If **Joshua** wants to or has the energy for it, he could exact this punishment immediately. He also could arrest **George** by tying him up and delivering him and the mule to a nearby Army outpost for a reward upwards of five hundred dollars (an equivalent of $9,600.00 in 2023).[323] Instead, **Joshua** rules that **George** and his companions must leave them at first light.

## Brown, Oliver & Roe

Among those who try to get a jump start into the Black Hills are the friendly **Brown** and **Oliver Trains**, along with the **Roes**. Because there is no mention of the departure in the **Brown** accounts, and no travel record exists

---

[323] Using the CPI Inflation Calculator from OfficialData.org

for the **Olivers** (other than this book), only **Martha Roe's** diary entries are included here. She claims her wagon train leaves the Fort on July 5, "in pretty good time." As expected, the initial leg of the journey is particularly difficult.

**Martha Roe**
*Roe Train*

"Drove about 5 M and camped for dinner [lunch] then started to climb the hills and mountains   verry steep hills to go down   we had to lock and bough back the waggons"
*(July 5)*

The limited description provided by **Martha** suggests her wagons do not have a brake system installed. To "bough back" on a downhill, they could secure a rope or chain to the rear wheel, then wrap the other end to a tree or similar anchor point uphill. By releasing slack in the line, the wagon can roll down slowly and with control. A simple illustration of this maneuver is comparable to a rock climber rappelling down a cliff (albeit on a smaller incline). The difficulty **Martha's** teams face are echoed by another diarist, Howard Stillwell Stanfield, who started into the Black Hills on May 22:

"We left the camp near Fort Laramie ... the road has been very rough and hilly ever since in some places very steep almost perpendicular so we have not made very good time."[324]

The process to get **Martha's** two wagons up and over the initial hills takes so long, they likely impede progress for all those who are behind them on the trail. It appears that after this challenge, the **Roes** resign to layover for the remainder of the day. They camp approximately eleven miles from Fort Laramie, near the "Good cold springs on right of road," as described in J. L. Campbell's emigrant guide.[325] Here, on the northern end of present-day Guernsey, **Martha** notes with Biblical awe that water comes, "out of the rocks," and blesses the thirsty among them.

---

[324] Howard Stillwell Stanfield, *Diary of Howard Stillwell Stanfield: Overland Trip from Indiana to California, 1864*, Ed. Jack Detzler (Bloomington: Indiana University Press, 1969).
[325] J. L. Campbell, *Idaho…*, 1864, 49.

**Martha Roe**
*Roe Train*

"Night came and found us in the midst of high rocky mountains on every side … was nearly suffocated for water[.]  we then felt the true value of water" *(July 5)*

## Jongewaard

Unlike the early-rising **Roes**, the Dutch **Jongewaard Train** stays near Fort Laramie until noon. Shortly after leaving, the Dutch are halted by the sight of the burial scaffold.

**Gerrit Roorda**
*Jongewaard Train*

"…traveled about 3 miles. There was an Indian buried in a cottonwood tree[,] wrapped in buffalo and buckskin[,] laying on some poles." *(July 5)*

**Gerrit's** employer, **Lutje Mars**, has two young stepsons whose curiosity goes a bit too far on this day. Thirteen-year-old **Peter Ellerbroek** and ten-year-old **John Ellerbroek** are a mischievous pair. For context, on June 12, **John** tried his hand at whipping the stock pulling the wagon **Gerrit** was driving. In the process, **John** loses his balance and falls over the buckboard. Then, both the front and rear wheels of the wagon crush him into the soft ground beneath. In **Gerrit's** daybook, he records, "the boy of **L. Mars** fell out of the wagon," but in **John's** later reminiscence, he places blame squarely on **Gerrit**; the hired man who "let" him do it.[326] Less than a month later, **John** is fully recovered and back to his impulsive ways.

**John Ellerbroek**
*Jongewaard Train*

"After we left Fort Laramie, we saw an Indian buried in a tree, with all his belongings: his bow and arrows, and old gun, and other things. Brother **Peter [Ellerbroek]** and I wanted the bow and arrows very badly, but our captain **[Cornelius Jongewaard]** told us not to touch them, for if we did we might all be killed, and we left them in the tree." *(408-409)*

---

[326] John Ellerbroek, "The Oregon Trail," in Charles Dyke's *The Story of Sioux County*, (Orange City: n.p. 1942): 408-409.

The detailed inventory creates suspicion that the boys climbed up the tree for a closer look. Though the exact consequences for the **Ellerbroek boys** disturbing the scaffold are unknown, **Cornelius'** severe warning hints at the general beliefs that consequences are expected.

The **Jongewaard Train** ends their day's travel after only three miles. They may be using the remainder of the day to make necessary modifications to their vehicles prior to attempting the steep climbs ahead or to check once again for any mail at the post office.

### Howard, Missourians & Virginians

With any hold up to the Dutch families at the graveyard, those in the **Howard** and **Missouri Trains** can easily pass them by. Still, their progress into the Black Hills is likely hampered by the slow-moving **Roes** trying to get up and over the first hill. From the **Ridgley Party, Albert Dickson** confesses that the wait in these traffic jams can be brutal. He writes, "I shall never forget what a tedious experience this was. Every wagon had to wait until the one ahead was out of the way" (108).

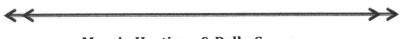

### Morris-Hastings & Pella Company

After the prior day's rest for their horses, **Sarah Rousseau** in the **Pella Company** looks forward to reaching a spot ahead where J. L. Campbell's guidebook says the trail "runs near the river," and is a, "good chance to camp."[327] When they arrive at this promising site, however, the emigrants are disappointed by what is left for late season travelers.

| | |
|---|---|
| **Sarah Rousseau**<br>*Pella Company* | "Passed over this morning a desolate[,] barren region of country. Seemingly not fit for man or beast. Very poor grass and little of it." *(July 5)* |

---

[327] J. L. Campbell, *Idaho…*, 1864, 49.

They noon near present-day Morrill, Nebraska (about six miles from the western state border). Here, the **Pella Company** is greeted by friendly Pawnee Indians from a nearby village.

| | |
|---|---|
| **Sarah Rousseau**<br>*Pella Company* | "Came by about 20 Wigwams, and as a matter of course[,] there [are] plenty of natives." *(July 5)* |

At the Pawnee village, **Dr. James Rousseau** purchases half of a Buffalo skin, then pays a craftsman $2.00 (an equivalent of $37.00 in 2023) to fashion the leather into a "shoe" or hoof covering for his lead horse. A simple explanation for this process can be found in **Albert Dickson's** account: "Whenever any of them [oxen] showed signs of becoming footsore we cut out pieces of sole-leather, one for each 'toe' and fastened them on with oxshoe nails. ...the leathers usually last as long as they were needed" (89).

In the afternoon, the **Pella Company** continues a short distance and camps for the evening near another village on the border of Idaho Territory (Wyoming). From here, the emigrants can see Laramie Peak out in the distance.

| | |
|---|---|
| **Sarah Rousseau**<br>*Pella Company* | "...Passed quite a village of Indians. I suppose there was at least 40 wigwams. I can't tell how many Indians. They make quite a curious appearance. Some about naked. And some dressed up in thick Buffalo skins while other have some kind of shirt or old dress." *(July 5)* |

**Sarah** claims they are camped among the Lakota-Sioux (Brulé, Oglala and Hunkpapa). It should be noted that, as a result of the Yankton, Dakota and Lakota-Sioux's forced eviction from Minnesota, the Pawnee people are generally at odds with their relatively new(ish) neighbors. In addition, she is informed that her people will soon be in "considerable danger" ahead, where the Blackfoot-Sioux are occupying land.

"Laramie Peak, ½ Day Beyond Fort Laramie." Sketch by Joseph Goldsborough, 1849. Huntington Digital Library, Western Americana Drawings Catalog [43513].

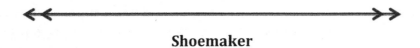

## Shoemaker

Still on the South Bank Trails on July 5, **Mr. Shoemaker** likely reaches the site of Chimney Rock where he is spotted by **George Forman** either that same evening or on the morning of July 6.

# Wednesday, July 6, 1864

### Ridgley Party

As soon as the sun's rays break through the dense, dark green and shadowy trees that give the Black Hills their nickname, **George Colburn** and his entourage leave the **Ridgley Party**—taking the stolen mule with them. **Albert Dickson** notes how peculiar it is that they head directly off into the surrounding forest, instead taking any visible trail.

By now, members in the **Ridgley Party** are fully convinced that **George** was "in league with" the Indians who attacked the emigrants from Missouri (96). **Albert** records that corrupt white men would sometimes rustle up chaos as needed to, "steer business in their direction" (97).[328] If this is what **George** has been doing, it seems he never bargains on emigrants fighting back. Rather, he depends on emigrants' fear of Indians being so debilitating that they flee or readily abandon their horses to save their scalps.

**Albert Dickson**      "We never saw them again." *(97)*
*Ridgley Party*

The **Ridgley Party** travels a total of eighteen miles, passing what remains of Bridger's Ferry, then camps near the North Platte River in present-day Orin,

---

[328] In a November 27, 2023 interview with Larry Cundall, descendant of the original Cundall Ranch owners est. 1917 (which includes the Alder Clump camp), he shared he has looked into these claims and long suspected there was a horse thieving crime ring organized by a white man and a local band of Indians. They may have established a base camp up on Sheep Mountain where they could look down on the emigrants coming through the prairie below and plan their terrorizing. Stolen horses would be taken back east to be traded or sold to emigrants who were none the wiser.

Wyoming. In the process, they also pass by the camp of the Missourians who were allegedly raided by Indians.

| **Albert Dickson** | "...there was nothing left but the ashes of extinguished |
| *Ridgley Party* | camp fires and some household goods thrown about." |
| | *(97)* |

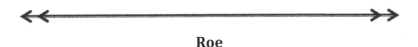

## Roe

After waking up near the cold spring, **Martha Roe** observes her surroundings with awe.

| **Martha Roe** | "Found ourselves hemed in on every side by high |
| *Roe Train* | mountains" *(July 6)* |

The **Roe Train** ventures ten miles around forested hills that continue to be unforgiving on their equipment and animals. Andrew Child's 1852 trail guide warns emigrants that after summiting a "short steep ascent," the road ahead is "sidling [dangerously sideways or sloping] and stony," and progress might be slow before reaching where the "Road Joins River"—a camp with abundant timber and grass.[329] This camp is found in Long Canyon where a stream crosses the road. If followed, thirsty travelers reach the North Platte River.

| **Martha Roe** | "got 10 M and came to the river where we camped all |
| *Roe Train* | afternoon ... took a good sleep then sewed a while" *(July 6)* |

In 1850, Byron McKinstry traveled this same route. His travel log from fourteen years prior aligns with **Martha's.** On June 23, 1850, he wrote about reaching Long Canyon: "After winding among the hills for about 10 m. we passed through a notch and descended to the river again. ... water was scarce on the route."[330] This "notch," as he calls it, is a popular place to lay over. At

---

[329] Andrew Child, *New Guide...*, 1852, 21-22.
[330] Byron N. McKinstry, *The California Gold Rush: [1850] Overland Diary of Byron McKinstry* (Glendale: Arthur Clark Co., 1975), June 23.

the end of **Martha's** July 6 diary entry, she claims, "bout 1 hundred waggons camped with us."

While **Martha** prepares dinner, the men in her company "fixed one thing and another" on the wagons. **"The Boys"** from the mining team take advantage of this opportunity to swim their cattle through the River to the south bank, where there is better feed available. **Martha** does not comment on the crossing here being risky or difficult whatsoever.

### Brown, Howard, Oliver, Roe, Missourians & Virginians

The large July 6 gathering in Long Canyon is suspected to include the twenty-seven wagons identified with the **Brown** (3), **Howard**, (17+), and **Oliver** (7) **Trains** as well as the **Missouri Train** with **two men from Virginia** and their unknown number of wagons. When this total is added to the **Roes'** two wagons, the remainder of one hundred vehicles is grossly unaccounted for. Even as a ballpark number, **Martha's** report is evidence that numerous, yet-to-be-identified travelers are not only taking advantage of this valley respite but are subject to the danger that awaits.

### Jongewaard

From just west of Fort Laramie, the **Jongewaard Train** finally enters the Black Hills on July 6. Like many before him, **Gerrit Roorda** remarks on the challenging terrain.

| | |
|---|---|
| **Gerrit Roorda**<br>*Jongewaard Train* | "We commenced traveling in the Black Hills. We had very steep hills to go up and down but we made 15 miles and got to the river." *(July 6)* |

This mileage brings the **Jongewaards** into Long Canyon with others who have gathered there. With their seven wagons added to the running total of twenty-nine, there is still plenty left for future researchers to discover.

## Pella Company

While it seems everyone else is finally in the fated Black Hills, on July 6, the **Pella Company** barely enters Idaho Territory (Wyoming). The night before, a spinster in their company, **Matilda Fields**, has a "sick spell" that **Dr. James Rousseau** treats. **Matilda** had made arrangements to work as **Sarah Rousseau's** aide, in return for transport and protection. **Matilda's** position is so essential to the wheelchair-bound diarist that there are more mentions in the trail diary about her than of **Sarah's** own children. In the morning, **Matilda** "feels a good deal better," but **Sarah** continues to document the frequency and regularity of her sickness, causing suspicion of a pregnancy

In addition to **Sarah's** verbose diary entries, supporting details of this leg of the journey are found in a letter from wagon master **Nicholas Earp,** dated April 2, 1865.[331] After careful evaluation, the author has found that everything **Nicholas** writes in his letter corroborates **Sarah's** story and vice versa.

| | |
|---|---|
| **Sarah Rousseau**<br>*Pella Company* | "Started on our journey again. Travelled about [11] miles and stopped to noon. But found there was no grass, so we went on. ... we are camped close by the river at an Indian Missionary Station.[332] Traveled 17 miles today." *(July 6)* |
| **Nicholas Earp**<br>*Pella Company* | "...on we went without any serious trouble[,] occaisonaly passing indions on the rout... " *(1865)* |

The seventeen mile distance brings the **Pella Company** to camp for the evening on Raw Hide Creek in the present-day city of Lingle, Wyoming. During the day, **Sarah** expresses rising concerns about the behaviors of Indians in the area. Her interpretation of their behaviors are unfounded.

---

[331] Nicholas Earp, Letter to James Copla, April 2, 1865, Ts. By Janelle Molony and Nicholas Cataldo. See the Appendix.

[332] This is probably a reference to Fort Bernard, a trading post once owned by Bernard Pratte and Joseph Bisonnette, located approximately eight miles east of Fort Laramie. Later, the American Fur Company operated the post.

| **Sarah Rousseau** | "Two group[s] of Indians passed by us at a small |
|---|---|
| *Pella Company* | distance which showed they were not friendly. When |
| | they feel friendly they will come around your waggons |
| | or tents." *(July 6)* |

## Forman & Shoemaker

At the back of this emigrant lineup is the solitary wagon of **Mr. Shoemaker** who, by July 6, is officially joined by **George Forman** at Ficklin's Springs telegraph station; a former Pony Express Station in present-day Gering, Nebraska.[333]

| **George Forman** | "We are joined here by an old Bachelor **Shoemaker** |
|---|---|
| *Lone Traveler* | with a load of leather and food, with a one yoke wagon |
| | like ours, and keep company with him to Laramie. He |
| | is bound for Idaho." *(July 6)* |

The "like ours" comment from **George** comes from his temporary association with a widow and her children that he is accompanying to Fort Laramie. **Mr. Shoemaker** continues to travel with **George** and the widow on the South Bank Trail system until they reach the Fort.

On arrival, **George** calls this station, "the only hut between Ash Hollow and Fort Laramie," where "a few soldiers [are] keeping the Line in order." Near the telegraph station is a larger military outpost which is nearly finished being constructed out of adobe bricks.[334] According to military records, manning this outpost is a special assignment and besides the four or five members of

---

[333] This "Scotts Bluff" Pony Express Station was in operation from 1860 to 1861, then it was repurposed into an Overland Stage Stop. Between 1861 and 1864, the station fell into disrepair and the Union soldiers try to make the most of it. By 1867, the Union abandoned this property for good. See more in the article, "An Eye For History: Fort Mitchell," *NPS.gov,* April 14, 2006. https://www.nps.gov/parkhistory/online_books /knudsen/sec2j.htm

[334] When completed in August, the outpost will be dubbed Camp Shuman, as Co. H is temporarily under the command of Captain Jacob S. Shuman. In September, however, the outpost is renamed Fort Mitchell after Brigadier General Robert B. Mitchell.

Company H, there were only a handful of local civilian "cowboys" in the general area.[335] **George** identifies the telegraph operator as 1st Lieutenant William W. Ellsworth of the 11th Ohio Volunteer Cavalry, who is also from Paris, Canada West (Ontario).

---

[335] See 1864 & 1865 "U.S. Returns from Military Posts: Soldier Lists."

# Thursday, July 7, 1864

### Townsend Train (Briefly)

For July 7, the author would like to pause the exploration of emigrant tales on the North Bank Trails for another detour up the Indian foot trail through the Powder River Basin. On this day, a second inciting event occurs on the would-be Bozeman Trail: The **Townsend Train** of one hundred covered wagons, captained by Absalom Townsend, choses to venture off the treaty-protected North Bank Trails with Rafael Gallegos as his guide (the interpretive guide John Bozeman explored with a year prior). It is believed Rafael charges a hefty fee and gathers his clients from upstream near the Platte Bridge Station in a similar scheme.

The **Townsend Train** starts north from a point near Richard's Bridge (in Evansville, a suburb of Casper, Wyoming). Where they depart, there are obvious warnings not to use the foot trail, but they all go ignored. A summary of what happens next is provided via an excerpt from the author's article, "1864: More Than Massacres," as published in the *Annals of Wyoming* (Fall, 2021).

> Following a respite near Richard's Bridge, Townsend decided to continue on, ignoring numerous "Beware of Indians" warnings painted on smooth rock surfaces, per passenger Adelia French's reminiscence.[336] Hers is a rare account to mention this danger alert.

---

[336] C. Adelia French, "Reminiscence, 1864," in Susan B. Doyle's *Journeys to the Land of Gold: Emigrant Diaries from the Bozeman Trail, 1863-1866*, 1 (Helena: Montana Historical Society, 2000), 239.

According to Frank Wager, another passenger, a group of Indians stopped their train just after crossing the Powder River (about fifty miles north of the Platte River, near present-day Kaycee, Wyoming).[337] The Indians warned the captain and his interpretive guides, John Boyer and Rafael Gallegos, not to proceed any further and instructed them either to turn around or else face harm. Wager recalled, "If we tried to go on, they would kill us all."[338]

After a handshake between Townsend and the braves' leader, the Indians receded. The emigrants then held a vote on whether or not to take their chances to press forward, despite the threat. They sized up the situation and opted to continue north, figuring they had the firepower to win, should there be a fight.

Seeing the wagon train once again on the move, the [Indians] became angry, drew their bows and arrows, and set fire to the grass around the train in a dramatic final warning.[339] Their menace was met with a counter-attack by members of the wagon train. The ensuing battle lasted nearly five hours and resulted in the killing of fourteen Indians and four whites.[340]

This July 7 event has since been called the Townsend Train Fight.

---

[337] Frank Wager, "Reminiscence, 1864" in *Journeys to the Land of Gold*, 248.
[338] Ibid., 248.
[339] C. Adelia French, "Reminiscence, 1864," in *Journeys...*, 240.
[340] Ibid., 241.

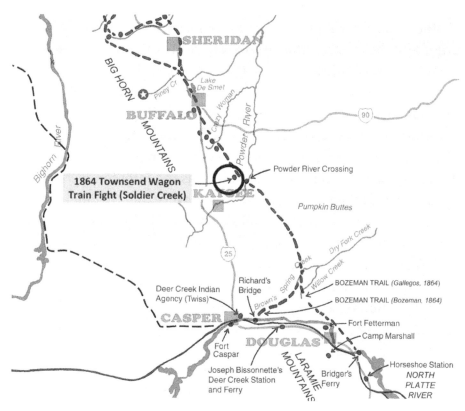

Partial view of the Bozeman Trail showing the location of the Townsend Train Fight and trailheads from Bridger's Ferry and Richard's Bridge. Reprint permission granted by Sylvia Bruner, Jim Gatchell Memorial Museum. Modified by author.

If the deep grooves that one-hundred and eighty-three wagons carve through the reserved lands are not enough to infuriate multiple tribal bands of Northern Plains Indians, and if the slaughter of one hundred sacred Buffalo near Bighorn River on July 4 is not enough to make them livid, then this outrageous incursion after a clear intervention could explain why the Sioux, Cheyenne and Arapahoe, are ready to retaliate. After the Townsend Train Fight, hundreds of Plains Indian hunters and warriors band together to address the matter. Contemporary research suggests the warrior society known as the Dog Soldiers also participates in this advance. Union soldiers have failed to curtail their own people and, unfortunately, instead of this being a lighter matter of trespassing and property destruction, a blood is debt is now owed.

Rather than allowing the author's conclusions to stand alone, readers are encouraged to hear from the voices of those directly affected. A 1993, television docu-series titled, "How the West was Lost," produced by the Discovery Channel, features interviews with descendants of Plains Indians. Episode four focuses on precipitating factors leading up to the Sand Creek Massacres of November 1864. The Bozeman Buffalo Massacre, the Townsend Train Fight and Platte River Raids are all considered in the mix.

In that episode, a Cheyenne man explains the interconnectivity with his people and the Buffalo, saying, "Once we were on the high plains, our dependance was centered on the buffalo. The buffalo became the chief source of subsistence. The buffalo was used for food, for clothing, for shelter and for tools."[341] Then, a Cheyenne woman shares that the roads made through their country, "split the buffalo herds that were very necessary to our survival as a people because Buffalo will not cross over grazed out land. And if you think of just a road being grazed out, you might think 'why can't the Buffalo cross over that?' But the grazed out land was two or three miles in width."[342]

Though the **Bozeman Caravan's** and **Townsend Train's** venture through the Powder River Basin might not constitute the creation of a road yet, **Albert Dickson** of the **Ridgely Party** does confirm the unmistakable damage caused by the wagon wheels. In his July 7 entry from where John Bozeman left the North Bank Trail, he writes that there are "deep imprints" that scar the land to the north (*Covered Wagon Days*, 1989, 101). With this in mind, the Cheyenne descendant's highly emotional response to such destruction created by Bozeman's Trail is valid.

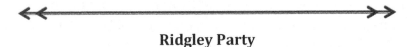

## Ridgley Party

July 7 brings members of the **Ridgley Party** a tinge of sadness as **Joe Donovan** and his partners leave to backtrack down to Bridger's Ferry. According to the research of Dr. Grace Raymond Hebard and Earl Brininstool, Bridger's Ferry was established pre-1859 and ended its operation in that year

---

[341] See minutes 4:00-4:00. No name is provided to identify the man being interviewed.
[342] See minutes 7:26-7:54.

with James "Jim" Bridger's acceptance of a guide role for Raynolds Expedition.[343] A map of the Bozeman Trail created by Dr. Hebard shows its early connection points at Fort Laramie, Bridger's Ferry and (by 1865) at Fort Fetterman, as well as its southernmost destination of Sedgewick, Colorado.

Anecdotal evidence has suggested that though there was no longer an official ferry operator in 1864, traveling parties could coordinate with others across the River or pay strong swimmers to help bring the ferry raft to whichever side of the River they were on or needed to go. Sometimes local bands of Indians would perform this duty with the expectation of a high-value compensation (usually sugar or alcohol). It is unclear how the **Donovan Team** makes their crossing. Once on the South Bank Trail, **Joe** can resume his original plan to go south to Colorado (via a different section of Bozeman's Trail) after being previously unable to cross the River near Fort Laramie.

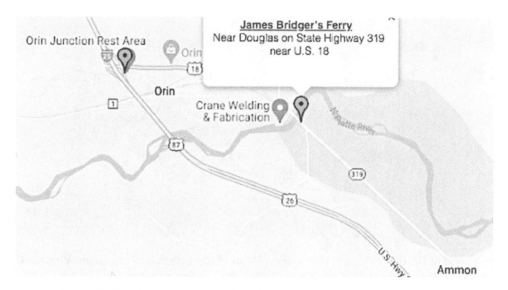

James Bridger's Ferry historical marker, erected in 1937. Google Maps.

---

[343] *The Bozeman Trail*, 1922, 37.

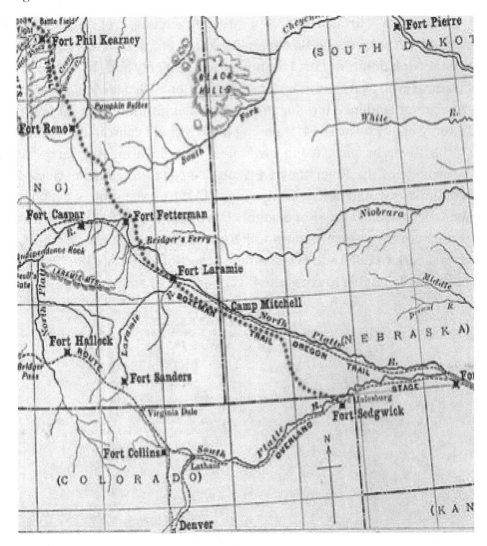

Partial view of Dr. Grace Raymond Hebard's "Map of the Bozeman Trail (from Virginia City, Montana to Fort Sedgwick, Colorado)," 1922. Permission granted by the University of Montana.

The rest of the **Ridgley Party (Ridgleys, Kellys, Buttons, and Smiths)** continue thirteen miles through what will eventually be Douglas, Wyoming, then up and over another steep ascent at McKinstry Ridge. They descend into the area the author has dubbed the North Douglas Bend (*see the map shown on July 4*). At this location, the North Platte River bends ninety degrees.

**Albert Dickson**
*Ridgley Party*

"...about the middle of the forenoon as we were passing over the ground where Douglas now stands, we noted the deep imprint of wagon wheels turning due north at right angles to our trail." *(101)*

Making such a distinct turn "due north" would lead emigrants directly off the North Bank Trail and into the Powder River Basin. This departure point is diagonally across the River from where Fort Fetterman will be established in 1865. Eventually, a historical trail marker is erected on the grounds of Fort Fetterman, marking the Bozeman Trail (*see the image shown on July 4*). The inscription reads: "the Bozeman Trail wound a long, twisting northwesterly route to the Montana goldfields."[344]

**Albert Dickson**
*Ridgley Party*

"Besides the road at our left was another note on a cleft stick[345] from the **Phillips [Boys]**, stating that they were going with Bozeman by this new route that he was laying out to Virginia City and urging us to catch up with them if possible. The message bore the date of July 1." *(101)*

By July 7, Bozeman's Train is beyond catching up with, but the enthusiastic note causes the remaining **Ridgley Party** to weigh their options.

**Albert Dickson**
*Ridgley Party*

"Here we halted until afternoon, turning the problem over in our minds, whether to follow Bozeman's party or stick to the old trail. ... To avoid crossing and recrossing the continental divide was itself a matter worth serious consideration ... Yet it might have taken weeks to overtake the Bozeman train..." *(101)*

The **Ridgley Party** ultimately decides not to take the risk into uncharted territory, citing the dangers of entering "Indian country" (*Covered Wagon Days,*

---

[344] "Bozeman Trail" transcription from The Historical Trail Marker Database.
[345] A "cleft stick" has been cut or split at one end so items such as a paper note can be pinned within the groove. It functions like a clothespin.

102). According to a write up on **Edward Phillips** by the Society of Montana Pioneers, the risk is worth the reward for **Edward,** who reaches Virginia City on August 2,[346] a month faster than the September 5 arrival date of the **Ridgleys**.

During the evening camp, passing emigrants report a robbery from last night, back at Alder Clump [AKA Box Elder Spring, presently near the intersection of Emigrant Hill and Patten Creek Roads in Glendo, WY].

| | |
|---|---|
| **Albert Dickson**<br>*Ridgley Party* | "Reports of their depredations reached us daily, and we were never free from apprehension." *(102)* |

This robbery is allegedly conducted by only one Indian. This solo operator manages to take five animals, both horses and mules, from two men leading a herd between the River and their camp. The circumstances oddly coincide with the July 6 departure of **George Colburn** and his team at that location, earlier in the morning.

## Missourians & Virginians

The **Missouri Train** with two men from Virginia have not been located for this day. If researchers wish to entertain the idea that they may have been the wagon train that suffered a loss by stampeded (as **George Colburn** in the **Ridgley Party** reported on July 5), then the **Missourians** may have sought safety in numbers in Long Canyon and secured some type of connection with a larger, well-armed traveling party, possibly matching the description of the **Howard Train.**

---

[346] Society of Montana Pioneers, *Montana Pioneers: Constitution, Members and Officers, with "Portraits and Maps,"* ed. James Sanders (Society of Montana Pioneers, 1899), 195.

## Brown & Oliver

The exact locations of the **Brown** and **Brown Oliver** are unclear for July 7, though they are likely trying to maintain some separation from Southerners (particularly the **Missouri Train**) on the trail.

## Jongewaard & Roe

Because of limited feed sources in Long Canyon, on July 7, **"the Boys"** (the mining team) in the **Roe Train** have to swim cattle across the North Platte River again to feed.

**Martha Roe**
*Roe Train*

"got breakfast and crossed the river and got the cattle [back over] and started bout 8 oclock..." *(July 7)*

Coordinating diary entries indicate the **Jongewaard Train** keeps pace with the **Roes** today. Leaving Long Canyon poses yet another bottleneck situation for wagon trains who choose to ascend the two and a half miles of switchback climbs up Emigrant Hill. Prior travel diaries hint that emigrants might need to thoroughly rest their stock animals prior to attempting the climb. In 1852, traveler John McAllister described the uphill haul as follows: "...[the] road turns down a hollow for some distance[.] it then turns to the right up a long rocky steep hill that is truly hard on the teams."[347] John Clark, another traveler from that same year, referred to this slope as a "Jacob's Ladder,"[348] or in other words, a steep path that bridges earth and sky. He mentions that some travelers get help overcoming gravity with the use of a windlass (a winch and crank more familiarly used to hoist or release a ship's anchor).

---

[347] John McAllister, *[1852] Diary of Rev. John McAllister: A Pioneer of 1852.* (Oregon Pioneer Association, 1925), July 4.
[348] John Clark, *Untitled 1852 Diary*, June 13. Available at the Newberry Library in Chicago, Illinois.

Another way to get up and over is for emigrants "to unload everything from their wagons at the bottom of the hill[, then] One by one[,] the wagons were pulled up the hill, empty, by multiple teams of oxen. The wagon's occupants then had to carry all their belongings up the hill to repack the wagons."[349] For parties unable or unwilling to tackle the Hill, a circuitous path to the east can be taken to avoid the challenge, albeit at the expense of going nearly eight miles out of the way. Both the **Roe** and **Jongewaard Trains** take on the challenge.

| | |
|---|---|
| **Martha Roe**<br>*Roe Train* | "drove bout 9 M and camped for dinner ... stopped bout 2 hours" *(July 7)* |
| **Gerrit Roorda**<br>*Jongewaard Train* | "We traveled about 9 miles and camped out on a spring in the bluffs." *(July 7)* |

The lunchtime break **Martha Roe** and **Gerrit Roorda** mention may be the same location Byron McKinstry found to be a delight on his 1850 journey. When on this section of the trail, he wrote: "passed some fine springs of pure cold water just before we reached the summit, say 9 m. from the River."[350] Though neither **Martha**, nor **Gerrit** make mention of it, at the top of Emigrant Hill, travelers pass by two small graves. One is unidentified, while the other is that of four-year-old Elva Ingram, who died from Cholera in 1852.[351]

After a quick bite, the **Roes** harness their animals who had just pulled their best up a trail that is "little better" than one from the day before (Roe, July 7). Both wagon trains continue another eight miles until the trail can access the water again in Sawmill Canyon, at the base of Baldy Mountain (which is marked as fifteen miles "to River" in Andrew Child's guidebook).

| | |
|---|---|
| **Martha Roe**<br>*Roe Train* | "camped for the night bout 5 oclock   got supper and went to bed." *(July 7)* |

---

[349] Sue Stafford, "Of a Certain Age…," *The Nugget News*, August 8, 2017. https://www.nuggetnews.com/story/2017/08/08/news/of-a-certain-age/27536.html
[350] Byron McKinstry, *The California Gold Rush Overland Diary of Byron N. McKinstry: 1850-1852*, annotated by Bruce L. McKinstry (Glendale, CA: The Arthur H. Clark Company, 1975). June 23, 1850.
[351] The Ingrams crossed the Plains in 1852 from Salem, Iowa.

**Gerrit Roorda**    "15 miles from the river." *(July 7)*
*Jongewaard Train*

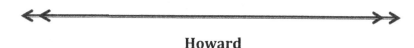

## Howard

Today, members in the **Howard Train** relish the sights around them. **Mary Howard Birks**, the newlywed daughter of the captain, **William Howard**, reminisces that, "no bride ever had a more romantic honeymoon."[352] While their spirits are up, the family sings and entertains all who are around them. Randall Lovejoy, a family historian and great-grandson of **Jeremiah and Mary Birks**, calls the **Howards,** "extremely musical people," in his 1988 genealogical essay.

## Pella Company & Union Army

In the **Pella Company, Sarah Rousseau** looks forward to leaving the "Indian Missionary Village" where Northern Plains Indians visit annually to trade peacefully and collect their annuities from the Indian Agency outside of Fort Laramie.[353] Despite earlier assumptions about ill-intentions of Indians, **Sarah** writes, "We were not disturbed last night by the Indians." Her anxiety is not fully relieved, however, and she is eager to get to the Fort, "where there is more to be feared by them."

**Nicholas Earp**    "...on we went with tolerable good luck and speed
*Pella Company*    considering the scarceness of grass for our animills
untell we got to ft. Laramie which we did on the Seventh
of July..." *(1865)*

---

[352] "The Howard Wagon Train," *The Genie* (1988), 202.
[353] In 1860, President Abraham Lincoln moved the agency to the outskirts of Fort Laramie and in 1864, William Bullock is the agent on duty in addition to managing the Sutler Store at the Fort.

**Sarah Rousseau**
*Pella Company*

"Having traveled about 6 miles this morning brought us opposite Ft. Laramie. ... Laramie has quite a picturesque appearance from this side." *(July 7)*

Like others before them, those in the **Pella Company** are alarmed by the sight of above ground burial methods on this side of the North Platte River, although **Sarah** writes about a different type of structure than the cottonwood tree setup mentioned by others before her.

**Sarah Rousseau**
*Pella Company*

"The Indians here have [a] rather strange way of burying their dead. They have 4 sticks about 10 to 12 feet high and they place their dead on top of them, it has a very singular appearance." *(July 7)*

"Dakota scaffold burial." Illustration from The Miriam and Ira D. Wallach Division of Art, Prints and Photographs: Picture Collection at the New York Public Library.

In the afternoon, **Nicholas Earp** and **Dr. James Rousseau** take a ferry across the River to visit the Fort and check for mail. The **Rousseaus** are expecting letters from their daughter Mary Ann back in Knoxville, Iowa.

**Sarah Rousseau**
*Pella Company*

"**Dr. [James]** has gone across to Fort Laramie to see if there is any letters for us. He has come back brought 2 letters with him." *(July 7)*

**Nicholas Earp**
*Pella Company*

"...we began to hear about depredations being comited by the Indians on trains but we were not seeing any of it and it was reported always behind or before us ... the crowd began to think it was all falce, and as they had bin before pretty mutch all the way..." *(1865)*

At the Fort, **Dr. James,** a former postmaster and government land surveyor,[354] asks about the conditions of the road ahead. Of more important interest to the wagon master, **Nicholas**, however, is the state of affairs with Indian relations. Prior to reaching the Fort, word about attacks on emigrants and homesteaders from elsewhere cause him to tighten up the security in the **Pella Company**. His reactions undoubtedly play into **Sarah's** fear. Though **Nicholas** receives the same reassurance of safety that the doomed **Kelly-Larimer Train** hears, he reserves his doubts and maintains a suspicion that the soldiers at the Fort are simply not taking his concerns, or their jobs, seriously enough. In addition, these particular soldiers are often recorded in travel accounts as capitalizing on emigrant fears and fatigue, and for exploiting the unseasoned traveler who makes such inquiries.[355]

Seeing how their safety is not even remotely a priority triggers **Nicholas** to respond in accordance with his former position as 3rd Sergeant and Provost Marshal. The role of Provost Marshal is primarily chief of military police.

---

[354] Dr. James Rousseau served as the first postmaster of Elm Grove in Liberty Township (Marion Co., Iowa). In addition, he operated a circuit route around the county as a Star Postal rider.

[355] One traveler (not included in this book), Katherine Dunlap, remarked of her experience at the Fort on June 20, 1864: "The soldiers are often very insolent to emigrants, stopping them of old soldier clothes belts, pistols, &c. They are no protection to emigrants at all." Her annotated diary is published online at http://www.thediaryofkatedunlap.umwblogs.org/.

National Park Services provides a historical job description for Union Provost Marshals at this time, citing: "The Provost Marshal dealt with prisoners of war, spies, and guerilla fighters, as well as the drunk, disorderly, or deserting soldiers, and even unhappy or disloyal civilians. The Provost Marshal had the authority to regulate military and civilian life under Martial law ... he could jail, punish, or even execute."[356] **Nicholas** performed these duties in Marion County, Iowa from 1861 to at least 1863, though he is well known to have also recruited, drilled and organized new soldiers into suitable companies.

On the evening of July 7, **Nicholas** causes a scene when he sees the general laziness of the recruits stationed at Fort Laramie who are supposed to be deterring any Indians from mischief and mayhem. **Sarah** reflects on this conflict in her July 8 entry, while **Nicholas** details the ruckus in his 1865 letter. First, for reader context, it should be noted that after the successful July 4 performance of singing minstrels performing in blackface where **Sgt. Lewis Hull** reports "seats [were] crowded," Fort Commander **Lt. Col. William O. Collins** requests a repeat production on the 7th.

| | |
|---|---|
| **Sgt. Lewis Hull**<br>*Union Army, Co. K* | "Acting secretary for the minstrels. ... Better fixed than before; seats raised [in price]. Admittance, front seats, 50 cents, back 25 and 15. ... Took in $107. **Colonel** pleased with the results; says there must be another show tomorrow night." *(July 23)* |

The soldiers at the Fort are reasonably distracted (as are many of the emigrants in the area who either attend or enjoy any catchy tunes from a distance). Ticket sales from this minstrel performance surpass $2,000 USD at today's rate.

| | |
|---|---|
| **Sarah Rousseau**<br>*Pella Company* | "We came pretty near having an unpleasant time last night. We have to keep close watch day and night over the stock. **Mr. Earp** went to see about the guards and he found they got up a dance ... And he told them they must quit their dancing and be on duty." *(July 8)* |

---

[356] National Park Services, "Prospects of Peace 1864 Tour: Provost Marshal, Chief of Military Police," http://www.nps.gov/places/provost-marshal-chief-of-military-police.html.

**Nicholas Earp**
*Pella Company*

"At least some of them a little slack in doing their duty when in camp in garding the stock[.] they began to be still morseso untell I began to scold some about it and told them that we would have to have a demonstration from the Indions which I believed would take place before long ... I would not care mutch if we did[,][357] so [long as] they did not hurt us[,] as I thought it would be the cause of them being more prompt in doing their duty..." *(1865)*

**Sarah Rousseau**
*Pella Company*

"**One soldier** told him [**Nicholas**] to mind his own business and ordered him off. ... He [**Nicholas**] used very profane language and could hardly be appeased. But he cooled down after a while and all was quiet." *(July 8)*

As **Nicholas** is no longer in a position of military authority, his complaint carries no weight. A military record has not yet been found to verify or expound on the claims that **Nicholas** started a verbal altercation with the guards on duty. Plenty of evidence, however, is available to elaborate on the military's drunken carelessness and dances while stationed there. The account of **Lt. Eugene Ware** offers one such look at the culture of the rowdy "Bedlam Boys" of Fort Laramie, as they were aptly nicknamed.[358] Many of these soldiers, though assigned to guard emigrants and the telegraph lines on the trails, are abundantly happy to not see any "real" war, while drinking their summertime away. In fact, even after this confrontation by **Nicholas**, on July 10, there is an encore of the entertainment where **Sgt. Lewis** admits, "Some disorder caused by there being too much whiskey on hand; some of the performers the worse for it."

---

[357] Nicholas' nonchalant, "I would not care much," comment about being attacked resonates as flippant, though when writing this letter seven months later, he knew exactly what dangers lay ahead.
[358] Eugene Ware, *The Indian War of 1864: Being a Fragment of the Early History of Kansas, Nebraska, Colorado, and Wyoming.* (Topeka: Crane & Co, 1911)

## Morris-Hastings

After a dramatic evening with the **Pella Company** at Fort Laramie, the **Morris** and **Hastings** families decide to separate from their associates and take the South Bank Trail system. Perhaps the two families from Davis County, Iowa felt that after this conflict, **Nicholas Earp's** leadership style was not to their liking. Evidence for their departure comes from **Sarah Rousseau's** diary entry on July 21, after she learns of their fate:

| **Sarah Rousseau** | "There was two families that traveled in our train. One |
|---|---|
| *Pella Company* | of them named **Morse [Morris]** and the other [**Arthur**] **Wright**.[359] They left our train at Laramie to go to the South side of the river" *(July 21, 1864 - in reflection)* |

## Forman, Shoemaker & Union Army

By July 7, **Mr. Shoemaker** and **George Forman** pick up speed and make well over twenty miles in one day, reaching the Indian village at Horse Creek, just before crossing the Nebraska border into Idaho Territory.

| **George Forman** | "Passed through the intricate small chalk cut canyons of |
|---|---|
| *Lone Traveler* | Scotts Bluff ... and camped at Horse Creek, 32 miles yet to Fort Laramie." *(July 7)* |

| **George Forman** | "At Horse Creek was a large Indian Village of their Skin |
|---|---|
| *Lone Traveler* | Teepees or Lodges, with the Indians having horse races. They are the best bare back riders I ever saw...." *(July 7)* |

---

[359] Arthur Wright is employed by Nelson Morris.

# Friday, July 8, 1864

### Ridgley Party - Epilogue

On July 8, with only five remaining wagons, the **Ridgley Party** allegedly leaves the North Douglas Bend. After the last evening's deliberations, **Joshua Ridgley** concludes they will continue due west instead of north on Bozeman's Trail. Fourteen-year-old diarist, **Albert Dickson** claims that by the end of the day, they reach present-day Casper, Wyoming. This destination is problematic as it implies traveling over forty miles in a day.[360] This is both infeasible and implausible.

| | |
|---|---|
| **Albert Dickson**<br>*Ridgley Party* | "...below us was the little stockaded post near the end of a long bridge of logs laid upon rock-filled log piers across the Platte. ... Mail, stage-coaches, freighters, and a stream of emigration passed here..." *(102)* |

While camped near the Platte Bridge Station, **Albert** receives news about "a battle between the indians and a large emigrant party down on the Leavenworth trail."[361] The details of the so-called battle supports either the **Ridgley Party's** arrival at later date, a five-day layover in the area, or may be a reference that should have been recorded at a different location farther down the trail.

---

[360] Again, at an ox's pace, this claim would require the wagons to be rolling for twenty-plus hours in this short window of time.

[361] *Covered Wagon Days,* 1989, 103. The "Leavenworth Trail" is one of the South Bank Trail's origins in Kansas.

Moellman, C., "Sketch of the Post at Platte Bridge in 1863," American Heritage Center. Shown on the right is Guinard's Bridge.

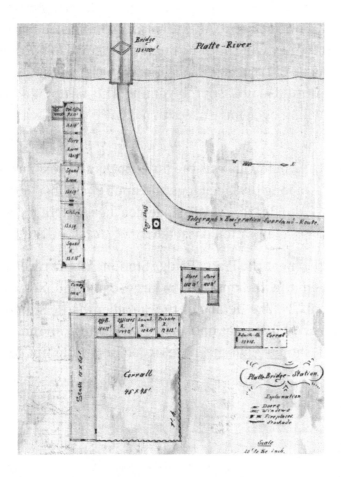

Collins, Caspar W., "Plan of Platte Bridge Station," Circa 1862-64. Colorado State University Library.

**Albert Dickson**
*Ridgley Party*

"Away out on the trail to the northwest somewhere it was that they had corralled for the night, when Indians swooped down upon them with their blood-curdling warwhoops. Of the prisoners taken all got away, I believe, except missus **Kelly** and her little niece - a sister's child left in her care - and another lady." *(103, quoting from a Mrs. Anna Birlew)*

After (impossibly) hearing about the **Kelly-Larimer** incident, the first attack on the South Bank Trails, the **Ridgley Party** continues west, unaware of how things escalate. They allegedly reach Independence Rock on July 12. It is much more likely they hear about the Platte River Raids on the morning of July 13 from this location. Major discrepancies such as these should cause readers to question more of the material found in *Covered Wagon Days*, especially if using in research applications.

A week later, near Fort Hall in Idaho Territory (state), the **Ridgley Party** breaks up. The **Ridgleys** and **Smiths** stay their course northward on the Montana Trail, reaching Virginia City on September 5. There, **Joshua** tries his luck as a miner but becomes disenchanted within a couple of months. He decides that farming is a better way of life for him after all and purchases a new plot of land in what would become Bozeman, Montana. In 1866, the **Ridgleys** return to Wisconsin to sell off their former property. During the visit, sixteen-year-old **Albert** learns that his mother has been widowed for a second time. He decides to stay home to help take care of her and his five younger siblings.

After a short stay in Montana Territory, the **Smiths** also return east, but end up resettling in Cedar, Iowa by 1870. **Sylvester** returns to farming, even into his old age. **Alonzo "Lon" Smith** marries a local girl and also starts farming.

From Fort Hall, the **Button family** heads south on the Salt Lake Road, but before reaching the Mormon settlement, they turn west onto the Humboldt River Emigrant Road that leads to Redding, California. They arrive in Redding some time in August, then continue south to Petaluma and settle about seventeen miles from where **Alfred** and **Albert Kelly's** brothers George and Seth reside in Santa Rosa. Pioneer sketches and obituaries claim **Isaac Button** erected one of the first homes on the historic D Street in September, where the travelers all eventually purchased properties. The industrial **Buttons** and **Kelleys** both become well-esteemed families in the area.

## Jongewaard

On the morning of July 8, the **Jongewaard Train** leaves the still slumbering **Roe Train** in Sawmill Canyon.

**Gerrit Roorda**
*Jongewaard Train*
"We had a pretty fair road … We saw singular looking rocks and hills all around us and arrived at the river at 5 o'clock." *(July 8)*

After overcoming "some steep and bad descents," as described in Andrew Child's 1852 travel guide, emigrants at this point can expect more sideling and sloping roads that pass Alder Clump/Box Elder Spring, cross the boggy Muddy Creek, then ease up on "tolerably good, but sandy" trails past this (22-23). Larry Cundall, former Glendo, Wyoming resident and owner of the cattle ranch that the Alder Clump campsite is located on has shared that, from Muddy Creek, the trail is "mostly downhill to the river."[362]

The description **Gerrit Roorda** gives for this day's journey places his company near the mouth of Lost Creek, on the north end of the present-day Glendo Reservoir. This is the first time all week that the **Jongewaard Train** puts a satisfactory distance behind them (about twenty-two miles). It is believed they are trying to reconnect with the Rysdam Train that left Pella, Iowa one week before them.

---

[362] Personal communication to the author, November 27, 2023.

### Brown & Roe

After sleeping in late, the **Roe Train** only scoots about a mile away from the congested hundred-wagon gathering at Sawmill Canyon. Joining them there is the **Brown Train.**

| | |
|---|---|
| **Martha Roe**<br>*Roe Train* | "We moved our waggons to a spring 'bout a mile from where we camped…" *(July 8)* |

By moving aside, faster wagon trains can clear out from the area. Perhaps **Mary Brown** and her son **Salmon** feel hopeful that the **Missouri Train** will take advantage of this clearance and skip ahead into the distance, never to be seen again. At the spring, **Martha Roe** describes spending the day cooking a "big dinner," with the help of **Alex Cathcart** (their cook), and **Salmon Brown** (whom she refers to simply as **"Mr. Brown"**).

| | |
|---|---|
| **Martha Roe**<br>*Roe Train* | "After doing up the work I took a sleep" *(July 8)* |

Since both **Martha** and her husband **Isaac** suffer considerably from chronic pain, these naps may be one of few ways they find relief while on the road.

| | |
|---|---|
| **Martha Roe**<br>*Roe Train* | "…when evening came there was 'bout 50 waggons camped with us making quite a little town" *(July 8)* |

### Oliver

The location of the **Oliver (AKA "Indiana") Train,** is uncon-firmed for this day, though they are suspected to be somewhat connected to the **Brown** and **Roe Trains** at this time.

### Howard, Missourians & Virginians

Also unclear are the locations of the **Missouri** and **Howard Trains,** though evidence places them behind the **Browns** and ahead of the **Pella Company** in just a few days, so readers might wonder if there is a layover or other reason for a delay.

### Pella Company

On July 8, the **Pella Company** leaves Fort Laramie very early in the morning without the **Morris** and **Hastings families**. Approximately four miles later, they stop at a local blacksmith.

| | |
|---|---|
| **Sarah Rousseau** <br> *Pella Company* | "Crossed Dry Creek. We are camped close by a blacksmith. We have to stay and have some work done. … The Blacksmith has a[n Indian] for a wife."[363] *(July 8)* |

Neither **Nicholas Earp** nor **Sarah Rousseau** explain what work must be done, though there is reason to believe the **Rousseaus** are re-shoeing a horse. After the work is complete, the **Pella Company** is ready for the same difficult hills that those ahead have complained about. They start up, "between 10 & 11 oclock," according to **Sarah**. She mentions the day being blustery ("a fair hurricane"), which probably increases the challenge of pulling canvas-covered vehicles uphill.

| | |
|---|---|
| **Sarah Rousseau** <br> *Pella Company* | "…passed over some dreadful bad roads, rocky and broken. We had some high hills to go over. … One high hill towering above another in their majestic appearance." *(July 8)* |

---

[363] There are multiple civilian business owners identified on the 1860 census of the Fort who were known to have wives from various local tribes. More on the enterprising families of the area can be found in James H. Nottage's article, "A Frontier Census: Fort Laramie in 1860," published January 9, 2023 at WyoHistory.org.

In the afternoon, the **Pella Company** gives their stock a well-earned rest in Long Canyon. **Nicholas** continues to press everyone to keep a vigilant watch for Indians.

**Sarah Rousseau**
*Pella Company*
"We had to keep pretty close together as the Indians are bad about stealing horses." *(July 8)*

Aligning with **Nicholas'** previous comment that every depredation happens either ahead of or behind the **Pella Company, Sarah** documents a horse robbery, just behind their wagon train.

**Sarah Rousseau**
*Pella Company*
"There is a man that was about 100 yards behind the rest[,] not thinking of danger[,] when some Indians came from behind the Bluffs, and took his four mules out of his waggon and ran them off." *(July 8)*

No one in the **Pella Company** sees or hears anything to validate that the robbery is caused by Indian mischief versus any other reason for an animal to run off (being spooked, looking for feed, etc.). **Sarah** blames the man for his own misfortune, owing to a lack of common sense.

**Sarah Rousseau**
*Pella Company*
"There is every opportunity to run them off, run them over the Bluffs and nobody could tell where they went." *(July 8)*

Further research is required to identify the **Man with Four Mules**. He is presumed to be stranded at the bottom of Long Canyon unless he can make arrangements to borrow spare horses or mules from another traveling party. He might even seek aid from a southbound company and return to Fort Laramie. No further mention has been found on him.

By evening, the **Pella Company** successfully tackles Emigrant Hill and corrals again in Sawmill Canyon where **Martha Roe** describes a "little town" being formed (July 8). Due to poor vegetation in the area, the **Rousseaus** consider crossing the horses over the North Platte River, as others have been doing, but by the time they arrive, it is too dark outside to cross safely. The **Rousseaus** (who do not have spare feed) try to give their horses a mixture of flour and water, but some refuse to eat the dough.

## Morris-Hastings

Back at Fort Laramie, the **Morris** and **Hastings** families regroup for their departure along the South Bank Trail system. These two families leave the Fort on either July 9 or 10 and keep a regular pace behind the **Kelly-Larimer Train**. (*For more on their story, see the Emigrant Tales from the South Bank Trails.*)

## Forman & Shoemaker

Finally, on July 8, **Mr. Shoemaker** and **George Forman** (with his temporary widow companion) reach Idaho Territory (Wyoming). **George** records the sights **Mr. Shoemaker** was probably quite familiar with on this leg of the journey.

**George Forman**
*Lone Traveler*

"We passed here into Wyoming Territory[364] and saw numbers of old stone and Adobe Ruins with Port or Loop holes, used by the old Overland stage or Pony Express... " (*July 8*)

Along the way, **Mr. Shoemaker** is repeatedly approached by Indians expecting to make trades. **George** observes these interactions with suspicion. He does not expect the widow he is traveling with to be hassled but considering how **Mr. Shoemaker** is carrying "a load of leather and food," as previously described, **George** is on the defensive.

---

[364] Wyoming does not become a territory until July 25, 1868. As a reminder to the reader, George's 1883 manuscript includes perspectives and knowledge that did not exist at the time of his travels.

**George Forman**
*Lone Traveler*

"...passed three other Indian Villages and had visitors from them all to buy flour. They would not take no for an answer. ... They were contemplating robbery I knew and wanting to find out if we were worth robbing, which we were not... " *(July 8)*

**Mr. Shoemaker** and **George** cover about sixteen miles before camping near present-day Torrington, Wyoming.

# Saturday, July 9, 1864

### Jongewaard

Out towards the front of the wagon train lineup today is the **Jongewaard Train**. According to J. L. Campbell's 1864 guidebook, their camp at Lost Creek is supposed to offer them "wood, water, and timber" (49) and Andrew Child's guide specifically mentions there being plenty of grass here, but this is not the case for late season travelers. Perhaps taking a cue from former campmates, the **Roes**, those in the **Jongewaard Train** swim their animals across the North Platte River again.

**Gerrit Roorda**
*Jongewaard Train*

"We laid by all day and had the stock across the river. Here we saw the wild sage growing in abundance..." *(July 9)*

### Oliver & Roe

Not far behind, the **Roes** pack out from Sawmill Canyon, but get separated from the **Brown Train** who lags behind. The **Roes** stop for lunch before reaching the sandy roads (Sand Draw) that kicks up a fair amount of dust when dry and may contribute to the **Roes** poor health.

**Martha Roe**
*Roe Train*

"Started in pretty good time[.] travail till bout 2 pm and we turned out bout 1 ½ h[ours] and got our dinners [lunches] and the rest went on till they came to the river bout 5pm[.] We came bout an hour later[.] I was sick all day with the head ache" *(July 9)*

The "rest" of the travelers are not clarified but likely include the **Oliver Train** who will soon be a good distance ahead of the **Roes**. Their evening camp is suspected to be at Alder Clump/Box Elder Spring (about fifteen miles behind the **Jongewaard Train**).

## Howard, Missourians & Virginians

The **Howard** and **Missouri Trains'** locations are unconfirmed for July 9. In **Howard** descendant, Randall Lovejoy's genealogical essay, there is no mention of the family seeing any Indians in the Black Hills, nor hearing about any depredations prior to the commencement of the Platte River Raids. This leads the author to believe they are, at least, somewhere ahead of the **Pella Company** for the day.

## Brown & Pella Company

Early this morning, the **Pella Company** leaves Sawmill Canyon camp without breakfast. About four miles north (approximately at Bulls Bend), **Sarah Rousseau** mentions running into familiar faces.

**Sarah Rousseau**
*Pella Company*

"...we came up with a train we had been in company with before. We did [not] know at first, but it might be the train the Indians had taken all their horses and left them a few days before..." *(July 9)*

No further information is provided regarding who, ahead of the **Pella Company,** was robbed of all their horses, but based on their location, readers might suspect this being a reference to the train of Missourians that **George Colburn** informed the **Ridgley Party** of. Certainly, these reports keep **Nicholas Earp's** head on a swivel and rifle close by.

| **Sarah Rousseau** | "...but it turned out to be the **New York train** we had |
|---|---|
| *Pella Company* | got acquainted with sometime back. They told us they |
| | had been laying over..." *(July 9)* |

So far, the **Browns** in the **"New York Train"** have done everything in their power to remain unidentified to most people. To date, only **Martha Roe** has identified them by name. It is difficult to say exactly when **Sarah** "got acquainted" with the **Browns**, as this is her one and only direct mention of them, though plenty of opportunities existed along the trail between Iowa and Idaho Territory (Wyoming).

In Al Reck's 1961 article series for the *Oakland Tribune*, he comes to the conclusion that after traveling alone (and likely trusting no one), the **Browns** "decided it was best to join another train heading for California."[365] The only California-bound travelers known to be in proximity of the **Browns** at this point are the **Howards** and the **Pella Company**. This detail also helps clarify that the **Oliver Train** is at Alder Clump with the **Roes**.

| **Sarah Rousseau** | "So here we have camped. ... But the Indians are around. |
|---|---|
| *Pella Company* | The men are guarding them. All well armed. The men |
| | have seen 5 or 6 of them, they are on horseback with |
| | guns on their shoulders. We know they are hostile |
| | because they keep aloof." *(July 9)* |

Beyond noticing that emigrants on the North Bank Trails are being eerily watched, readers should note that the thieves operating in this area are probably unaffiliated with the army of approximately three-hundred that is currently heading south from the Powder River Basin. Local history enthusiast and ranch owner, Larry Cundall has shared that he has long suspected a "horse thief ring" in this area. He has found archaeological evidence near his ranch on Sheep Mountain that suggests a white man's square-shaped tent was pitched amongst circular teepees.[366] He believes this may have been a hub for those participating in the scheme.

----

[365] Al Reck, "Indians Terrorize..." in *Oakland Tribune*, 1961, 4-5.
[366] Personal communication to author, November 37, 2023. Sheep Mountain is about ten miles northeast of Bulls Bend, as the crow flies.

## Forman & Shoemaker

Still not in the Black Hills yet, **Mr. Shoemaker** and **George Forman** reach Star Ranch, AKA "Five Mile Ranch," about twenty-two miles from the territorial border.

**George Forman**
*Lone Traveler*
"Made Beauvais Ranch 5 miles from Fort Laramie on the edge of the Fort Reservation of 10 miles square inside of which no one was allowed to camp." *(July 9-10)*

From **George's** observations during his visit to Fort Laramie, nothing **Nicholas Earp** said to the army guards on July 7 had any effect.

**George Forman**
*Lone Traveler*
"The soldiers had been paid off on 4th July[367] and were having a glorious time." *(July 9-10)*

By the end of the day, **Mr. Shoemaker** parts ways with **George** and ferries over to the North Bank Trails. *(For more on George Forman's Story, please see the Emigrant Tales from the South Bank Trails.)*

---

[367] According to Sgt. Lewis Hull's 1864 diary, the paymaster arrives on July 9. This discrepancy might be a simple transcription error.

# Sunday, July 10, 1864

### Jongewaard & Oliver

Like on prior Sabbaths, the **Jongewaard Train** observes only a partial day's rest. After just a few hours of travel, they stop approximately in present-day Orin, just before the road rises up to overtake another rocky ridge.

**Gerrit Roorda**
*Jongewaard Train*
"We traveled until about noon. ... found a place to stop and laid over until morning. Here we found large cottonwoods." *(July 10)*

Based on future mentions of the **Oliver Train,** they are presumed to be in the same vicinity, though not necessarily with the **Jongewaard Train**. They might even continue on past Orin.

### Howard, Missourians & Virginians

The **Howard** and **Missouri Trains** are unable to be located for this day, though evidence from July 13 places them ahead of the **Pella Company**.

### Brown, Roe & Pella Company

The **Roe Train** once again remains in place at Alder Clump/Box Elder Spring. **Martha Roe** relishes another opportunity to sleep in "pretty late" (July 10). Mid-morning, they are joined by the **Brown Train** and the **Pella Company**.

| | |
|---|---|
| **Sarah Rousseau**<br>*Pella Company* | "Started and came about 8 miles. To the right of the road we saw as we thought at first a number of indian ponies, but it turned out to be emegrants, a great many of their company." *(July 10)* |
| | "Here, there was plenty good grass and water..." *(July 10)* |

**Sarah Rousseau** describes the camp at "Alder Creek" as having a "good spring," where they can water their horses and fill up any containers they may have. Even though the mileage is less than ideal for the **Pella Company**, they wisely take the opportunity to let their horses fill their bellies before continuing over, "twenty miles of bad mountanous roads and very poor prospect[s] of getting good grass for our horses" (July 10). **Sarah's** guidebook warns about the trail being sandy, then rough, "steep and craggy," and mountainous, for upwards of thirty-two miles.[368] Similarly, Andrew Child's guide says to expect a "flint and cobblestone hill," followed by steep banks that make accessing the River difficult.[369]

| | |
|---|---|
| **Martha Roe**<br>*Roe Train* | "After the usual work is don **Mary [Brown]**[370] and I ascended one of those high mountains or legges [ledges] of rock ... when we came back red the bible sung  and went to the spring " *(July 10)* |
| **Sarah Rousseau**<br>*Pella Company* | "...we did our washing[,] Sunday as it was." *(July 10)* |

Because **Sarah** is wheelchair-bound, she relies on **Matilda Field** to help her with the laundry. In the past, **Matilda** has also washed the clothes of the **Rousseau's** teamster, **Tom Ellis**, but today she refuses. As a result, he gives her (and the entire camp) an earful.

---

[368] J. L. Campbell, *Idaho...*, 1864, 49.
[369] *New Guide...*, 1852, 22-23.
[370] This is the second direct mention of Brown Train members being with and personally known to Martha.

**Sarah Rousseau**
*Pella Company*

"Our trip has been made exceedingly unpleasent on account of **Tom Ellis**, his continued profanity whenever he was near. A more wicked man I never saw, and one more ungentlemanly. I believe he will leave ... as **Mattie** won't do his washing any more, he has treated her so unmanly cursing her all the time." *(July 10)*

**Martha Roe** overhears the conflict and records a similar impression.

**Martha Roe**
*Roe Train*

"...camped with some duck that swore awfully" *(July 10)*

A "duck" is a common English slang term for a "mate" or "lover." As **Martha's** husband **Issac** is from Lincolnshire, England, she might be borrowing one of his expressions. After the argument, **Martha** busies herself with more chores.

**Martha Roe**
*Roe Train*

"I baked bread  then supper  then chatted a while  then prayer  then bed" *(July 10)*

At the end of the day, **Martha** records that **John and Sam**, two men from their mining outfit, attend a dance. Thought here are dancers and musicians in the **Pella Company** (see July 4), the **Browns** are probably responsible for this evening's entertainment. Their family's musicality is later highlighted in a September 29 news article in Nevada's *Gold Hills Daily* that reads:

> "One feature in the immigration is very noticeable; that is, the great musical genius it exhibits. We saw none [in **the Brown Train**], either male or female, who would not sing on the least invitation–the males having voices like handsaws, and the females like night-owls."[371]

_____

[371] "The Brown Family," 1864, 2.

## Shoemaker

**Mr. Shoemaker** seems to cover extraordinary distances once he is in the Black Hills. Based on the next recorded sighting by **Martha Roe** on July 13, he will have traveled about eighty-five miles in four days' time. This averages out to around twenty-one miles per day. Using this average daily travel speed, on July 10, **Mr. Shoemaker** may be ending his day in Deadhorse Canyon, just after summiting Emigrant Hill.

# Monday, July 11, 1864

### Oliver

The location of the **Oliver Train** is unclear for July 11, but evidence from July 12 suggests they are still ahead of the **Jongewaard Train**, perhaps reaching the North Platte River in present-day Douglas, Wyoming by evening.

### Jongewaard

Again on July 11, the **Jongewaard Train** does not travel far, perhaps due to the terrain. After rumbling over a rocky ridge east of present-day Irvine, Wyoming, they take a midday break.

**Gerrit Roorda**
*Jongewaard Train*

"We camped out on the bluffs and drove the stock to the bottom as there was no grass on the bluffs." *(July 11)*

Andrew Child's guidebook advises that there is a "little feed near the river,"[372] but the **Jongewaard Train** has few other options but to try. **Gerrit Roorda** likely accompanies the cattle a few miles down to the North Platte River somewhere near present-day Douglas. He offers little explanation for why the **Jongewaards** do not continue on, other than a brief remark that "it rained a few drops." McKinstry Ridge, the next hill past Douglas is considered a "steep and craggy ascent,"[373] and any sign of inclement weather could be a deterrent for continuing on, although no one else on the trail today seems to

---

[372] *New Guide...*, 1852, 23.
[373] J. L. Campbell, *Idaho...*, 1864, 49.

be concerned about the weather. The detour to get grass might also take up too much time to make the next climb feasible.

## Howard, Missourians & Virginians

The location of the **Howard and Missouri Trains** also remains unclear for July 11. They are suspected to be either approaching or camping in present-day Orin, Wyoming.

## Brown, Clark, Pella Company & Roe

In the morning, the **Roe Train** rises early to tackle what they heard would be "24 M without water" (July 11), though trying to round up their stock on the other side of the North Platte River causes a setback. The **Roes** have repeatedly taken their stock across to the south side of the North Platte River for better grazing opportunities. To do so from Alder Clump/ Box Elder Spring, "The Boys" may have led the animals about six miles northeast of camp toward present-day Sandy Beach Dune or Cottonwood campground.

**Martha Roe**
*Roe Train*
"Going to start early but the cattle being gon ... we found them could not get the cross the river for more than an hour" *(July 11)*

The **Brown Train** is presumed to remain in the company of the **Roes** and **Pella Company** today. In the **Pella Company, Sarah Rousseau** writes that **Tom Ellis** holds to his threat from the day prior and takes off with "another family by the name of **Clark**." This is a reference to **William** and **Mary Clark**, a Mormon couple heading to Provo, Utah, who have been joined with the **Pella Company** since June 2.[374]

---

[374] The Clarks joined the Pella Company in Omaha, Nebraska with their son-in-law Robert Parker. Due to today's events, they will be singled out in the headings from now on.

| | |
|---|---|
| **Sarah Rousseau**<br>*Pella Company* | "It has been the most pleasant day I have spent since I left home. We have heard no swearing. All has been quiet and pleasant." *(July 11)* |

Though some people, such as **Sarah** and **Matilda**, will find relief from **Tom's** absence, the lack of a teamster puts more strain on **Dr. James Rousseau**. For reader clarity, the **Rousseaus** have two vehicles: a standard prairie schooner ("wagon") and a Landeau ("carriage"). Later diary entries refer to **Nicholas Earp**, or one of his sons, driving the **Rousseau's** heavily loaded prairie schooner (with undesirable results), but for the time being, the family must rely on an ill-equipped fourteen-year-old daughter, a twelve-year-old son, and Sarah's aide, **Matilda Field** to pick up the slack.

Once the wagon trains get going, **Martha Roe** is pleasantly surprised that the earlier predictions about a lack of water are "not so."

| | |
|---|---|
| **Martha Roe**<br>*Roe Train* | "Travailed bout 7 M and came to the river camped for noon ... Then proceeded bout 6 or 7 M farther and came to the river where we camped for the night[.] pretty good feed and water" *(July 11)* |

**Sarah** reports a similar story of traveling thirteen miles over "some rough roads." They all end their day where Lost Creek meets the River. **Sarah** considers this spot "a very pretty place." Here, company teamsters can ford or swim horses and cattle over to the south bank, saving them from needing to dip into any packed feed supplies.

| | |
|---|---|
| **Sarah Rousseau**<br>*Pella Company* | "The girls had to do the men's work. The **Dr. [James Rousseau]** is pretty tired to-night. We must try and get someone else to go with us. " *(July 11)* |

Once settled, **Sarah** records their evening being disturbed. It should be noted, however, that **Martha's** diary does not contain any mentions of the following.

| | |
|---|---|
| **Sarah Rousseau**<br>*Pella Company* | "...after driving our horses across the river to feed[,] some one gave the alarm, that Indians were around. And that a gentleman in a train close by had just lost three of his horses[,] all that he had. He saw them [Indians] cut the |

ropes they were fastened with and ran them off before they could get assistance." *(July 12, in reflection)*

**Sarah** does not provide clarifying details on who the **Man Robbed of Three Horses** is or anything about the wagon train he is associated with. It seems she does not know him well enough to do so. Further research is encouraged.

| **Sarah Rousseau** *Pella Company* | "Well it caused a great deal of alarm. They sent word over the river to the guards that the Indians were about and they all commenced right away to gather up their teams to bring them back and form a correle..." *(July 12, in reflection)* |
|---|---|

Word of the robbery reached the **Clarks** ahead who rallied for protection and to help where they could. **Dr. James Rousseau** had sent all of the family's horses across the river because the **Rousseaus** did not have a backup feed supply (see July 8).

| **Sarah Rousseau** *Pella Company* | "...consequently he had no horse to go after them. And he left them to those who were going after theirs ... there being so many of them to bring, it took them till[sic] dark ... and ours were left behind" *(July 12, in reflection)* |
|---|---|

Under the cover of night, **Sarah** laments, "the horses could not be seen anywhere." Just when **Sarah's** heart drops and she admits, "of course I felt afraid they would be run off by the Indians," a friend comes to the rescue. **Robert Parker** extends an offer to go back over the River to find her horses. Because he was one of the guards posted for his horses on the other side of the River, he believes he knows the last place the **Rousseau's** horses were seen.

The fact that he is willing to take on this dangerous task speaks to his impeccable character and bravery. It also indicates that the **Clarks** (with **Tom Ellis**) are still within range of hearing the alarm signals fired by the **Pella**

**Company**. They may be keeping just far enough ahead to maintain peace between **Tom** and **Matilda**.

**Sarah Rousseau**
*Pella Company*

"The Messrs. **[Robert] Parker, [William or Richard] Curtis and [John] Hamilton** went over to see if they could get them. But it was too dark for them to see and they stayed all night." *(July 12, in reflection)*

### Shoemaker

Keeping with the average travel speed of 21 miles per day, on July 11, **Mr. Shoemaker** might reach Muddy Creek or a spring near Red Canyon, on the north side of present-day Glendo Reservoir. Or, as trail conditions permit and the help of his horses allows, he may be even farther, perhaps joining or passing those camped at Lost Creek.

# Tuesday, July 12, 1864

### Oliver

Today the **Oliver Train** overcomes McKinstry Ridge then descends to the North Douglas Bend. As they descend, they might get a glimpse of the steady North Plate River winding left and right, flowing back towards Fort Laramie. At the base of the ridge, a trickling creek lures them to the River's edge. This would make a lovely place to rest and eat lunch.

By late afternoon, the **Oliver Train** is suspected to have continued approximately eight to ten miles along the lowlands bordering the River. Right below the entrance of a ravine,[375] the **Olivers** are assaulted and robbed. Because there is no first person account to expound on this claim secondary reports must fill in the blanks. When **Sarah Rousseau** from the **Pella Company** reaches this point on July 17, she records:

**Sarah Rousseau**
*Pella Company*

"...we saw a paper staked to the ground. **Mattie [Field]** got out to see what it was. It stated that the **Oliver train** had lost 8 head of horses[.] no lives lost, but had a very narrow escape." *(July 17)*

---

[375] School Section Draw runs northward from here and the location of the Kelly-Larimer attack on Little Box Elder Creek is four or five miles due south of this spot.

It is entirely possible that the **Oliver Train** is an early victim of the Northern Plains Indians' ire that also descends on the **Kelly-Larimer Train** and others on the South Bank Trails. It is also plausible that this attack occurs after the **Kelly-Larimer** incident. The **Oliver Train** may be caught up in the subsequent chasing down of anyone who may have witnessed any portion of the event, including the late night dash over the river and up through Powder River Basin.

The site where this attack happens is considered by other trail diarists to be the halfway point between the Bend and Deer Creek garrison. It is also located nearly opposite from where Box Elder Creek meets the North Platte River. Presently near this location, there is a public campground on the North Bank of the River called Bixby Public Access which touts year-round camping, fishing and hunting. In an effort to remain concise, the author will borrow the campground name and refer to this halfway point as "Bixby Point."

**Abbie Brown** claims in her memoir that after being attacked, the **Olivers** retreat east, back to the North Douglas Bend, where they will gather with other emigrants (including the **Browns**) for safety. No mention of a tussle or theft is found in Emery Oliver's Oral History from 1992. One could argue that if relatively few horses are lost and everyone survives, perhaps the tale could be long forgotten over one hundred and fifty years' time.

### Man with Three Mules

About eight miles from the North Douglas Bend, but still a short distance east of Bixby Point, there is another assault and robbery on July 12. An unidentified man is "shot all to pieces," according to the trail marker warning later seen in this location.[376] It is unclear if he lost his three mules in the attack, or if he is merely left with three mules after it.

---

[376] See Sarah Rousseau's diary entry for July 15.

The author suspects the **Man with Three Mules** is rescued by the **Oliver Train** while they are retreating.  When **Martha Roe** later meets this man, she details his condition.

| **Martha Roe**<br>*Roe Train* | "[Indians] shot the man with arrows[,] once in the leg[,] once through the arm below the elbow[,] and a flesh wound above the elbow[,]  and one wound in the brest[,] a glancing shot and thinks the dart in his side[.]  I think it fatal" *(July 13)* |

### Jongewaard & Seven Wagon Train

On the morning of July 12, the **Jongewaard Train** proceeds up and over McKinstry Ridge, followed by a short trip through the lowlands of the North Douglas Bend.

| **Gerrit Roorda**<br>*Jongewaard Train* | "We had a mountainous road in the forenoon but in the afternoon we traveled along the river. We pass two very nice springs. We all felt first rate." *(July 12)* |

This "first rate" feeling does not last long, according to **John Ellerbroek's** recollection.[377]

| **John Ellerbroek**<br>*Jongewaard Train* | "There was a small wagon train ahead of us and the Indians swooped down on them and took every hoof they had, so they could go no farther." *(405)* |

---

[377] Readers should bear in mind that John's reminiscence from 1942 is that of an eighty-eight-year-old remembering the event as a ten-year–old. His story is found in Charles Dyke's *Story of Sioux County,* pages 402-411.

**John Ellerbroek**
*Jongewaard Train*

"One of their party had caught an Indian pony and he rode back on the dangerous trail to inform us of their plight. ... they were waiting for us to come along and pick them up." *(405)*

A July 13 diary entry for **Martha Roe** clarifies that this party that lost "every hoof" had seven wagons in it. Moving forward, for a lack of a better option, these travelers will be identified in this book as the **Seven Wagon Train**. Those in the **Oliver Train** likely aide and corral with this party after their attack on the same evening. Further research is encouraged to identify who this wagon train might belong to. Based on the date, time, location and level of aggression shown towards the **Oliver Train, Man with Three Mules**, and the **Seven Wagon Train**, all three of these attacks are attributed to the army of Northern Plains Indians from the Powder River Basin.

**John Ellerbroek**
*Jongewaard Train*

"This occurrence put us on our guard more than ever."
*(405)*

In response to the news, **Cornelius Jongewaard** reassigns wagon driving duties to women so that men can be constantly armed and ready to fire upon any potential threat.

**Gerrit Roorda**
*Jongewaard Train*

"The girls drove the teams for us." *(July 12)*

**John Ellerbroek**
*Jongewaard Train*

"When we came up to them, they were camped on a river..." *(405)*

The **Jongewaard Train** meets the stranded **Seven Wagon Train** and others approximately where the freshly carved Bozeman Trail leads north.[378] When **John** takes into account his surroundings this evening, his imagination gets the better of him.

---

[378] For context, on the south side of the North Platte River is the junction of La Prele Creek, and the future site of Fort Fetterman (constructed in 1867).

**John Ellerbroek**  "...as usual, the captain [**Cornelius Jongewaard**] put out
*Jongewaard Train*  a double guard ... There was a deep gulch on one side of
the camp and the Indians seemed to have spied us and
had hidden in the gulch." *(405)*

He further remarks, "we were always ready for a fight."

## Howard, Missourians & Virginians

By the end of the day, the **Howard** and **Missouri Trains** may be tackling
the eight or ten mile climb up and over McKinstry Ridge and corral near the
same creek the **Oliver Train** likely nooned at earlier. There are no mentions
of the other attacks by **Howard** family descendants.

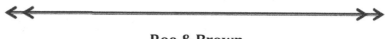

## Roe & Brown

The **Roe Train**, along with the family of **John Brown**, leave the **Pella
Company** at their morning camp on Lost Creek.

**Martha Roe**  "Started pretty good time   drove bout 12 M and camped
*Roe Train*  on the river bank under a large cotton wood tree ...
started and drove bout 7 M and camped bout four oclock"
*(July 12)*

Considering **Martha Roe's** mileage estimate and a familiar mention of
aged cottonwood trees, it is believed they take their lunch break on the north
end of present-day Orin. By the end of the day, the **Roes and Browns** approach
what is now Douglas, Wyoming.

**Martha Roe**  "...I washed a large washing on the bank of the Platt[,]
*Roe Train*  then got supper and went to bed" *(July 12)*

## Shoemaker

If keeping to an average pace, **Mr. Shoemaker** might also be descending into present-day Douglas, Wyoming; joining the other campers by the end of July 12 with a string of horses. It is also possible that he camps on the far end of Douglas, along the bluffs near the base of McKinstry Ridge.

## Clark & Pella Company

The **Pella Company** and **Clarks** are detained at Lost Creek this morning while waiting for **Robert Parker**, **William (or Richard) Curtis**, and **John Hamilton** to return from across the North Platte River after a late night searching for the **Rousseau** horses.

| | |
|---|---|
| **Sarah Rousseau**<br>*Pella Company* | "**Mr. Parker** acted the part of a gentleman and friend to us which I shall always remember with gratitude."<br>*(July 12)* |

When these men return, **Sarah Rousseau** quotes Bible verses and sings praises over the sight of them.

| | |
|---|---|
| **Sarah Rousseau**<br>*Pella Company* | "...in the morning good fortune smiled on us, they found them [the horses] and brought them back. Oh how rejoiced I felt... " *(July 12)* |

It is suspected that **Robert** rejoins the **Clark family** and rides out ahead of the **Pella Company**, as there is no further mention of him in this day's events.

| | |
|---|---|
| **Sarah Rousseau**<br>*Pella Company* | "...passed over some very rough roads and got to the river, being some 9 miles where we stopped for noon."<br>*(July 12)* |
| **Nicholas Earp**<br>*Pella Company* | "...about 50 miles above Laramie[,] one day in camp for noon in the bend of Platt River... *(1865)* |

The afternoon stop puts the **Pella Company** in present-day Orin, Wyoming, in the valley of Shawnee Creek.

**Nicholas Earp**
*Pella Company*

"...the grass being verry pore on the side that we war campt on[,] I rode across the river and found that on the other side that thare was good grass[,] so I gave the order for the stock to be turned over the River. My hands [ie. **Charlie Capley**[379]] took my horses and all the cattle over..."[380] *(1865)*

**Nicholas Earp**
*Pella Company*

"the ballance turned some of thirs over sutch as they could drive over after the rest[,] but some would not go over and some said they would rather thirs would stay on the side they war on than to put them into the River[.] so thare was some of the stock on one side, and some on the other[.]" *(1865)*

After being shaken up over the near loss of the **Rousseau's** prized carriage horses the night before, they are likely among those who "would rather thirs would stay."

**Nicholas Earp**
*Pella Company*

"I gave orders to those that went across the river that in case that I gave the alarm to git hold of thir horses picket rops as quick as possible and bring them across the river into camp." *(1865)*

Despite **Nicholas'** anxious preparations, all seems to be peaceful, and the campers quickly relax.

---

[379] Charlie is the son of James Copla/Capley in Pella, IA (whom this letter is sent to).
[380] The cattle belong to Israel Curtis.

| | |
|---|---|
| **Nicholas Earp**<br>*Pella Company* | "We had been in camp but alittle[sic] while[.] **J. B. Hamilton**[,] **I. C. Curtis**[,] **Dr. Russaw** & my self war seated on the bank of the River talking and I happened to look around behind me and about four hundred yards off I saw a Squad of men on horse back galoping towards us[.]" *(1865)* |
| **Sarah Rousseau**<br>*Pella Company* | "We had hardly got our horses out to eat when the alarm was given [that] the indians were on us..." *(July 12)* |
| **Nicholas Earp**<br>*Pella Company* | "I sprang to my feet and sang out ["]Indians[!] to arms boys[!"]  *(1865)* |
| **Sarah Rousseau**<br>*Pella Company* | "...every man was for his gun and revolver and try to catch their horses as there was a regular stampede in every direction..." *(July 12)* |
| **Nicholas Earp**<br>*Pella Company* | "...we all rushed to the waggons and got our guns and ran to meet the red skins who by this time was amongst the horses that war on our side of the river[,] hooping and yelling, like indians shure enough[.]" *(1865)* |
| | "At the commencement of the fun[,] according to directions[,] I hollowed for the stock on the other side to be brought over [the river]..." *(1865)* |
| **Sarah Rousseau**<br>*Pella Company* | "**Tom Ellis** had left us a day or two before and we couldn't get another hand at present. **The Dr. [James Rousseau]** and the girls **[Matilda Field** and **Sarah Elizabeth Rousseau]** and our little boys **[John and Albert Rousseau]** were all we had to see to ours." *(July 12)* |

As a reminder to the reader, **Tom Ellis** is presently with the **Clark family**, whose location is presently ahead of the **Pella Company**, although at a farther distance than they had been before.

| | |
|---|---|
| **Sarah Rousseau**<br>*Pella Company* | "The indians made a rush by on the Bluffs, our men firing on them as they passed. Oh what an exciting time, the bullets flying in every direction & horses running as hard as they could." *(July 12)* |
| **Nicholas Earp**<br>*Pella Company* | "we met them and began to shoot at them…" *(1865)* |
| **Sarah Rousseau**<br>*Pella Company* | "I was left alone in the carriage, the rest of them all helping. It is impossible to describe my feelings at such a time and place in the situation I was. Helpless." *(July 12)* |
| **Nicholas Earp**<br>*Pella Company* | "we soon checked them up and turned them back[.]" *(1865)* |

Artist concept of the Pella Company's robbery in Orin, Wyoming, on July 12, 1864. Sketch by Manjula Karunatilaka, 2021. Copyright, Janelle Molony.

While **Nicholas** is engaging with the thieves who charge boldly at them, he doesn't realize that there are others nearby hoping to capitalize on the distraction. After chasing a few off, he rides returned to the corral and learns he is being two-timed by more Indians sneaking up from a different direction to steal horses right from underneath the emigrants' noses.

**Nicholas Earp**
*Pella Company*

"...while one of them was in the act of trying to lasoe one of the **Hamiltons** mares[,] I leveled the rifle I got of [E.F.] Grafe[381] at him and at the crack of the gun he fell forward in his saddle and turned his horse round and ran off[,] badly wounded, I am shure[.]" *(1865)*

"...the yells of the Savages and the firing of the guns fritened our horses so that it caused them to stampede and ran down apast the camp[.] in spite of all that we could do[,] they took back down the road[.]  The Indians[,] seeing that[,] ran round and got in between us and the horses and ran them off[.]" *(1865)*

**Sarah Rousseau**
*Pella Company*

"They run four of our horses off and five of **Mr. [John] Hamiltons** and a filly belonging to **Mr. [Israel] Curtis**." *(July 12)*

This attack is noticeably well coordinated. In February of 1865, **Lt. Col. William O. Collins** reports on the strategy and skill of those they are chasing down, writing: "The Indians of the Plains are the best skirmishers in the world. In rapidity of movement, sudden wheeling and hanging over steep and difficult

---

[381] Mr. Ernst Frederick Grafe (pronounced like "Graph") was born 1819 in Hanover, Germany and served in the Union army during the Civil War. At this time, he is living in Lake Prairie Township in Marion County, Iowa.

ground, no trained cavalry can equal them. ...We were not strong enough to charge or scatter."[382]

## Pella Company & Man Robbed of Three Horses

Just when the **Pella Company** feels like the storm has passed, they are joined by another traveler who riles up **Nicholas'** sense of justice.

**Sarah Rousseau**
*Pella Company*

"Another gentleman came in after us, belonging to another train, was unhitching his horses. They were taken with the harness on." *(July 12)*

This man is believed to be the same person that reported an incident on the evening of July 11. One discrepancy that might unravel that claim is found in **Sarah's** prior mention of the **Man Robbed of Three Horses**. She writes that he lost "all that he had" (July 11). Either this man obtained a replacement animal, or this is a separate person with a very similar story. Further research is encouraged.

**Sarah Rousseau**
*Pella Company*

"This gentleman held a consultation to see if they had better follow them [Indians] up, it took some time before they could decide, at last they decided that ten of them should get their horses and arm themselves, and follow after them." *(July 12)*

"**The Dr. [James Rousseau]** and all the married gentlemen staid to get all the waggons in Corelle while the rest were looking after the horses. They made the Corelle large enough to put the horses in when they should be brought up. It was very laborious work." *(July 12)*

---

[382] Lt. Col. William O. Collins, "Report February 15, 1865," transcribed in Yellowstone Genealogy Forum, RootsWeb.com, published April 21, 2004.
Https://sites.rootsweb.com/~mtygf/county/rescue_mudsprings.htm

The unmarried men in this pursuit are unnamed in any account from the **Pella Company**.[383] Those who make chase do not know how long they'll be gone, how far they'll have to go, or what other surprises will meet them along the way. The decision to pursue armed robbers who know the area far better than the emigrants requires significant consideration on behalf of the many women and children who are left behind anxiously waiting.

| | |
|---|---|
| **Sarah Rousseau**<br>*Pella Company* | "Here we are in the wilderness … not enough team to go on with, and don't know how long it may be before the rest of them may be taken." *(July 12)*<br><br>"Oh how desolate my feelings under such circumstances." *(July 12)* |

Not long after the men depart, one returns with his horse in poor condition.

| | |
|---|---|
| **Sarah Rousseau**<br>*Pella Company* | "One of the gentlemen that had three of his horses taken in their harness shot his horse accidently with his revolver and had to turn back with it." *(July 12)* |

No information is given as to the final condition of the replacement horse (wounded or dead). Despite the loss of a most enthusiastic fighter, **Nicholas** sticks to the plan.

| | |
|---|---|
| **Nicholas Earp**<br>*Pella Company* | "I took ten men [now nine] and persued them [Indians] untell dark but without effect[.]the conciquence was they got ten head of our horses[:]   5 of **Hamiltons**[,] 4 of **Rusaws** & one of **Curtises**['.]" *(1865)* |

---

[383] Ten unmarried men, plus the two leaders, might include: 1) the Man Robbed of Three Horses, 2) Nicholas Earp, 3) James Earp, 4) Wyatt Earp, 5) Richard Curtis, 6) Levi Tucker, 7) Charles Capley, 8) Mack, and two others who cannot be established.

| **Sarah Rousseau**<br>*Pella Company* | "The party came back at dark without our horses, hearing about them at the train we left at our camping place in the morning [on Lost Creek] … if they had been half an hour sooner they could have got them as the indians had just gone past with them on the other side of the river" *(July 12)* |
|---|---|
| **Sarah Rousseau**<br>*Pella Company* | "They [the Indians] had intended crossing there [at Lost Creek] but happened to see their train and they went further down to cross." *(July 12)* |

Based on the discoveries made by Larry Cundall about a potential hub for a horse thieving operation out on Sheep Mountain, readers might speculate on this being the initial destination for the stolen goods before being herded elsewhere for an illegal sale. Deterred from crossing, as the Indians were, the next plausible location for them to cross the North Plate River is down by Bulls Bend, where **Sarah** had recorded being watched by them on July 9.

| **Sarah Rousseau**<br>*Pella Company* | "We will have to try and make some arrangement to go on. I think it likely we can get two yoke of oxen to put on our big waggon[sic] and get a driver and let the horses go … we think it very unlikely we shall ever get to see them if we should go after them." *(July 12)* |
|---|---|

**Sarah** sympathizes with her husband's predicament after this event. At the age of fifty-two, **Dr. James Rousseau** has no adult sons to help him with the care and coordination of two vehicles (one covered wagon and one carriage) and approximately eight horses.[384]

The **Man Robbed of Three Horses** is never mentioned by **Sarah** again. While many emigrants feel morally obligated to rescue those who are stranded and band together, no evidence supports him staying with the **Pella Company**. When emigrants help out by sharing their animals, this increases the strain of travel on everyone. Previously non-working spares that might be swapped out

---

[384] His eldest son John James is only twelve and has been raised with upper class comforts, including attending school instead of laboring on a farm.

for a sick or tired animal, if shared, now have to face constant demands and run a greater risk of burnout. To adjust for this, wagon masters might slow the speed or reduce distance traveled to go easy on the animals.

Alternatively, as seen in **Sarah's** diary, a desperate victim might try to buy animals off a passing wagon train... at the proverbial cost of an arm *and* a leg, if necessary. The families in the **Pella Company** presently do not have the luxury of making any sales to or accommodations for anyone else on the trail, no matter how great the offer.

# Wednesday, July 13, 1864 (part 1)

### Shoemaker - Epilogue

**Mr. Shoemaker** is suspected to leave his camp quite early. While mileage specifics are impossible to confirm without additional evidence, on July 13, he passes through the North Douglas Bend where the **Jongewaard Train** is preparing their breakfast. Some distance past the Bend, **Mr. Shoemaker** is confronted by hundreds of Northern Plains Indians in his way. These could be a detachment from the same group that robbed the **Oliver Train** at Bixby Point. These Indians make off with twenty-eight of his horses.

**Sarah Rousseau**
*Pella Company*

"...we heard about train that they call the **Batcheler** had 28 head of horses take the day after we lost ours."
*(July 17)*

From July 13 on, there is no mention of the whereabouts of the **Mr. Shoemaker** and his lone wagon loaded with leather and food. Whether he made it or not to his destination in Montana or Idaho Territory is also unknown.

### Jongewaard

On the morning of July 13, the **Jongewaard Train** is still camped on the western end of the North Douglas Bend, presumably with the victims of yesterday's attacks somewhere nearby. Teamsters and guards from the

**Jongewaard Train** let the cattle and horses out from the double-guarded corral to feed on the south side of the North Platte River. The teamsters are identified as **Gerrit Rysdam,** who is responsible for **Lutje Mars'** animals, and the following: **Arie Jongewaard, Isaac DeVries, Barend "Ten" Broek,** and **Teunis Burgraff.**

| | |
|---|---|
| **John Ellerbroek**<br>*Jongewaard Train* | "...in the morning[,] the guard came in for breakfast while they left the horses and mules and cattle [to] graze...." *(405).* |

From **John Ellerbroek's** reminiscence, it sounds like **Gerrit** and the other teamsters left the animals completely unattended. Right at this moment of vulnerability **Gerrit** explains, "We had a good deal of trouble with the Indians" (July 13). While distracted by food, the **Jongewaard Train** is ambushed by a small band of eight Indians.[385]

| | |
|---|---|
| **John Ellerbroek**<br>*Jongewaard Train* | "...the Indians came like a windstorm and stampeded all our horses, mules, and cattle, except a few." *(405).* |
| **Gerrit Roorda**<br>*Jongewaard Train* | "They came unexpected upon us and drove 7 of our horses off." *(July 13)* |
| **John Ellerbroek**<br>*Jongewaard Train* | "...they pulled the pickets out or broke the ropes or the Indians cut them, and we had only three horses and two mules left." *(405)* |

Using the figures provided by **Gerrit** and **John,** we learn that the Dutch families had twelve steeds to start with, while the majority of their wagons were drawn by mostly unbroken oxen.[386] Further details of the attack come

---

[385] This headcount comes from Martha Roe's notes on July13.

[386] Wealthy and early-start emigrants might have had the first choice of yoke-ready cattle from providers back in Iowa. Unbroken animals required on-the-job wrangling; a physically demanding skill not every emigrant had the patience or strength for.

from **Cornelius Jongewaard's** daughter **Jana** (then, only one-year old) who relays her story to Charles Dyke in 1942.

**Jana Jongewaard**
*Jongewaard Train*

"When going through the mountains, the Indians shot at [us] from behind the rocks with bows and arrows. But except for wounding a couple of oxen, they did little damage. [We] had lined up the canvas covers with [our] feather beds so as to protect the women and children, and while the arrows penetrated the canvas, they sank harmlessly in the feathers." *(411)*[387]

It doesn't seem plausible that the women and children prepared their wagons in such a manner mid-crises. The more likely conclusion is that this work was done on July 12 as a response to coming upon other emigrants who were previously robbed and stranded. While those in the defensive corral secure their loved ones and possessions, an offensive team kicks into action. As a reminder to the reader, the wagon train has only three horses and two mules at their disposal.

**John Ellerbroek**
*Jongewaard Train*

"...three of our men jumped on the horses and went after them. ... [**Arie**] **Jongewaard** also hastily ferried several men across the river, two on a horse, and they also went after them. The horsemen went as fast as they could with the men on foot following." *(405)*

**John's** attention to detail serves historians well. With his story, we can confirm that most of the grazing stock had been left on the south side of the river.

_____

[387] Jana Jongewaard Bogaard in Dyke's *Story of Sioux County*, 1942, 411.

**John Ellerbroek**

*Jongewaard Train*

"As the Indians could not keep the [unbroken] animals together[,] our men soon overtook them and they had a gun fight which sounded in the distance like the firing of a bunch of firecrackers, for we boys had followed the men to see what was going on." *(405)*

"The Indians shot the bridle from the horse **Arie Jongewaard** was riding and shot it in the leg so that it spurted blood at every jump[,] but they [the teamsters] tied a bandage around it as soon as they could and it was all right. ... Another horse was so badly wounded, that it fell dead when near the camp." *(405-406)*

Three useful mounts remain. But the fight is not over.

**John Ellerbroek**

*Jongewaard Train*

"While the fighting was on, my stepbrother, **Isaac De Vries** went around a little hill to head the Indians off, and they all came his way, but they did not see him, as he hid behind some rocks. Before they came to him, they stopped to give battle to the three men[388] that followed them." *(406)*

"...when **Isaac** saw them and they came on again, and were within range, he also began to shoot and he shot one who fell from his pony. But the other Indians put him [back] on and tied their wounded comrade to his pony." *(406)*

---

[388] These men are still believed to be Arie Jongewaard, Isaac DeVries, Barend "Ten" Broek, and Teunis Burgraff.

Though not a confirmed kill, **John** does note that the man who is tied to the pony flops around on the horse while his animal retreats.

**John Ellerbroek**
*Jongewaard Train*

"When the Indians fled, they took along the horses they could handle, but we got most of our horses back. However, we lost one of our finest horses, Young Prince." *(1942, p. 406)*

If there were twelve "mounts" (horses and mules) to begin with, the final loss might be four animals, as follows: One horse (Young Prince) from **Lutje Mars**; one horse that dropped dead; and two horses (one team) from **Cornelius Jongewaard**. This count leaves nine reclaimed mounts (eight unwounded).

"With that," Dutch Immigration expert, Brian Beltman writes, "the Indians departed, abandoning the livestock. Except for a few horses, including the best team belonging to **Captain Jongewaard**, the emigrants recovered most of their animals."[389] Iowa historian and biographer, Charles Dyke also concludes, "After that, they had no more trouble with the Indians or horse thieves."[390] **John's** account also confirms this result, but the "excitement," as he calls it, is far from being over. After the Indians are out of sight, the men regroup and strategize.

**John Ellerbroek**
*Jongewaard Train*

"...it was decided to send three men to one of the little forts and see if we could get the soldiers to help us get our horses back and three of our men volunteered to go to the fort." *(406)*

Brian Beltman claims, "Three of the Dutch-Americans ... headed for Deer Creek Station where 40 soldiers were encamped, to report their run-in with the Indians."[391]

---

[389] Brian Beltman, 1997 dissertation, 127-128.
[390] *Story of Sioux County*, 1942, 411.
[391] Brian Beltman, "Civil War Reverberations: Exodus and Return Among the Pella Dutch During the 1860s" in *The Dutch-American Experience: Essays in Honor of Robert P. Swierenga,* Eds. Hans Krabbendam and Larry J. Wagenaar (2000, VU Uitgeverij, Amsterdam), 129.

**Gerrit Roorda** *Jongewaard Train* — "Three of our boys went after some soldiers. They went part of the way." *(July 13)*

**John Ellerbroek** *Jongewaard Train* — "When they had gone about half of the way,[392] they saw a big cloud of dust coming … They were soldiers from the fort [Deer Creek], but they had a [Black man] with them with whom the men mistook for an Indian and they thought that they [the soldiers] were Indians." *(407)*

Until conclusive evidence suggests otherwise, the Black rider is suspected to be the teen **Andy Lawrence** from the **Kelly-Larimer Train**, who was last seen on the eve of July 12, fleeing from the site of his father's death and the destruction of the wagon train camp on Little Box Elder Creek. His whereabouts for the remainder of the night are undocumented, though it is believed while **Josiah Kelly** ran east, **Andy** ran west to the military station. In the morning, **Andy** leads these military scouts back towards the scene of the murders.

For nineteen-year-old **Issac DeVries**, the thought of confronting more Indians with only three riders causes him to wheel about. This is a mistake.

**Gerrit Roorda** *Jongewaard Train* — "They saw some horsemen take after them…" *(July 13)*

**John Ellerbroek** *Jongewaard Train* — "As our men did not give the right signal and went back as fast as they could, the soldiers mistook them for horse thieves … and gave pursuit." *(p. 407)*

[392] The halfway point is approximately at Bixby Point, on the opposite side of where the North Platte River connects with Box Elder Creek.

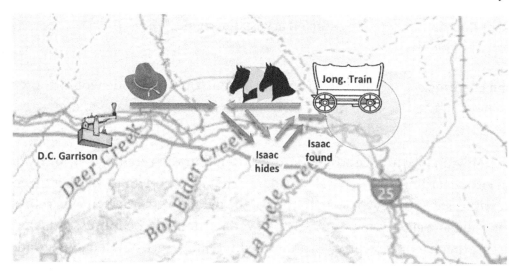

Author's interpretation of the skirmish between the Union Cavalry and three men from the Jongewaard Wagon Train. U.S. Geological Survey (USGS), "Topographic Map of Converse County, Wyoming," modified by author.

In his later reminiscence, **John** explains that there are white antagonists on the trail who either coerce, partner with, or pose as Indians to conduct robberies. Keen readers might once again reflect back on the behaviors of **George Colburn** from the **Ridgley Party**. In some cases, **John** reports, the robbers, "could sell them [horses] to agents of the Southern states for the [Confederate] army" (1942, 406). **John** further confirms that Union soldiers stationed in the area are operating under a command to capture and hang all horse thieves on sight and that civilians who help capture a horse thief are incentivized by an award of five hundred dollars (the modern-day equivalent of $9,580.00 in 2023).[393] Brian Beltman sums up this twist with, "[the] pursuers now became the pursued."[394]

**John Ellerbroek**
*Jongewaard Train*

"The soldiers cornered the men in a bend of the river, but our men jumped into the river ... [they] swam across with the soldiers after them." *(407)*

---

[393] Using the CPI Inflation Calculator from OfficialData.org
[394] 1997 dissertation, 127-128.

| | |
|---|---|
| **Gerrit Roorda**<br>*Jongewaard Train* | "…they started across the river…" *(July 13)* |
| **John Ellerbroek**<br>*Jongewaard Train* | "…the horse on which **Isaac De Vries** rode would not jump [into the river] and he tried to escape to one side…" *(407)* |

Moving forward, contradictions are found in the retellings of **John** and **Gerrit** regarding the chase. Readers should note that neither were eyewitnesses to the event — both hear of the details from the men who return. If any added weight is to be given to one version, it might be **John's**. As **Isaac's** stepbrother, he may be privy to additional retellings or extended details later in life. Both accounts agree, however, that the cavalry fires on the emigrants first (unprovoked and without a clear accusation or evidence of a crime). According to **Gerrit's** day book, **Isaac's** horse is shot while he is crossing the North Platte River. **John's** reminiscence, however, suggests **Isaac** does not make it across the River until much later.

| | |
|---|---|
| **Gerrit Roorda**<br>*Jongewaard Train* | "…one of them [soldiers] shot **Isaac DeVries'** horse while he and **Teunis Burgraff** and **Ten Broek** were crossing the river." *(July 13)* |
| **John Ellerbroek**<br>*Jongewaard Train* | "…one of them [soldiers] shot his [**Isaac's**] horse[395] and it stumbled and fell. … He ran away as fast as he could … hid in a gulch and they could not find him." *(407)* |

In the gulch, **Isaac** covers himself in sand and waits for the danger to pass. From where he lies, he can see the chase continue through the leaves of a shrub.[396] While the soldiers continue to chase after **Teunis** and **Ten** on the south side of the river, **Isaac** stays put until he feels it is safe to move out from his hiding place.

---

[395] John later specifies that the horse Isaac rides is a race horse.
[396] John Ellerbroek, 1942, 407.

**John Ellerbroek**
*Jongewaard Train*

"**Isaac DeVries** took to the brush and as he heard the Indians in the timber, he pulled off his boots for fear that they would make too much noise." *(407)*

These Indians might be the same few seen prowling around Little Box Elder Creek to find and kill **Mary Hurley Kelly** (*See July 13 from the South Bank Trails*).

After members of the 11th Ohio Volunteer Cavalry cross the river, it becomes unclear if, or how much, **Andy** engages in the skirmish they started. It is plausible that he abandons the pursuit and continues back down the South Bank Trail to view the remains of the Little Box Elder camp, then heads east to the gathering at La Prele, where he announces that everyone in his wagon train is (or must be) dead.

**John Ellerbroek**
*Jongewaard Train*

"The soldiers again cornered the men [**Teunis** and **Ten**] in a bend on the other side of the river and again they jumped into the river and tried to get across [to the North Bank]. But the soldiers tired of chasing them to catch them alive, began to fire at them while they were crossing the river." *(407)*

This time, **Ten's** horse catches a bullet as soon as he comes out of the water. When the horse falls, it pins **Ten** underneath its body.

**John Ellerbroek**
*Jongewaard Train*

"The soldiers then came up and pulled him from under his horse and learned from him who they were." *(407)*

**Gerrit Roorda**
*Jongewaard Train*

"**Teunis** went right back to camp and did not know where **Ike [Isaac]** and **Ten Broek** were." *(July 13)*

Once the soldiers realize their mistake, they quit their chase, collect the saddles of both dead or dying horses and, as **John** tells the tale, they "went away." Alternatively, **Gerrit** writes that two soldiers accompany **Ten** back to the camp "about half past ten," and confess that they "killed two horses for us," and that they had no idea where **Isaac** was.

| | |
|---|---|
| **Gerrit Roorda**<br>*Jongewaard Train* | "We started, 9 of us, to hunt for him **[Isaac]** but did not find him." *(July 13)* |

This ordeal would be talked about on the South Side Trails for days to come, perhaps because of details shared by **Andy** when he gets to Le Prele Creek *(See George Forman's remarks on July 15).*

### Man with Three Mules, Oliver & Seven Wagon Train

In the **Jongewaard Train** narratives from July 13, there is no inclusion of those in the **Oliver Train**, the **Man with Three Mules**, or the **Seven Wagon Train** that had joined together the night before. A count of wagons made by **Martha Roe** confirms that they are still present when she arrives at this place. Readers can speculate that being wounded and lacking horses, these victims are incapable of fighting alongside the **Jongewaard Train** in the morning but could very well be part of the search effort for **Isaac** later in the day.

# Wednesday, July 13, 1864 (part 2)

### Brown & Roe

Unaware of the immediate danger around them, the **Brown** and **Roe Trains** leave from present-day Douglas, Wyoming, and tackle the difficult McKinstry Ridge together. Perhaps they have this precarious terrain to thank for not being a victim of an attack. Another theory is that they are overlooked because their three wagons are ox-drawn and the North Plains Indians are, for the most part, uninterested in cattle.

**Martha Roe**
*Roe Train*

"Up this morning ... started and drove bout 9 or 10 M and camped on the river bank after going through some of the most mountainous countrie I ever saw." *(July 13)*

"**Mrs [Mary Brown]** and **Miss [Abbie] Broun** and I and children took a cutoff through the hills and mountains that shortened our road 3 or 4 M then came together at noon ... Stopped bout 2 h and moved on bout 3 or 4 M and all calm." *(July 13)*

After lunch, they descend the ridge into the North Douglas Bend where the **Jongewaards** and others are waiting for the safe return of **Isaac DeVries**.

**Martha Roe**
*Roe Train*

"The first thing we know[,] a man came up and gave the alarm of an attack of the Indians ahead that we should hurrah up and get out fire armes for action[.] we drove as fast as we could and drove on a huddle with the rest." *(July 13)*

### Brown, Jongewaard, Oliver & Roe (& Others)

**Abbie Brown**
*Brown Train*

"As Indians were getting numerous, we thought it best to join some train, especially as we were hearing of murders being committed." *(1916)*

We went in with a small train from Indiana **[the Olivers]**, some of whom were tinctured with colored blood … They seemed to know who we were and were very friendly." *(1916)*

"As several emigrants were killed the night before we joined them, we felt we ought to get in a larger train." *(1916)*

This last comment from **Abbie Brown** corroborates the date of their arrival at this location. It also reveals that the cavalrymen who brought **Ten Broek** back after their "skirmish" must have told the emigrants about the **Kelly-Larimer Train** incident they were supposed to be investigating. Beyond this, the emigrants in camp exchange stories from their own recent experiences.

**Martha Roe**
*Roe Train*

"…learned that they [the Indians] had stampeded and took 28 horses **[Shoemaker]**   all the horses from one trane of 7 waggons **[Seven Wagon Train]**   and had attacked **a man with 3 mules**…" *(July 13)*

"while they **[the Jongewaards]** was on guard there was 8 Indians that shot[,] had a little skirmish…" *(July 13)*

Because the morning attack on the **Jongewaard Train** is conducted by a much smaller band of Indians, and at a greater distance from Little Box Elder Creek it is questionable as an inclusion in the Platte River Raids initiated by Indians from the Powder River Basin. Readers are encouraged, however, to revisit the details of the **Kelly-Larimer** incident where a portion of the war chief's army (up to half) detaches into smaller bands, deploys to different areas in the Hills, then sends up smoke signals from the tops of hills. Emigrant diaries also confirm seeing Indians stalking them or watching from high places for a potential opportunity to strike. These details certainly do not support the war chief's claims to **Josiah Kelly** or **William Larimer** that they were in the area to hunt buffalo, antelope or deer.[397]

| **Martha Roe** | "[We] appointed guards for all night   formed a large |
| *Roe Train* | currell[sic] with 28 waggons[sic] ..." *(July 13)* |

This collective of terrified emigrants is believed to include the following parties, adding up to exactly twenty-eight vehicles:

- **Oliver Train**
- **Jongewaard Train**
- **Man with Three Mules**
- **Roe Train**
- **Brown Train**
- **Seven Wagon Train**

## Brown & Oliver

Despite the risk of a second attack, the **Oliver Train** abandons the security of the large gathering. Joining them in their departure is the **Brown family** with their few cattle and a wagon full of prized Merino sheep. Maybe they think the worst must be over and the soldiers are now on the case. Maybe they simply believe they can squeeze in another few miles before the sun goes down.

## Howard, Missourians & Virginians

Also coming around the Bend on July 13 are the **Howard** and **Missouri Trains**, with the two **Virginians.** Details of the **Howard Train** experience come from the family historian Randall Lovejoy, who is the great-grandson of

---

[397] See the South Bank Trail events from July 12, or Sarah Larimer's memoir on page 42.

**Jeremiah** and **Mary Howard Birks**.[398] In 1988, he publishes his compiled research in an essay for the genealogical journal, *The Genie*.[399]

**Randall Lovejoy**
*Howard Train*
*(descendant)*

"[**The Howards**] had traveled for a long time when they came to the Platte river country, where there was a reported to be very warlike tribes of Sioux Indians." *(1988, p. 202)*

According to Randall's retelling of the story, when passing those gathered in the Bend, the **Howards** are adequately warned of the potential to run into an army of warriors but continue west anyways.

## Brown, Howard, Oliver, Missourians & Virginians

As predicted back in the North Douglas Bend camp, the stretch of trail leading to Bixby Point and to the garrison, is teeming with activity.

**Abbie Brown**
*Brown Train*

"We had not traveled many hours before we saw a band of Indians coming. There were 250 Sioux on horseback, armed to the teeth with guns and lances, which shone wickedly in the sun and made us feel our doom was near." *(1916)*

This is an absolutely clear reference to the conglomerate army of Sioux, Cheyenne and Arapaho that terrorized several emigrant parties on the night before and this very morning. It might be that on this evening, the **Browns, et al.** sighted much of the army on their way back north after committing numerous depredations on the trails. While the following encounters are presented in tandem, it should be noted that they could be happening one after the other, or simultaneously but in proximity. The correlations are difficult to

---

[398] James Randall Lovejoy (1927-2003) composed two key documents on the Howard family history. One such item of great interest, but with limited access is, *The House of Howard: A compilation of the genealogy of the Howard Family by many members*. Private distribution was made within his family prior to his passing.
[399] Randall Lovejoy, "The Howard Wagon Train," in *The Genie*, 1988, 202.

ignore, however, and future evidence points to this interaction forcing the travelers with opposing views together.

| | |
|---|---|
| **Randall Lovejoy**<br>*Howard Train*<br>*(descendant)* | "One evening a large band of painted warriors circled on their horses around the **Howard camp**." *(202)* |
| **Abbie Brown**<br>*Brown Train* | "They rode in and out among our wagons, trying to estimate our strength, preparing to stampede our stock and then massacre us, as that was their mode of warfare." *(1916)*<br><br>"One of them made a grab at **Mr. Brown's sister's** hair and when she screamed, [he] laughed as though it was a great joke. ... At last the captain [unclear who] ordered the train stopped and the men got out their guns" *(1916)* |
| **Randall Lovejoy**<br>*Howard Train*<br>*(descendant)* | "The men quietly got their guns and kept a close watch although **William Henry Howard** advised them not to make the first hostile move." *(202)* |

In a later editorial in the *Oakland Tribune*, Al Reck adds that the Indians may have "practiced all their devices they knew to intimidate the whites,"[400] though there neither family historian suggests there is any immediate threat to harm anyone beyond the hair pulling. **Abbie's** fear echoes other stories she has recently heard. She refers to the antagonists as "huge, powerful specimens" who look "as cruel as death" (1916). Comparatively, the **Howard family** historian reports that the Indians are calculative with their approach, which is reminiscent of the **Kelly-Larimer Train's** experience.

---

[400] "Indians Terrorize," January 22, 1961, 4-5.

**Randall Lovejoy**
*Howard Train*
*(descendant)*

"The **Indians** showed a friendly attitude and began coming into camp. ... **The Howard women** had already prepared dinner when the Indians came into camp. Feeling[s] had run high when the Indians began taking seats and helping themselves to the meal." *(202)*

With the known wagon trains combined, there are at least twenty-seven vehicles with one-hundred-sixteen known souls (the **Missouri Train** being a complete mystery to the author and not included in this count). Of those travelers, there are at least twenty-six adult males who are ready to put up a sudden and fierce display of resistance. While admirable, they are outnumbered and wise to show restraint.

**Randall Lovejoy**
*Howard Train*
*(descendant)*

"The Indians finally make known their purpose. They wanted to buy **Nancy Howard**, **William Henry's** [**Howard's**] daughter." *(202)*

According to Randall, fourteen-year-old **Nancy** has long, blonde hair and is a considerable beauty. During the day's travel, she had been riding a horse behind her father's wagon, which increases her vulnerability to any type of advancement. This purchase offer infuriates **William**.

**Randall Lovejoy**
*Howard Train*
*(descendant)*

"...the men were eager to open fire, but older heads prevailed." *(1988, p. 202)*

In the **Brown Train, Salmon Brown** may have given his wife a signal to stay back or hide. Before this, his daughter pleads with him.

**Abbie Brown**
*Brown Train*

"Our little 4-year-old girl [**Cora**] said, 'Papa, don't you shoot. If you do they will kill all of us.'" *(1916)*

The Indians may have continued to profess their friendliness and enjoy looking around at whatever the emigrants might have that they want to buy (or eat). So far, there are no other hostile moves or signs of aggression except from the emigrants. Al Reck speculates that, "the emigrants [were] holding their ground and making a display of guns that convinced the Indians they were prepared to die fighting if necessary."[401] The Indians insolently stayed in the camp while carefully eyeing the men who were obviously ready to engage at any moment. Finally, **William**, a reverend and son of the seventy-year-old **Howard Train** captain, **Charles Howard**, approaches someone he believes might be leading this army.

| | |
|---|---|
| **Randall Lovejoy**<br>*Howard Train*<br>*(descendant)* | "**William Henry [Howard]** walked over to where a fine-looking Indian, a noble specimen of his race and evidently the **chief**, stood conversing with the white men. **William Henry** called his attention to the rude behavior of his people, upon which the **chief** gave a low whistle." *(202)* |
| | "At the [**chief's**] call, his warriors hastily arose and followed him out of camp, mounting their ponies and riding hastily away." *(202)* |
| **Abbie Brown**<br>*Brown Train* | "Fortunately they did not have to shoot. The Indians all fell into line, dropped their heads and never stirred until our train moved on." *(1916)* |
| | "When our train moved on, the Indians moved on, too, single file and we watched them until they were out of sight. I supposed if we had not joined that train that morning we would not have lived to tell this tale." *(1916)* |

Al Reck adds, "**Mrs. Salmon [Abbie] Brown** was convinced it was because they dreaded the potentialities of the guns in the hands of the white men that the Indians permitted them to move on."[402]

| | |
|---|---|
| **Randall Lovejoy**<br>*Howard Train*<br>*(descendant)* | "After this incident, **Nancy [Howard]** was forbidden to ride her horse and was instructed to remain inside the wagon." *(202)* |

---

[401] Ibid.
[402] "After Harpers Ferry," *Oakland Tribune*, May 21, 1933.

## Pella Company

Many miles south, back by present-day Orin, Wyoming, the **Pella Company** regroups from the loss of ten horses the night before. Fortunately, the **Curtis family** has a small herd of cattle with them and may have loaned replacements to the **Rousseau family**; a debt that could be paid upon arrival in California, if it is ever it paid at all. After distributing their remaining stock animals and perhaps shifting items inside the wagons to redistribute the weight begin pulled, they start heading north again.

| | |
|---|---|
| **Nicholas Earp**<br>*Pella Company* | "Next morning[,] on we went…" *(1865)* |
| **Sarah Rousseau**<br>*Pella Company* | "I feel very sad. But still I am thankful that it is no worse. … Left camp rather late. … Our appearance in the train to-day seems rather strange. Instead of our four pretty horses we have 2 yoke of oxen, which we were glad to get…" *(July 13)* |

**Sarah's** usual awe and appreciation for nature dies out as she describes the next leg of the trip from Orin to Douglas as being over "a desolate wilderness."

| | |
|---|---|
| **Sarah Rousseau**<br>*Pella Company* | "I never saw a more barren broken apparently worn out country in my life." *(July 13)* |

She ends her lament by cursing the very land of Idaho itself for not being the "rich beautiful contrie" she was expecting. After only ten miles of travel, the **Pella Company** settles down to camp in present-day Douglas, Wyoming.

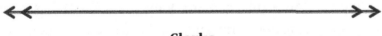

## Clarks

The **Clarks**, with **Tom Ellis,** are not too far ahead of the **Pella Company** on July 13. At most, they might end their day in the North Douglas Bend, but later details prove that is not so likely.

# Thursday, July 14, 1864

### Kelly-Larimer (Kidnappees)

Twenty five miles above the North Platte River, survivor-kidnappees from the attacks on the **Kelly-Larimer Train** at Little Box Elder Creek await an arduous ride towards the Bighorn Mountains and Powder River Indian Village. On the evening of July 13, **Sarah Larimer** and **Fanny Kelly's** captors camped in the Pine Gulch Ravine, where they could refresh themselves before facing a long day's ride across dry land. That same night, **Sarah Larimer** and her young son **Frank** begin their desperate escape from captivity.

| | |
|---|---|
| **Sarah Larimer**<br>*Kelly-Larimer Train* | "With a silent prayer to God for protection, I awoke him [**Frank**] and we proceeded upon the journey..."<br>*(Larimer, 93)* |

Under the cover of night, the escapees trek across a series of accordion-fold hills to the west. Just before any ray of light can expose their July 14 location, **Sarah** hides with her son under a rock projection inside a canyon. They try to sleep through the heat of the day and will continue their plight at dusk. During the entirety of her escape, **Sarah** is cognizant of her surroundings, attentive to cardinal directions, and somewhat knowledgeable about what is edible to stay alive (including eating an uncooked toad).

### Jongewaard, Man with Three Mules & Roe

"After a dreary nights rest," **Martha Roe** remarks on waking up on July 14 in the North Douglas Bend feeling relieved there were no "depredations" in the night, "nor one Indian" in sight. When preparing to leave the large gathering place, however, those in the **Roe Train** are shocked by an unforgettable sight.

**Martha Roe**     "after breakfast picked up and got ready to start when
*Roe Train*          there was seen Indians in all directions" *(July 14)*

She does not clarify how long these Indians stayed around, but it is not long enough for anyone in the **Jongewaard Train** to notice. If the **Roes** had any thoughts to leave separately this morning, those plans are immediately changed. They rally all eighteen wagons together and leave as one unified force, hoping that their size will make them less vulnerable to a repeat attack. Chances are, with the lack of horses amongst them, this group is no longer an attractive target. Those who suffered losses over the last two days rearrange their outfits and make do with the animals they have left.

**John Ellerbroek**     "While the loss of the horses was much deplored, we
*Jongewaard Train*      had plenty of oxen and we could go on." *(408)*

**Martha Roe**     "our trane was more than half mile long" *(July 14)*
*Roe Train*

**Gerrit Roorda**     "We traveled about 8 miles." *(July 14)*
*Jongewaard Train*

According to J. L. Campbell's guidebook descriptions, the emigrants travel over "High, rolling, barren country for some distance, followed by, "Low lands bordering upon the river."[403] The distance cited by **Gerrit Roorda** brings the emigrants approximately to Bixby Point, where they find the **Browns, Howards and Missourians, etc.** shaken up, but unharmed.

**Brown, Howard, Jongewaard, Roe, Missourians & Others**

**Abbie Brown**     "We were soon overtaken by a train of eighty wagons and
*Brown Train*       they seemed anxious for us to come into their train on
                    account of the Indians." (1916)

---

[403] *Idaho...*, 1864, 49.

**Gerrit Roorda**      "Our train consisted of about 80 wagons." *(July 14)*
*Jongewaard Train*

More and more emigrants gather here than can presently be accounted for. [404] One theory about some of the extra vehicles is that they include the **Wood Freight Train (AKA "Salt Lake Train")** led by **Captain Wood** (*Also see July 18 from the South Bank Trails*). If this party had, "fought the Indians three days in the Black Hills," according to **George Forman** (July 21), it might have been between the North Douglas Bend and Bixby Point (where the Northern Plains Indians may have descended from the so-called Bozeman Trail). Those three days might encompass July 12 through 14. If this is the case, the **Wood Freight Train** would add six vehicles to the total count. Further research is encouraged.

**Martha Roe**      "...camped bout 2 h ... evry man takes his pistol and rifle
*Roe Train*            and holdes his horses to eat grass..." *(July 14)*

At this midway stop, **Martha** sees notices posted along the trail with mentions of attacks and various deaths. Even though these North Bank travelers are in the vicinity of the so-called "massacre" at Little Box Elder Creek, there have been no official communications regarding that tragedy other than what might have been shared with the **Jongewaard Train** after their skirmish with the cavalry.

**Martha Roe**      "...did not see any [more] Indians[.] we sent scouts out
*Roe Train*            on the hills to see if they were concealed anywhere but
                      none could be seen." *(July 14)*

When the emigrants feel sure they will not run into any immediate trouble, most families chose to move on to the garrison.

---

[404] Known wagons trains that contribute towards this number are as follows: Brown (3), Oliver (7), Howard (17), Jongewaard (7), Roe (3), Seven Wagon Train (7), Man with Three Mules (1). These add up to forty-five vehicles, plus an unknown number from the Missourians & Virginians.

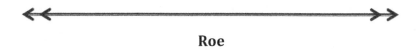

## Roe

**Martha Roe**
*Roe Train*

"Well[,] picked up our things and started ... drove to dark and camped for the night [.] kept no guard this night."
*(July 14)*

The **Roe Train** finishes their day between four and six miles further west and camps near the Lower Ferry of the Platte. Proximity to the soldier station might be one reason the **Roes** feel comfortable enough to sleep through the night with every eye closed.

Bruff, J. G., "Ferrieage of the Platte above the mouth of Deer Ck.," July 28, 1849.

## Brown, Howard, Missourians & Others

The **Brown, Oliver, Howard** and **Missouri Trains** bypass the **Roes** and stop almost directly opposite of the military station at Deer Creek. It is believed the **Seven Wagon Train** and **Man with Three Mules** also proceed west.

Moellman, C. "Deer Creek Station, I.T. [Idaho Territory]," 1863, University of Wyoming/American Heritage Center.

## Jongewaard

Unlike the others, the **Jongewaard Train** does not move from Bixby Point. Because this is the last place **Teunis Burgraaf** and **Ten Broek** saw **Isaac DeVries**, they might be hoping for his safe return, or be sending men over the river to search for him again. Once again, **Gerrit Roorda's** day book and **John Ellerbroek's** reminiscence disagree on critical details.

| **John Ellerbroek** | "For two days he [**Isaac DeVries**] wandered through |
|---|---|
| *Jongewaard Train* | the brush and along the river ... As the train had waited for him all this time ... they gave him up for lost." *(407)* |

| **Gerrit Roorda** | "**Isaac DeVries** ... came back to camp this morning." |
|---|---|
| *Jongewaard Train* | *(July 14)* |

| **John Ellerbroek** | ...when **Captain Jongewaard** had given orders to |
|---|---|
| *Jongewaard Train* | break camp ... **DeVries** appeared on the river bank opposite the camp and signaled his people to get him." *(407)* |

It is remarkable that **Isaac** survived this ordeal with hundreds of Indian warriors still canvassing the area. Historian Brian Beltman asserts, "**Jannetje [Van der Meer DeVries Ellerbroek Mars]** surely prayed thankfully that her firstborn had been spared."[405]

| **John Ellerbroek** | "...there was great rejoicing, and his stepfather, **Lutje** |
|---|---|
| *Jongewaard Train* | **Mars**, and another man each mounted a mule and, leading a horse for **DeVries** to ride, swam across the river to get him." *(408)* |

After an incredibly stressful few days, **Isaac** is too tired to stay on his own horse and the **Mars family** has a good, hard laugh over the picture of **Lutje**, a forty-three-year-old, "long-haired and hewhiskered" man returning to the North Bank Trail system on a stubby-legged mule with his fully grown stepson riding behind him with arms wrapped around his midsection (Ellerbroek, 408).

| **John Ellerbroek** | "All declared that it was the bravest deed that **Lutje** |
|---|---|
| *Jongewaard Train* | **Mars** had ever done." *(408)* |

At the end of the day, the **Jonewaards** are met by another unidentified wagon train.

---

[405] 1997 dissertation excerpt, 127-128.

**John Ellerbroek**
*Jongewaard Train*

"That night[,] another big wagon train came in and they wanted to help us to get our horses back with the aid of soldiers" *(408)*

It is unclear if this wagon train is heading east and is being escorted by soldiers, or if they are heading west and simply planning to involve soldiers when they get to the garrison. In **John's** story, he adds that the soldiers in question are reluctant to go any farther east because, "over the hills[,] the Indians were thicker than flies" (408). This report might have been shared by any one of the wagon trains that reached Deer Creek earlier in the day.

## Clark & Pella Company

Starting on July 14 from their camp back in Douglas, Wyoming, the **Pella Company** are the last folks in this book to come over McKinstry Ridge. When on the Ridge, **Sarah Rousseau** sees the feared collective of Northern Plains Indians that **Martha Roe** felt surrounded by that morning.

**Sarah Rousseau**
*Pella Company*

"After we started this morning, we saw a number of Indians[406] on the opposite side of the river. They had stampeded some horses and were taking them off." *(July 14)*

The horses seen with the Indians on the south side of the North Platte River could have come from any one of wagon trains robbed during these Raids. Perhaps **Cornelius Jongewaard's** best race horse is amongst the herd. It is believed that those in the **Clark family** either see the same view or hear the following gunshots and fall back to rejoin the **Pella Company**.

---

[406] The phrase "a number of" means an uncountable number, a collection, many or a lot.

**Sarah Rousseau**
*Pella Company*

"All the men got their guns and revolvers ... the **Dr. [James Rousseau]** and **Mr. [Levi] Tucker**[407] started on foot toward the river to see if they could get a shot at them. ... **Mr. Tucker** fired on them." *(July 14)*

"When they got back to the train, they said if they had been on horseback, they could have crossed the river and got the horses. The indians and horses seemed tired down." *(July 14)*

Why **Levi Tucker** risks instigating a battle might be explained by **Sarah's** claim that "they [the Indians] have been following us up[stream] fifty or sixty miles," presumably at a calculated distance (July 14). This behavior might make anyone feel paranoid, especially after having fought them once already.

**Sarah Rousseau**
*Pella Company*

"The guards went along side of the train all day. ... We had to be very watchful." *(July 14)*

While passing "dangerous" roads with high cliffs on both sides, **Sarah Rousseau** is convinced there is nothing but doom hidden behind every rock and tree. This is reminiscent of **John Ellerbroek's** feeling while coming through the same approximate location. Finally, the **Pella Company** descends into the North Douglas Bend. There, like others before them, they are disappointed by the lack of viable feed sources near the river.

**Sarah Rousseau**
*Pella Company*

"Came to the river and watered our horses ... but found that there was no grass so we went on some further, found a little grass and camped." *(July 14)*

**Nicholas Earp**
*Pella Company*

"...we camped again for noon in a bend of Platt River[,] situatied a good deal as before[,] only we had all our stock on the same side of the River that the waggons was on and we had our guards properly posted & pickets out..." *(1865)*

---

[407] Levi Tucker (1833-1926) was born in Ohio, lived in Knoxville, Iowa and is a family friend to Joh Hamilton. He is a farmer by trade and his motive to take this overland journey is unknown.

| | |
|---|---|
| **Sarah Rousseau**<br>*Pella Company* | "...had *plenty* of guards watching." *(July 14, emphasis added)* |

On this day, **Nicholas Earp** takes extra precautions to keep the stock closer by, hopefully dissuading the Indians from attacking them twice (assuming they had enough horses left to still be an attractive target). He also remarks in his letter that, "it was no trouble *now* to get the men all to do thir duty" (1865, emphasis added). Because of this extra effort, the emigrants enjoy their midday camp undisturbed, at least for a little while.

| | |
|---|---|
| **Nicholas Earp**<br>*Pella Company* | "we had not bin in camp long untell the Sentinels gave the alarm that the Indians was coming[.]" *(1865)* |
| **Sarah Rousseau**<br>*Pella Company* | "They came as before, full speed to stampede our horses, but we were ready..." *(July 14)* |
| **Nicholas Earp**<br>*Pella Company* | "...I ordered the horses to be brought inside of the Corell[sic] by the gards... the women all turned out to help get the horses into the Corel..." *(1865)* |
| **Sarah Rousseau**<br>*Pella Company* | "When they came this time[,] two of the women came and gave us their babies to take care of, they screaming poor little things ... The women having to run and catch the horses while the men are keeping the indians off." *(July 14)* |

The babies **Sarah** mentions are likely **William** and **Frances Curtis'** toddler, **Holman**, and **Rev. Israel** and **Lucy Curtis'** newborn, **Penelope**. Without her husband around, **Sarah** and the babies are left to whatever immediate protection her nearly twelve-year-old son, **John James** can provide. Beyond **Sarah's** son, other men and young adults who remain posted as guards over the women and children are as follows: **Wyatt** and **Morgan Earp** (teens), **Rev. Israel Curtis** with sons **William** and **Richard, Stephen Hays,** and **William Clark.**

| | |
|---|---|
| **Nicholas Earp**<br>*Pella Company* | "...we who was not on gard gathered our guns and rushed to meet the Indians" *(1865)* |

**Sarah Rousseau**
*Pella Company*

"...they appeared determined to make a rush on us by circling around a little. ... The Sioux Indians display a great deal of daring and bravery. They make a dash among the whites seemingly not caring for anything, stampede the horses and take them off." *(July 14)*

**Nicholas Earp**
*Pella Company*

"when they got as clost as we entended them to come[,] we comenced poping away at them..." *(1865)*

**Sarah Rousseau**
*Pella Company*

"Several of the men ... caught a horse and took their guns and followed after them at full speed[,] firing at them as they went." *(July 14)*

Artist illustration of the second attack on the Pella Company, July 14, 1864 near McKinstry Ridge. Sketch by Manjula Karunatilaka, 2021.

One major distinction for today's events is found in the number of Indians involved. **Nicholas** estimates, "they ware about 4 to one of us," which pits them up against forty men (1865). This is a drastically different number from the reported eight who robbed the **Jongewaard Train** at this same location.

In the initial defense, one man who charges off with **Nicholas** accidently shoots and kills his own horse. **Sarah** claims he was attempting to shoot at an Indian and failed, but, "Luckily our men were close at hand and saved him from the dreadful fate that awaited him" (July 14). Though no one names this rider, speculation points to him being **James Earp, Nicholas'** eldest son on this journey.

**James** recently mustered out of the Union army with a crippling shoulder injury. If called to join in the chase, he would be limited in his ability to simultaneously maneuver a horse and shoot with any degree of accuracy, having only one fully functional arm. Considering **James'** physical limitations, it remains a mystery to the author why **Nicholas** did not enlist the help of his younger son **Wyatt** for such a critical time as this.

| | |
|---|---|
| **Nicholas Earp**<br>*Pella Company* | "...soon [we] succeeded in checking them and putting them to flite[.]they ran of[f] about a half amile and stoped and turned round as tho they war not satisfied[.]" *(1865)* |
| **Sarah Rousseau**<br>*Pella Company* | "The Indians turned on them and they had a regular fight... they shot their bows and arrows, the men bringing 2 of them back with them." *(July 14)* |
| **Nicholas Earp**<br>*Pella Company* | "I said[, ']boys they are not satisfied[.] lets satisfy them[!']" *(1865)* |

**Nicholas** quickly calls more men to join in the fight. Of interest is the naming of **Tom Ellis**, who had separated himself from the **Pella Company** days prior.

**Nicholas Earp**
*Pella Company*

"so I ran to the waggons and [j]umped upon a hors[e] & said[,'] we'll make them then leave thare[.'] **Dr. Rusaw**[,] **T.J. Ellis**[,] **James Earp** and a young man by the name of **[Levi] Tucker** that was with **[John] Hamilton** & two other men that got in with us followed suit..." *(1865)*

**Sarah Rousseau**
*Pella Company*

"The **Dr. [James Rousseau]** was one of the men that went on horseback after them[.] he recognized one of the Indians we bought some Elk Skins from,[408] and which appeared the most friendly kind." *(July 14)*

If **Dr. James Rousseau** can truly recognize one or more of his attackers, then this evidence supports the theory that this particular group of bandits is not related to the large army from the Powder River Region. Instead, they are linked to the horse thieving operation that other diarists claim supports the Confederacy.

**Nicholas Earp**
*Pella Company*

"...off we charged after the Indians[.]" *(1865)*

When the Indians see the emigrant squadron rushing after them, they wheel around for combat.

**Nicholas Earp**
*Pella Company*

"on we went in full persuit of them untell they found we war about to over take them[.] they then faced about to give us battle[.]" *(1865)*

"I gave orders to form line of battle and we went into a general engagement[.] they undertook to flank us first to the right and then to the left but they found out they could not for they had [met] thir match[.]" *(1865)*

As the battle continues, and as **Nicholas** claims, "the arrows flew and the bullets [whizzed]," he presses his men forward very carefully, making note of how the enemy maintains a perfect gap between them that is just beyond range of their

---

[408] On July 2, near Chimney Rock, Sarah records: "when we stopped the Indians came to us. We had quite a time with them. They had skins to sell and Moccasins. We bought 1 skin and we gave a dollar and a quarter … They appeared very friendly."

bullets. At this point, **Dr. James** pulls out his "marine glass,"[409] and focuses his gaze on one of the assailants who appears to be leading the attack.

| **Sarah Rousseau** | "[Dr. James] saw **a white man** that he saw the other side |
|---|---|
| *Pella Company* | of Laramie[410] and wanted to trade horses with him[,] Charlie[411] being some lame..." *(July 14)* |
| **Nicholas Earp** | "the man who seemed to be leading the band and gaving |
| *Pella Company* | orders was **a white man**..." *(1865)* |

The fact that **Dr. James** recognizes two different individuals from somewhere between the state border and the Fort adds to the suspicion that there has been a concerted effort by these thieves to target and follow emigrants for several days in anticipation of the right opportunity to strike.

Readers might guess that this white man is **George Colburn**. If so, when he disappears at Fort Laramie on July 3 to go west (like he tells the **Ridgleys** he is doing), then he'd have to travel fifty miles east to have an encounter with the **Rousseaus**. Then, he'd have to make a return trip, plus go an additional twenty and thirty miles past the Fort by July 5. This is simply not possible in the timeframe he is gone. It is more likely that this particular white man is just another accomplice.

| **Sarah Rousseau** | "**The Dr.[,]** the instant he saw him told the men to shoot him |
|---|---|
| *Pella Company* | as he was a white man." *(July 14)* |
| **Nicholas Earp** | "he hollowed out[, ']**Earp** shoot that man on the roan |
| *Pella Company* | horse..."[412] *(1865)* |
| **Sarah Rousseau** | "He [**the white man**] heard him, he supposed, as he made a |
| *Pella Company* | quick move to get out of the way. ... They fired a good many shots, but did not know if they hit him." *(July 14)* |

---

[409] Also called a maritime telescope or spyglass.
[410] See possible trade interactions from July 2 through July 5.
[411] Charlie is one of Dr. James Rousseau's favorite horses.
[412] Earp, 1865.

**Nicholas Earp**
*Pella Company*

"I leveled on him [**the white man**] and at the crack of the gun[,] he fell to one side of the horse but caught in the mane and recovered again then wheeled his horse and lumbered over the hill as fast as his horse would take him[.]" *(1865)*

**Nicholas Earp**
*Pella Company*

"The rest immediately took to flight following him[.]" *(1865)*

**Sarah Rousseau**
*Pella Company*

"Our men scared them off completely." *(July 14)*

**Nicholas** claims the reason they do not pursue the bandits farther is because, "we had exhausted all our shots."[413] After watching to see that their adversaries were not turning back for a third round, the men of the **Pella Company** collect evidence from the scene (including two arrows).

**Nicholas Earp**
*Pella Company*

"[We] saw by the blood on the trails that we had woonded 4 of them[.]" *(1865)*

That night, **Sarah** processes what she has witnessed and how the trauma is affecting her. Her dissociative response is familiar to what might be diagnosed today as Post-Traumatic Stress Disorder.

**Sarah Rousseau**
*Pella Company*

"...I can't account for my feelings. I fear that I am getting some stoical. I sit in the waggon and see all that is going on and it don[']t appear to move me ... I must acknowledge I feel afraid some of the time." *(July 14)*

At some point, folks back in Iowa receive word that the **Pella Company** is massacred, but this rumor is later corrected in the newspapers.

---

[413] Ibid.

It is reported that a party of emigrants from Marion county, in this State, were a few weeks ago massacred near Fort Laramie. Among the party were Hon. I. C. Curtis and family of Pella. Mr. Curtis was well known and widely esteemed as a public man in this State, and served with distinction in the Legislature. We should be glad to learn that the report is unfounded, and that no such tragic fate had befallen them.

"News from the Plains," *Quad-City Times,* August 8, 1864, 2.

**Kelly-Larimer (Kidnappees)**

When the sky darkens again, **Sarah Larimer** leads **Frank** southeast into a valley with a stream of undrinkable muddy water. They follow this stream for a few miles until it turns east, then continue walking south over dry and desolate hills [*see map on the following page*].

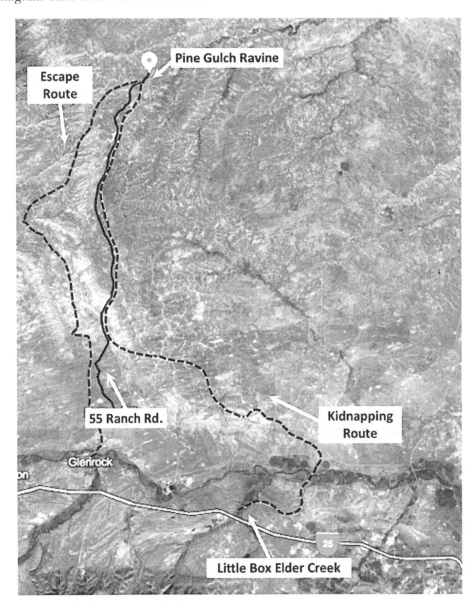

Map of Sarah Larimer's kidnapping and escape. Satellite Image of Converse County, Wyoming from Google Earth, 2022. Modified by author.

# Friday, July 15, 1864

### Brown, Howard, Oliver, Missourians & Virginians

After a stressful week, the traveling group consisting of the **Olivers, Browns, Howards, Missourians,** and **Virginians** lays over near Deer Creek garrison to recuperate. Daniel Rosenberg, a scholar and biographer of *Mary Brown: From Harpers Ferry to California*, has determined that it is during this time spent together that, "**Mary [Brown]** would find out that the greatest threat came not from the Indians whose land she crossed, but from certain men in white skins."[414]

| | |
|---|---|
| **Abbie Brown** | "We thought that our troubles were over, but as it |
| *Brown Train* | proved[,] they had only just begun." *(1916)*[415] |

The ominous feeling **Abbie Brown** conveys is supported by rumors and secrets being passed between campers, primarily with the **Howard** and **Missouri Trains**. These secrets include the **Brown's** true identity being discovered.

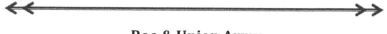

### Roe & Union Army

**Martha Roe** starts her Friday morning in sight of the Lower Ferry of the Platte. This operation has been described in detail in the July 14 chapter from the South Bank Trails section of the book. Here, someone who just crossed

---

[414] Daniel Rosenberg, *Mary Brown...*, 1975, 21.
[415] Abbie Brown, "Across the Plains," *Lake Placid News*, Sept. 29, 1916, 5-7.

over the river tells **Martha** about the tragedies that have occurred on the other side.

| **Martha Roe**<br>*Roe Train* | "There was a trane just across the river informed us that the Indians stampeeded a horses and mule trane and taken 65 horses  10 mules  plundered the waggons  captured 2 womin and children  killed 3 or 4  wounded 2  and this trane buried 5 men out of there trane[.]" *(July 15)*[416] |

Perhaps the description of the **Kelly-Larimer** incident reminds **Isaac Roe** that they should not be so relaxed with their guard watch, as they were the night before. The **Roes** move in closer to the growing emigrant encampment forming opposite the North Platte River from the Deer Creek military garrison.

| **Martha Roe**<br>*Roe Train* | "Stopped for dinner [lunch] then concluded to stay till Monday ... got supper[.]  some soldiers and **a doctor** came from the fort[.] **the girls** sang and then to bed[.]  kept guard[.]" *(July 15)* |

The doctor has since been identified as **Dr. Alfred Ferdinand Zeigler**, Assistant Surgeon posted at Deer Creek. [417] The identity of "the girls" could be from the **Redfern** family who are loosely mentioned in **Martha Roe's** diary, or this may be an indication of reconnecting with the **Brown Train**.

---

[416] This death toll includes all the known bodies found at Little Box Elder Creek except for Mary Hurley Kelly.

[417] The official Post Surgeon (stationed at Fort Laramie) is Lt. General George C. Underhill, of the 11th Ohio Volunteer Cavalry. He comes up on the South Bank Trails with the soldiers who were called in for reinforcements.

## Jongewaard

After a night's stay at Bixby Point with an unidentified "big wagon train," the **Jongewaard Train** is eager to leave the Black Hills of Idaho far behind.

**Gerrit Roorda**          "We traveled about 8 or 10 miles over a sandy kind of
*Jongewaard Train*        road. We passed Deer Creek station ... on the south
                          side of the river. ... The Indians are pretty bad here."
                          *(July 15)*

The Indians they see are most likely wives and families of the soldiers at the garrison. This includes **Cpt. Levi Reinhart's** second wife and son. **Gerrit Roorda's** last comment hints at the overall distrust these Iowans now feel towards any and all Indians, but **John Ellerbroek** captures the trauma response of the emigrants before they approach a large number of Indians a short distance outside the garrison. Before they get too close, **Cornelius Jongewaard** gives orders to be on the defensive and that, "every one who had a gun should fire it," as a way to both warn those ahead that they are fully armed and to make sure every gun is in working condition (409).

Readers might wonder if the shots fired are what draws the attention of "some soldiers and a doctor" to cross the river and investigate (Roe, July 15). The **Jongewaard Train** ends their day camped approximately two to four miles west of where a crowd is gathering across from Deer Creek garrison.

## Pella Company

On July 15, **Sarah Rousseau's** diary entry lacks its familiar vibrancy. After mentioning the hard rain and heavy winds that likely kept her up all night with arthritis pain, she records the **Pella Company** making a late start to their day.

**Nicholas Earp**          "The next morning we started on a gain[.]" *(1865)*
*Pella Company*

**Sarah Rousseau**
*Pella Company*

"Traveled over some high, rolling, barren country."
*(July 15)*

**Sarah** quotes directly from J. L. Campbell's 1864 description of the sixteen mile stretch between the North Douglas Bend and the Lower Ferry of the Platte (presently in Glenrock, Wyoming). Instead of covering all sixteen miles, though, the Pella Company stops to noon just east of Bixby Point.

**Sarah Rousseau**
*Pella Company*

"As we were riding along to-day **Mattie [Field]** saw a stake with a paper attached to it. ... There was written on it to be careful here, one man was shot all to pieces, and horses run off. I hope when we get to the Ferry of the Platte there will not be so much danger." *(July 15)*

The identity of the man "shot all to pieces" is probably the **Man with Three Mules** who was attacked here on July 12.

**Sarah Rousseau**
*Pella Company*

"The **Dr. [James Rousseau]** had just gotten his horses out to feed when the news was that **Mrs. [Jane] Hamilton** was sick." *(July 15)*

With this announcement, the wagon train relocates one mile west, where grass is more abundant. Here, they find enough room to raise a tent to accommodate the birthing of **John Hamilton's** first (and only) biological child. **Nicholas Earp** also notes this birth.

**Nicholas Earp**
*Pella Company*

"nothing of any consequence hapining from that to Salt Lake[,] only **Mrs [Jane] Hamilton** brought forth a fine boy..." *(1865)*

**Sarah** and **Nicholas'** writings are the only known places where the child's birth (and any proof of existence) is preserved. The baby is never given a name in their writings, but **Sarah's** claims the delivery process is not difficult and the baby arrives in a matter of hours. **Nicholas'** comment that he is a "fine boy," also suggests a healthy birth. No further comment is made on this child (ie. short life, illness, or other explanation for his mysterious disappearance). He is unlisted on future census records, unfound in birth or grave records, and missing from ancestry and genealogical databases for the family. Further research is encouraged.

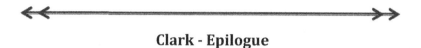

## Clark - Epilogue

No mention is made by either writer in the **Pella Company** on where the **Clark family** and **Tom Ellis** might be on July 15. They may have gone ahead to the garrison. The next mention of the **Clarks** appears in **Sarah Rousseau's** diary on July 27, near Devil's Gate, when she writes: "**Mr. [Robert] Parker** left **Mr. Clark** and is now travelling along with us." As the **Clarks** are **Robert Parker's** in-laws, this could be an awkward parting of ways. It is presumed that **Tom** continues to Salt Lake City with the **Clarks** then eventually heads out on his own to California. Perhaps, by then, he finally cleans up his swearing habit because in 1870, he is found in the U.S. Census working as a school teacher in Los Angeles and by 1871 he marries a local gal and becomes a family man.

The **Clarks** end their journey in Provo, Utah where Mary Clark Parker delivers her second child by **Robert** on August 15, 1864. **Robert** remains with the **Pella Company** until August 31, when he goes home to see his wife. The **Pella Company** gets detained in Fillmore (about one hundred miles south of Provo) due to their late season travel and delays in the Black Hills setting them up to cross the Mojave Desert across Nevada during dangerously hot conditions. They must wait a month for temperatures to drop. When it is time to resume, the paying job of a teamster is still available with the **Rousseau family**. On October 6, **Robert** rejoins the **Pella Company** and escorts them through the Mojave Desert, helping out however he can.

The **Parkers** have nine children together, but Mary dies shortly after the last birthing, along with her child. After this, **Robert** packs up his home and young children and moves out to California, settling in Redlands, where he retires in the same small community that the **Rousseaus** and descendants remained for multiple generations. His grandchildren eventually move to

Phoenix, Arizona in 1919 where the Rousseau-Molony descendant line also settles in the 1980s.

### Kelly-Larimer (Kidnappees)

Again, **Sarah Larimer** waits for the sun to go down before coming out of hiding with her son **Frank**.

| | |
|---|---|
| **Sarah Larimer** <br> *Kelly-Larimer Train* | "... night hovered over the hills as we resumed our journey." *(Larimer, 99)* |

On July 15, they travel approximately ten miles south, staying concealed from view amid dark shadows of rolling hills located to the west of Sage Creek.[418] Towards the end of the overnight trek, **Sarah** discovers that hope and help is not too far away.

| | |
|---|---|
| **Sarah Larimer** <br> *Kelly-Larimer Train* | "I caught a glimpse of the valley we had so long been approaching. ... Perhaps we were nearing the emigrant road, and much nearer the fort than had been supposed." *(108-109)* |

Before daylight of July 16, **Sarah** and **Frank** hide and sleep again.

---

[418] Approximately where present-day 55 Ranch Road runs North-South.

# Saturday, July 16, 1864

### Jongewaard

On July 16, the **Jongewaard Train** hastily reconfigures their outfit for an early departure. Both **Gerrit Roorda** and **John Ellerbroek's** accounts say the families were fine to continue on with the remaining oxen they had. When ready, **Gerrit** records that they leave without delays, accompanied by twenty additional wagons that were also camped northwest of the Deer Creek garrison. The families associated with the twenty vehicles that join the **Jongewaards** have not yet been established.

| | |
|---|---|
| **Gerrit Roorda**<br>*Jongewaard Train* | "We passed the lower bridge and the cut off to East Bannack." *(July 16)* |

The distance the **Jongewaards** cover is between twenty-eight and thirty miles. This is certainly a reflection of the desperation many surviving emigrants feel when leaving the area. The cutoff **Gerrit** mentions is presently known as the Bridger Trail, which links the Oregon Trail at Red Butte in present-day Casper, Wyoming to the popular Montana gold mining cities of Deer Lodge, Virginia City, and Bozeman. As Pacific-bound travelers, the **Jongewaards** will not use this cutoff. Instead, they will proceed south on the Mormon Trail, following the Sweetwater River to South Pass.

Map of the North Platte River and the Sweetwater River tributary flowing west from below Casper, towards the base of the Wind River Mountain Range. Modified with USGS National Map and NASA SRTM data. Wikipedia Commons (Shanon1, 2019). Permissible use.

## Brown, Howard, Oliver, Missourian & Virginians

This unlikely conglomerate also leaves their North Bank camp across from Deer Creek garrison on July 16. Altogether, the known wagons in these groups adds to more than twenty-seven. Over the next week, this group travels as far as the Sweetwater River, approximately forty-five miles south of the Lower Platte Bridge & Station. Though they are no longer in the "Black Hills," the story of the fleeing New Yorkers, misfit Sympathizers, and hostile Rebels is not quite over. The continuation of their story picks up on July 19, in the diary of **Martha Roe**.

## Roe & Unidentified Train

Back across the North Platte River from Deer Creek garrison, the **Roe Train** stays for another day in a camp that now resembles a small town. A remarkable cook (see the feast she creates on July 4), **Martha Roe** prepares a jackrabbit potpie for lunch while some of the men ferry over to the south side of the river and inquire about trail conditions.

**Martha Roe**
*Roe Train*

"The horse teams from our trane went over [to the garrison] this morning[.]" *(July 16)*

"This morning findes us still unmolested but still rumors of depredations arrives[.] we faired better than any other trane[.] we have never had an attack yet[.] I do not know the reason…" *(July 16)*

Joining the sprawling North Bank camp this afternoon is an unidentified wagon train with fourteen or fifteen vehicles.

**Martha Roe**
*Roe Train*

"…they had an attack[.] shot an Indian pony[,] took the saddle and blanket[.]" *(July 16)*

This sounds similar to the report that reached the **Jongewaard Train** on July 12, however the unidentified wagon train from that day was "small" and had "caught" a pony, using it to ride out and warn others behind them.[419] From the observations of South Bank Trail traveler, **George Forman**, on July 15 there is also a "freight train" that had a reported "skirmish" on the North Bank Trail, approximately fifteen miles north of Le Prele Creek. Then again, this large train is not necessarily from the North Bank Trail. They may have recently crossed over

---

[419] John Ellerbroek in Dyke's, *Story of Sioux County* (1942), 405.

the river. Without additional details, it is impossible to make a conclusive connection.

The unidentified train also spots a terrifying sight that has yet to be mentioned by others.

**Martha Roe**
*Roe Train*

"...[they] found a dead man[,] side of the river with 3 or 4 arrows in him[,] his face all cut up with tommahalks[.] he had been dead about a week[.] considerable excitement prevailed" *(July 16)*

Clues that might be giving them a one week guess on the corpse could be a bloated and green-hued abdomen that starts early in the purification process. If this is the case, moderner researchers must also consider that the warmer summer temperatures accelerate the stages of decomposition, which more realistically places this man's actual date of death between July 9-13.

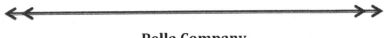

## Pella Company

Still at Bixby Point in the lowlands opposite Box Elder Creek, the **Pella Company** rises on July 16 to the joyful sounds of a newborn's cries. **Sarah Rousseau** is in a particularly good mood after a harrowing week.

**Sarah Rousseau**
*Pella Company*

"This morning bright and clear. ... Merciful God watched over us..." *(July 16)*

**Sarah** claims the wagon train is "detained" because of **Sarah "Jane" Hamilton's** recent childbirth. It is likely that the women in the **Pella Company** wagon train advocate for at least one day's rest on **Jane's** behalf, even though women of this time typically enjoy a longer puerperal (post-partum) bedrest. While camped, the women cook up a hearty meal and wash the dirty laundry in the cold waters of the North Platte.

| | |
|---|---|
| **Sarah Rousseau**<br>*Pella Company* | "About 4 oclock this afternoon … we saw plainly[420] there were some horsemen on the other side of the river…" *(July 16)* |

The formal approach of these men puts some in the **Pella Company** on edge. If an attack were to ensue, they would be more vulnerable under present circumstances. Besides the new mother and child, the emigrants must consider their reduced ammunition supply after two recent engagements.

| | |
|---|---|
| **Sarah Rousseau**<br>*Pella Company* | "The **Dr. [James Rousseau]** and a good many other men gathered on the bank with their guns… The **Dr.** looked through the Marine glass and discovered them to be soldiers" *(July 16)* |

**Nicholas Earps'** letter to James Capley contains no further comment on the trip until the events of August 12, so his actions are told from **Sarah's** point of view. **Nicholas** apparently demands that the squad of soldiers cross the river to be identified. **Sarah** notes that the soldiers are being led by a Lieutenant who is also a surgeon. He has just come from there to stop any trains from leaving their camps, "until further orders."[421]

The **Lieutenant/Surgeon** tells the **Pella Company** about the **Kelly-Larimer** incident, citing the murder of fourteen men, two wounded, three women and one child captured. This announcement is nearly verbatim to the warning that **George Forman** heard on July 14 at La Bonte Creek.[422] If this **Lieutenant** is **Dr. Alfred Ziegler**, the assistant surgeon stationed at Deer Creek garrison, it seems odd that he is repeating outdated information even though, "…he said he dressed the wounds of the men," and likely would have received updated numbers while doing so (Rousseau, July 16).

**Sarah Larimer** later confirms that **Dr. Alfred Ziegler** most definitely should have heard at least one first-person testimony from her husband.

---

[420] The "plainly" comment differs from other instances where Dr. James Rousseau views things far off through his "marine glass" (telescope).

[421] This is the same order conveyed to the wagon train on the South Side Trail near La Prele Creek.

[422] He recorded that, "two trains had been attacked and 14 men killed and two women and three children taken captive" (Forman, July 14).

**Sarah Larimer**
*Kelly-Larimer Trian*

"**Dr. Zeigler,** the post surgeon, was very skillful and efficient in his care, and my husband was rapidly recovering." *(123)*

After delivering the sad news and detainment instructions, the soldiers extend their stay through a meal (whether they were invited to or not is a separate issue).

**Sarah Rousseau**
*Pella Company*

"The **Lieut.** and his soldiers took supper with us. ... He enquired if we had lost any horses. **Dr. [James Rousseau]** told him 4..." *(July 16)*

Readers might assume that **John Hamilton** and **William Curtis** also reported their loss of six additional horses. After dinner, the **Lieutenant** concedes to the **Pella Company** moving forward in the morning despite the stay-in-place order but only approves them going as far as twenty miles (not to go past Cole Creek on the far side of the garrison).

## Kelly-Larimer

**Sarah Larimer**
*Kelly-Larimer Train*

"Arriving on the bank of the stream under the cover of night, we sought the shelter of some bushes, for the mighty river rolled between us and the fort." *(110-111)*

On the evening of July 16, **Sarah Larimer** and her son **Frank** carefully wind their way down what is now called Monkey Mountain, situated north of Glenrock, Wyoming. On seeing numerous campfires, tents and all sorts of commotion on the north side of the river, **Sarah** hesitates to approach until...

**Sarah Larimer**
*Kelly-Larimer Train*

"...a most joyful and welcome sound greeted our ears – one in which there was no mistake – our own language, spoken by some boys who passed, driving cattle. We arose ... and soon saw a man who was approaching with two horses, and called to him. ... I endeavored to explain to him why I thus unceremoniously addressed him, but he interrupted me by saying, 'Oh, yes, I already have heard of the Indians' outbreak, and that you were carried away; but no one ever dreamed of your coming back by yourself.

Two companies of soldiers have arrived at Deer Creek, just beyond the river, on their way to chastise the red scoundrels.[423] But, come along with me, and I will take you to the train, where there are ladies.'" *(111)*

Since this man already knows who **Sarah** is, she jumps at the chance to find out what else he knows.

| | |
|---|---|
| **Sarah Larimer**<br>*Kelly-Larimer Train* | "'Your husband,' he replied, 'was wounded, but not fatally, and is beyond the river, in the fort.'" *(111)* |

The unidentified man who greets **Sarah** probably sets her and **Frank** upon his horses and leads them to where the **Roe Train** and many others are camped for the evening.

**Kelly-Larimer, Roe & Union Army**

| | |
|---|---|
| **Martha Roe**<br>*Roe Train* | "...just after supper in came one of the womin [**Sarah Larimer**] and children that was captured by the Indians[.] she came a long ways and were tired and faint[.]" *(July 16)* |

If Martha Roe has any leftover Jackrabbit stew, she might warm up a bowl for the weary travelers.

| | |
|---|---|
| **Sarah Larimer**<br>*Kelly-Larimer Train* | "We soon arrived at the place where the women were, and were introduced and cordially welcomed. Never before was I so glad to see ladies. They were, of course, all strangers to me, but, not withstanding, they seemed as sisters..." *(112)* |

---

[423] Companies E and H of the 11th Ohio Cavalry.

"Very soon hundreds of persons flocked to see us and inquire of what manner we had effected to escape, and how we found our way back ... Many of these good people were Germans,[424] and, as they conversed among themselves, expressed a very great hatred to the Indians. I felt almost persuaded that they were as much imbittered against the savages as myself ... This train had come from Iowa"[425] *(112)*

**Martha Roe**
*Roe Train*

"her husband is across the river to the fort[,] wouded[.] she did not know anything about it[.] staid all night with us[.] ... We all went to bed rejoicing ... " *(July 16)*

**Sarah Larimer**
*Kelly-Larimer Train*

"As the waters were too high for us to cross that night, a soldier, by the name of **[William] Sparks**,[426] who happened to be there, kindly offered to cross the river and inform my husband of our safe arrival, when **Mr. [Josiah] Kelley** immediately came over to inquire the fate of his family..." *(113)*

By now, **Josiah Kelly** knows his wife's body is not amongst the ruins, and he has been informed that **Mary Hurley Kelly** was seen alive on July 13, although new rumors are circulating.

**Martha Roe**
*Roe Train*

"...the other women [who] had left the camp[,] her little girl [**Mary Hurley Kelly**] recaptured by some more Indians[.] kept guard" *(July 16)*

**Sarah** cannot offer proof that either **Fanny** or **Mary** is still alive, nor can she say where her kidnappers might have moved to since she left Pine Gulch. She relates, "I was able to give him **[Josiah]** no very encouraging information" (113). What little she shares fuels **Josiah's** continued search and rescue attempt.

---

[424] Sarah's meaning might also be broadly applied as, "Europeans" or "Immigrants."
[425] The Roes are from Grinnell, Iowa.
[426] William Sparks is a soldier in Company E under the command of Levi G. Marshall. He entered the service on June 8, 1863 and was sent to Fort Laramie in "Dakota Territory." He is approximately twenty-two years old in 1864.

# Sunday, July 17, 1864

### Jongewaard

On the far side of Casper, Wyoming, **Gerrit Roorda** records reuniting with friends and relatives from back home. The Dutch families in the **Rysdam Train** have been laying over near the Platte Bridge Station (eventually named "Fort Caspar"). Historian and biographer, Toni Rysdam-Shorre explains in her book, *Gerritt... A Dutchman in Oregon,* that **Gerrit Rysdam,** and three wagons departed from Iowa a week in advance of the **Jongewaard Train**. While the **Jongewaard-Rysdam Train** stays here for the rest of the day, the unidentified twenty wagons who came with them presses on.

### Kelly-Larimer & Roe

Early on the morning of July 17, **Sarah Larimer** and her son thank the **Roes** for their hospitality and cross over to the south side of the North Platte River with an escort. **Martha's** account contains no mention of **Josiah Kelly.**

**Martha Roe**
*Roe Train*
"[Sarah Larimer] went on with some horse teames in the morning" *(July 17, transcribed as 16)*

The **Roe Train** plans their usual layover for the Sabbath. After a harrowing few days, **Martha Roe's** writing reflects a newfound cynicism.

**Martha Roe**
*Roe Train*
"Got up this morning and found no scalpes lost" *(July 17)*

"Returning to Civilization," illustration in Sarah Larimer's memoir, *The Capture and Escape, Or, Life Among the Sioux,* (1870), page 132b. This same illustration is found in Fanny Kelly's memoir, though it is labeled as Fanny's return to Fort Sully (the more likely application).

## Pella Company

Though traditionally a non-traveling day for the Baptists and Methodists in the **Pella Company**, on July 17, they take advantage of the minimal travel allowance they were given the day before. The emigrants leave Bixby Point around six in the morning.

**Sarah Rousseau**
*Pella Company*
"When we had gone a short distance we saw a paper staked to the ground." *(July 17)*

**Sarah Rousseau** asks her aide, **Matilda Field**, to go find out what the paper says. Here, they learn about the fate of several wagon trains and travelers who were ahead of them during the Raids.

**Sarah Rousseau**
*Pella Company*

"...the **Oliver train** had lost 8 head of horses no lives lost, but had a very narrow escape." *(July 17)*

"And we heard another train they call **the Batcheler** had 28 head of horses taken the day after we lost ours." *(July 17)*

These attacks have since been accounted for in the Platte River Raids toll, but **Matilda** notices one more that is relatively new.

**Sarah Rousseau**
*Pella Company*

"We saw *another* written paper that told of a man being found dead[,] killed by the indians[,] he had several arrows shot through him." *(July 17, emphasis added)*

This last notice might be about the same body **Martha Roe** learned about on July 16 (the "**dead man** side of the river with 3 or 4 arrows in him"). It is presumed that the unidentified wagon train that found this body also left the note. The **Pella Company** continues west to where hundreds of wagon trains from both the east and west now camp across from the soldier station.

**Sarah Rousseau**
*Pella Company*

"There[,] we heard that one of the captured women [**Sarah Larimer**] made her escape from the Indians and had just arrived here... We don't know how reliable the statement is as we did not see the woman." *(July 17)*

From here, **Dr. James Rousseau** rides his horse back down to the Ferry of the Platte and crosses over the river, "to see about **John [Rousseau]'s** mare" (July 17). By then, another traveling party had visited with the military and reported that they picked up two horses, "which answered the description of **John['s]** mare and one of **Mr. [John] Hamiltons**." If these two horses can be reclaimed, that reduces the **Pella Company's** total loss from ten animals to eight.

**Sarah Rousseau**
*Pella Company*

"**The Lieut.** [who spoke to **Dr. James**] said… they thought of getting two or three hundred soldiers and what men they could from the different trains and go to their Indian village [and] take all the horses … It is supposed there can't be less than a thousand horses stolen." *(July 17)*

Several regiments arrived late last night from Fort Laramie and are awaiting orders to head out. These troops are preparing for an expedition while two or three hundred additional soldiers are still anticipated coming in from Fort Kearny in Nebraska.

**Sarah Rousseau's** mention of the Army keeping a tally of stolen horses matches a report from South Bank Trail traveler, **Garland Mahan** in the **Mahan-Moore Train**. On July 17, he states that the 11th Ohio seeks to receive, "several 1000 head of stock." When **Dr. James Rousseau** returns to the **Pella Company**, they relocate two miles west, away from the crowds.

### Pella Company, Roe & Union Army

Stirring up the North Bank crowds today is **William Sparks,** the same soldier who informed **Sarah Larimer's husband** of her arrival. It appears **William** is beginning the resource recruitment process. Soldiers have been encouraged to recruit every available horse and to commandeer any useful weapons and ammunition that emigrants might have on them. Removing a firearm from any of the emigrants who have just heard about or experienced a tragedy firsthand is justifiably met with resistance.

**Martha Roe**
*Roe Train*

"**Mr Wm Sparks**[,] a soldier came[,] was there a while and took a revolver from **a dutchman**[.][427] others interfered and came verry near being shot by **Sparks**[.]" *(July 17)*

---

[427] This "dutchman" is not yet identified. If man is associated with the Jongewaard-Rysdam Train, it is unclear why he became separated.

Many emigrants are vehemently opposed to this government-approved theft and likely hide firearms and ammunition as best as they can to avoid being stripped of their personal protection, despite being sympathetic to the cause. Others are simply fed up with the situation and take off.

**Sarah Rousseau**
*Pella Company*

"There is a train just passed and in one of the wagons, there is a man the Indians shot their arrows in three different places. He said he was driving his own team ahead of the train..." *(July 17)*

The identity of this man sounds like with the **Man with Three Mules** in the North Douglas Bend. Without additional details, this conclusion cannot be confirmed. If the wagon train the **Rousseaus** see is attempting to leave camp, they would be violating the order to stay in place.

In addition to ensuring the safety of those on the road, the 11th Ohio has an alternative motive keep people nearby: they need volunteers and supplies for the impending expedition. From the South Bank Trails, **George Forman** reports that between July 18 and 20, "our trains are ordered to furnish a number of men and horses with 12 days cooked rations to go with the soldiers." **Cpl. Hervey Johnson** writes from Deer Creek on July 18 that, "if they [emigrants] wont [volunteer,] then we will 'press them into service.'"

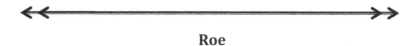

**Roe**

After witnessing this conflict, **Isaac** and **Martha Roe** ferry over the North Platte River to see the "fort."

**Martha Roe**
*Roe Train*

"pretty soon a company of Soldiers came ... they was from Ft. Laramie and had come to fight the Indians." *(July 17)*

In an August 6 letter to an Ohio newspaper, one soldier reports from Deer Creek that the plans evolve from a conservative horse and captive recovery into something much more aggressive. The soldier, William Boardman, writes: "**Col. [William O.] Collins** sent a party of about 150 men, with two mountain howitzers, to pursue and chastise any war party that they might encounter."[428]

The **Roes** return to their North Bank Trail camp and devote the rest of the day to Bible reading and singing followed by an afternoon nap before another wonderful supper prepared by **Martha** with the help of **Alex Cathcart**.

---

[428] William Boardman, "Correspondence of the News, August 6, 1864," letter to editor, in *The Highland Weekly News*, Oct 20, 1864, 1. [See the Appendix]

# Monday, July 18, 1864

### Jongewaard

Today, near Casper, Wyoming, the dual **Jongewaard-Rysdam Train** reconfigures their outfits to continue to Oregon together.

**Gerrit Roorda**
*Jongewaard Train*

"Some of our friends that had lost their stock went with us. They had lost 9 horses and mules and had been here 3 weeks Saturday." *(July 18)*

"The name of our friends are **Mr. [Gerritt] Rysdam** with his son and 2 daughters, **John** and **Cornelius Blokland** and **A.** and **J. Vander Meulen**. They had started one week before we did." *(July 19, reflective)*

While separated by time and distance, the **Rysdam Train** was also attacked and robbed in the Black Hills, albeit prior to the Platte River Raids. Though the **Jongewaards** are able to recover from their attack by redistributing stock animals, the **Rysdam Train** suffers a significant delay. Their biographer writes, "The **[Rysdam] train** stayed at Deer Creek until such time as **Gerrit [Rysdam]** was able to purchase a team of oxen and a team of cows."[429] Moving forward, this blended group will be called the **Jongewaard-Rysdam Train**.

Details of the **Rysdam Train's** attack are found in the accounts of **Jana Jongewaard** and **Mary Ellerbroek-Hornstra**, though a brief summary is included here:

---

[429] Rysdam-Shore, *Gerrit...*, 1985, 73.

While corralled for safety, **Magdalena Rysdam Earp van Rossum** hides her four-year-old daughter by Virgil Earp, **Nellie Jane**.[430] She tucks the girl down inside a clothing trunk and tells her to be quiet.[431] Depending on who tells the story, **Magdalena's** second husband **John van Rossum** either runs away in fear and dies at the hands of the attackers, abandons the family and takes on a new identity, or gets lost and dies from other consequences. **John's** sister, **Dirkie Jongewaard,** later reports back to Iowa relatives that he died, and the presumed two-time widow **Magdalena** picks up a third husband when in Oregon.[432]

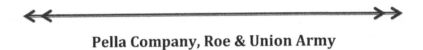

### Pella Company, Roe & Union Army

On July 18, the **Roe Train** is more than ready to leave Glenrock, Wyoming. After multiple days of rest, **Martha Roe** claims, "our oxen well recruited" and that in the morning, they are "ready for [their] journey." In the meantime, the **Pella Company** is still trying to reclaim the two horses that matched the description of the **Rousseau's** and **Hamilton's**. Today, **Dr. James Rousseau** returns to the garrison to check if those horses have been turned in.

| | |
|---|---|
| **Sarah Rousseau**<br>*Pella Company* | "The **Dr.** got back but did not bring the horses. They [the Army] told him the train had not come up yet…"<br>*(July 18)* |

Despite the travel ban, when **Dr. James** returns, the **Roe Train** has left camp. With them when they leave may be the **Dutchman** who fought **William Sparks** to keep his weapon. After an easy five or six miles, the **Roe Train** stops for lunch near present day Big Muddy Creek. Along the way, the mining team

---

[430] In 1860, Magdalena and her very non-Dutch beau, Virgil Earp, both under the age of 18, eloped using pseudonyms to keep the matter private. When the family discovered her pregnancy, patriarchs Gerrit Rysdam and Nicholas Earp resolve to terminate the relationship one way or another. Since they cannot officially annul a marriage they canno find records of, they concoct a tale of Virgil's death while he was out fighting in the Civil War. At the time of these attacks, Virgil is still very much alive.

[431] Toni Rysdam-Shorre, *Gerrit… A Dutchman in Oregon* (1985), 73.

[432] Ibid. Further research shows that John van Rossum returned to Iowa and started a new family.

that makes up the second wagon falls behind and **Martha** remarks on having to wait up for them.

Back across the garrison, **Sarah Rousseau** writes that some people are so anxious to leave that they make a mad dash in the afternoon. From her diary, readers can see how seriously the Union Army takes the detainment order.

| **Sarah Rousseau** | "After all the warning the soldiers have given them. |
|---|---|
| *Pella Company* | Two soldiers have just gone by riding as hard as they |
| | could to stop the train that has gone ahead." *(July 18)* |

**Sarah** does not identify who from the camp had caught the attention of the soldiers. After seeing the chase, however, she shares: "it is presumptuous for us to go on yet, as we were told not to go" (July 18). Nothing in **Martha Roe's** diary indicates them being stopped or warned by soldiers.

Over on the South Bank Trail, more soldiers reach Deer Creek garrison, along with approximately five hundred covered wagons with thousands of civilians. The pending Army expedition increases the nervousness of those around. **Sarah** claims rumors spread through the emigrant camp about there being two thousand "wicked" and "bloodthirsty" Indians up north (July 18). Emigrants fear that not only will the Army be outnumbered and slaughtered, but that their advancement will invite retaliation on everyone back at Deer Creek.

For a second time today, **Dr. James** goes to the garrison in the evening to see if the train with their horses had come in yet, "but it had not" (July 18). With that, **Sarah** considers her son's mare to be gone for good.

| **Sarah Rousseau** | "The **Dr. [James]**said when he returned [to camp] that |
|---|---|
| *Pella Company* | we might go on. **The Lieut.** said the order [to stay put] |
| | had been countermanded. We would have to defend |
| | ourselves." *(July 18)* |

The lifting of the protective order must have come from either **Cpt. Levi M. Reinhart,** post commander, or **Lt. Col. William O. Collins,** district commander. Two days later, **Sarah** clarifies much more being said in that day's exchange.

**Sarah Rousseau**
*Pella Company*

"**The Lieut.** told **the Dr.** to kill every one of them [Indians] that came about, friend or foe." *(July 20)*

### Roe & Wood

The **Roes** finish out their day with another six or seven mile journey to Claude Creek on the outskirts of present-day Brookhurst (near Casper, Wyoming). **"The Boys"** in the mining team that lagged behind catch up with them here.

**Martha Roe**
*Roe Train*

"they came up[,] passed by and camped bout a M west of us with some freighters[.]  our trane consisted of 14 waggons." *(July 18)*

The freighters gathered in the area are not identified by Martha but may be the **Wood Freight Train** (*See the Emigrant Tales from the South Bank Tales on July 17-18.*) Once settled in for the night, there is a celebration of sorts amongst survivors of the Raids. The **Roes**, who were never attacked, believe the worst is behind them.

**Martha Roe**
*Roe Train*

"After supper had conciderable fun[.]" *(July 18)*

# Tuesday, July 19, 1864

### Jongewaard-Rysdam & Roe

Starting on July 19 from near Casper, Wyoming, the **Jongewaard-Rysdam Train**, takes off at a much slower pace than usual. From here, they average only ten miles per day. This may be **Cornelius Jongewaard's** response to having to support additional wagons with whatever stock animals they have to share, though **Rysdam** family biographer, Toni Rysdam-Shorre, writes that the patriarch, **Gerrit Rysdam**, acquired two oxen and two cows to help pull his five or six vehicles.[433]

The **Roe Train** also leaves from the Casper area on July 19 and **Martha Roe** writes that they quickly, "came up with the rest of one trane," that might be the **Jongewaard-Rysdams**, though no mention is made of the **Roes** in **Gerrit Roorda's** daybook. The other possibility is that they rejoin the **Browns** and **Olivers**, who are still trying to put up with their unlikely travel mates.[434]

**Martha Roe**
*Roe Train*

"[that train] was glad to see us[.]said that we should drive slow and they would come with us" *(July 19)*

Together, this collective will follow the Sweetwater River which leads southwest to the Wind River Mountain Range.

---

[433] *Gerrit...*, (1985), 73.
[434] Though the Wood Freight Train is also there, they do not leave until July 21, per George Forman.

## Pella Company

Back in Glenrock, thousands of emigrants are glad to be released from the detainment order applied on July 16. The **Pella Company** leaves promptly at sun up.

**Sarah Rousseau**
*Pella Company*

"Started from camp about six oclock ... After traveling a short distance we got somewhat of a fright[,] some of the men thought they saw indians coming..." *(July 19)*

This is the second time in three days that the men of the **Pella Company** assume that *any* approach on horseback is an immediate danger: a prominent symptom of PTSD. They quickly circle the wagons into the defensive position **Nicholas Earp** taught them. After climbing up a bluff to get a better look at the incoming threat, **Nicholas** discovers their reaction to be a false alarm. No clarity is offered as to what was really seen, but perhaps the **Pella Company** second-guesses the camp of Indian wives and family members outside of the garrison, just like the **Jongewaard Train** did days before.

While they reconfigure to leave again, **Sarah's** twelve-year-old son runs up to say that the party who found his and **Mr. John Hamilton's** mares has just come up. Two men from the unidentified wagon train bring the horses to where the **Pella Company** is stopped. After the stressful ordeal, the **Pella Company** stops traveling for the remainder of the day. That night, the rest of unidentified wagon train rolls in and joins them, as do many others who are glad to get any small distance away from the Black Hills.

# Wednesday, July 20, 1864

### Pella Company

After a harrowing week, members of the **Pella Company** are eager to relaunch their California venture. **Sarah Rousseau** records that on the morning of July 20, one hundred wagons ban together with them under the advisement of the post commander at Deer Creek.

**Sarah Rousseau**
*Pella Company*

"…we will all join into one train as we hear there is so much danger with the Indians." *(July 20)*

While waiting to roll out, **Sarah** catches the gossip being passed around camp. One train on the south side of the river was robbed of sixty horses and only four were recovered. In another story, a man was approached by a "friendly" Indian asking for bread. When this individual turned to get the item from his vehicle, the Indian shot him at point blank range, then robbed him.

**Sarah Rousseau**
*Pella Company*

"…I think of how often we have done the same thing…" *(July 20)*

Folks in the long wagon train aim to reach the Platte Bridge Station by day's end, but Mother Nature stirs up a storm in the late afternoon that disrupts dinner and causes everyone to hunker down for another night.

## Union Army

In Nebraska, **Brig. Gen. Robert B. Mitchell** holds a peace council today at two o'clock. He hopes to form a truce with and gain information from local tribal bands who might have been involved in the ongoing assaults, but the entire demonstration is a failure.

Despite the **Brigadier's** most earnest efforts, historical patterns of betrayal have eroded any confidence the Northern Plains Indians have that a fair solution to this problem can be found – or kept. By 1864, the Army has created a legacy of ill-motivated treaties and flawed peace agreements that have not been honored. In Wyoming, the Sioux and Cheyenne people are particularly sensitive to these betrayals involving the constant encroachment on their prized hunting grounds. Besides, any message of peace is already being undermined by troops currently heading to the Powder River Indian Village with their howitzers (AKA "mountain canons") in tow. By midday, one lethal engagement already takes place (*see the Emigrant Tales from the South Bank Trails*). With this in mind, the **Brigadier** has no credibility to back his peaceful promises.

After all is said and done, the July 19-20 pursuit toward Powder River and Wind River marks the launch of the 11th Ohio Volunteer Cavalry's first offensive action against the Northern Plains Indians. When Irving Merrill, a historian and descendant of **Julius Merrill,** studied this event, he found that it was "the marshaling of the *largest* force of the 11th Ohio Cavalry to ever take the field in a single action against the Indians."[435]

The **Brigidier's** Department of Kansas counterpart, Major General Samuel R. Curtis,[436] also contributes to the Union's offensive response by shoring up the military's presence along the North and South branches of the Platte River leading to Colorado, even though the Major General needs every

---

[435] Irving Merrill, "The Civil War in the West: The 1864 Trail Season," *Overland Journal*, vol. 9, no. 4 (Winter 1991), 22. Emphasis added.
[436] In 1864, this department includes Kansas, Nebraska Territory, most of Colorado Territory, Indian Territory (Oklahoma) and a slice of Arkansas.

man he can keep on the battlefield to win against Confederate Major General Sterling Price.

News of this rallying spreads fear and hate across the country and promotes an indiscriminate violent stance that is echoed in military and political communications leading up to the Sand Creek Massacres in Colorado in November.

### INDIAN DIFFICULTIES.

Our news from the Plains is no better. The Indians have made a simultaneous attack on the immense commerce of the Plains, from Marysville to Fort Laramie, from Junction City to New Mexico.

They murder all whom they meet. At least one hundred white persons have already been scalped. These Indians are invariably led by white men, and the fight on the Plains is as surely against rebels as are the battles at Atlanta and Petersburg.

Gen. Curtis is not less active than heretofore. He has sent forces direct to Fort Kearney and has himself gone to Omaha to organize a Western expedition.

Gen. Blunt is active at Fort Riley.

*Extermination* is the word.

"Indian Difficulties," *The Leavenworth Times*, August 16, 1864, 2.

### Roe

On July 20, the **Roe Train** has one final interaction with the **Dutchman** who argued with **William Sparks**.

**Martha Roe**
*Roe Train*

"Lade over this afternoon[.] **the dutch** killd a calf[.] **Isac [Roe]** got 13 lb of it[.]" *(July 20)*

### Jongewaard-Rysdam - Epilogue

As the **Jongewaard-Rysdam Train** proceeds slowly toward South Pass, they'll have one more encounter with the **Pella Company** before they take a cutoff towards the Pacific Northwest. When they reach the end of their 5-month journey, some families find rich farm land in the Grande Ronde Valley of Oregon and establish a Dutch-friendly safe-haven in the area. The families of **Gerrit Rysdam, John van Blockland,** and the **van der Muelens** settle in Union County. Others, including **Gerrit Roorda**, continue west to Portland, then eventually move south into the Willamette River Valley.

Once settled in Oregon, **Magdalena Rysdam Earp van Rossum** delivers a son by her second husband who is shamefully long-gone by now. Then, despite the efforts made by **Gerrit Rysdam** and **Nicholas Earp** to separate **Magdalena** from her first non-Dutch husband, **Virgil Earp**, she picks up another non-Dutchmen named Thomas Eaton as her third husband.

Most of the families mentioned in this book return to Iowa by 1870. In a later record by Allie Brunia, **Gerrit Roorda's** niece, she adds, "Of those who went to Oregon in 1864, some returned the next year but the majority stayed five years, until the Transcontinental Railway was completed" (Roorda Family History, 1984, 61-62). Many bide their time, waiting out the political demands of United States citizenship and consequential draft registration. Those embittered by the Iowa governor's ultimatum to register or leave the "country," return to Iowa with confidence after his removal and the cessation of war.[437]

---

[437] Governor Samuel Kirkwood issued a demand for all unnaturalized aliens to register, even though the Pella draft rolls were never lacking volunteers.

# Thursday, July 21, 1864

### Pella Company - Epilogue

On July 21, the **Pella Company** finally reaches the Upper Platte Ferry and Ford. A short distance later, they rest at the Platte Bridge Station (Fort Caspar).

**Sarah Rousseau**
*Pella Company*
"This is a soldier station and where the Telegraph stops and post office. ... There, we met a gentleman that traveled in a train that left us below Laramie, his name was **Northrop**." *(July 21)*

**Sarah Rousseau** clarifies that **Mr. Northrop** left with **Nelson Morris** to take the South Bank Trails. As a reminder to the reader, the **Morris** and **Hastings** families were in the immediate vicinity of the brutal July 12 attack on the **Kelly-Larimer Train** at Little Box Elder Creek.

**Sarah Rousseau**
*Pella Company*
"**Mr. Northop** told us this morning ... **Indians** killed **Mr. Wright**. We used to call him Buck Skin as he wore buckskin breeches fringed down the side." *(July 21)*

**Mr. Northrop** goes on to say that it was **Nelson Morris** who was approached by an Indian asking for bread. This detail corrects what **Sarah** previously heard about the driver of the **Morris'** wagon being "shot dead."

**Sarah Rousseau**
*Pella Company*
"Meanwhile **Morse's wife** took the lines[,] turned as quick as thought[,] and went back as hard as she could ... while **her husband** was throwing the things out of the waggon to lighten it." *(July 21)*

**Mr. Northrop's** recall mostly aligns with what **Fanny Kelly** preserves in her memoir. He also shares with **Sarah** on what he believed happened to the **Kelly-Larimer Train**:

| | |
|---|---|
| **Sarah Rousseau**<br>*Pella Company* | "The people all massacred and waggons burned. They found the body of a little girl." *(July 21)* |

The fact that he knows **Mary Hurley Kelly's** body had been found suggests the **Morris-Hastings Train** remained at Deer Creek from July 14 until at least July 17. Surely, in this exchange, **Sarah** informs **Mr. Northrop** that she knows of at least two escapees returning to safety and that the rescue mission for the third captive has begun.

While camped near the station, the **Rousseaus** are approached by two men selling horses at sky high prices. **Dr. James Rousseau** purchases two heads at $300 USD each (approximately $5,800 per horse in the year 2023). For comparison, **Rushville's** account says heads of cattle go for about $250.[438] With their fresh horses, the **Pella Company** continues south along the Sweetwater River towards South Pass.

Five days later, the **Pella Company** learns through a telegraph announcement near Devil's Gate that, "the soldiers and Sioux Indians had a fight. The soldiers captured 200 head of horses." **Sarah** is convinced that her horses must be in that small collection, out of the thousands reported stolen in the Raids. The fight **Sarah** is referring to has since been identified as the July 25 attack on Platte Bridge Station in Casper, Wyoming. The way the event is presented is that a large band of armed and angry warriors approached the station and provoked the soldiers, including **Lt. Casper Collins**, son of **Col. William O. Collins**.

**Cpl. Hervey Johnson** of Company G, wrote of this incident in a letter, stating that when, "the Indians tried to run off even more horses near the garrison, the soldiers responded by, "peppering them" (July 25, 1864). He goes on to say that, in retaliation, "Our boys destroyed all the lodges and every thing the indians had ... you may think that they are receiving rough treatment from us, but it is nothing compared with what is their due."

---

[438] Rushville, "En Route for Idaho, August 2, 1864," letter to the editor in *The Weekly Herald and Tribune*, September 8, 1864. [See the Appendix]

Because of the narratives of **George Forman** and **Chief Bill Grass**, readers know this is not a truthful retelling.

On July 28, the **Pella Company** passes by fellow Iowans in the **Jongewaard-Rysdam Train** near the South Pass Station. There doesn't appear to be any social reconnection between the old friends beyond brief mentions on paper. As a reminder to the reader, **Nicholas Earp** and **Gerrit Rysdam** are in cahoots to keep **Magladena Rysdam Earp van Rossum** from discovering the truth about **Virgil Earp**. It would not behoove either party to socialize much under such conditions. From there, the **Jongewaard-Rysdam Train** veers west on the Lander Cutoff, while the **Pella Company** continues south along the Mormon Road to Fort Bridger in Utah.

When the **Pella Company** reaches Salt Lake City, **Matilda Field** finds herself in a compromising situation with a local gentlemen, then decides it is best to stay in Utah with him. Her borderline criminal encounter with him becomes a national news sensation that ends up being reported in the New York Times.

| | |
|---|---|
| **Nicholas Earp** <br> *Pella Company* | "we got to Salt Lake on the 12 day of August when we ought to have bin thare by the first[.] ... we could not go to California on the Southern Rout untell about november on account of having to cross the Great American desart because it would be to hot ... So, we lay by nine weeks[,] waiting for the wether to get cool enough.." *(1865)* |

The Pella Company takes up a short-term residency about a hundred miles south in Petersburg (commonly called Corn Creek Settlement, presently in Fillmore). While there, the integrity of the **Pella Company** deteriorates when **Nicholas**, as acting wagon master, accuses members of the Pavahant-Ute tribe of injuring one of their cattle. After a tense moment of conflict with Chief Kanosh, **Nicholas'** reputation as a leader is ruined.

**Sarah Rousseau**
*Pella Company*

"He still shows us more and more every day what kind of man he is." *(November 25)*

From that moment on, **Sarah** writes that **Charlie Capley,** a Confederate draft evader who was carefully smuggled out of the country by the **Earps,** leaves the demoted wagon master and "is going the remaining part of the way with us" (November 26). Presumably, **Charlie** serves as a replacement teamster for the **Rousseaus,** though **Robert Parker** may also fill that role starting in October.

The **Pella Company** resumes their journey to San Bernardino, California on the Old Spanish Trail with a desperate flight across the Mojave Desert that takes an irreparable toll on the horses. Fatigue, loss of supplies, and resentments continue to tear the long-time friends apart. The **Rousseau** horses die while trying to make it up the Cajon Pass. The **Rousseaus** are left stranded while everyone else passes them by, causing **Sarah** to believe she and her family would die by starvation. Fortunately, a surprise hero comes back for them with fresh horses and emergency supplies.

The **Rousseaus** reach San Bernardino on December 18, 1864, on a "very cold freezing morning." All four original families (**Earp, Curtis, Hamilton** and **Rousseau**) are considered pioneers of the Valley. The **Hamiltons** return to Iowa after the Civil War. There, **John Jr.** becomes visibly sick with tuberculosis and dies in 1871, leaving everything to his wife. No children are identified in his will. **Sarah Rousseau's** unabridged diary has since been recognized as a historical treasure of the American West.

**PIONEER WOMEN.**
ERECTED IN MEMORY OF THE PIONEER WOMEN
OF THE SAN BERNARDINO VALLEY WHO DARED TO
TRAVEL ACROSS THE COUNTRY BY OX TEAM AND
COVERED WAGON TO HELP LAY THE FOUNDATION
FOR THE BUILDING OF THIS STATE.
DEDICATED APRIL 16, 1977 BY THE
SAN BERNARDINO SOCIETY OF CALIFORNIA
PIONEERS, ORGANIZED JANUARY 21, 1888
CHRISTIAN R. HARRIS, PRESIDENT

"Pioneer Women Marker" in Glen Helen, California, erected by the San Bernardino Society of California Pioneers. Photo credit: Michael Kindig (2013), used with thanks.

### Brown, Howard, Oliver, Roe, Missourian & Virginians

After their one day rest at the Platte Bridge Station, the **Roe family** starts west again with the **Browns, Olivers,** and their unlikely companions (the **Howards, Missourians** and **two Virginians**). Along the Sweetwater River, it appears the **Roe's** connection with the **Browns** is as comfortable as ever.

| | |
|---|---|
| **Martha Roe**<br>*Roe Train* | "We left the Platt this morning … camped by a good spring and good feed[.] **Cap [Salmon] Broun** and **[Rodney] Clark** kept guard[.]" *(July 22)* |

The longer this collective remains together, the worse relations get between the Northerners and Southerners (and Sympathizers). Despite their political differences and initial gut feelings against remaining in company with the Southerners, **Abbie Brown** reports that her family "traveled with them for several days."[439]

---

[439] Abbie Brown, "Across the Plains," *Lake Placid News*, Sept. 29, 1916, 5-7.

Like the **Jongewaard-Rysdam Train** does, this collective slows their average pace to between twelve and fifteen miles per day. This means it takes twice as long as expected to reach the South Pass at the base of Wind River Mountain Range. Losing four days of progress in the Black Hills and upwards of ten more days being encumbered by a large company is a huge setback for the **Brown family**. Compared to the others in this collective, the **Browns** have the least resources to sustain the journey at this pace, or to replenish two weeks of food and feed that should have lasted them through to Idaho already.

To make matters worse, newspapers are now printing tips from other travelers about the celebrity family on the move. With their identity now exposed, there is an opportunity for a Rebel intervention at any point. As some see it, **Mary Brown** (who has been absolved of guilt in the violent demonstrations led by her husband) is harboring two fugitives (or antiheroes). Many Confederates and Southern Sympathizers still believe that both **Salmon Brown** and his sister **Annie** need to receive their comeuppance. Under such conditions, the **Browns** now have targets on their backs. After coming over South Pass, they become particularly anxious to break away from the crowd.

**Abbie Brown**
*Brown Train*
"We had not been with this train long before we felt that there was something wrong." *(1916)*

Around this point, the Northern California and Montana-bound emigrants anticipate taking either the Lander or Sublette Cutoff through Idaho. Per Frederick Lander's original map, the "New Worked Emigrant Road," he marked out departs from very near the former Pony Express Station at the end of the pass.[440] Based on the descriptions given in various trail accounts, however, it seems there are numerous unofficial paths carved out where emigrants who may have second-guessed their turn simply make up for it with an impromptu shortcut through the sand and shrubs of the Colorado Desert. It is possible that these alternative routes offer tempting escapes for the **Browns**.

---

[440] F.W. Lander, W.H. Wagner, T.S. Wagner, "Preliminary Map of the Central Division Ft. Kearney South Pass & Honey Lake Wagon-Road," Philadelphia, Dept. of the Interior, 1858.

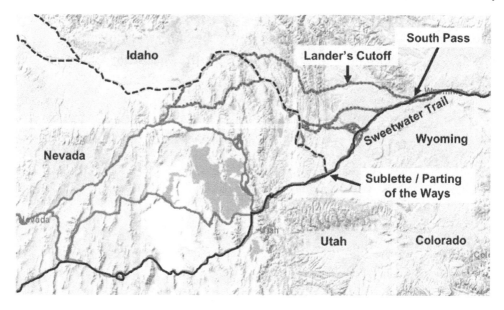

Multiple departures points lead northwest from the Sweetwater Trail. Generated by NPS National Trails Historic Trails Viewer, marked by the author (2023).

Sandra Weber, author of the biographical sketch, "Mary Ann Day Brown, Widow of John Brown," writes that, "When a group of Confederate sympathizers discovered they were the family of **John Brown**, trouble started. [**Abbie** wrote,] 'Little Dick, and the best two ewes, we have reason to believe, were poisoned by a rebel."[441] Though the malicious act is never formally pinned to the **Howards** or **Missourians**, it puts the **Browns** more on guard. Finally, on August 7, the **Browns** and **Olivers** make an unannounced departure from the group.

**Martha Roe**     "**Broun** and **his train of friends** left us this morning[.]"
*Roe Train*          *(August 7)*

Five days later, the **Roes** have a passing encounter with the **Browns** along Lander Road, then on August 16, they share a final camp together after navigating a canyon pass into the Salt River Valley (presently Star Valley on the Wyoming-Idaho border).

---

[441] Found in *The Adirondack Almanack*, March 26, 2016.

**Martha Roe**

*Roe Train*

"Had splended roads down the Salt river bottom ... camped with the **Broun train**[.]" *(August 16)*

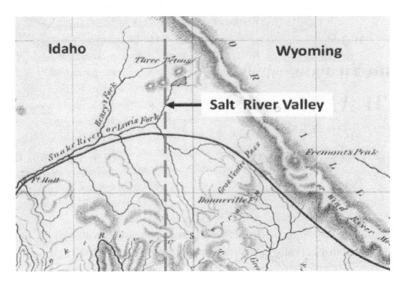

Thomas. S. Wagner, "Map of the South Pass of North America," Philadelphia, Sower, Barnes, & Co., 1860. Partial view, marked by author.

## Roe - Epilogue

The **Roe Train** heads due north form Star Valley to their final destination in Bannack, Montana Territory.[442] There, **Isaac** and **Martha Roe** move in with **Isaac's** brother William, who had staked a claim on Grasshopper Creek two years prior and had done very well as a miner.[443] **Isaac** opens a mercantile with items he brought on the overland journey and the store is rather successful. **Isaac**, though not as highly educated as his wife, becomes an esteemed businessman. Biographers lavish praise on him as "exhibiting ...

---

[442] Montana becomes a territory in May of 1864.

[443] A descendant reports that on William's first day panning, he collected $40 in gold dust—the equivalent of $780 in 2023.

every manly virtue and quality of heroic endurance ... endowed by nature with wonderful talents," such as business savvy.[444]

In 1867, William Roe purchases two hundred heads of cattle and the brothers abandon the mercantile to start up Isaac Roe & Bro., a livestock dealership and butchery. From this venture, **Isaac** "amassed wealth,"[445] but does not live long to enjoy it. In 1873, he dies from typhoid fever, leaving **Martha** and their two young children to the protective care of William. **Martha** remarries in 1880 and retires to Bozeman. She is considered an "estimable wife,"[446] and one of the earliest of pioneer women to settle in Beaverhead County. Her obituary mentions that she was devout in her Methodist Evangelical faith and hosted traveling ministers at her home until the local church was built. Presumably, as one of the wealthiest women in the most lucrative mining town (prior to the boom in Virginia City), **Martha** might have been noticed for something other than her piety, though little to nothing has been published on her life or adventures to date.

## Brown, Howard, Oliver, Missourian & Virginians

As much as the **Browns** wish to put a substantial distance between themselves and the Southerners, it is risky to make that happen with their tired animals and three rickety wagons. As this large collective continues heading northwest through Idaho, **Abbie Brown** reports that their circumstances become more dire:

**Abbie Brown**
*Brown Train*

"Our **Indiana friends** found out that they [**the Howards or Missourians**] had planned to kill us and told us of it. We hardly knew whether to believe them or not, but **two**

---

[444] "Isaac Roe," biographical sketch in, *Progressive Men of Montana*, ca. 1903, 1193.
[445] A Prominent Bannackite is Gone…," Isaac Roe obituary in *Helena Semi-Weekly Herald*, November 27, 1873, 2.
[446] "Mrs. Loughridge, Pioneer, is Dead," Martha Freeman Roe Loughridge obituary in *The Anaconda Standard*, May 13, 1920, 10.

> **young men from Virginia** came to **Mr. [Salmon] Brown**
> and corroborated the story." *(1916)*

It's possible that the **Olivers**, AKA the **"Indiana Train,"** do some investigating into the poisoned sheep and that, in the process, learn of darker intentions. In Daniel Rosenberg's study of this event, he concluded that when the **Virginians** confess to the **Browns**, they "defected" from their Missouri associates.[447] Randall Lovejoy, a descendant of the **Howard Train** has also found support for an extended threat on John Brown's daughters (**Annie, Sarah, and Ellen**). Someone in the **Howard family** spoke of wanting to further smear the name of John Brown by making him a "grandpa to a secessionist grandchild."[448]

In a letter home to her sister, **Abbie** also accuses the **Howards**, writing, "There was a train of Tennessee rebels of the worst kind got us into their company and were going to kill **Salmon**, and doubtless the rest of us."[449] In another retelling, she specifies that the threat conveyed was for her family to be "slain in their sleep," which is a direct reference to the zealous murders committed on pro-slavery voters by John Brown and his son **Salmon**, with blades, at night, in Pottawatomie, Kansas.[450] That raid marked the beginning of what would be coined the "Bleeding Kansas" period.

Over the next ten days, one of the wagons belonging to the "Tennessee rebels" requires a major repair. When the **Howards** stop to address this, **Salmon** takes the opportunity to break away from the would-be murderers and rapists. The **Brown** and **Oliver Trains**, dash away.

**Abbie Brown**
*Brown Train*

"As we did not stop, several of the men got out their guns. … For some reason they did not think it was a favorable

---

[447] "Mary Brown: From Harpers Ferry..," American Institute for Marxist Studies, 1975, 21.
[448] "The Howard Wagon Train," in *The Genie,* 1988, 203.
[449] Abbie Brown, "My Very Dear Sister," October 9, 1864, Published by *The Liberator*, November 25, 1864.
[450] "After Harpers Ferry," *Oakland Tribune*, May 21, 1933. A word of caution: The source cited within the editorial is a story by Abbie Brown in the January 25, 1913 issue of *The Outlook* news magazine in New York. The 1913 article ("My Father, John Brown") was actually by Salmon Brown and does not contain the detail shown.

time for the attack and they allowed us to go over the hill..." *(1916)*

The **Browns** and **Olivers** flee with "all possible speed," **Abbie** shares, even traveling nonstop through the night. The next day, on a downhill, one of their wagons tips over and requires an emergency fix. As the men scramble with the work, **Abbie** writes that she never takes her eyes off of the road behind them. When the **Howard and Missouri Trains** are seen out in the distance, the Northerners leave in a panicked state, "stopping to eat and sleep as little as possible."[451]

They are able to stay ahead in the chase until they reach Camp Conner, a military garrison in Soda Springs, Idaho. The distressed parties share with the California infantrymen that their lives are in danger and need protection. The **Oliver Train**, proven not to be involved in the conflict, leaves Camp Conner and heads directly to Oregon.

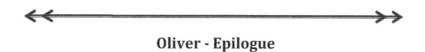

## Oliver - Epilogue

On the way to Oregon and away from the troubled trails, **Hiram Oliver's** son and daughter-in-law, **Elial** and **Nancy**, deliver a daughter in Nez Perce County, Idaho.[452] **Idaho May Oliver** (born July 29) is an example of many instances when parents along the route use a place name for their child. In other trail diaries, popular baby names incorporate an idyllic creek or spring system such as "Willow," "Sage," "Hope," or "Sandy." "Idaho," is the Territory's made-up name with no meaning. As a teen, **Idaho** changes her name to Ida.

The **Olivers** settle in Grand Ronde Valley in mid-September where **John van Blockland** of the **Jongewaard Train** ends up being a close neighbor. In Oregon, **Hiram Wesley Oliver** builds the first sawmill in Grande Ronde Valley and is credited with land surveying and laying out road through very mountainous areas. His sons work at the mill until they venture into their own

---

[451] Abbie Brown, "Across the Plains," *Lake Placid News*, Sept. 29, 1916, 5-7.
[452] Joseph Gaston, "James A. Stephens" in *The Centennial History of Oregon, 1811-1912*, 4, (Chicago: The S. J. Clarke Publishing Company, 1912): 60-63.

diverse careers. In Portland, **William Lower** becomes a wholesale merchant with H. L. White & Co. while his two married daughters move away to settle elsewhere with their husbands. **Benjamin Shonkwiler** picks up work as a teamster, then by 1875, he relocates his family to Pomeroy, Washington, where he gets nominated for town constable in 1882.[453] **William Johnston** takes up farming in The Dalles, but eventually retires back in Portland.

Emery Oliver, a great-grandson of **Elijah and Catherine Oliver**, explains in an oral history interview that, "**Joseph Oliver** stayed through Winter because his wife was pregnant; then went on to the Willamette Valley. **Elial Oliver** went on with the rest of the wagon train to Portland. He later moved back and farmed in Pomeroy, Washington."[454] **Joseph's wife, Mary Jane**, also records in her 1918 memoirs, saying: "In '64 started acros the plains in an ox team the 11 of may[.] arrived in Eastern Oregon near summersvill in September ... lived there 2 years moved to Portland in '67."[455] With the family crossing state lines, the **Olivers** are considered pioneers in both Oregon and Washington.

In 1935, **Hiram's** grandson Frank Wesley Oliver majors in education at the Oregon State College. While there, he donates family heirlooms to their museum collection, including a two hundred year old powder horn that was presented to **Elijah and Catherine** as a wedding gift by Ovid Boone (Catherine's father and Daniel Boone's brother) and was carried across the Plains with them in 1864.[456]

### Brown, Howard, Missourians & Virginians

When the **Howards** and **Missourians** arrive at Camp Conner three hours after the **Browns**, the tension thickens. **Howard** family historian, **Randall Lovejoy's** confirms that his family reconnects here with, "John Brown and his

---

[453] He declines the nomination through an announcement published in the *Pomeroy Republican,* September 16, 1882, page 7.
[454] "Oral History interview, 2002," by Marshall Kilby and Eugene Smith for the Oregon History Project, (La Grande: Eastern Oregon University, 2004).
[455] Mary Jane Oliver, personal note dated 1918, as composed from the Patton Home for the Aged and Friendless in Portland, OR. (Shared on Ancestry.com February 17, 2008 by user "Pearsey.")
[456] "Family Relics Given to Museum," in *Daily Gazette*, January 7, 1935.

family, in three or four dilapidated old wagons."[457] Once together, all the emigrants are lined up and the infantry commander, **Cpt. David Black**, immediately orders them to recite the "Oath of Allegiance" as proof of their loyalty to the Union. **Abbie** claims that, "Of course, we were glad to do so, but the rebels hated it like poison."[458]

Instead of complying, seventy-year-old **Charles Murphy Howard** responds to the order with a list of his contributions to the Union beginning with his volunteering in the War of 1812, then serving with the Tennessee Mounted Gunmen in 1814 (neither claim being confirmed with evidence). Following his father's lead, **William Henry Howard** adds claims that their ancestors came to America on the Mayflower (which has since been confirmed), and that their innocence is to be believed because he is a Christian minister and wouldn't lie.

| | |
|---|---|
| **Randall Lovejoy**<br>*Howard Train*<br>*(descendent)* | "In deference to **Charles'** age, the train was allowed to pass without having repeated the oath. ... the commander of the fort ordered an army escort to accompany the two groups [in opposite directions] to maintain peace..." *(203)* |

All was not peaceful, however. Before parting, the **Browns** have their suspicions confirmed.

| | |
|---|---|
| **Abbie Brown**<br>*Brown Train* | "One of the rebels told **Mr. [Salmon] Brown** ... if they could have caught us the night we left them[,] there would have been bloody work." *(1916)* |

---

[457] "The Howard Wagon Train," in *The Genie,* 1988, 203.
[458] Abbie Brown, "Across the Plains," *Lake Placid News*, Sept. 29, 1916, 5-7.

## Brown - Epilogue

Though both the Northerners and Southerners initially intended continuing through Idaho to Northern California, the **Browns** are rerouted south to Salt Lake City by an escort of six soldiers who witnessed the fear and threats on their family. One, Lt. Shoemaker would later regal readers of the *Union Vedette* and *Santa Cruz Sentinel* with the assassination plot he was privy to.

THE FAMILY OF OLD JOHN BROWN ESCORTED BY SOLDIERS ACROSS THE PLAINS TO CALIFORNIA.—The Camp Douglas (U. T.) Union Vedette of 27th August gives the following interesting item:

By a letter from Camp Connor, near Soda Springs, Idaho Territory, we learn that Lieut. Shoemaker, of Company H, stationed there, with five men of the command, had been sent out as an escort to the family of John Brown, of Harper's Ferry notoriety. The family consists of the widow of Brown —his two daughters and one son—the only one who has not been killed, and is now emigrating to California. They were under the impression that the son was in danger of assassination at the hands of certain parties who were on his track, and requested the escort at the hands of Capt. Black, who commands Camp Connor.

"The Family of Old John Brown Escorted by Soldiers Across the Plains to California." Editorial in Santa Cruz Weekly Sentinel, September 10, 1864, 2.

From Salt Lake City, the **Browns** continue west on their own, through Nevada, and up north into Red Bluff, Tehama County, California, like they originally planned.

**Abbie Brown**     "We reached Red Bluff a hungry, almost barefoot, ragged
*Brown Train*        lot…" *(1916)*

When news of the family makes it back East, the *New York Tribune, Brooklyn Daily Eadle, the Boston Commonwealth* and many other print sources report the same late September story:

> "There is a painful rumor, not yet confirmed, that after leaving Missouri, it having been ascertained that they were John Brown's family, they were pursued by Missouri guerillas, captured, robbed, and murdered."

These claims are later retracted when an October 3 article from *The Red Bluff Independent* reports:

> "ARRIVED – A large emigrant train from the East, by the Plains across, arrived in town this forenoon. Among the number was the wife, son, and three daughters of John Brown, the hero of Harpers Ferry notoriety, the frightener of the great state of Virginia…"

In California, the **Browns** received a warm welcome amongst other liberals, but they face yet another challenge: "They were destitute," writes Al Reck.[459] Residents in Red Bluff donate clothes and pantry items to assist the family through their first Winter. Once settled, **Salmon Brown** begins a livestock breeding and butchering business with his surviving Merino sheep. After six years in Red Bluff in Tehama Co., **Mary Brown** and her daughters join **Salmon** and **Abbie** in Humboldt Co. and where there is cooler weather on the coast.

---

[459] "John Brown's Family Comes West—Chapter 1," *Oakland Tribune*, January 8, 1961, 4-M.

For a while, **Mary** scratches out a living as a lay nurse[460] while her daughters get involved in education. Her eldest daughter, **Annie Brown** marries and resumes teaching African-American children, as she had been doing back east.[461] **Sarah Brown** becomes a schoolteacher in Antelope Valley, until she takes a job in San Francisco at the U.S. Mint. She is later fired because of her association to John Brown. In 1876, **Ellen Brown** marries a schoolteacher, as family stories convey, but on a later U.S. Census, his is listed as a school janitor.[462]

When the transcontinental railroad is complete, **Mary** makes one last trip back to New York and visits the grave of her late husband. She is suspected to be battling cancer and knows her time is limited. When she returns to California, she passes away peacefully in 1884. **Salmon** eventually retires his family to Portland, Oregon. Then, in 1913, he releases an essay confirming his everlasting support for his father and family, where he recalls, "our family was long buffeted from pillar to post. Efforts to forget were fruitless. ... I feel that no apology is needed on behalf of John Brown, husband and father[,] kind and true..."[463] Sadly, in 1917, **Salmon** falls from a horse, becomes paralyzed and after being bedridden for two years, commits suicide.[464] By this time, his sisters **Sarah** and **Ellen** have also passed away.

Once again, the legacy of the **Brown family** is transferred to the memories, letters, and care of the two last standing women who loved their men. **Salmon's wife Abbie** composes a personal memoir in 1914 and releases it in 1916. A full transcription of it has since been republished in the *Overland Journal*. **Annie Brown** becomes an activist who, "would defend **Brown's** raiders—their couth as well as their motives—for the rest of her life."[465]

---

[460] Sam Hanson, "Threats, Then Friends, For John Brown's People," in *Los Gatos Daily Times*, March 26, 1953, 7.

[461] Her husband is Samuel Adams (1829- 1914) from Ohio.

[462] Her husband is James Fablinger (1852-1925) from Illinois.

[463] Salmon Brown, "My Father, John Broan," *The Outlook*, January 25, 1913, 215-217.

[464] Fred Lockley, "Observations and Impressions of the Journal Man," *The Oregon Daily Journal*, May 29, 1919, 8.

[465] Bonnie Laughlin-Schultz, *The Tie That Bound Us: The Women of John Brown's Family and The Legacy of Radical Abolitionism*, (Cornell University Press: New York) 2013. 58.

## Howard - Epilogue

The Camp Conner intervention also sours **Charles Howards'** plan to go to Northern California. For nearly two hundred miles, the **Howard Train** is escorted due north, toward Oregon and Washington. Once their Army escorts releases them, the family settles in Oregon's Grande Ronde Valley in October. Most of the wagon train members stay through the winter and the men reenter a life of farming, perfectly happy to be away from the political upheavals that prompted their westward journey in the first place.

From there, individual family disperse across the Pacific Northwest: some in Oregon (Umatilla Co., Yamhill Co., and Willamette Valley), some in Washington (Walla Walla), and others in California (Shasta Co., Solano Co., and even Tehama Co.). According to descendant Randall Lovejoy, this is when, "the **Howard Wagon Train** began to disintegrate."[466]

Only two years after leading his family to across the country, **Charles Howard** dies from apoplexy (a stroke) at the age of seventy-two. Oddly, when his sons **Charles** and **James** reach the age of seventy-two, they also die from strokes. **"Dr." Wyatt Wherry** never establishes any form of medical practice. **Rev. William H. Howard** continues preaching in the Methodist Evangelical faith for the next twenty years and is considered a friend to everyone he ever meets. **Jeremiah Birks** becomes a well-known stock raiser, but his brother eventually returns to Iowa.

The **Scroggin** family become well-known pioneers in the Grande Ronde Valley. **Pleasant Scroggin** goes into banking and becomes the senior partner in the firm, Scroggin & Wortman. When both **Pleasant** and his wife **Sarah Howard Scroggin** pass away, their children erect a polished granite monument in their memory that is, at the time, the largest in the state, south of Portland. According to one news article, it stands eighteen feet high on a six foot by six foot base.[467]

---

[466] "The Howard Wagon Train," *The Genie,* 1988, 203.
[467] "A Handsome Monument," *The Sunday Oregonian*, June 14, 1896.

By 1870, at least four family units make it to their original destination in Tehama Co., California. Coincidentally, this happens to be right around the same time the **Brown family** decides they must move out of the area. **Howard Train** diarist, **Alfred Kennedy**, settles in Seattle, Washington and works as a school teacher. After his 1931 death, a distant cousin saves his diary, though by the 1980s, it disappears entirely, causing it to become "the object of many a search."[468] Descendants are encouraged to continue the search.

---

[468] Randall Lovejoy, "The Howard Wagon Train," *The Genie,* 1988, 206.

# Afterword

**Janelle Molony, M.S.L.**

Between the dates of July 8 and 16, at least thirty-five threatening or violent encounters with Northern Plains Indians occurred in the Black Hills of Idaho (ie. Wyoming's Medicine Bow Forest), as supported by immediate eyewitness or other authoritative accounts. Reported losses are as follows:

| | |
|---|---|
| 8 | Emigrants Killed |
| 8 | Emigrants Injured |
| 4 | Emigrants Kidnapped |
| 1 | Indian Killed (unconfirmed) |
| 7 | Indians Injured |
| 261 | (Counted) Horses and Mules Robbed (though the military reports thousands) |
| 7 | (Uncounted) Reports of "All" Stock Robbed |

To maintain perspective on this week of losses, it is important to remember that on July 4, Bozeman's Caravan annihilated one hundred Buffalo along Bozeman's Trail. Then on July 7, the Townsend Train provoked a battle with Plains Indians,[469] resulting in the death of fourteen warrior-hunters who were acting within their right to preserve and defend their choice hunting grounds. Regardless of any justification the Plains Indians may have had, the unsuspecting families in their crosshairs did not deserve to be the victims of such depredations. They were, as you have seen, reputable pioneer families (doctors, clergy, lawyers, merchants, photographers, farmers, and widows). They were hopeful people seeking a fresh

---

[469] Susan Badger Doyle claims those responsible were "primarily Northern Cheyennes, joined by some Oglalas and other Upper Platte Sioux." Cited in *Journeys to the Land of Gold: Emigrant Diaries from 1863-1866*, 1 (Helena: Montana Historical Society Press 2000), 153.

start, a medical miracle, or an escape from the effects of the Civil War and guerilla violence.

Though historian Susan Doyle did not use the same body of material to draw her conclusions, she and I agree that, "emigrants passing through the tribes' territory did not directly cause the Indian wars. Rather, the military intervention … did that by escalating the situation."[470] Immediate consequences of the Raids were imposed on Northern Plains Indians without any evidence of wrong doing. This includes ten of **Chief Bill Grass'** men killed or wounded and twenty-two of his tribe's women and children being held hostage in exchange for **Fanny Kelly** during the July 25 Battle of Platte Bridge.

Starting in August, depredations escalated past the boundaries of Medicine Bow Forest, extending east into Nebraska Territory, following the South Platte River into Colorado Territory, and even causing chaos as far south as the Arkansas River in Kansas. As the War for the West continued, all semblance of human decency eroded with inflammatory remarks being made by Army leaders and politicians that spread like wildfire in news media. Genocide became the publicly advertised solution to silence the anger expressed by Plains Indians over broken promises. With this in mind, as one military combat strategist has put it, "it is easy to understand their violent resistance. …the stage was set for long periods of violence, broken only by intermittent lapses of peace, until one side finally achieved permanent dominance."[471]

---

[470] Doyle, *Journeys…*, 5.
[471] Charles Collins Jr., "The Sioux and the Great Plains," in *Atlas of the Sioux Wars,* 2 ed. (Combat Studies Institute Press: Fort Leavenworth, Kansas, 2006).

THE INDIAN TROUBLES.—The Denver correspondent of the Atchison *Free Press* attributes the Indian outbreak to the fact that the ranch-men along the Platte have swindled the Indians most barbarously. Stealing stock on the Fort Laramie road has been more extensive than along the South Platte. A party of Cheyennes and Sioux came to Beaver Creek a few days ago, and boasted that they had taken 1800 head of stock, and were bound to have twice as many more before quitting. Many think it is the determination of the Indians to clean the whole road this fall, and the way they have been proceeding for the past two months, would naturally lead a person to this belief.

"The Indian Troubles," *The Weekly Herald and Tribune*, August 11, 1864, 2.

In November, Colonel John Chivington, headquartered in Denver, decided to take drastic measures to address the so-called uprising. He encouraged approximately 750 innocent Southern Cheyenne and Southern Arapahoe chiefs, women, children and elderly to gather at Big Sandy Creek in Colorado, where they were told they would be spared from the punishment that was to be inflicted on those involved in the violent acts. Once there, the Colonel betrayed them in one of the most cruel and controversial events in the Army's history. Starting on the morning of November 29, and lasting for nearly eight hours, his troops mowed down over two hundred people in what has since been coined the Sand Creek Massacre.

After this barbaric demonstration, Dr. Grace Raymond Hebard and Earl Brininstool concluded, "the Cheyennes, without a home, and enraged with our government, sent a pipe of peace to the Sioux and the Northern Arapahoes, inviting them to enter into a joint war .... The proposition of a united war was, in

December, 1864, accepted by the leaders of both the Sioux and Arapahoes. Thus the three tribes joined forces ... and swept the Oregon Trail for two hundred miles..."[472] Later researchers would find additional agreements between even more tribal bands: "And it so appears that the Kiowas, Apaches, Arapahoes, Cheyennes, with the Bruele, Ogalalah and Missouri Sioux agreed to drive the white people out of their domain by any means that they could devise. The Indians had plenty of firearms and ammunition and their raids were well planned and timed and ingeniously carried out."[473]

With the massive numbers and far-reach of the united tribes, traveling on the trails became so dangerous this Fall that stagecoaches had to be rerouted and freighting operations had to cease. Telegraph lines were destroyed, ranches were burned down and smaller Army posts abandoned. "Practically all the stations and ranches were burned from Julesberg to Kiowa station with the exception of Little Blue station," writes one historian. [474] Pioneer settlers and entrepreneurs uprooted in fear. Many fled back east along the trails. As one example, Nebraska's lightly settled Hall and Merrick counties became ghost towns almost overnight.[475] "Farms were abandoned and implements of agriculture left to rust and destruction. Only the more valuable variety of stock was taken, such as horses and cattle; hogs and cats were turned loose to shift [fend] for themselves."[476] By the end of 1864, Plains Indians had gained "complete possession" of the West.[477]

---

[472] Grace Raymond Hebard and Earl Brininstool, *The Bozeman Trail*, 1. (Cleveland: The Arthur H. Clark Company, 1922), 129-130.

[473] John Ellenbecker, "Indian Raids on the Little Blue River," *Advocate-Democrat*, Jan. 20, 1927, 6.

[474] Ibid.

[475] Clark E. Persinger, *A History of Merrick County, Nebraska*, (Central City: The Nonpareil Press ,1898): 35.

[476] Alfred T. Andreas, *History of the State of Nebraska: Merrick County, vol. 1*, (Chicago: The Western Historical Company, 1882).

[477] Hebard and Brininstool, *The Bozeman Trail*, 131.

# Appendix

## Newspaper Articles & Letters

| Author | Date | Page |
|---|---|---|
| Boardman, William | Letter dated Aug. 6, 1864 | I |
| Davenport, William | Letter dated Aug. 1, 1864 | V |
| Earp, Nicholas | Letter dated April 2, 1865 | VII |
| Edwards, Haywood | Diary (July 1864) | XIV |
| Forbis, Amanda | Biographical sketch, 1893 | XVI |
| Grass, Chief John | Oral History (1915) | XVIII |
| Hull, Lewis B. | Diary (July 1864) | XX |
| Johnson, Hervey | Letter dated July 25, 1864 | XXV |
| Johnson, Hervey | Letter dated July 26, 1864 | XXVIII |
| Kelly, Josiah S. | Letter dated Aug. 15, 1864 | XXIX |
| Larimer, Sarah L. | Letter dated Aug. 1864 | XXXII |
| Logan, James | Letter dated Aug. 1, 1864 | XXXIV |
| Logan, James | Letter dated Aug. 9, 1864 | XXXIX |
| Lucas, William | Oral History (1926) | XL |
| Phillips, Elenor | Obituary from June 11, 1892 | XLII |
| Rockwood, A. L. | Letter dated July 25, 1864 | XLIII |
| Rushville, (NFN) | Letter dated July 29, 1864 | XLVII |
| Rushville, (NFN) | Letter dated Aug. 2, 1864 | XLIX |
| Taylor, Noah D. | Letter dated July 5, 1864 | LII |
| Editorial | *Union Vedette*, Aug. 13, 1864 | LIII |
| Editorial | *Chico Weekly*, Sept. 3, 1864 | LIV |
| Editorial | *Daily Union Press*, Sept. 8, 1864 | LV |
| Editorial | *Gold Hill Daily*, Sept. 29, 1864 | LVI |

# William Boardman, Letter, Aug. 6, 1864

**(Correspondence of the News.)**
Letter from the 11th O.V.C. – A Fight with the Indians – Lieutenant Brown, of Co. E, Killed – Emigrants Murdered by the Indians, &c., &c.

DEER CREEK TELEGRAPH STATION,
Idaho Ter., Aug. 6th, 1864

DEAR NEWS:

Your readers have been informed, doubtless, by Telegraph, of the recent Indian depredations on this road, but perhaps a detailed account may not be uninteresting. During the month of June, and up to the 12th of July, all the disturbances were on the north side of the Platte. Several trains had been attacked and their stock run off, and a few emigrants killed and wounded.

On the 12th of July, a train of six wagons, camps on little Box Elder Creek, about fourteen miles below this post, on the south side of Platte, were attacked by about forty Indians, and four emigrants killed, two wounded, and two women and two children taken prisoners. One of the women, **Mrs. [Sarah] Larimer**, escape about a week afterwards, and made her way to this post, with her little boy. The other woman, **Mrs. [Fanny] Kelly**, has never been heard of. The little girl was found not far from where captured, pierced by arrows, and her scalp taken. This has been the most serious occurrence on the road. I suppose that about eighteen emigrants have been killed and wounded along the road since the 12th of July.

On these facts be known at Fort Laramie, **Col. [William O.] Collins** sent a party of about 150 men, with two mountain howitzers, to pursue and chastise any war party that they might encounter. The Expedition went as far as Wind River. On the second day out, **Lieutenant John Brown**, of Co. E, with a party of five men, while scouting about nine miles from the command, came suddenly upon a party of about seventy-five Indians, herding about 150 head of stock, which they were taking to their villages.

**Lieut. Brown** and party immediately attacked them. In changing his position for what he though a more favorable one, the Indians closed in on the small party, who bravely stood their ground as long as possible, but were soon compelled to retreat, but not before the **Lieutenant** was pierced by two arrows.

The rest of the party[,] supposing the **Lieutenant** to be killed, retreated to the main command, who pursued the Indians as far as possible, in the condition their horses were in, but were unable to overtake them.

In two or three days[,] the expedition returned to this post, bringing the body of **Lieut. Brown**, which was recovered the next day after the skirmish.[478] When found, he was not yet dead, but breathing his last[.] a short time after he was taken to camp. The Indians stripped him of all clothing except his hat and boots, took his horse, two gold watches, and some $40 in money. One arrow struck him in the small of the back, and only lacked an inch or two of penetrating his body. Another arrow went into the back of his neck, and came through his throat. An Indian arrow makes a terrible wound, which most generally proves fatal.

During the latter part of May last, **"Old Grass,"**[479] one of the Platte Sioux chiefs, with a party of seventy-five warriors, started up the road from Fort Laramie, ostensibly for the purpose of fighting the *Utes*, (a war-like tribe some 200 miles above here) and hunting buffalo.

It was not more than two weeks after until we began to hear of Indian depredations on the other side of the Platte. It was thought by many at the time, that he was going for the purpose of disturbing emigration.

The day after the Wind River Expedition returned[,] news came from Platte Bridge (28 miles above here) that "Old Grass" and his party were there, asking permission to pass down to Fort Laramie. **Capt. [Levi G.] Marshall**, commanding the expedition, sent word to the troops stationed there to hold them until his command could come up and take them prisoners, acting on the suspicion that they had been engaged in the recent depredations.

---

[478] His entrails were removed, insides salted, and he was buried in the sand on July 21, but Hervey Johnson's squad collected his body on their way back from Wind River to be properly buried with honors.

[479] Hervey Johnson names him Bill Grass.

Serg't Meriom,[480] commanding at Platte Bridge during the absence of Lieut. Bretney, with **Capt. Marshall's** expedition, went to the camp of "Old Grass" with 12 men, to have a talk with him and engage his attention until **Capt. [Marshall** should come up.

**"Old Grass,"** however, probably "smelling a mice," raised the war-whoop, down came their wigwams, and in a few minutes the whole Indian party were on their way to the hills.

Serg't Meriom and a party immediately pursued, and the Indians made a stand near the foot of the bluffs, and a sharp skirmish of about three-quarters of an hour ensued, resulting in the Indians being dispersed, with 10 or 12 killed and wounded; the loss of about 40 of their ponies and several wigwams, with only one man wounded on our side, Chavil St. Clair, Co. G., who was struck in the leg by a rifel ball. Private John Bennett had his horse shot from under him, and private Dab [Dob] Moppins had his horse wounded. **Capt. Marshall** and his command arrived too late to take part in the affair.

**"Old Grass"** was wounded twice, but made his way to the ranch of Maj. Twiss, some 4 miles above this post; where he lay for some two or three days. **Capt. [Levi M.] Rinehart** wished to place a guard over him, but Maj. Twiss' promised to be responsible for his safe keeping, and as the Major was considered "O.K." no guard was placed over the Chief. Two or three days ago a party of Indians came near Maj. Twiss' ranch and endeavored to run off a herd of ponies, belonging to Mountaineers. This was near where hay is being cut for this post. One of our men who was stationed there, was fired on by three Indians, and had three bullet holes put in his blouse, but he succeeded in getting away. Word was brought down the post as soon as possible, and our boys started after them, but arrive too late, the Indians having made good their retreat, carrying off with them **"Old Grass."**

No Indian disturbances of consequence have since happened, but we keep a sharp look-out. There will probably be Indian depredations along the road during the whole Summer. We have been kept on the move for the last five weeks, and are getting a pretty fair experience of frontier life.

---

[480] 1st Sargent. Henry D. Merwin.

There has been more trouble with Indians this Summer than at any time since the road was established, probably owing to the heavy emigration to Bannock. Should anything further of interest occur, I will keep your readers posted. The company is in very good health, and always "cocked and primed" for redskins. More anon.[481]

W.F.B.

**Source Citation**: Boardman, William F. "Correspondence of the News," August 6, 1864 letter to editor, *The Highland Weekly News*, Oct 20, 1864, 1.

---

[481] This expression means something like, "I'll be in touch soon," or "You'll hear from me again later."

# Wm Davenport, Letter, Aug. 1, 1864

**From the Plains.**
PLATTE Harbor, Idaho Ter.
August 1st, 1864

Mr. R. H. Miller[482] – Dear Friend:

I write to give you the melancholy information of the death of Martin Ringo. Owing to some difficulties we had with the Indians below Fort Laramie[,] at Scott's Bluff[,] the emigration formed themselves into large companies. Our company, consisting of the **Martin brothers** and **Jas. Reed** of Clay county, **Forbes, Irvin, Lucas** & Co., from the Platte and Buchanan counties, – **Beauvais** & Co., from St. Joseph, with **Mr. Ringo and family**, and others, making in all about 70 wagons, have been traveling together for mutual protection.

We passed through the Black Hills[,] where the Indians have committed most of their depredations this season[,] without being molested, and camped the night of the 29th of July, about three miles this side of Deer Creek, and about twenty-four miles from this point. Shortly after dark[,] a gentleman by the name of **Davis**, from Kansas, went out about fifty yards from the camp to look after his horses that were picketed out, and an Indian shot and wounded him in the right arm and side, making a painful tho' not dangerous wound.

The Indian succeeded in stealing three horses – one from **Mr. Davis**, one from **Mr. Irvin**, and one from **David Morris**. There was only one Indian seen, and I think his only object was to steal horses. The shooting of **Mr. Davis** created considerable excitement in camp, as we expected to be attacked by Indians in force.

The whole company stood guard during the night so as to be prepared in case we were attacked. Just after daylight on the morning of the 30th ult., **Mr. Ringo** stepped outside of the wagons, as I suppose, for the purpose of looking

---

[482] Robert H. Miller is the editor of the *Liberty Tribune* and the brother-in-law of Martin and Mary Ringo by marrying Mary's sister Enfield.

around to see if Indians were in sight and his shot gun went off accidentally in his own hands, the load entering at his right eye and coming up out at the top of his head. At the report of his gun[,] I saw his hat blown up twenty feet in the air, and his brains were scattered in all directions. I never saw a more heart rendering sight; and to see the distress and agony of his wife and children was painful in the extreme.

**Mr. Ringo's** death has cast a gloom over our while company, and his wife and children has our sympathies. The ladies in our company are very kind and attentive to **Mrs. Ringo**, and every gentleman in the company is disposed to do anything in his power to make her comfortable, or promote her interests.

**Mr. Ringo** was a very mild, pleasant and unassuming gentleman, and was duly appreciated by our company – all of whom esteemed him highly. He was buried near the place he was shot in as decent a manner as was possible with the facilities on the [P]lains.

**Mrs. Ringo** thinks of going to Salt Lake and of disposing of her outfit at that point and taking the stage from there to California. There is a portion of our company that are going to California via Salt Lake; the larger portion are going to Idaho via the South Pass, and a portion of them are going by Bridger's Cut-Off, sixteen miles from here.

We do not anticipate any further [sic] Indian troubles on our journey, as there is no report of their committing any depredations beyond this point. We are going to travel in sufficiently large companies to protect ourselves; and by keeping strict guard[,] we do not expect to be molested – their only object being to steal horses.

Our company are all enjoying excellent health.

Your Friend,
WM. DAVENPORT.

**Source Citation**: Davenport, William. "From the Plains," letter to editor dated August 1, 1864, *Liberty Tribune*, September 16, 1864.

# Nicholas Earp, Letter, April 2, 1865

April 2nd 1865
James Copla

Dear Sir[,]

after a long elapse of time and agreate deel of anxiety waiting for aletter from you in answer to one I wrote to you from Corn Creek Utah Territory and finding out from Charleys letter that he just received from you that you had not received any letter from me[.] I embrace the present opertunity of wrighting you a nother letter to let you know how it is with me and family and all the friends.

myself and family we are all well as are all of the friends that came across the plains with me and we hope these few indifferent written lines may find you all well when they come to hand together with all enquiring friends

now James as you did not get my other letter that I rote to you in whicth I had given you a full account of our trip and the incidents thare to as far as Corn Creek Territory 1.75 miles South of Salt Lake[.] I will endeavour to gave a slite history of the trip through and some of the occurrencies that took place on the trip but cannot give it in full detail for two mutch time has elapsed for me to remember all sufficient to do so and it would take more time and paper than I have to spare at this time[,] but I will try to satisfy your mind to some extent and the many others that I know are ancious to heare from us[.]

well hear we go across the Missouri River as you know we had to do to cross the plains[.] just before we got to the River at the crossing place[,] little **Allen Curtis** fell from the mule waggon and it ran over him and came verry near killing him but we crossed over and he the boy got well and on we went with tolerable good luck and speed considering the scarceness of grass for our animills untell we got to ft. Laramie which we did on the Seventh day of July just one month & Seven days from the time we crossed the Missouri River and on we went without any serious trouble[,] occaisonaly passing indions on the rout untell we got about 50 miles above Laramie[.]

when we got to Laramie we began to hear of depredations being comited by the Indians on trains but we were not seeing any of it and it was reported always behind or before us and[,] as we did not see any of the occurances[,] the crowd began to think it was all falce, and as they had bin before pretty mutch all the way or at least some of them a little to slack in doing their duty when in camp in garding the stock[.]they began to be still morseso untell I began to scold some about it and told them that we would have to have a demonstration from the Indions which I believed would take place before long and I would not care mutch if we did[,] so they did not hurt any of us as I thought it would be the cause of them being more prompt in doing their duty and cause them to see the necesity of more care and vigilance[.]

and sure enough[,] when about 50 miles above Laramie[,] one day in camp for noon [July 12] in the bend of Platt River[,] the grass being verry pore on the side that we war campt on[,] I rode across the river and found that on the other side that thare was good grass[,] so I gave the order for the stock to be turned over the River[.]

my hands took my horses and all the cattle over[,] the ballance turned some of thirs over sutch as they could drive over after the rest[,] but some would not go over and some said they would rather thirs would stay on the side they war on than to put them into the River[.] so thare was some of the stock on one side, and some on the other[.] I gave orders to those that went across the river that in case that I gave the alarm to git hold of thir horses picket rops as quick as possible and bring them across the river into camp.

so we had bin in camp but alittle while **J.B. Hamilton   I.C. Curtis   Dr. Russaw**, & my self war seated on the bank of the River talking and I happened to look around behind me and about four hundred yards off I saw a Squad of men on horse back galoping towards us[.] I sprang to my feet and sang out ["]Indians[!] to arms boys[!"]and we all rushed to the waggons and got our guns and ran to meet the red skins who by this time was amongst the horses that war on our side of the river[,]  hooping and yelling like indians shure enough[.] we met them and began to shoot at them and we soon checked them up and turned them back[.]

while one of them was in the act of trying to lasoe one of the **Hamiltons** mares[,] I leveled the rifle I got of Grafe[483] at him and at the crack of the gun he fell forward in his saddle and turned his horse round and ran off[,] badly wounded

---

[483] This expression might be edited to read "I leveled the rifle that I got off of Ernst Grafe." At this time, Mr. Ernst Frederick Grafe (pronounced like "Graph") is living in Lake Prairie Township in Marion County, Iowa. He was born 1819 in Hanover, Germany and served in the Union army during the Civil War.

I am shure[.]  but, the yells of the Savages and the firing of the guns fritened our horses so that it caused them to stampede and ran down apast the camp in spite of all that we could do[.]  they took back down the road[.]  the Indians seeing that[,]ran round and got in between us and the horses and ran them off[.]

at the commencement of the fun[,] according to directions[,] I hollowed for the stock on the other side to be brought over[the river,] and as soon as it could be got over[,] I took ten men and persued them [Indians] untell dark but without effect[.]  the conciquence was they got ten head of our horses[:] 5 of **Hamiltons**[,] 4 of **Rusaws** & one of **Curtises**[.]

next morning [July 13] on we went and the second day [July 14] after they had made the first raid on us[,] we camped again for noon in a bend of Platt River[,]  situatied a good deal as before[,] only we had all our stock on the same side of the River that the waggons was on and we had our guards properly posted & pickets out for it was no trouble now to get the men all to do thir duty[.]

we had not bin in camp long untell the Sentinels gave the alarm that the Indians was coming[.]  so I ordered the horses to be brought inside of the Corell by the gards that was garding them[.]  the women all turned out to help get the horses into the Corell while we who was not on gard gathered our guns and rushed to meet the Indians[.]

when they got as clost as we entended them to come[,] we comenced poping away at them and soon succeeded in checking them and putting them to flite[.]

they ran of[f] about a half amile and stoped and turned round as tho they war not satisfied[.]  I said[, "]boys they are not satisfied[.]  lets satisfy them[!"]  so I ran to the waggons and gumped upon a hors[e] & said[, "]we'll make them then leave thare[."] **Dr. Rusaw**[,] **T.J. Ellis**[,]  **James Earp**[,] **Richar[d Curtis,]** a young man by the name of **[Levi] Tucker** that was with **[John] Hamilton** & and two other men that got in with us[,] followed suit and off we charged after the Indians[.]  when they saw we war making for them[,] they wheeled about and off they put[.]

on we went in full persuit of them untell they found we war about to over take them[.]  they then faced about to gave us battle[.]  they ware about 4 to one of us[.]  I gave orders to form line of battle and we went into a general engagement[.] they undertook to flank us first to the right and then to the left  but they found out they could not for they had thir match[,]  so they then began to gave bac[.]  the arrows flew and the bullets wised[.]  they began to gave back to keep out of range of our guns[.]

we rushed on[.] When **Dr. Rusaw** put his mareen glasses to his eyes and discovered the man who seemed to be leading the band and gaving comand was a white man[,] he hollowed out[, "]**Earp**[,] shoot that man on the roan horse[,] he is a white man[!"]  as I was the closest to them[.] and I leveled on him and at the crack of the gun[,] he fell to one side of the horse but caught in the mane and recovered again then wheeled his horse and lumbered over the hill as fast as his horse would take him[.] the rest immediately took to flight following him[.]

we had exausted all our shots so we had to stop the persuit but saw by the blood on the trails that we had woonded 4 of them[.] so that was the last time we was attacked by the Indians

The next morning [July 15] we started on a gain[.] nothing of any consequence hapining from that to Salt Lake[,] only **Mrs Hamilton** brought forth a fine boy afew days after war attacked by the Indians[.]

We got to Salt Lake on the 12 day of August when we ought to have bin thare by the first[.] then we ascertained by the old Salt Lake freighters that we could not go to California on the Southern Rout untell about november on account of having to cross the Great American desart because it would be to hot before tate time to cross it[.] So, we lay by nine weeks[,] waiting for the wether to get cool enoughf and at the proper time we took up the line of martch again and on the 20th day of December we landed in San barnardino after along and tedious trip[.]

I got through with all the stock I started with but one of the mares died at utah lake with the colic[.] comparitivly in good order[,] my blind horse at the beaver dam two hundred miles from San Barnardino fell down abank about fifteen feet high and disabled himself so that I had to leave him[.]

now for what I am doing[.] I succeeded in Renting afine farme the 3rd day after I got to San Barnardino and on the 25 day moved out to it about 10 miles from San Barnardino[.] it has ten acres in peach & apple orchard & 35 in grapes[.]

Oh dont I wish you and many others of my friends was here to help me to eat apples peaches & graps this fall & drink wine[.] I got here a month to late to get in as large a crop as I wanted to[.] the people was most done sowing when I got on my farm[.]  I have 12 acres in wheat[,] 18 in barley which is now in the boot[484] & I have 20 acres now planted in corn[,] ten of which is large enough to plow & shall plant 8 more this week[,] then I shall be done planting[.] Letis [lettuce] large anoughf to eat of our own sowing but we have had lettis & cabage all winter which

---

[484] This phrase can be understood as "in storage."

was growing here when we came[.]   we have our peas stuck and onions large anoughf to eat of our own planting[.]

I set out 20 lbs of onion sets and about a quarter of an acre in onion seeds[.] my potatoes is large anough to work[,] peaches as large as small birds egs[.]  This is the finest climate in the world altho I don't know that I shall stay here and think I shall not for I did not start from home expecting to stop here[.] but when we got heare[,] we ware all so near run through that we could not go any longer[.] I no of places in California that I like better than I do here[,] but if a man has got him a place here[,] after the first year[,] he can live as easy as any place in the world and as pleasant[.] but I expect to go higher up in California or into Arisonia or to Sonorh[,][485] one or the other[.]

Now James[,] I expect you to expect for me to gave you an account of the Country and prohaps to advise you whether to come here or not[,] which I cannot do at this time any more tha[n] I could when I was thare[.]  I no that thare is places in California that I can recomend to any person but those places I have not seen cince I have bin here[,] but as soon as my crop is harvested[,] I shall look round & see something about whare I shall go or whare I like the best[.]  I dont like this part of California as well as I do some other parts and then thare is no chance to get land hear without buying second handed[,] altho I would rither stay hear on rented land than to be in Iowa on land of my own[,]  and I can make more at that[.]

Just imagine that you dont have to feed any thing winter or somer[,] only the animals you keep up to work[.] all the ballance you rais is for sale and you can rais stock without any expense[.] and thare is another satisfaction in being hear is we are mutch more free heare than theare[.] we can say what we please heare and none dare molest or make us afraid[.] I have enjoyed my self here cince I have bin hear and seen more peace and freedom than I did the last three years I stayed in Iowa[.] heare people that are Seces make no boan in saying so[.] they hollow for Jef Davis when they please[.]

Now friend Copla[,] I would like to see you verry mutch and all the rest of my old friends and neighbors[.] gave my respects to Dr. Henry Keables[,]  John Welch[,]  Port Welch and all of the Welch family that is thare[,] John Roark[,] Peter Bousquet [and] John Nollen[.] tell Nollen and Bousquet that I rote them both a letter and have not had a word from them[.] also to Hospers & all the debenports

---

[485] Sonora, California was an established mining boomtown in Northern California.

[Davenports,]    Mr. Fisher[,]   R. Hamilton[,][486]  E. F. Grafe  and all others of my friends that is thare[,] tell them all to write to me[.] this letter is entended for them all but as soon as I can[,] I will write to them separately[,] as soon as I find out who is thare to write to[.]

I want you James to answer this letter as soon as this comes to hand and let me know who all has left thare[.] now I will say to you that **Charles [Capley]** was a good boy on the road and mutch liked by all the train[.] he was the best hand in the train[.] you need not gave your selves any uneasiness about him[.] he is sivil and attends to his own business[.] he is well[.] he is living with me at this time[.] he cannot want while I have any thing[.]

let me now everything that you that you[487] think will be of any importance to me[.]

**John Hamilton** is on a farm about 5 miles from me[.]  **Curtis** and **Rusaw** is in the San Bernardino and are all well[.] my wife sends her respects to Mrs Coplea & Mrs Swader[.]

beleave me as ever[,]  your cincear friend[,]
N. P. Earp

**Source Citation**: Earp, Nicholas. "Copy of a Handwritten Letter from Nicholas Earp to James Coplea, April 2, 1865." Transcription by Janelle Molony and Nicholas Cataldo, November, 2023. Pella Community Memory Database, Pella Public Library [Identifier: 2019.1.62.11].

---

[486] Robert Hamilton is related to John Hamiltion who is in the Pella Company with Nicholas Earp.
[487] This is not an error. In the original letter, he repeats "that you" twice.

# Haywood Edwards Diary, July 1864

**[Relevant Selection Only]**

July 15        Got alarmed at the Indians and got with a large train [**Ringo Company**] & camped at Gricklin's Ranch 5 miles east of Scots Bluff.[488]

July 16        Past Scots Bluff & camped 3 miles west of them.

July 17        Camped 2 miles west of a creek called Horse Creek.

July 18        Nooned at the Cold Springs & camped 5 miles west of them on a small branch to the right of the road.

July 19        Travelled till noon and camped at t ranch 9 miles east of Fort Laramie.

July 20        Past Lorina [Laramie] and camped 5 miles west of the fort.

July 21        Went 7 miles and camped on the bank of Platt. Laid by in the evening.

July 22        Went 20 miles and crossed the principal chain of the Black Hills and camped on the bank of Platt.

July 23        Remained on the same place and rested our cattle and gathered kearns.[489]

July 24        Nooned on the hill west of Horse Shoo Creek and camped on Elkhorn Creek. Went 16 miles.

---

[488] Ficklin Springs Pony Express Station (turned telegraph station) is in Gering, Scotts Bluff Co., Nebraska.

[489] An early transcription note suggests these are "cow chips."

July 25    Traveled over hills & camped on a creek called Labonta.

July 26    Crossed a ridge of 6 miles in the forenoon and camped
on a small creek. Laid by in the evening. Water plenty.

July 27    Went 10 miles & camped on a small creek.

July 28    Traveled half the day & camped on a a creek called the Laperell.

July 29    Camped 4 miles west [east] of Deer Creek. Nooned at
Deer Creek. Had 3 horses stolen & one more wounded by the Indians.

July 30    **Mr. Ringo** shot himself. We buried him and went
5 miles. Camped.

July 31    Camped 5 miles east at the bridge on Platt.

August 1    Traveled half the day & crossed the river & camped 1
miles west of the bridge.

August 2    Remained on the same place & rested our cattle.

August 3    Traveled half the day & went 8 miles and
camped at Red Buttes.

**Source Citation:** Edwards, Haywood. *The Diary of Haywood Edwards, May 30, 1864 to October 31, 1864*. Typescript by A.W.D. in the Missouri Collection (f-238; box #SUNP-2507; C3982). Available at the State Historical Society of Missouri Research Center-Columbia.

# Amanda A. Forbis, Sketch from 1893

**[Relevant Selection Only]**

I was born in Stanford, Lincoln County, Ky., on the 35th of September, 1817. my ancestors for several generations were southern planters, and I grew up on my father's plantation where I was born. My lineage is American of Scotch origin. My maiden name was America Perrin, and I was educated at Isette female college at Cynthiann, Ky. On December 13, 1836, I was married to Jonathan Franklin Forbis, who was also born in Stanford, Ky., and who knew me from infancy.

In January, 1841, we left our native state, and then began our pathless westward March. We first settled in Platte County, Missouri, then a new state with unknown resources, where we spent 20 years, carving out of the wilderness a home, a farm, for we were farmers by nature, in a locality which from 1861 to 1864 was the common battleground of the rebellion, harassed by both sides, protected by neither, and the theatre of the most appalling scenes of fratricidal warfare. Our farm horses were taken for Calvary uses, our produce for the commissary, our lambs devastated, and we were finally driven to again resume our westward way.

May 18, 1864, we started with ox-teams for Oregon via Idaho, which then included the territory embraced in Montana, and after four months' travel through the country, infested by the war-like Sioux, under the chief, Black Kettle, we arrived at Virginia City, in Alder Gulch, the present county seat of Madison county, Sept. 21, 1864 .

Emigrant trains, westward bound, in those times were compelled to travel together for protection against the Indians, and while crossing the plains of Nebraska, our train was so long that one end could not be seen from the other. Bodies of murdered travelers were often seen lying by the roadside, partly devoured by wild animals. Work animals died in great numbers from drinking alkali water, and carcasses fairly indicated the way to the bewildered pilgrims. But we became so accustomed to carnage, that we could detect a stench of the decaying human body from that of the beast. Many of these murders were committed by whites, to obtain the victims money or goods, and were attributed to Indians.

But still we made merry. Men and women, old and young, would gather round the campfires and sing familiar songs to the accompanying notes of the guitar.

On one occasion one of our party [**Mr. Davis**] was shot by an Indian that had crept almost into the circle without being discovered by the guards. Males, young and old, had guard duty to perform.

I recall an instance when a mere boy [**Johnny Ringo**] was standing night guard at the wagon next to mine. He was so exhausted by the heat and fatigue of the day's travel that he would fall asleep at his post, and at intervals through the night his watchful mother [**Mary Ringo**] would arouse him by a gentle call from her wagon. She did not sleep that night, but kept watch in place of her boy, and awakened him only when she feared he would be discovered neglecting his duty. His father [**Martin Ringo**] was killed only a few nights previous while on guard duty at the same wagon.

To describe the striking and trying scenes of Alder Gulch in the "palmy days" is hardly within the scope of this sketch. To chronicle the acts of the vigilance committee; to describe the flour riots of 1865, when a citizens' committee examined each house to see if anyone had more flour than was necessary to subsist upon until freight trains shall arrive in the spring, and if a surplus was found it was taken for those who had none; when the miners' meeting was the legislator, the court and the executioner; All these must be done by the one whose task it is to write the early history of Montana.

Gold was plentiful. Nearly $100,000,000 were in time taken from this one gulch. Provisions became exhausted during my first winter in Montana, and could not be obtained, as Salt Lake City was the nearest supply point, and freight wagons the only means of transportation; hence the anomalous spectacle of a community of 20,000 people, rolling in wealth, and destitute of the necessities of life.

In May, 1865, we moved from Alder gulch to Last Chance gulch—now Helena—and settled upon a farm, where we lived for 14 years, cultivating the soil, the most productive I have ever known. The richer placer mining districts were practically worked out by 1870.

**Source Citation:** Forbis, America A. "Women Pioneers." Autobiographical sketch for the World's Fair of 1893, in *The Anaconda Standard*, February 17, 1895, 12.

# Chief John Grass, Oral History from 1915

**[Told by John Grass to Col. Alfred Burton Welch, about 1915]**

"A long time ago I was a sub-chief of a band of Sihasapa. We were south of here and on Moreau creek in camp. A large band of Hunkpapa, with many tipis, came to make us a visit. We made a great feast for them for there was much game and we had made a good killing. We saw a woman standing apart [**Fanny Kelly**]. She had a light skin and we thought that she was white, but, until we heard her voice, we could not be sure."

**Uses Him as a Shield, father of John Grass**
"That night my father, who was head chief [**Chief Bill Grass**], had a man crawl around to where we saw her go into a tipi, and he listened there. By and by he went in by crawling. She talked white talk. He came back and said so. Then we were afraid. We wanted that white woman but we did not want to fight for her if we could help it, for there were more Hunkpapa men there than we had Sihasapa. So we did not know what to do."

"But we called several warriors and wise old men into my father's tipi after it was dark and they came easy and talked low voice. It was decided not to fight right away but to try another plan."

"The next day we sent for eight of the best warriors of the Hunkpapa to come to my father's tipi. They did not know what it was about, but they came. They were brave men for they could see that we were uneasy about something. When they came we gave them much to eat and some fine clothes and some feathers and we smoked some tobacco. We did not have much tobacco then and it was good to smoke."

"When we smoked my father said, "We want that white  woman." They said that she did not belong to the people but to one man who owned her. Then they made this plan: We would give each one of these brave eight men a horse. They were to help get her for us. So they said, "Yes," and went away."

"They went to this one man who owned her and the headman said like this, "We want that white woman and will buy her." He said, "No, you can not have my white woman. One of them get lonesome and die. I want to keep this one.""

"Then they said, "You give us this woman. We will give you eight horses for her. There is one other thing you can do. You can keep the white woman and we will bury you today (ostracize him).""

"Then he said he did not want to die that day, and that he would trade. So we got the white woman for sixteen horses. These horses were all my own horses and they were good ones, too. We did not have to fight anyone. We had very wise men with us."

"After a long time we took the white woman to Fort Sully and gave her to the white people there. She was glad to be with white people again and talk her own tongue. She stayed there some time and then, once she was gone, and I did not see her there again."

"The Hunkpapa had attacked a wagon train to the west of the Black Hills and killed all the people but two white women. One got lonely and died after a while. The other one we bought as I have told you about. She had been with them for about one summertime. One time when I was in Washington to see the President, and my picture was in the paper there, this woman [**Fanny Kelly**] came to see me. I knew her. She was happy. I cannot pronounce her name very well. My father and I did this thing. I am glad about it. Men know if it."


**Note added by A.B. Welch (adopted son of Chief John Grass):**
This was **Fanny Kelly**, who has written a book upon her experience while with the Sioux as a captive. She pays high tribute to John Grass as a savage gentleman.


**Source Citation:** Grass, John. Oral History to Col. Alfred Burton Welch in 1915. Transcribed by Everett Cox. Published as "Fanny Kelly Story," in "Oral History of the Dakota Tribes 1800's-1945," *Welch Dakota Papers,* 2011. https://www.welch dakotapapers.com/2011/11/chief-john-grass-2/

# Lewis B. Hull Diary, July 1864

## [Relevant Selection from Fort Laramie]

June 30    Company and general inspection; review and muster
           for pay. Quarter master department changing hands.

July 2     A heavy storm during the night blew our pine down and
           overturned several chimneys.

July 3     Finishing the arbor again, making wreaths and decorating the
           rooms for the Fourth. Arrest of some emigrants for making a
           disturbance.

July 4     The 88th anniversary of the Declaration of Independence, the day
           when every American heart should swell with pride and gratitude
           toward those noble men who gave their all to establish a free and
           independent government as an inheritance for future generations.
           Little did they think that there would be millions at this day trying
           to overthrow and destroy the fruits of that seven years of toil and
           blood; but so it is. May they not succeed, is our daily wish.

           A salute of fifty guns was heard at noon; then we had a splendid
           dinner: roast beef, veal, mutton tongue, pies, cake, etc. Table neatly
           spread and decorated with wreaths and ornamental cake stands.
           The officers were invited to dinner with us, but having mess dinner
           of their own, none but the officer of the day, Lieut. Pettijohn,
           responded. Officers and ladies visited our quarters and praised our
           taste very highly. Quite nice, a spread eagle of cedar in each room
           and one at the top of the arbor.

           Boys were very busy putting up seats and canvas for the
           performance tonight. Copied programmes. Great rush around the
           door. Seats crowded. Performance good, consisting of pantomime,

burlesque, songs, etc. Salute of fifteen guns heard after eleven. Fine sight.

July 7      Acting secretary for the minstrels. Weather quite cool for July. Boys getting ready for another performance tonight. Better fixed than before; seats raised. Admittance, front seats, 50 cents, back 25 and 15. Sold tickets. Show good. Took in $107. **Colonel [William O. Collins]** pleased with results; says there must be another show tomorrow night.

July 9      Paymaster here. Finishing payrolls; none to be mustered as veterans.

July 10      Mail in. Letter from Mae. Paid off in evening. Six of us received the veterans' bounty, an order having been received from the adjutant general. Paid from date of enlistment up to the present time after deducting advance pay. Received $100, $50 bounty, and $13 a month regular pay, the paymaster not having received an order to pay me $16 a month.

Another entertainment last night. Some disorder caused by there being too much whiskey on hand; some of the performers the worse for it.

July 13      Dispatches received from up the road that the Indians are killing the emigrants at different places. Company E and some men from Company I, and twelve men from Company K and two pieces of artillery sent up. **General Mitchell** is expected in a few days. An escort going to meet him tomorrow. News from down the road that there is trouble with the Indians. Mr. Lorey writes from the agency that the place will probably be attacked tonight by a large body of Missouri Sioux, each with a hundred warriors. Considerable excitement. Sitting up late writing and waiting for news.

July 14      Still excitement. **Gen. Mitchell** telegraphs to send no escort. Herds to be brought in at night and strongly guarded. Two of Co. A sent with a dispatch.

July 15        No Indians around here yet. A dispatch from Fickland[490]
that Indians attacked that place and that there are 60 or 70 emigrants corralled there. Think they can hold out until reenforcements arrive from here. Co. B gone down to help them through. Co. A men report a large body of hostile Indians advancing in this direction.

July 16        No news; apprehensions beginning to abate.

July 19        Croughan and Woods went out with the mail as far as Mud Springs. Going to stay there awhile.

July 20        Heavy rain.

July 21        Detailed for guard. Row at taps; took one man to the guard house.

July 22        Remainder of government train came in from below. Two deserters from Co. I last night, Carter and Baker. Took Grace, Co. I, to the guard house for making a disturbance.

July 23        Dispatch received that Lieut. Brown, Co. E, was killed in a charge on the Indians over near Powder river; his body shot full of arrows and scalped.

July 24        Co. B going over on the Rawhide after a party of Indians.

July 25        Co. B came back, having taken one scalp.

A detail of 15 men of Co. K to go over on Rawhide to bring in what plunder was left at the Indian camp. I thought I would go along. Sergeant Channel, Co. B, took charge. Two other Co. B boys with us; all on ponies. Started at three o'clock. Two ponies gave out at Beauvais, leaving our party at sixteen. At Bordeaux we were joined by two Indians. Crossed the Platte without accident a mile below the ranche. Struck a northeast direction and in about seven miles came to where the dead Indian was. Found several old saddles,

[490] Ficklin Springs Pony Express Station (turned telegraph station) is in Gering, Nebraska.

lariat ropes, robes, paint, and other Indian paraphernalia. A dead one lay in the sun scalped.

Our Indians took what they wanted and we burned what remained, then struck for the river. Reached it at sunset, crossing where it was deep and swift. Two B boys got set off; got a complete ducking. Had some milk and biscuits at the ranche and came on up to the fort, arriving after 11 o'clock. Several ponies tired out. Mine fell with me; no damage done though.

July 26    Reported fight on Upper Platte bridge. Several Indians killed. Detailed for guard, but as I was tired, Corporal Martin took my place.

July 27    **Gen. Mitchell** came in from Kearney with an escort of 7th Iowa. Salute of seven guns heard in honor of his arrival. Agent in. Says it was a friendly Sioux that Co. B killed. Indians talking of revenge. Mail in; received six letters and two papers.

July 29    Boys came in from scouting. Reeshaw says the fighting is a humbug. Change reported in this department; Maj. Wood to command the post. Lieut. Reeves to be inspector general in the department. Salute of 13 guns heard before tattoo. Was ordered to help. Don't know what it was for.

July 30    Went out riding ten miles up the river. Stopped at a train. Had dinner of peaches, sardines, crackers, and pickles. Went across to the Laramie, where Co. B had camped for the night. Boys came in from the scout. **Lieut. Brown** dead; shot with two arrows, one in the back and one in the neck. Lived till morning.

**Source Citation**: Lewis B. Hull, *The Diary of Lewis Byram Hull, 1864-1866.* Edited by Myra E. Hull. Topeka: Kansas State Historical Society, 1938). Published as "Soldiering on the High Plains: The diary of Lewis Byram Hull, 1864-1866," in *Kansas Historical Quarterly*, vol. VII, No. 1, pages 3-53, February, 1938.

# Hervey Johnson, Letter, July 25, 1864

Deer Creek
July 25th 1864

Sister Sybil,

We returned yesterday from our Indian excursion, and as I may go away soon I thought I would write now. I don't know when the mail will go out so I can send it,[491] the indian troubles have made it very irregular.

There was no trouble along the road while we were out; but yesterday evening two of our Company horses and several emigrants horses were stolen at a place called Horse Shoe Station, where four of our boys are staying sixty five miles from here.

We were gone five days[.][492] there were about one hundred and sixty of us, thirty of co G. a detachment of Co E, the whole of Co H, detachments of Cos I and K, and two pieces of artillery. We started out in a northeast direction, the remainder went north.

We saw no Indians though we crossed several trails that had been made by large herds of horses that they had been running off.

A small squad of Co E ran into a band of Indians forty or fifty, in the afternoon [of July 20] and attacked them, they were overpowered and compelled to retreat. The **second Lieutenant [John Brown]** who was in command of the squad was shot off his horse[.] the arrow going in near the spine at the small of his back. I saw the arrow after it had been taken out, it was shot in six inches[.]

After the **Lieut**. was shot[,] the other boys made for this command which was four miles off[.] They reported what they had seen and the whole command started after them. They got [in] sight of them but night coming on they were compelled to give up the pursuit. They did not get into camp till next morning. The

---

[491] Lewis Hull at Fort Laramie clarifies that the mail is received every 15 days.
[492] July 19-23.

**Lieut**. was left out all night supposed to be killed. Our camp was on a creek about thirty miles from here.

Next morning [July 21] an ambulance was sent, to bring in his **[2ⁿᵈ Lt. John Brown's]** body, when they got to the place he was still alive and his clothing all taken off except shirt and boots, two arrows in his body, one through the next and one in the back. The feather was cut off the one through the neck and it was drawn through. They gave him some water to drink and it ran out at the wound in his neck. They tried to pull the arrow out of his back but the barb pulled off and was left in his body but was afterwards taken out with an instrument. He was brought into camp and died next morning [July 22]. His entrails were taken out and the place filled with salt[.] he was buried in a shallow sandy grave.

We left the place and went on camped again then next day reached Wind river. No Indians there[.] Scouts were sent out in three different directions but found nothing, camped on wind river for the night, left at half past two in the morning to come home[.] came back by the place where the **Lieutenant** was left[.] staid all night, took up his body and started for Deer Creek before daylight, arrived here and buried the **Lieutenant** with military honors five days after his death [July 27].

Night before last two of the boys from Platte Bridge came down and told us that the Indians were coming in there and wanted to go down to the fort to get something to eat. They said they saw a heap of bad Indians with a heap of ponies but would not go with them because they were bad Indians. Co E was just starting to the fort. The captain turned them back with the artillery. Several of our boys went from here too.

The Captain[']s plan was to take the chief and some of his best men prisoners and keep them so till they would tell who it was that was committing depredations along the road, and where the stock was they had taken, and if they would not tell, to kill them and their squaws and papooses[,] burn their lodges and take their ponies.

Our first Lieutenant[493] who was with us on our wind river expedition and who also has commanded of the troops are the bridge was here at the time the news came that the Indians were there. He was very angry at it, because he gave the Sergt.[494] whom he left in charge imperative orders to shoot any Indians who

[493] Lt. Captain Henry C. Bretney.
[494] 1ˢᵗ Sargent. Henry D. Merwin.

came about. He hastened up there to the bridge[,] mounted his men and went out and pitched into the Indians. We have not yet learned weather any body was hurt of not.

The Indians ran away with the boys after them, they got a citizens hat that the chief wore. It was a perfect blunder on the part of the Lieutenant and I hope he will be courtmartialed because he acted contrary to express orders[.]

If he had [done] according to orders they might have got all the Indians there was there and their ponies, besides perhaps finding a great many horses that had been stolen and bringing the thieves to justice, but as it is[,] I doubt if they have got a single Indian or retaken a single horse.

**Source Citation**: Hervey Johnson, Personal correspondence to Sybil, July 25, 1864 in *Tending the Talking Wire: A Buck Soldier's View of Indian Country, 1863-1866*, ed. William Unrau (University of Utah, 1979).

# Hervey Johnson, Letter, July 26, 1864

26th.

A portion of the troops who went to the bridge yesterday [July 25] have returned. They had a fight with the Indians, captured several horses, sixteen or seventeen squaws, who are held as hostages for that woman that was taken by the Indians some time ago[.][495]

An old Indian chief has been sent out to bring her in, he says he knows where she is. If he does not bring her in[,] those squaws will *go up*.

Several of our horses were killed in the fight and one man wounded. His name is St Clair, he lives in or near Marshal, he was shot through both legs below the knees with a slug. Our boys destroyed all the lodges and every thing the Indians had and they are making their way towards the fort[,] back of the mountains. You may think that they are receiving rough treatment from us, but it is nothing compared with what is their due.

The very next morning after they came there[,] they tried to run off the Government horses at the bridge, and at the same time were making friends with the boys there. The boys couldn't see it in the same light that the red skins did so they went to peppering them.

I must come to a close. I wish you could send me a pair of suspenders and a small necktie ... write often[.]

Hervey Johnson

**Source Citation**: A continuation of the July 25 letter to Sybil Johnson, as previously referenced.

---

[495] A reference to Fanny Kelly from the Kelly-Larimer Train.

# Josiah S. Kelly, Letter, Aug. 15, 1864

From Josiah S. Kelly, mailed from Fort Laramie, Idaho Territory

To Rezin W. Kelly in Montgomery, Ohio

Deer Creek, Idaho Territory
August 15, 1864

Dear Brother (R.W. Kelly)

It is with a sad heart that I undertake to write to you of my awful bereavement. It was on the 12th day of July that we was attacted by the Indians. My wife **[Fanny]** and her niece[,] a little girl about eight years old[,] carried off prisoners. My load and 4 head of horses taken and destroyed. There was 5 wagons of us traveling together, 6 men and a boy **[Andy]** about 15 years old.

We were attacted by between 75 and 100 Indians who came to us about two hours before sundown and staid until we stoped for the night[.] about sundown we had just unhetched and were going about to get supper wen they fired on us killing three and sevrly wounding two of our men the first fire. I hapened to be about 20 feet from the wagons kindling a fire when they shot.

At the report of the guns I sprung to my feet and saw there a man fall dead and two shooting at me with bowes and arrows and I had not a thing to fight with, my gun being in the wagon. I ran for a ravine close by which I ran down a ways and got into a thicket of brush and concealed myself until it was dark[,] when I tried to make my way back to a creek about 7 or eight miles back where I expected to find some trains camped. But finding the road picketed I took through the hills and got lost and did not reach the trains until day light next morning. I could get no help from them except to bury the dead and haul the wounded to deer creek station distant about 13 miles[.]

I cam to this station and tried to get help to rescue the priseners but they could not spare a man. 50 men stationed here to gard the post. Telegraffed to Fort Laramee and in one week two hundred and fifty soldiers arrived. I started with them to go to Powder River village[.] went to Wind river about 60 miles north of here when the officers in command concluded they were not strong enough to go to their village and came back and returned to the Fort[.] Powder River village is supposed to be from 150 to 200 miles north of here.

The first day out I in co. with three soldiers struck the trail that they went with the priseners we know from papers dropped along it. Followed it about 12 miles when we ran onto about 50 Indians with a large drove of horses we got close onto them before we saw them, just as we saw them they started for us.

We broke for the command which we supposed was about three miles to our right but found it to be about seven miles distant. The Indians ran us about four miles. We made several stands but they were trying to out flank us on both sides and surrounded us so that we dare not stand longer than to make one shot. One of our party **Lieut. Brown** was killed by them. He fell ten feet from me.

The Indians were by us thick. All that saved us was our horses out winded theirs. When we reached the command[,] the command went for them but did not get in sight of them until nigh sundown[.] they ran then until some time after dark but don't know as they killed any of them.

Got back here on Sunday and Monday went up to Platte Bridge 25 miles from here. Met a party of Indians coming down[,] wounded one Indian[,] took one man and 22 squaws and children priseners. They claimed to be innocent and friendly but said they knew that the Indians at Powder River village had a white woman prisoner. They sent the Indian after her and told him if he brought her in fifteen days they would all be set free and if not they would all be shot.

In a few days after[,] a french man came and claimed all but one squaw and her children as his family[.] there were given up to him. The 15 days was up about four days since and the Indian has not returned[.] his sqaw and children are stil held prisenor. **[Brig.] General [Robert B.] Michel** arrived at Fort Laramee some days since as I understood to go with an expedition against the Indians but now[,] as I am informed[,] that Maj. General Curtis has forbid his making any move against them. What it means I don't know.

Since our attact there has been nineteen persons found murdered by the Indians between here and where they attacted us a distance of 13 miles. I wil not mention that at the time that they attacted us[,] they took a **Mrs. Lariner** and her son about eight years of age priseners who made their escape the second night out.

She says that when they started from the wagons they put **Fannie** on a horse and **Mary Herly**, her niece[,] on behind her and soon after they started, close to the road[,] **Fannie** sliped **Mary** off in the brush and told her to go hide and stay there until she would see some wagons going long the road and go to it. We have since found **Mary** shot with two arrows, scalped and tomahawked.

What I have suffered since that time[,] no press of tongue can express. But O God only knows the sufferings of my poor wife in the hands of those Savages. **The Colonel** of this Reg. the Ohio 11th can teels his men if they see one[,] they must not shoot at him but motion him off.

Write as soon as you rec. this direct to Fort Laramee, Idaho Territory

Your Brother,
J. S. Kelly

**Source Citation**: Josiah Shawan Kelly, "letter to Rezin Wells Kelly, August 15, 1864," in *Genealogy of the John A. Kelly Family,* transcribed by Henry Pelton and Dwight Yates (Ohio: Private Publication, 1950). Reprint permission granted by Barbara Yates-Romine.

# Sarah Larimer, Letter, Aug. 1864

Mrs[. Sarah Jane] Taylor[,]

Dear madam[,] You may be surprised to receive a letter from an unknown friend, yet many unexpected things occur in this life. And I feal it a painful duty to communicate to you the sad tidings of the death of your husband who fell by the hand of a barbarious savage, July 12, one hour befor sundown.

**Mr[.] Taylor** had been with us one month. As he was not a man of many words he had told me but little of his family. Yet I had enquired of this children, which he said numbered eight. I believe he said his past address was Burlington[,] Kansas. The twelfth of July[,] when not yet camped for evening[,] we were attacted by eighty or one hundred Indians (I did not count them and as they were in more than one company the exact number is not known)[.] Our train numbered eleven, being six men one boy two women and two children. So you see our force was not sufficience to contend against so many[.] **Mr[.] Taylor** and two others fell dead at the wagons[.] My husband [**William**] and one other were wounded but are recovering, two men escaped unhurt.

**Mrs[.] Kelley** of Genevea[,] Kansas and her little niece a child of eight years[,] our son of seven years and myself were taken prisnors. The little niece they afterward killed[.] **Mrs[.] Kelly** is stil missing, but my son and I made our escape after being with them two nights and one day. They traveled with us forty five or fifty miles. We walked back.

**Mr[.] Taylor** was taken and placed in the ground with three others (One man not of our train being found dead not far from our wagons) in the afternoon of the next day. He was covered with a buffalow robe[,] the last thing of clothing being left in our wagon. We heard of their grave today it is undisturbed.

A Revolver and some other things **Mr[.] Taylor** had left with **Mr[.] Ely** of Burlington[,] Kansas which he agreed to make right with you[.]

I would be glad to receive a letter from you at your earliest conveniance[.] our Address is Fort Laramie[,] Idaho Territory. We have returned eighty miles.

We were of Iola[,] Allen Co[.,] Kansas.

I feal to sympathize with you in this[,] your bereavement and with those dear children who are left fatherless. I was left fatherless when a child.

Sarah L Larimer

N B[496]

Not knowing your first name[,] I address in your husband[']s.

**Source Citation:** Sarah Luse Larimer, "Letter to Sarah Jane Taylor (undated, circa August, 1864)," typescript illustration in Randy Brown, "Attack on the Kelly-Larimer Wagon Train," *Overland Journal* 5, no.1 (1987): 26.

---

[496] "N.B." at the close of a letter is an abbreviated Latin expression "*Nota bene*," meaning to "take note," or "note well." It is a near equivalent to the modern day expression, "For your information," abbreviated as "FYI."

# James Logan, Letter, Aug. 1, 1864

**"From the Rocky Mountains"**
South Pass, Idaho Territory, August 1, 1864

DEAR FRIENDS:

I improve the present opportunity to fulfill my promise of "writing often," as near as the circumstances will admit, for we have been for several hundred miles passing through a country in which there is no post office, or any other accommodations. As you will see by the heading, we are now on the western slope of the Rocky Mountains under the shadow of peaks which are covered with perpetual snow, and which is the source of many fine streams of water.

We find plenty of good springs as cold as ice, but don't need it so cold up here as you do down in the States, for it is plenty cold up here all the time, except when down in some deep hollow between high hills where the cool breeze can't reach you; at night it is universally cold enough to sleep under two or three blankets. We generally have found plenty of grass by hunting for it, and waiting till our stock could eat enough and we have learned to do entirely without wood except sage brush and Buffalo chips. For this country is nothing but mountains and deserts–entirely bare of every thing like timber and almost so for grass, except up the valleys.

On the mountains[,] part of the way[,] we find some Pine and Cedar. We have traveled up valleys almost all of the way[.] first[,] South Platte to Lolesburgh or Overland City. Next[,] over to North Platte and headed it out in the Rocky Mountains.—Next[,] over Sweet Water which we head out here at the summit of Rocky Mountains at South Pass where we find the water running west to the Pacific Ocean.--

We have had a very pleasant trip, all have kept well in every thing in pretty good shape. I broke down 1 wagon, went ten miles to get it mended. Next[,] to the Provost Guard at Fort Cotton Wood[.] seized animal in hopes to get to keep it, but I beat them, by laying by one week, and having plenty of brandy and knowing how to serve them.

They take away a great many mules, horses, guns and pistols, saddles &c., leaving the emigrants bare. I kept my other stuff out of sight or I would have lost two mules, one gun and a saddle. There are quite a number of these Soldier stations, watching what they can see from the emigrants, saying they are here for their protection. I lost a very fine horse worth $300 at Independence rock, near Devil's gate.

The destruction of cattle on the road is awful; dying by the wholesale and will average near five to the mile. The stench is terrible, can hardly get out of it, they die of conjestion caused by the Alkalie dust, water &c., they have to encounter in such large trains. They drop dead in the yoke, often both oxen. It is not so bad on horses and mules.

I found Atchison a good place to start from–A very nice young thriving City. Every thing reasonable in price and plenty of it[,] cheaper than to carry it from home. If I should start again[,] I would do quite different. In the first place[,] I would get very light one horse wagons and put on to each four of the best mules I could find, not younger than four years old. Load light[.] take only what I was compelled to use on the road, and altogether to four mules[,] not over eighteen or twenty hundred pounds.

Would start over land from home and never shipped by Rail or River[.] start by the first of May[,] lay in necessaries at Atchison, except provisions which I would lay in plenty of at Seneca at least flour, bacon, corn meal, potatoes, butter, eggs, and oats, and corn which is much cheaper, have to be hauled to the River for sale except to supply the emigration.

About Seneca is the last farming country of any note on the road, but you can buy any thing you want all along the road as far as Overland City, by paying very high for it.

The country through Kansas is very [*words missing*] .... En-countering awful hail storms, heavy sand, precipitious rocks, deep sloughs and Rivers, dying off valuable stock, breaking down wagons, encountering the Alkalie regions of dust and poison water. We count it all joy, forwith good appetites our faces westward to the land of promise, where we hope to enjoy liberties of thought and speech, to which we were strangers in the land of despotism, from which we are willing exiles fleeing to the mountains and valleys of the far, far west, we are prepared to enjoy it and make light of all these apparent difficulties.

For convenience sake we travel in large crowds[,] have fiddling[,] and Sam seen once or twice each week[.] in a calm laugh and joke, tell of our troubles where we once counted our homes where we lay our dead parents, brothers, sisters and many dear children and glorious ancestors in the old church yards was once dear to us, but now universally dedicated to miscegenation[.][497] And the countless damnable doctrines of hell for the persecution of those who stand firm to the faith and doctrines taught by Christ on the Mount and handed down to us through our forefathers by their blood through the battles of the Revolution; which scenes will once more have to be re-enacted if ever our fallen, degraded and once happy country is relieved from the approaching darkness, which can be even felt and make the true patriots heart bleed to think of the past.

Glance at Mexico, and other disorganized despotic countries– but digression, these things are so deep in my thoughts by night and by day[,] I could not help it.

There is a great deal of the scenery on the road[.] we can see Chimney Rock fifty miles away which looks like the Shot Tower in St. Louis, only much higher. Also Court House Rock where a large party of us enjoyed the once glorious 4th of July in remembrance of the past. I ascended its steep and rugged sides several hundred feet to the summit where I planted the Stars and Stripes[,]  a beautiful emblem of past greatness and prosperity, which flag we named the Phoenix[,] it having risen from the ashes of the one the Abolitionists burnt for me at Centralia.

Big and Little Blue River[,] South and North Platte, Big and Little Sandy streams; abounding and fish, are very rapid and nearly straight. Our road runs the entire way up them except passing over from the one to the other where grass and water is very scarce and no timber. We have not seen a skirt of timber since leaving the Missouri River, over which I could not throw a finger stone, and these only a few cotton woods down next to the water.

For hundreds of miles not a twig anywhere, the streams rushing along through the wide prairies or desert which are inhabited by hostile Indians, who appear very friendly until they get a chance to steal. There are several tribes who have declared war against the emigrants and are stealing everything they can lay hands on and killing all who they find defenseless. In Idaho from Laperell and Deer Creek to Port Bridges,[498] they have made a general and almost simultaneous descent on the emigrant.

---

[497] Miscegenation is the interbreeding of races.
[498] This might read Fort Bridger, Utah Territory. This 1842 fur trading outpost on Blacks Fork is now in Uinta County, Wyoming.

The train I was mostly traveling with, lost fifty-two head of stock at one time[.] I had refused to travel with them preferring to be alone which saved my stock[,] although in great danger with four wagons  and sixteen mules in the mountains, [and with] only myself and my three teamsters[.]  they happened to miss me which was the only train that escaped for many miles.

Each way I was within seven miles of trains who lost every hoof. **Hawley and Rockwood** of Centralia lost all[,] which was mostly the result of carelessness having no armed men with the stock.

I adopted the rule of having two men with the best arms marching around my stock night and day when not in motion[,] which the Indians watched like an eagle, and finding stock out without the proper guard (always in the night)[,] they come out of the mountains with a whoop and yell [at] our trains and drove them [horses] off whilst we would rather they had come on for we was ready and anxious to learn them a lesson.

The soldiers ordered us to halt and keep all back until there was near five hundred wagons together then two hundred soldiers[.] With two pieces of artillery[,] move on through them[,] passing many horrid sights of burnt trains, destroyed goods &c., whilst the advance guard found in one place **four dead men** and buried them. Each shot through with arrows[,] scalped and tomahawked.

We found **a little girl and man** shot through with two arrows each, scalped and tomahawked and we buried them. When we arrived at the Deer Creek Post, we found **several wounded men**, one of whom will die, and a lady [**Sarah Larimer**] that had been captured with her **little boy six years** old had escaped and just returned faint[,] on foot[,] sore[,] carrying her boy four days and nights whilst another lady [**Fanny Kelly**] that was carried off who tried to escape has not yet returned[.] perhaps recaptured and killed.

Fortunate for these families who had lost their stock[,] their came in **a large drove of mule from Salt Lake City** going to the Missouri River for Freight which could not proceed with safety[,]  conducted by **Capt. Wood** who kindly took some twenty wagons with families on to Salt Lake City. But **Hawley** and **Rockwood** of Centralia were both left behind and what has become of them I can't say it, except that **Rockwood** has hauled to Independence Rock and dropped. Since those troubles[,] we have traveled in large trains and had no trouble.

Although the gold diggings of Idaho are yielding well to those who have claims, the field is not extensive enough for the tremendous rush[,] consequently[,] the thing is over done and many financially ruined.  Some returning before winter and a great many going on to California, Oregon &c., while there are large prospecting parties all over the Territory. They are prospecting right here and in fact some of our train is out with pick and shovel into the mountains whilst others are hunting game, guarding stock &c.

There is a party of Californians here who say the prospect is very good and in fact bring in many valuable specimens of both Silver and Gold, and I'm laying in their winter's provisions, preparing to lay up for winter and open out here next spring.

Some of our party are about to lay up and join them, but as for me[,] although I know there is gold here as yet[,] it has been no temptation to stop, for my face is set for the setting sun until stopped by the Pacific ocean in some quiet valley home, with fruits and flowers, rippling springs and humming bees for me to make a final rest; to spend my days in peace, away from the noise and bustle of business, annoyed No More by glistening bayonets and clamoring for spoils.

**Source Citation:** Logan, James. "From the Rocky Mountains" letter to the editor in *Salem Weekly Advocate* (Salem, Illinois) November 10, 1864.

# James Logan, Letter, Aug. 9, 1864

FORT BRIDGES, Aug. 9th, 1864 [Fort Bridger, UT]

Have no opportunity to mail the above[.] I left it open until now, and if I have the time and space would add many incidents and items of interest. But we'll leave it for a future occasion when[,] if you wish to come[,] I will give every item that would be of advantage to any one outfitting for the Plains.

I think it's possible that I may winter in Carson Valley, or some where in Nevada where I can live cheaper than in California, where every thing as we understand is so very high in price on account of drought. These thoughts have been hurriedly jotted down without thought as to form, but if you think there is any thing in them worth attention you may place it in form and revise it and make such use as you think proper.

It is directed to no particular person but intended for any of my numerous friends, particularly A. J. Percy, A. B. Fry, J. M. O'Melveny, Esquire Howell, the McClellans, Moores, Smiths, Lyman and others.

Hoping to hear from all at Salt Lake.
I am &c., JAS. I. LOGAN

**Source Citation**: A continuation of the August 1 letter, as previously referenced.

# William Lucas, Oral History from 1926

## [Relevant Selection Only]

My full name is **William Thomas Lucas**. I was born on March 18, 1850, and so and passed my 76th birthday. My birthplace was Buchanan County, Missouri and my parents were **George J. Lucas**, a native of Ohio, and **Sally Thomas Lucas** of Kentucky.

We were Southern sympathizers, and as Buchanan county is on the border, and Kansas is a Northern state, there was a good deal of bitterness and ill-feeling. It was not exactly a pleasant place to live, under the circumstances, so in May, 1864, when I was fourteen years old, we left Missouri for the West —for Montana.

THE EMIGRANT TRAIN

In our particular train there were sixty to seventy wagons, occupied by our friends and neighbors, but when we passed through country where it was known that the Indians were hostile, we doubled up until there were from two hundred to three hundred wagons—formidable array for anything short of a good-sized army of Indians to tackle.

I fancy they knew that as well as we, because we had little serious trouble. The stock in our particular Missouri train was made up of horses and mules, and we drove our cattle with us.

You know, I rather imagine the union army wanted that stock of ours pretty badly. I shouldn't wonder but what a force had been sent out to pick it up, but my father had learned his strategy as a captain in the confederate army, and they didn't get it.

THE HORSEBACK BRIGADE

My father was, naturally, made captain of our train, and had as his first Lieutenant a man who had served as Lieutenant under him in the war[.] Father organized a sort of flying squadron, a horseback brigade, which attended the slow moving train on either flank, scouted far in advance along our line of march, and also acted as rearguard.

Because we were Southern sympathizers[,] they dubbed us "the left wing of Price's army," but once we got out of the neighborhood where they had so much acquisitive interest in our horses and mules, we were not molested.

We had two or three little scrap[e]s with the Indians and some other mishaps, but nothing really serious. We reached the territory of Montana the latter part of September, after having been more than four months on the way, and took up land.

## MOVES TO CALIFORNIA

After four years there, herding cattle and doing more dairying as well, I came to California in 1868 and have never, except accidentally and incidentally, been out of the state since. And I don't want to go. We settled in Woodland, Yolo County, and I went to Hesperian college.

**Source Citation:**  Lucas, William T. "Fifty Years and More in Santa Barbara."   Oral History Transcription by Michael Phillips, *Santa Barbara News-Press*, May 1,  1926, 4.

# Elenor Phillips, Obituary, June 11, 1892

DIED

Phillips. - At her home, on Ruby valley June 5th 1892, of general debility, Mrs. Elenor, wide of Edward Phillips, aged 79 years, 4 months, and 16 days. Mother Phillips was among the first lady residents of Madison county, having come here to join her husband, who had come a year or two before, in the early sixties.

**Source Citation:** "Elenor Phillips," Obituary in *The Madisonian,* (Virginia City, MT), June 11, 1892, page 3.[499]

---

[499] Only the relevant portion is included here.

# A.L. Rockwood, Letter, July 25, 1864

**"From the Plains: A Thrilling Letter of Adventures of an Emigrant Party. Indian Atrocities–Hardship and Suffering of the Women and Children"**

From a private letter, Sweet Water Bridge, 106 miles East of South Pass, July 25, 1864

DEAR —:

We know you must feel very anxious about us by this time, for we suppose you have heard of the troubles up here among the Indians, and I expect they are multiplied considerably by the time they reach you.

We have struck a hard run of luck lately, although **Anna**, **Henry** and **myself** never enjoyed better health than now.

On July 14th the Indians stampeded about sixty head of stock from our train, while they were feeding about one and a half miles from our camp. they got every animal I had, except the two Jacks and Jimny, and succeeded in getting them all off. The first we heard of any trouble among the Indians, was about midnight of the 13th, some soldiers were passing, and said that the Indians had attacked and captured a train above, the day before and murdered six men, and we're all about us.

We had seen no sign of them, but never the less we gathered in our stock and guarded it well till daylight, and about 6 o'clock we turned them out to grass, and about 7 a.m. the Indians came out of the hills near by and got within a few feet of the men on guard before they were discovered.

**Henry** was out with my stock, and also the other man that was with me. I had been on guard all night, and had laid down by the wagons to sleep. When I sent the stock out[] I put a long rope on Kitty (a favorite mare), and told him not to let go of it, but if there was any alarm or danger to mount her and come to me at once. He had but just got on the feeding ground, and sat down on the grass to mend his moccasin, with the rope in his hand, when he heard a horse galloping in the direction of our camp. He looked up, and there was an Indian within a few feet of him. The Indian yelled and scared the mare; she broke the rope, and a way she went with the rest.

If I could have got them there, with her [Kitty] and my rifle[,] I could have recovered the whole of the stock in a few hours, as there were only about ten or twelve Indians in the gang. The boys that went out forgot to take the revolvers, and there was but one revolver out at the time. The man who had it emptied it at them, but does not know as he done any damage. The other boys ran into the herd, and tried to head them to the camp, and one of the teamsters got an arrow into his hip pretty badly, but it's now nearly well.

We lay there where we were till there were near five hundred wagons come up, and about one hundred and ten soldiers, and on the 15th we moved up to a creek about ten miles, where we could get plenty of water, and lay there two days for the military to fool around and do nothing. They could have had two hundred volunteers, and there were over one hundred of them, and two mounted howitzers, and the trail perfectly plain to follow, but they would not go.

After waiting two days on the creek, we moved up to Deer Creek, twenty miles, between military station and telegraph office. The emigrants volunteered their teams to move our wagons to that point, thinking we would be safer there than on the road.

On reaching there **Captain Granger** and **myself** learned there had been a train of six wagons and sixty loose mules left there that morning for Salt Lake. (**Capt. G** is the man who owned the most of the train we were in company with.) We mounted a couple of mules and started after them. We overtook them [**the Wood Freight Train**] at Platte bridge, twenty-eight miles; stayed over night with them, and they sent back thirty-one mules to help us.

They had already picked up about seven wagons in the same fix, and they only had that many animals to spare. When we got back to Deer Creek Station, we found they had started out with one hundred soldiers and ten days' rations, to try to recapture the stock.

We learned when we came to Deer Creek back on the 13th, the Indians, about 30 and number, had surrounded a train of three or four wagons [the **Kelly-Larimer Train**], six men and their families, professing to be friendly Indians, and kept on with them for a few miles, and then demanded their supper. The emigrants were in their power[500] and therefore stopped to comply with their demand, and, as they were making a fire to cook it, the Indians commenced the attack and killed or wounded all but one white man [**Josiah Kelly**] and a negro

---

[500] Meaning overpowered.

[**Andy Lawrence**]– they both commenced to run on the first alarm, and made their escape to some willows on the bank of the stream, and it be night, they got to the station.

A force was sent out in the morning and they found two of the men there badly wounded with arrows, and three dead, and two women and three children missing, and the wagons burned and stock gone. They bury the dead and remove the wounded to the station, but sent no one in pursuit. Four days after, as we were moving up, we took another road which passed about two miles to the right of the scene.

Near the road we were on, was found one of the children [**Mary Hurley**], a little girl six years old, with several arrows in her body and scalped. We buried her as well as we could and passed on. That happened about fifteen miles from the Deer Creek Station, and, when within about six miles of the station, we found a man beside the road shot with arrows and stripped of all but his pants. He had been dead, I should think, about four days, but we cannot find out anything about him. He was buried he lay.

At Deer Creek, we found the two wounded men and one of the women [**Sarah Larimer**] came in the night before we got there, bringing her little boy [**Frank**] with her. She had made her escape in the night, and had travelled two nights and part of the last day and came in safe. Her husband [**William Larimer**] was one of the wounded and is likely to recover. The other wounded man [**Gardner Wakefield**] was a single man and is probably dead before this.

We lay a while before we moved on, and for a week after they commenced they were stealing the stock and attacking the trains all up and down the Platte River for fifty miles, and no one to stop them, and the Emigrant had to rely on his own protection.

I didn't hear of them killing anymore, but there were a great many wounded and different trains, and as I near as I can find out they have captured above 2,000 head of horses and mules from the emigrants.

We got the mules from the **Salt Lake Train**. And **Granger** and **myself** started our wagons. We offered to the families that were with us enough to move two of the three families, but they preferred to stay and await the return of the expedition, thanking to recover their stock, or part of it, but I had seen enough to satisfy me there was no hope, and I came to the conclusion that we could expect no help from any man, or the Indians receive any damage from one who is keeping from one to three squaws to sleep with and raise families by,[501] and therefore thought it best to take the first chance to go on.

We moved on to this place, eighty miles from Deer Creek, and reached here Saturday night [July 23]. My big Jack was taken sick Saturday afternoon. And I had to stop with him, and the train went on and left me, and here I am. The Jack is some better, and I hope we'll be able to travel by the 1st of August.

I have succeeded in buying one yolk of broken-down cattle and a yoke of broken down cattle and a yoke of cows by paying heavy for them, and hope to be able to raise another yoke of cattle, although it is doubtful, as they are dying by the thousands along the road. It will take all the money I have and my watch to get us to Salt Lake, if the cattle I have leave to reach there, but we will work through some way sure.

[July 25:] We are now camped at a military and telegraph post at Independence Rock, four hundred miles from Salt Lake. I wish to God I could get to the authorities and let them know how they work out here. I will write you when I strike the mail route at Fort Bridger, as it is uncertain about a letter reaching you from here. There is no help for the emigrant from those here, but the opposite.

Yours, ever, A. L. Rockwood

**Source Citation**: Rockwood, A. L. "From the Plains" letter to the editor, *Chicago Tribune,* (Chicago, Illinois) September 10, 1864.

---

[501] Referring to some the soldiers at Deer Creek Garrison who have families with local Plains Indians women.

# Rushville, Letter, July 29, 1864

**[Relevant Selection Only]**

**"Crossing the Plains."**
Crossing the Platte—Incidents Along the Route

Correspondence of the Morning Herald.
BORDEAU'S RANCH, NEAR FT. LARAMIE, July 29, 1864[502]

Again I have the pleasure of writing you a short communication from this God-forsaken country. When we left home[,] we expected by this time to have been almost to Virginia City, Idaho. What a short-sighted creature man is; he literally knows nothing of the wants of to-morrow.

...

After we left the South Platte and travelled several days, we all at once found ourselves amongst the Missouri and Minnesota Sioux. They are doing considerable mischief along the toure of travel from here to Deer Creek, one hundred miles above Fort Laramie. You have learned, no doubt ere this, by telegraph of many of their depredations. We have been travelling for the last sixty miles in the immediate vincinity of their raids, but as yet have had no trouble with them.

Men are collecting in large trains for the purpose of travelling with greater safety. – Our train now numbers sixty-nine wagons and that is as small a train as can get along safe. We travel slow and with caution.

This morning we had a false alarm and made ready for a fight, but no Indians appeared, and our boys (through mistake)[503] fired on two friendly Indians, but happily the thing will pass by without any serious difficulty.

---

[502] This date is believed to be in error. Mr. Rushville reaches Fort Laramie by July 20, per the accounts of Davenport and Ringo. The corrected date might read "July 19."
[503] Parentheses added.

Our train is composed of our own, **Capt. Hodges**, **Doctor [Addison] Gutherie's**, of Platte County, and **[Calon] Morris**, of Clay county. We all get along very smoothly, but travel slow.

[July 19:] We are now stopping a part of a day to patch up some wagons made in Chicago. There is very little good grass here, as no rain has fallen for some time. We expect to reach Laramie to-morrow, and perhaps then we may hear from home.

...

I think we are plenty able for the Indians, although they fight under may advantages. The troops along the route do all they can to favor the emigrants.

I forgot to mention that **Floyd** and **Farris**[504] of Buchanan, are travelling with us with their trains. We are all well and shall write you again soon.

RUSHVILLE.

**Source Citation**: Rushville. "Crossing the Plains, July 29, 1864" letter to the editor in *The Morning Herald* (St. Joseph, MO), August 9, 1864.

---

[504] Mathias Ferris.

# Rushville, Letter, Aug. 2, 1864

**"En Route for Idaho. The Indians"**
The Indian Troubles–An Emigrant Accidentally Kills Himself–Cattle Dying on the Route–Rough Times Generally

Correspondence of the Morning Herald.
DEAR CREEK POST, IDAHO, Aug. 2, '64

Since my last to you from near Fort Laramie, we have passed through an exciting period. We are now one hundred and twenty miles above Laramie, near where the Indians, a short time since, burnt five wagons, and killed several men and children, and took some women prisoners. Small trains are attacked almost daily, until but few small trains are now traveling the road.

Night before last[,] one of our men, well near the Corral, was fired upon by an Indian, and badly wounded, but not fatally; his name was **D. C. Davis**, from Kansas. During the excitement that followed, before we could get our horses inside the Corral[,] they managed to steal three of them.

The same night that **Davis** was wounded, a man belonging to our train, from Gallatin, Daviess County –**Martin Ringo**– discharged his shot-gun accidentally, and blew the top of his head off. He leaves a large and helpless family, on their way to California.

Our train is composed of about seventy wagons, owned by a number of different men. **Mr. Beauvais**, formerly of your city; **Mr. Milette,** of Deer Lodge Valley, Idaho; The **Morrises**, of Clay County; **Davenport**, of Clay, and many other families of small trains. We left **Mr. Farris**[505] and **Capt. Hodge** back on Horse Shoe Creek, trying to recuperate and rest their cattle.

---

[505] Mathias Ferris' Shipping Company is mentioned in George Forman's journal as the first employer he hired on with, then abandoned one day later.

A great number of cattle have died in the past hundred miles, or since we left Fort Laramie. Many large trains cannot move until they can get cattle either from the States or Salt Lake.

If a man wants to buy anything from a ranch man along here, he has to pay about four prices for it.  Work cattle are worth two hundred and fifty dollars per yoke and everything else in proportion.

We are holding a council to-day to determine whether we shall go by Bridge's new Cut Off–thereby saving the distance in travelling to Virginia City, some three hundred miles–or go the old beaten route, up Sweet Water (where cattle are dying by thousands,) to South Pass.

There are a number of mule wagons line[d] at Deer Creek, that cannot move, -- the Indians have taken all their mules and horses.  There has been a vast amount of suffering caused by the Indians along the road. They do not molest any cattle. The telegraph dispatch came to Platte Bridge yesterday evening [Aug. 1], that Deer Creek Station had been attacked, and, up to last night, it had not been contradicted. We do not know whether the Post was captured or not. There were some fifty soldiers at the Post. We are near Platte Bridge Station, which is protected by twenty soldiers; they are somewhat alarmed but appear to think they will not be captured. You can at once appreciate the danger we might be in.

But our entire train feel confident that we will not be attacked, and that if nothing else will satisfy them but a fight with us, we can whip them very easily. What troubles us most is our cattle dying so fast, also, as to myself, I have been lucky. I have not lost one out of twenty-one head that I started with.

It was a sad scene we went through, the morning **Mr. Ringo** shot himself. Most of us had been up the entire night, watching for an Indian attack. We were close to some brush near North Platte, and could not tell how many of our foes were lying in the brush, waiting for day to dawn are they begin the attack.

Just as day dawn began to streak the East, myself with others were standing against our wagons, listening at the crack of every Bush around us, and, every now and then, could hear **Davis**, the wounded man, grown most piteously. All at once, a loud report of a shot gun was heard a few wagons passed us, and a cry was heard from a bystander that a man was shot in the head. A moment and all was as silent as the grave; then came in loud, mournful whale from a female [**Mary Ringo**], and a cry of anguish from the children, that husband and father was killed. A few soon rushed to the spot and acertain that his own gun killed him.

We spent part of the day in digging a grave up on the hill close by, and left him to rest until the resurrection morn.

RUSHVILLE.

**Source Citation**: Rushville. "En Route for Idaho, August 2, 1864" letter to the editor in *The Weekly Herald and Tribune* (St. Joseph, MO), September 8, 1864.

# Noah D. Taylor, Letter, July 5, 1864

Nebraska, July the 5th, 1864
in camp near Fort Laramie

Dear wife[,]

I take my pen in hand to inform you that I am well and harty at preasent and hope thease few lines may find you and the children all injoying the same kind Blessings[.] I have nothing of importance to rite to you[.] I am driving a four horse teem for a man By the name of **Larimis** from Iola Allen County Kansas[.] we are About half way to Banock though we are within 30 miles of the Lines of Idaho Territory[.][506]

the old man **Ely** is About one Day and A half Behind in Company with some are Teems from Kansas[.] we have Bin Detained on account of hy waters[.] we was five Days Crossing the South fork of the platte river[.] they was ten wagons in our Company[.] we made a ferry Boat out of four wagon Beds and ferryed our selves[.] they was three or four hundred wagons Crossed in the same way[.] Hear was several men got Drowned at that one plase[.]

we have not had any trouble with the Indians as yet[.] they Appear to Be very friendly[.] they will shake hands and say 'how how how how[.]'

Tell Mr Jackson that I have not seen the first d - - m Buffalo yet   But I take in A antilope About every other Day[.]

Sarah Jane[,] I don't now whither I will have the chance to rite any more ___ Before I get through[,]So nothing more at present[,] But Remains your Husband until Death[.]

N D Taylor

**Source Citation:** Noah Daniel Taylor, "Letter to Sarah Jane Taylor, July 5, 1864," illustration in Randy Brown, "Attack on the Kelly-Larimer Wagon Train," *Overland Journal* 5, no.1 (1987): 23-24.

---

[506] The border town of Henry, NE is about thirty miles from Fort Laramie.

# Unsigned Editorial, Aug. 13, 1864

**[Credited to either Mr. Northrop or Nelson Morris of the Morris-Hastings Train]**

## Indian Massacres in July

It will be remembered that early in July we briefly chronicled the fact that emigrants had been attacked by Indians on Deer Creek, 100 miles west of Fort Laramie. From one of the emigrants, who fortunately escaped and is in this city in destitute circumstances, we have learned the following particulars, with the names of the killed and wounded:

The attack was made on the 12th of July last by a band of Sioux and Cheyennes at Box Elder, above the mouth of Dry Creek, on the North Platte.

LIST OF KILLED:

**Noah Taylor**, from Coffee county, Kansas; **Mrs. Sharp** [sic], from Woodman county, Kansas; **Arthur Wright**, Minneapolis, Hennepin county, Minnesota; colored boy **Frank**, Kansas; - - **Wakefield**, Woodson county, Kansas, formerly from Maine; **William J. Larrimer** [sic], of Allen county, Kansas, was wounded in the thigh. His wife and child were taken prisoners by the savages, and were in durance [duress] two days. On the fifth day they came into Deer Creek all right.

**Mrs. Fanny Kelly** and niece were taken prisoners. The former is supposed to have escaped, but the niece (a child) was found murdered and scalped. Our informant only escaped by belaboring his horse into a gallop and eluding the savages.

**Source Citation**: "Indian Massacres in July," editorial in the *Union Vedette* (Camp Douglas, Utah), Aug. 13, 1864, 2. Accessible through UtahDigitalNewspapers.com

# Unsigned Editorial, Sept. 3, 1864

**[Credited to either Mr. Northrop or Nelson Morris of the Morris-Hastings Train]**

**MASSACRES ON THE PLAINS.** – The Salt Lake Vedette gives the following account of an Indian massacre, on the Plains, east of that city:

It will be remembered that in July we briefly chronicled the fact that emigrants had been attacked by Indians on Deer Creek, one hundred miles west of Fort Laramie. From one of the emigrants, who fortunately escaped and is in this city in destitute circumstances, we have learned the following particulars, with the names of the killed and wounded.

The attack was made on the 12th of July last by a band of Sioux and Cheyennes at Box Elder, on the mouth of Dry Creek, on the North Platte. The following were killed:

**N. Taylor**, from Coffee county, Kansas; **Mrs. Sharp** [sic], from Woodman county, Kansas; **Arthur Wright**, Minneapolis, Hennepin county, Minhsota [sic]; colored boy **Frank**, Kansas; **Mr. Wakefield**, Woodson county, Kansas, formerly from Maine; **William L. Larrimer** [sic], of Allen county, Kansas, was wounded in the thigh. His wife and child were taken prisoners by the savages, and were in durance [duress] two days. On the fifth day they came into deer creek all right. **Mrs. Fanny Kelly** and niece were taken prisoners. The former is supposed to have escaped, but the niece (a child) was found murdered and scalped. Our informant only escaped by belaboring his horse into a gallop and eluding the savages.

**Source Citation:** "Massacres on the Pains," editorial in the *Chico Weekly Chronical-Record* (Chico, CA), Sept. 13, 1864, 1.

# Unsigned Editorial, September 8, 1864

## Further Indian Atrocities

**Charles Long**, who recently arrived at Kansas City from Salt Lake, with a train, writes to the Kansas City Journal a narrative of his adventures, from which we make these extracts:

On the 22nd ult.[507] we camped at Deer Creek station. Here we found **Gardner Weakfield**, and **Larimer** wounded. The former in a condition not expected to live, the last to recover – both of Allen county, Kansas. This was a party attacked by the Indians on the 12th of July at Little Box Elder, ten miles east of Deer creek. The Indians at first came up to the party and pretended to be friendly. They asked for something to eat, and while some was being prepared, the Indians commenced firing on the party, killing three, and wounding the above two.

They took the women and children along as prisoners. One, a **Mrs. Larimer**, with a little boy, seven years old, got away from the savages in the night and returned safe on the fifth day to Deer Station.

**Mrs. Kelly**, the other lady, had not been heard from since she left. **Mr. Kelly** was out at the time with a squad of soldiers in search for her. The little girl of **Mrs. Kelly** was found killed and scalped.

**Source Citation:** Long, Charles, "Further Indian Atrocities" in the *Daily Union Press* (Louisville, Kentucky), Sept. 08, 1864. Reprinted from the *Kansas City Journal*.

---

[507] This abbreviated term, "ultimo," refers to a date from the month prior to the date of letter composition. With this in mind, readers can deduce that the wagon train Charles Long is associated with reached Deer Creek Garrison on August 22, 1864.

# Unsigned Editorial, Sept. 29, 1864

THE BROWN FAMILY. – The newspapers have lately announced that the family of old John Brown were coming over the plains, bound for California. They were out in Humboldt country last week, as will be seen by the following extract from a letter written by a gentleman who was visiting the emigrant highway, and who resides at Unionville:

We also saw the family of John Brown, of Harpers Ferry notoriety, consisting of the widow, one son and two daughters. **Mrs. [Mary] Brown** is a very matronly-looking lady of about forty; the son's age is about twenty-six years, and the daughters fifteen and seventeen. They had some fine stock with them, including three imported merino sheep.[508]

One feature in the immigration is very noticeable; that is, the great musical genius it exhibits. We saw none, either male or female, who would not sing on the least invitation–the males having voices like handsaws, and the females like night owls.

**Source Citation**: "The Brown Family," editorial in *Gold Hill Daily News,* (Gold Hill, NV), September 29, 1864.

---

[508] The Browns started with six.

# About the Author

Janelle Molony, M.S.L. is an award-winning author and recognized family historian with ties to Iowa, Wyoming and Arizona's territorial history. She has received various honors for her research findings, as published in numerous academic journals and topical magazines. When she isn't digging into her own family's past, she writes for the local newspaper circuit and supports various preservation initiatives with historical societies and museums around the country.

For more books by Janelle Molony, or to contact her about a speaking engagement, please visit her official author website:

**www.JanelleMolony.com**

# Coming Soon

**From Where I Sat**  (fiction, in development)
Website JanelleMolony.com/RousseauProject
Social Media @RousseauProject

Escaping the Civil War is extra hard when one's family is tied up in political schemes. To avoid the next round of drafts, a grand plan brings four families from Pella, Iowa together for the greatest adventure of their lives on the Overland-California trail. Between the endless starry nights and daytime gunfights with menacing Indians, Mrs. Sarah Rousseau logs the wagon train's progress in her pocket diary. As a wheelchair-bound woman, she's not able to help when supplies run low and desperate choices must be made before they reach the snow-covered mountains standing between them and their California dreams. All she can do is write down *whatever happens next.*

# Now Available!

**The 1864 Diary of Mrs. Sarah Rousseau** (non-fiction, 2023)
JanelleMolony.com/RousseauDiary
Social Media @RousseauProject

The <u>only</u> descendant-vetted and approved, unabridged edition of Sarah Rousseau's 1864 journey across the American West. Read how the Pella Company faces fierce enemies, quicksand, hailstorms, poison water, and the blazing sun. Feel the budding romance between youths. See who has enough mettle to survive. And meet the surprise heroes who restore the emigrants' faith in humanity.

**Awards and Recognition**: As seen in the *Oskaloosa Herald & San Bernardino Sun*, and *Wild West Magazine*, 3rd Place in History (BookFest, 2023), Pulitzer Prize Nominated (2023).

## Poems from the Asylum

(non-fiction, 2021)
JanelleMolony.com/PoemsFromTheAsylum
Social Media @SevenYearsInsane

After noticing she no longer needed to eat or drink in 1927, St. Paul, Minnesota, Martha Nasch's doctor claimed she just had a "case of nerves." With a signature from her husband, Martha was committed against her will to the asylum. She spent nearly seven years in the Minnesota hospital during the Great Depression and tried to escape twice. Martha's award-winning poems from behind bars include shocking eye-witness accounts of patient treatment and a long-suffering adoration for her only child.

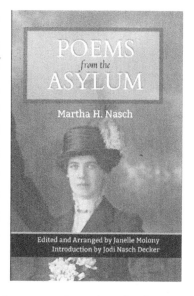

When not a soul believed Martha's story, she sought an explanation for her mysterious condition that led her to a spiritual answer for the mystifying curse. Would her findings make her a metaphysical guru of the Breatharian lifestyle, or would she become the laughingstock of her Depression-era family?

**Awards and Recognition**: As seen on ABC TV's *Minneapolis Live!,* in the *St. Peter Herald* and *Minnesota Genealogist,* 2nd Place in History (BookFest, 2022), 3rd Place in Biographies (BookFest, 2022), Merited Woodticks Poet Award (League of Minn. Poets, 2021), Honorable Mention (Arizona State Poetry Society, 2021)

## Un-Adoptable? Faith Beyond Foster Care

(non-fiction, 2020)
JanelleMolony.com/AdoptionToLife
Social Media @AdoptionToLife

When an adoptive mother is presented with a foster child that doesn't fit the description, quick-thinking helps her navigate a situation that was set up to fail. Faced with either turning her back on the child or turning to God for help, she fights for what she believes to be right.

Molony opens her heart to the reader with an authentic and relatable tale of a couple doing everything they can to help their foster son find his place in the world through faith, hope, and acceptance.

**Awards and Recognition**: As seen on ABC TV's *Sonoran Living Live!*, in *Foster Focus* and *Fostering Families Today* Magazines, Amazon Bestseller 2020, National Indie Excellence Award Finalist 2020, Readers' Favorite 5-Star Rating, Arizona Authors Association 2020 Literary Contest Winner, Perfect Score from Writer's Digest Self-Published Book Awards.

An honest review of your reading experience is
highly appreciated!
Please share your opinions of this book with the
location of your purchase
and on social media.

Made in the USA
Middletown, DE
27 January 2024